The Five Sedgwicks

The Five Sedgwicks

Pioneer Entertainers of Vaudeville, Film and Television

MICHAEL ZMUDA

McFarland & Company, Inc., Publishers
Jefferson, North Carolina

All photographs are from the author's collection, except those provided by Edward Hutson and Niles Essanay Silent Film Museum.

LIBRARY OF CONGRESS CATALOGUING-IN-PUBLICATION DATA

Zmuda, Michael, 1958–
The five Sedgwicks : pioneer entertainers of Vaudeville, film and television / Michael Zmuda.
      p.   cm.
Includes bibliographical references and index. Includes filmography.

ISBN 978-0-7864-9668-6 (softcover : acid free paper) ∞
ISBN 978-1-4766-1781-7 (ebook)

1. Sedgwick family. 2. Sedgwick, Ned, b. 1868– 3. Sedgwick, Fenie, b. 1872– 4. Sedgwick, Edward, 1892–1953. 5. Sedgwick, Josie, 1898–1973. 6. Sedgwick, Eileen. 7. Entertainers—United States—History—20th century. 8. Motion picture actors and actresses—United States—History—20th century. I. Title.

PN1998.2.Z68 2015   791.4302'8092273—dc23   2015011464

BRITISH LIBRARY CATALOGUING DATA ARE AVAILABLE

© 2015 Michael Zmuda. All rights reserved

No part of this book may be reproduced or transmitted in any form or by any means, electronic or mechanical, including photocopying or recording, or by any information storage and retrieval system, without permission in writing from the publisher.

On the cover: *left to right* Edward (in the car) in a behind-the-scenes photo from *Parlor, Bedroom and Bath*, 1930; Eileen (superimposed) in *The Riddle Rider*, 1924 (author collection)

Printed in the United States of America

McFarland & Company, Inc., Publishers
Box 611, Jefferson, North Carolina 28640
www.mcfarlandpub.com

For those who encouraged me, thank you.

Table of Contents

Preface	1
One. Medicine Shows and Gas-Lighted Theaters	3
Two. Tank Towns and Four-a-Day Vaudeville	20
Three. Orange Groves and Shootouts	43
Four. Dynamite's Daughter, the Ramblin' Kid, and the Diamond Queen	75
Five. The Saddle Hawk, Lightnin' the Police Dog and Leo the Lion	108
Six. The Rise of the Almighty Studio System and the Fall of the Silent Film	147
Seven. The Business of Laughter During the Depression Years	175
Eight. A Hollywood in Transition and the Fate of the Silent Idol	200
Nine. Nazis, Country Bumpkins, and a Couple of Redheads	226
Ten. Journey Beyond the Silver Screen	239
Sedgwick Family Filmography	251
Bibliography	257
Index	259

Preface

A number of years ago I acquired a pair of silent era one-sheet movie posters that promoted a series featuring Lightnin', the Police Dog. One of the posters especially sparked my curiosity: an illustration of a blonde-haired female about to be rescued from the clutches of two villains by her charging German Shepherd companion. The apparent damsel in distress turned out to be Eileen Sedgwick, a film star who made many daredevil escapes in numerous Universal serials throughout the 1920s. I soon discovered that my initial conception of Eileen as a "damsel in distress" was far from accurate. As a protagonist, she could escape from cliffhanger situations just as well as, or better than, any of her male counterparts.

Eileen, along with her brother Edward and sister Josie, started making silent movies during Hollywood's formative period, launching successful careers in the entertainment industry. By the late 1920s the Sedgwick siblings were all well-known motion picture personalities: Edward was satirized by actor Harry Gribbon as an overtly enthusiastic comedy director in King Vidor's 1928 silent comedy hit *Show People*; Josie was a star of Western films and was presented the honorific title of Queen of the Roundup; Universal Films promoted Eileen as their "Queen of the Serial."

The members of the Sedgwick family, individually and together, are among the unsung heroes of the early history of filmmaking in Hollywood. This book is a tribute to the family's contribution to the entertainment industry. Their work experiences took them from vaudeville to silent films, through the studio era of the great movie companies, and into the Golden Age of television. Although their innovations are not always visible, they have helped in diverse ways to form the foundation of today's movies and television shows. In writing this book, my desire was to document the Sedgwick family's involvement on screen and behind the camera, and relate their experiences to the reader.

I owe a great deal to the late Edward Hutson, Eileen's son, for sanctioning this undertaking and encouraging me to write about his family. Edward continued the family tradition of working in the business, being employed at Fox Studio's art department for over 50 years. He passed away in 2015, just before this book went to press.

His uncle Edward's unpublished memoir *And Then There Were Five*, which describes the Sedgwick family's involvement in vaudeville, was an invaluable source. I've incorporated a great deal of this journal throughout the first two chapters. Considering the talent that Edward had for storytelling, it is likely that he may have occasionally embellished particulars.

However, the timeline and locations that he detailed in his recollections appear to be accurate. In the early 1950s Edward Sedgwick submitted his family's story to motion picture studios as a spec script for a possible film project. It is thought that Paramount passed on developing it, and instead produced the similar-in-nature film *The Seven Little Foys* (1955) starring Bob Hope as Eddie Foy, the father and head of a successful vaudeville family.

Edward Hutson was also very generous in sharing his mother's photographs collected throughout the family's career. The assortment of early images that are included in this book helps document an important era in the development of entertainment in the United States.

An acknowledgment of thanks also goes to Robert Rowe, as I greatly benefited from my conversations with him. He was instrumental in setting up my first meeting with Edward Hutson.

Finally, mention needs to made of the archives I utilized, including UCLA's Film & Television Archive and the American Film Institute's Louis B. Mayer Library, which I got to look at rare film footage, scripts, and industry publications. Popular fan publications published during the silent-era period were also a great reference source. Internet access to archived newspaper publications was an important tool in confirming vague references and dates. Gratitude also goes to an elusive group of film collectors who, over the years, have cared for and laboriously restored "lost" films, eventually making their collections, including several *Lightnin'* shorts, available to the public.

CHAPTER ONE

Medicine Shows and Gas-Lighted Theaters

The letterhead of "The Five Sedgwicks" proclaimed that they could sing, dance, and act. Dramatic sketches; comedy afterpieces; specialties between the acts; repertoire or stock company—they could do it all. The letterhead, printed in garish green and gold designs, was patterned to catch the eye of the small town vaudeville show manager, with vignettes of each family member smiling hopefully at the prospective buyer of their manifold talents. The father, Ned. The mother, Fenie. The elder sister, Josie. The younger one, Baby Eileen, the Child Wonder. The inimitable comedian son, Edward.

"We were pretty good," Edward Sedgwick proudly wrote of his family's talents in his memoirs.

> Ask anybody who got around the tank towns in the early part of the century. And tanks they were. We never played anything else. Why? Well, there were many reasons. The principal one, my Dad. He wanted no part of the big city show business. He would have no truck with Broadway at all. Maybe, under his veneer of brash Texas bravado there lurked an inferiority complex. He and I battled continuously on this score. His direct antithesis, I was Broadway at heart. Worshipped everything it represented. Envied all the artists who were on the Big Street. I followed them assiduously in the *New York Clipper,* the *Dramatic Mirror, Billboard,* and theatre magazines. I plotted, planned, prayed, for a chance to get our gang Up There—somehow. But it was not to be...

After marrying in 1890, Ned and Fenie developed a repertoire of acts and started their entertainment career, which would eventually lead them to the vaudeville stage. Ned and Fenie traveled with other entertainers and on occasion joined stock companies, performing the majority of their shows in gas-lighted dives or makeshift theaters that were conveniently located near stops along the Southern rail routes.

The couple entered vaudeville as the mode of entertainment was going through a transitional period where the industry was refining and redefining its form. Early vaudeville, originally referred to as "variety," was only introduced to amusement-seekers in the United States about 70 years earlier, sometime before 1820. This form of variety show entertainment, which evolved out of Europe, originally presented predominately male-oriented acts that were considered inappropriate for female audience members. The standard fare of the early shows, which were often performed in music halls or under tents, included a collection of

The Sedgwicks' letterhead proclaimed, "We are prepared to furnish a variety of Interesting Comedy Playlets full of singing, dancing and novel features." Entertainment critics unanimously agreed in their newspaper reviews (courtesy E. Hutson).

unrelated acts which might have featured "a singer of topical songs, an acrobatic couple, a tightrope walker, a sidewalk 'patter' pair, and perhaps a very rough comedy sketch."

It wasn't until after the Civil War that vaudeville managers started to give thought to improving their performances in order to attract entire families, a previously ignored subset of potential theatergoers. Entertainers needed to realize that to appeal to the masses—and especially to the growing middle class postwar population who had expendable money—vaudeville had to become wholesome.

One of the first businessmen to understand and invest in this concept was Tony Pastor. On July 31, 1865, he opened Tony Pastor's Opera House at 199–201 Bowery in New York City, where he introduced clean vaudeville. One of the sacrifices he needed to make was the sale of alcoholic beverages during performances. Because a large part of the revenue of a typical variety performance could come from beer sales, sacrificing this surefire source of profit seemed absurd to the majority of businessmen. Ignoring their advice, Pastor went on to successfully demonstrate that it was indeed possible to provide improved vaudeville acts to families without the drink bar, and without jeopardizing admission sales. Although it proved to be a successful experiment, the average vaudeville manager didn't believe that it was something that could be duplicated on a large scale, so vaudeville continued to follow its previous bawdy style. During the 1870s and the early 1880s, vaudeville was on the decline and was classed even lower than the circus, from which many of its acts had been hired.

Aside from Pastor, there were some other showmen who believed that vaudeville could actually be revitalized and transformed into a profitable business. By the early 1880s B.F. (Benjamin Franklin) Keith, who had previous experience working with various circuses, had already opened a successful storefront curio museum in Boston. He joined forces with E.F. (Edward Franklin) Albee II and on July 6, 1885, opened the Bijou Theatre, which became one of the early adopters of the continuous variety show. Continuous variety, or continuous vaudeville as it was to become known, was designed to run 12 hours straight, and often went from ten o'clock in the morning until close to midnight, seven days a week. Before the inception of the continuous vaudeville show, shows ran at fixed intervals, with several hours of downtime between each show. With the continuous vaudeville show, a theatergoer could enter the theater at any time and stay until they reached the point in a show where they walked in, as acts were rotated throughout the day.

With the advent of this polite form of vaudeville, the rough-and-tumble acts were being replaced with refined acts that attracted quality performers, many drawn from the legitimate stage. It also attracted audiences made up largely of women and children. Following Keith's success, F.F. (Frederick Freeman) Proctor, who was also influential in pioneering the method of the new style of vaudeville, opened the Twenty-third Street Theatre in New York City, using the slogan, "After breakfast go to Proctor's; after Proctor's go to bed."

In an article written for the November 1898 issue of *National Magazine*, Keith, known as "the father of vaudeville," described his original goal in creating a reputable version of the primarily risqué variety show. "Two things I determined at the outset should prevail in the new scheme. One was that my fixed policy of cleanliness and order should be continued, and the other that the stage show must be free from vulgarisms and coarseness of any kind, so that the house and entertainment would directly appeal to the support of ladies and children—in fact that my playhouse must be as 'homelike' an amusement resort as it was possible to make it."

Keith's idea of creating a "clean and respectable house and entertainment" was also ridiculed by many who thought it would be too costly to implement without charging a high entrance fee to make up for the lost revenue due to the ban on sales of alcoholic drinks. Keith explained that his solution was dependent on creating a well-rounded program, one that would satisfy all levels of theatergoers:

> The advent of dramatic players into my theatres has been distinctly beneficial, in that it has added the element of novelty, which is the essence of vaudeville, and has attracted the attention of a desirable class of patrons whose previous knowledge of a variety entertainment had been very vague and largely governed by tradition. As to the sort of entertainment which seems to please most, light, frothy acts, with no particular plot, but abounding in songs, dances, bright dialogue and clean repartee, seem to appeal most to the vaudeville audiences of the present time. But, it is quite evident that a thoroughly good program, in its entirety, is what draws the public, rather than individual acts, the rule being proven, however, by occasional exceptions, notably the Living Picture production, the song-sheet novelty and the Biograph, the most improved of the motion-picture inventions, and a very few of the leading performers who have novelties to offer. The most marked improvement is the tendency of artists to keep their acts clean and free from coarseness, and to do away with the ridiculous costumes, which were formerly a glaring defect of nearly all vaudeville entertainments. Added to this is the closer attention paid to stage setting and scenic embellishment generally.

In the May 1920 issue of *Theatre Magazine,* E.F. Albee, Keith's business partner, described vaudeville as "our American national theatre":

> To say that vaudeville is our most nationally representative form of theatrical entertainment is not overstating a condition that has been in process of forming and becoming permanent for more than a third of a century. There are many reasons and causes for this attitude of the American public toward vaudeville on one hand, and of vaudeville toward the public on the other. To begin with, the diversified, contrasted and all-embracing character of a vaudeville program gives it in whole or part, an appeal to all classes of people and all kinds of tastes. For its patrons it draws upon all of the artistic resources of every branch of the theatre—grand opera, the drama, pantomime, choreography, concert, symphony, farce and all of the kindred fields of stage entertainment.
>
> In addition to this wide diversity of its attractions, the personnel of its army of artists is as cosmopolitan as the population of the cities and towns of the United States. Not only are all the arts represented in vaudeville, but all of the nations and races of the civilized world are also represented by and through some characteristic form of expression.

* * *

Ned, born in 1868 and christened Edward W. Sedgwick, was one of eight children. His parents arrived in America from Ireland and settled in New Orleans, Louisiana. With a few of his siblings, Ned made his way to Galveston, Texas, where he readily found work as a longshoreman. He started his show business career by accompanying medicine shows that traveled throughout the countryside. The typical troupe program offered comedy, music, jugglers and other novelties along with their tonics, salves, and miracle elixirs. As a "physic" show actor with the Hamlin's Wizard Oil Company, Ned's job at the end of each show was to drum up an attentive audience who would be cajoled into purchasing a bottle of Hamlin's Cough Balsam, Blood & Liver Pills, or Wizard Oil—guaranteed to cure headaches, earaches and toothaches. He also traveled with the famous Kickapoo Indian Show, whose Kickapoo Sagwa Vegetable Tonic promised to eradicate diseases, and in the process make the stomach sound, regulate the liver, strengthen the weak heart, cleanse the clogged system and enable the kidneys and bowels to perform their proper functions.

Edward Sedgwick noted that when Ned performed with the Kickapoo shows, he "put on the 'black' [minstrel makeup], played a banjo, jigged, did an Irish clog dance. Quick-changed to a savage redskin: 'Big Chief Peep in the Blanket.' Lectured on, and sold, the concoction at a dollar a bottle. For the 'blow off' he would battle the local heavyweight champ, four rounds. The yokel to get fifty bucks if he lasted the full distance. They never did. My old man packed an awful wallop." Ned actually was a skilled boxer who once lasted four rounds with Bob Fitzsimmons, a boxer who went on to win the world's middleweight championship in 1891 and the heavyweight crown in 1897. Ned's poor eyesight kept him from becoming a real contender.

Born in 1872 as Josephine Walker, Fenie's family also relocated from Louisiana to the Galveston area. She too had theatre in her blood: A talented singer, she performed with church choirs, and was prominent in all civic entertainment. Fenie was experienced in the sentimental ballads that the public demanded, ones that dealt with homely, familiar subjects. Her tunes were the type that consisted of simple but strong melodies—tearful ballads in which the words and music were written without much form, rhyme or reason.

Fenie and Ned were childhood sweethearts. Ned had a lot of trouble getting to see her after he returned from his tour with the traveling medicine shows. He wasn't welcome in Fenie's home and had to fight three of her six-foot brothers before he was able to get through the door. Edward described his parents' courtship, which led to their 1890 marriage: "They went out. They strolled. They walked to a lake pavilion. They spooned. They danced. Won a prize for the best waltzing couple. They were in love. Real honest to goodness love, these two kids. She confided she had saved nearly a hundred dollars—enough to get married on. But Dad wouldn't go for that. He'd make his pile."

But the fortune wasn't to happen, as an event came up that would change their plans. The Sooner Dramatic Company came to town. Ned knew the manager, Mike Sooner, and was able to get a job for both—twenty dollars a week and cakes. And so began their career in vaudeville.

Eventually promoting themselves as "Repertoire Vaudeville Artists," they toured small Southern towns with illustrative names such as Sweetgrass and Hillsburg. As their routines expanded, so did their reputation, and eventually promoters started contacting them to fill out openings on their vaudeville bills. As their family grew, they ventured into cities such as Beaumont, Shreveport, and Memphis to do "legitimate" vaudeville in larger theaters. Ultimately, they would make it to the big-time vaudeville circuits in Chicago and New York City, but that was still a while off, and like all troupers of the time, they first had to pay their dues by working the dives as they built their credentials in vaudeville. They spent their honeymoon in horrendous boarding houses. They played all kinds of parts, most of the time with no salary. It was rugged but they loved it. They were together.

They studied drama with a veteran of the Wallacks-Daly era. From 1852 until 1887, Wallack's Lyceum was the most fashionable theatre in New York City. The plays that James William Wallack presented catered to an audience that wanted to venture into a glamorous world of charming men and striking women. Wallack provided a profusion of such escapism with exceptionally high production values. Daly's Theater, one of Broadway's first, is still referred to as "one of the most distinguished theaters in the history of American stage." The skilled old hand taught them all that he learned working at these institutions, including poise and characterization. He imbued in them the traditions of the theater. Studying Shakespeare was rough on Ned, who only had a third-grade parochial school education. It was difficult enough for him to read and write, which made it even harder to comprehend the verbiage of the prominent playwrights of the period. Fenie's first-year-high school education helped them enough to get through the ordeal.

Ned and Fenie made an effort to perform in only clean venues. That wasn't always possible, as they were desperate for work, jumping at any theatrical opportunity presented to them. Every so often a performance would end up with Ned brawling with an audience member, the fight most likely instigated by a crude remark made by a theatergoer to Fenie as she sang a spiritual on stage. Edward described one incident that almost got his father in trouble. "The curly-mustached 'heavy man' made a ghastly mistake in one little town. He made a pass at Mamma. Dad heard about it. She tried to save the poor ham's neck. No go. Six or eight of the local constables and towners pulled my old man off him. He was a mess. But they did pretty good jobs with prop teeth and fixing bones, even in those days."

Within a couple of years they had their first child, Edward. Soon after came Josie, followed by Eileen. Literally, the three children were born into show business. Although scholarly references commonly note that the Sedgwick siblings were all born in Galveston, Texas, Edward's memoir reveals that they were born in different states while the family was en route to performances. Their births didn't slow the act down one step. Whether they were born with an innate talent to perform, or the proximity to the theater rubbed off on them, they were all acting and singing onstage from the first possible moment.

With the announcement of Edward's arrival, Ned and Fenie consulted with each other and decided that it would be best if she returned home. Fenie made the final decision: She would stick with the troupe. It was the only time in Fenie's memory that Ned ever admitted he was afraid—afraid for her.

Edward, born on November 7, 1892, and christened Edward Martin Sedgwick, described his untimely birth:

> I picked a fine time to arrive. One night, in a badly lighted railroad coach, Mamma shook her sleeping spouse with the dreaded news. Things were happening. Woman passengers gathered. The conductor advised they were only a short distance from the little southern town of Sweetgrass. She held on until the train pulled into the station. Dad was having one fit after another. Threatened to kill everybody on the whole railroad if she didn't make it. A bit of pardonable hysteria at these precious times. She was tenderly carried to a private boardinghouse. The troupe went on without them. Dad, with all his other problems, dared not to tell her that Mike Sooner had fired them both—and fined them a week's pay. He ran into Mike some time later. What do you think? Yes, he also wore store teeth from then on. Crooked nose, too.
>
> Somehow, I had messed up the birth schedule. A bit premature. Mamma went down deep into the shadows. I shall always bless colored mammies. It was one of these rare specimens of the great creation that made it possible for us both to survive. Despite grave shaking of heads. Dire predictions—which nearly drove my Dad nuts. The colored girl came through. She wrapped him in swaddling clothes; used an oven for an incubator. Breathed the very life into the infant. And Dad's progeny was off to a wobbly start.
>
> I've always had the feeling my four-pound entrance weight did something to the huge, fighting man. Also, I was the cause of his nearly losing her. Our lifelong feud probably had its inception right here. In his book, I suppose, I was expected to come out throwing punches. But one misguided soul made a sly remark regarding this discrepancy. He barely succeeded in ducking a right cross that would have torn his head off. He yelled for mercy quickly. Dad stomped away, furious.

The local doctor, who had a limited knowledge of advanced obstetrics, advised them that Fenie should not be moved for a few weeks. In the meantime, Ned was frantic to raise some money. A traveling salesman by the name of Sam Henoch introduced him to a Mr. Steinworth. Steinworth was an organizer, representing the Improved Order of Red Men, a national fraternal order, with Tribes scattered across the United States. Steinworth gave Ned an opportunity to sell memberships, making a two-dollar commission on every new member he signed up. Ned made six dollars in the first day. The Red Men became an important organization in the Sedgwicks' future, bailing them out of several tough situations that they experienced while performing throughout the south. In return, Ned and Fenie became active members, often performing successful plays that benefited the organization. Ned would eventually become the Deputy Great Sachem of Galveston and act as a state organizer for Texas and Louisiana, with Fenie becoming a Past Pocahontas of Texas.

They spent the following spring on the outskirts of Shreveport, Louisiana, performing summer stock in an amusement park. Edward's cradle was the tray of a Taylor trunk. Ned was busy writing and singing parodies to popular songs of the day. Although their wages and living conditions were far from adequate, Edward described his parents as living in bliss. "He and Mamma were the feature of the show with their between-act specialties. Thirty a week double — and getting it. On the side, Dad played a little baseball with a semi-pro club. Coached a colored heavyweight into a main event spot. What a summer. They were in the chips. At times Dad got a little hard to handle. But Mamma straightened him out quick. They were more in love than ever. As far as they were concerned, this little paradise could go on and on."

A sudden "Norther" brought a heavy storm to the area, hitting the open-air theater during a performance. The fragile building started to come apart at the seams, giving Ned little time to get Fenie and Edward out before it collapsed. Fenie assisted in feeding and caring for storm casualties and got a civic citation for her help. The family's generosity became a trait which they would be known for.

The Sedgwicks went on to perform in *East Lynne*, a popular play based on the 1861 bestselling novel by Mrs. Henry Wood. At nine months, and weighing twenty-eight pounds, Edward played the baby in the Victorian melodrama. After *East Lynne* completed its run they were again anxious for work and, against Fenie's advice, joined a road company of the infamous *Black Crook*. *Black Crook* was the first American blockbuster musical, a five-and-a-half-hour extravaganza that originally opened in Niblo's Garden on Broadway in 1866. Fenie's fear became a reality, as Edward explained:

> In Pine Bluff, Arkansas, a gang of the "Oh! You kid!" boys made some obscene remarks when Mamma made her entrance clad in most revealing tights. Dad went over the footlights. It took all the money they had saved to bail him out. It was a pip of a brawl. Did Mamma pull the "I told you so" routine? No, sir! She agreed with him. Once again looking for employment. Not in that burg. They high-tailed it across the river into Memphis, Tennessee—but real fast.
>
> Dad caught on at Persicas. A box house of ill repute, located in the tenderloin district. He "Blacked Up" and put on afterpieces. (Nigger acts.) "The Ghost in a Pawnshop"; "Over the River Charlie"; and other famous old minstrel farces of that era. Mamma was never allowed to go near the joint.
>
> Not to be outdone, and over his most vehement protests, she got a job singing with the new Magic Lantern. Her sweet sentimental voice, accompanying the illustrated song slides, caused a mild sensation in a little Main Street house. "White Wings"; "The Passing Policeman"; "The Baggage Coach Ahead"; a few of the favorites. This was the first time they had been separated. Friction developed. Jealousy. But when the "grouch bag" is empty, any means of filling it is proper.

The owner of the Magic Lantern theatre had a big crush on Fenie and made a move on her. Fenie fought him off, bouncing a makeup box off of his head and knocking him out.

She thought she had killed him, and in near hysteria fled to Ned, who was performing at Persicas.

> Just ready to go on, his burnt cork makeup smeared her tear-stained face. Strong arms comforted her. Johnny Persica saved a bad situation. He convinced Dad to go on with the show. Soothed Mamma with his rough Italian sincerity. Offered her a job with him. Now the girls, in this line of show business, were expected to hustle wine sales. Working on "cork privileges" they picked up quite a bit of easy money. Dad exploded. Offered to lick Persica. Smash his joint. He yanked Mamma away. Quit on the spot. What a guy!

For the time being, Ned and Fenie ended their theatrical career and returned home to Galveston, and to the criticism and jibes of relations and friends. Ned joined the police force but made an awful law enforcer, as he slugged too many offenders. Desperate to provide for Fenie and Edward, he took a job as a longshoreman, doing heavy manual labor along the docks and loading bales of cotton into the holds of ships. They were doing all right and the two refused to talk about show business ... that is, until Ned badly injured his back. Joe Niemeyer, the owner of the Mascot Theatre, learned that Ned wasn't able to do anything physical for some time. Niemeyer convinced him to work at the Mascot, a somewhat shady venue, to produce afterpieces. The job fell through, as the reform candidate won the local election and closed all places of the Mascot's ilk.

Ned developed an idea and called the other actors from the Mascot together with a promising plan. They would put on a little variety show and play the towns nearby on a commonwealth plan, an agreement when all members of the act split the profits. He called this mixed-bag show "Sedgwick's Comedians."

In the meantime, Fenie was training Edward for the stage. "In her spare time she was teaching me to recite. With gestures! I could sing a few folk songs, even hop the buck a little. Under her tutelage I was advanced far beyond my years. I learned plenty! But my biggest thrill was always when Mamma rocked her chair and sang 'Jubilo' or 'Golden Slippers' as I harmonized." Fenie convinced a reluctant Ned to incorporate an act she came up with into his show. "Do an encore with me, made up in exact replica of his character. We sang one chorus of an old Irish ditty, 'Just Over,' and jigged a few steps. It stopped the show. The first time he had ever taken a back seat for anybody—and he loved it. Chip off the old block stuff. Very wisely Mamma allowed him to take the credit for 'his big idea.'"

Although the performances were successful, "Sedgwick's Comedians" only lasted for several weeks. The commonwealth plan wasn't working out too well, as there were too many bosses, as well as too many headliners.

One of the members who joined the troupe was an old dramatic actor who became Edward's tutor. Edward described him as a Rhodes scholar and a Phi Beta Kap from Harvard. "Must have been a family split somewhere. He was, in every particular, a gentleman. On occasion, he would take a nip too many and hold forth on the higher planes. Dad had a profound respect for his education. I adored him, and learned fast. The foundation of all my learning certainly came from old—well, he called himself Forrest Booth. Not a bad parlay in the dramatic Derby."

In a town named Manitou, located in Oklahoma up near the border of Indian Territory, the troupe got into financial trouble. The majority of the members took off, leaving Ned in charge of the situation. The town justice confiscated their trunks.

Fenie, who was pregnant with their second child, announced that Josie was ready to join the family. Ned swore he would risk anything to get their baggage released and send Fenie back home. "It was providence that catapulted him into Sam Henoch, selling his territory. On his insistent advice Dad called on the local Lodge of Red Men. Then and there he learned the great value of benevolent organizations. Not only did a brother lawyer front for him, but also a darn good doctor took charge of Mamma. He ordered that she was not to be moved under any circumstances. They also gave Dad the authority to go out after new members."

Forrest Booth had remained with them, and through the good graces of an elderly librarian he set up a class for dramatic readings and lessons. When Ned dropped in to watch him at work with a student, he hit upon another idea. His plan was to stage a home talent show, with the belles and beaux of the town to play parts, and other local talent to back up as a chorus of singers and dancers. Ned and Booth were to be the only professionals involved. He conferred with leaders of the Lodge and the Chamber of Commerce, who went for his pitch.

The life of the American Indians was the theme of their pageant (Edward "borrowed" it later in his life when he became a film scenarist). With rehearsals started, the advance sale of tickets would give them enough to pay their room and board and get professional medical attention for Josie's birth. Edward recalled that the thrills of opening night were enhanced by Josie's timely entrance:

> Of course it would have to happen. The night of the big show and Josie arrived simultaneously! Dad running between the two spots like a maniac. Through the grace of the Lord, and noble assistance from some real people, both events came off O.K. Mamma was all right. Her first daughter pushed the scales up to twelve pounds. The M.D. gave a clean bill of health. A gang of amateurs had a grand time. Albeit, there was many a slip between the cup and the final curtain. Dad and Booth played so many parts they ran into themselves getting on and off. The family cut from the profits was a healthy one.

Born March 13, 1894, Josie was christened Josephine Sedgwick. "Josie was the Old Man's heart. From the very first her temperament appealed to him. She swung with both hands at the slightest pretext. Hot-tempered. She squawked about everything that didn't go just her way. He loved it. He did not in the least approve of my methods of evading a battle with glib talk. But Mamma did. She was glad that I had not inherited the hair-triggered belligerency of my father."

Edward, skilled with a vivid imagination and a thirst for knowledge, became a natural scholar. Ned liked to brag to his friends about his "smart son" and showed him off. In many saloons and gambling houses Edward became the center of attraction with his "quips of the times."

Along with Booth, the family joined a rag trick (show under canvas) which came into town short-handed. Performing repertoire, actors had to be willing to participate in up to twelve plays in a two-week stand, with plays changing every night. The pay was $25 a week, plus cakes.

For the most part they enjoyed trouping through the southeast. Fenie and Ned doubled in brass, with Fenie on alto horn and Ned on bass drum. The fanfare started each morning with a parade, followed by a concert in front of the main entrance before each performance.

Tent show life proved to be rough—Fenie, especially, grew to despise it. On one occasion, as Edward described, while performing in Bodie, Alabama, a gang of locals decided to get in for free. "The 'Hey Rube' call! What a scrap. Showmen used stakes and crowbars. Dad stuck to his fists. He had a swell time. Once he went down under pressure. From out of nowhere, Mamma arrived with a club. She laid out a few. Dad got on his feet. Wow—did he go! I had myself a little fun, conking one or two. Perched on a prop box I swung a heavy cane of Dad's. Missed once, and fell off. I scrammed back to watch Josie. So help me, at her tender age she wanted in on the scrap."

The local law got involved and brought the melee under control. That night Fenie set her foot down firmly and demanded that they give their two weeks notice without delay. At first Ned protested, but then realized the tent show was too rough for the family. Ned and Booth immediately headed out for Birmingham, scouting for work.

Josie now occupied Edward's spot in the Taylor trunk tray. "She was beginning to get plenty fresh. Still heads up with Dad. Tried to give Mamma some of her lip and got a good wallop in return."

Ned and Booth returned with an offer: A friend of Booth's was producing the famous English play *The Celebrated Case* using a third-rate company at the Opera House. Fenie was given the lead role; Ned the character lead; Booth directed and played the Old Colonel; Edward was cast as an English five-year-old. "The plot centered around the boy," Edward explained. "If he recognized his father, a spy, he would be the cause of his execution. I loused up the first couple of shows. I would not accept a strange ham as my Dad. Mamma was patient. The Old Man steamed. But when I finally got up in the thing I stole the show. Got all the notices."

Although the one-night-stand outfit required a lot of travel, the nice people they worked with made it a happy experience. Fenie enjoyed the "refined" atmosphere of the "legitimate" theatre. The luxury of legitimate theatre meant a full-evening drama that utilized trained actors and skilled producers, which greatly distinguished it from that of the lowly vaudeville and burlesque fare. The show pulled them through a fairly successful season, and they closed in Danville, Virginia. Given the chance to return to Drury Lane, Booth left the company to return to England. It was a sad parting of the ways. The Sedgwicks never heard from him again, and he passed away the following year in London.

By the spring of 1898 the Sedgwicks had a productive little stock company of their own. As they played in a store show in Lake Charles, Louisiana, the newspaper headlines announce rumors of war with Spain. On April 25, the Spanish American War started.

> Dad came up with a brilliant idea. We closed our little show and quickly framed an act with a war theme. Our first taste of vaudeville. It was a dandy act. Cuba background; Red Cross tent. Mamma was a picture as a Clara Barton nurse. Off stage battle effects. Dad staggered on as a wounded rider. In Mamma's arms, he sang "Break the News to Mother." I finally got to be a drummer boy. My high tenor voice warbled "Goodnight Dolly Gray." Mamma soothed the soldier with "Sleep, Kentucky Babe." We harmonized. A little patriotic dialogue. A sock finale. Dad giving a fairly good impersonation of Teddy Roosevelt. Mamma, doubling as Columbia, guarded a little Cuban refugee. Me again. Josie made her stage debut as a Red Cross nurse. She was just past three. As she toddled out waving a flag, we all burst into the stirring "Hot Time in the Old Town Tonight." The house came down. We killed 'em!

At six years old, Edward became thrilled as his family finally had their first taste of big-time theater. "This was it! I could smell Tony Pastor's—Proctor's. We played several small-time theatres, broke in the act good. Agents were calling. Real booking was offered. It was suggested we go to New York and try out. Dad turned every offer down cold. He argued that we were much safer in this environment. He and I had our first battle. I got pretty fresh. He handed me rather roughly."

Fenie lost her temper with Ned, but in the end Ned got his way and they didn't go to New York City. As the war petered out, so did the act. There were a few weeks of layoffs, which again meant financial hardships.

Ned hit on another idea. The family would become independent of other actors and tour on their own. Ned just needed some time to write a series of sketches for the four of them. They decided to stay with Fenie's sister in Clebourne, Texas, for a while. Edward, who was put in school, described Clebourne as small-time life: "Corn-fed gals. Hay-pile lads. Deliver me!"

The Sedgwicks went back on the road with Ned's sketches. They started out playing small towns, with sketches changed every night. That way they could play to the same scanty, show-hungry audience every night.

Edward was at an age where he voraciously read "dime novels" (also known as "nickel weeklies" because of their half-dime price). He devoured titles such as *Liberty Boys of '76*, *Diamond Dick* and *Nick Carter Stories*. The booklets contained sensational detective stories and astounding wilderness adventures, which most likely influenced the derring-do silent films that he would be writing and directing as an adult. Ned discouraged Edward's choice of reading material and warned him that he "would go nuts reading that trash." "So I went underground. Chic sales, badly lighted rooms after hours, my libraries. Mamma wouldn't interfere, but Josie found my cache. I lost four priceless novels. Got a twenty-two pistol and was going to blast her. The disaster only adverted by the Old Man's interception. My first real licking. And Josie watched. Mamma dragged her away. She popped off and Mamma clouted her. We were a jolly little family. Just high-spirited. If you like that kind of stuff."

In the fall of 1898 the Sedgwicks prepared for the arrival of their third child. Ned was determined that this birth should be without the tumult of the others. Fenie suggested that she return to her sister's house in Clebourne. Instead, Ned booked himself, Edward, and Josie into a small city vaudeville house, where he framed a special act for them. Fenie was to have her next baby in the security of a hospital of a nearby town.

> We came into Hillsburg [Hillsboro, Texas] on a horse-drawn bus. It was quite a good-sized town. Lots of cotton. But the Katy R.R. bypassed the place by ten miles. Selection of the wrong site through stupid politics. The error was never rectified. A locoed steer leaped the right of way fence. The bus horses panicked and bolted. The driver lost the reins. It was a wild ride, bouncing and careening around sharp turns.
>
> Mamma tried to keep together as Dad fought with the driver to halt the team. Finally he had to do it himself. On the outskirts of town the bus lost a wheel. A crash landing. No one was badly hurt. But Mamma was out cold.
>
> They carried her away in a flat bed farm wagon to a small inn. The hastily summoned doctor found suspicious signs. Eileen was on the way. It was fortunate he was a good man for Mamma was in trouble. Dad went through his same routine. I was old enough to get in on this one.
>
> Josie was placed in my custody and we were both watched over by an old witch, who lived adjacent to the inn. What a horrible dame! She scared hell out of me with ghost stories and fearful predictions. Josie was too young to get them, or too tough, or both.

To make matters worse, someone stole their "grouch bag," filled with all of the family's earnings. Ned became frantic. He was able to get the local Red Men to advance enough money to pay for food and lodging for a few days.

On October 17, 1898, Eileen Sedgwick arrived. She was in rough shape, and Fenie was hurting as well. The doctor suggested surgery for Fenie, but in those days patients were hesitant to have any kind of surgery performed. The doctor warned Ned that she could never have another child, and that she needed a lot of immediate care.

> "Dad went into a huddle with the Tribe. Desperation inspired his greatest brainchild. A cotton carnival. A big amateur show. Three days of celebrations. Sham battles between "Indians" and the local company of State Militia. The civic leader of [Hillsboro] proved to be a go-getter. He went for the idea one hundred percent. So did the committee. This was to be a really big thing, all under the auspices of the Red Men. Dad was allowed to draw money against the proceeds. His well-established sideline of hustling members for the order also paid off. He was bubbling with enthusiasm when he came to see Mamma. She was a pretty sick girl, but game to the core. She said she would be up and about to help him with this show. And she did.
>
> What a three days! What a cotton carnival! What a beating the Old Man took. So did we. There was no Forrest Booth to help. Dad had to handle the amateur actors alone. Hustle ads for the big souvenir program. Paint signs. Gather enough costumes for the outdoor stuff. He discovered a young man in town, Charlie Brown. He had spent a few months on a black top show with a carnival. He was made assistant and proved invaluable. Josie and I escaped from the witch. Brrr—I'm still a little scared in the dark. What a character! It all rolled right off Josie's knife. What a gal!

As preparation went on for weeks, Ned became an important man in the town, which cost him pounds in weight and put many a line in his face. Fenie attended the last few rehearsals. She insisted on playing the Indian Princess in a little sketch that Ned created, "The Chief's Revenge."

> At last the great day arrived—and with it headaches. As it started, Eileen became very ill. I got hit in the face with a baseball. Catching without a mask. Had a shiner the size of a hen's egg. Josie decided she did not want to sing a duet with me and I didn't blame her. We were both backhanded—we sang. And for a climax, two of the better actors were called out of town.
>
> The parade started at ten in the morning. The streets were so jammed with out-of-town visitors, the horses and cotton floats could hardly get through. A couple of yokels were knocked down making practical jokes. A few horses acted up when the Silver Cornet Band blasted. That was understandable. They were awful!
>
> Then the Main Event—The Sham Battle. I shudder to this day when I think of some of the episodes. Several scores of mounted savages were to attack the Courthouse. The defenders were the Boys in Blue. Naturally, they had to be the victors. When rescued by a hard-riding relief force, these choice Cavalrymen were to chase the Indians away. Flag-waving. Patriotic songs. Hundreds of rounds of blank ammo had been distributed. All set for a tremendo. It sounded swell ... but...
>
> To bolster up their morale, several of the more festive-minded lads had loaded up on "red eye." Some of the other troops had over indulged at a "beer bust." Their intentions were of the best. The shrill notes of the bugle rent the air. Yipe! The first group of bareback-riding savages hit the square. Their guns firing promiscuously. War whoops echoing up and down the streets.
>
> This unaccustomed bedlam panicked the mounts. Synthetic aborigines were tossed about and catapulted all over the square. The horses bolted. Crashed into stores—tore through clusters of decorations. Some of the better riders hung on. Their mounts charged up the Courthouse steps. Then the defenders opened fire. More Indians bit the dust—more spilled horses. Dad, riding among the flashing hooves, attempted to get some semblance of order. He sure had guts! It took a couple of guardian angels to keep him in one piece. What a mess! The most amazing thing about the fracas, no one was seriously injured. Just a lot of bruised fannies and a lot of peeled-off skin. They all thought the affair was a huge success. The onlookers had a grand time. Success or no success, I never want to see another scramble like it.
>
> Mamma had a difficult time getting through the show that night. Weak, and concerned about Dad, to say nothing of what the local actors were doing to the art of histrionics. It was all so new

to her. A lot of emotion, too. As a surprise, and in honor of Eileen's advent into the family, Dad had scratched off a little song and called it "And Then There Were Five." He sang it himself. I thought it was lousy. Dad was deeply hurt. Mamma was furious—nearly twisted my ear off. I made a mental note not to press her too far. Maybe I was becoming a little too fresh.

But I went great in the show. My black eye was not conspicuous in Bowery makeup. I took four bows. What a ham I was. Josie did all right, too. Mamma had a little episode with the young blade of the town, who played the soldier lover. He got a bit too amorous in the love scenes. She smacked his face good when they came off. I, accidentally, stuck a spearhead in his leg. It was a good thing Dad was too busy elsewhere to catch any of this. That show would have ended with a bang!

Everything happened that usually happens in one of those affairs. Mishaps—stalled actors. But the locals thought they were good. Their families and friends agreed. They paid a lot of money to be in on the deal.

With a friendly sendoff by the townspeople, the Sedgwicks left with the "grouch bag" bulging. They were returning to Galveston. Ned needed to attend to the settlement of his father's property, which was found to be worth a lot more than had first been estimated. Although he had resented returning to domestic life, he saw an opportunity to improve the family's situation. They purchased a house with a nice-sized yard on the shore near the Gulf of Mexico. Edward described the healthful home atmosphere as a welcome relief.

> Such a contrast to ten years of playing tanks—battling around jerkwater towns. But somehow the new environment caused us to lose perspective. We all overplayed our hands a bit. Mamma secured a hired girl. Dad started raising prize chickens. Black Cochins with giant feathered legs. One old hen, the largest chicken I ever saw, got a crush on him. Ever the showman, he named her Madame and trained her to do tricks. She followed him around like a dog. I was scared to death of her. She knew it and gave me the business. I got a dog—my first one. Dad brought him to me. Brownie was swell—licked the dog next door. But it was all so marvelous. Home, companions, room to play—all the everyday things most poor show kids are deprived of.

Ned and Fenie enrolled Edward at St. Mary's College, a Jesuit school, where misery became part of his education. "Brother, were they tough. Mabel Tidd was my first girl friend. Over the back fence she listened sympathetically as I complained of my harsh treatment. But I must be brave and take it. Oh—did I take it. Mamma, also, patiently listened to my woes and gave the proper amount of consolation. Dad scoffed. This world had no place for whiners and weaklings."

Josie didn't fare any better, as she was enrolled at a parochial school where she gave them trouble on her first day. "Those Sisters were well versed in the handling of tough kids. She was knocked down a peg or two. Came back swinging. It had to be her way or no dice.

"Eileen was just about ready to toddle. Nothing bothered her. Eat and sleep—her only contributions."

Josie and Edward were invited to their first birthday party. She was dressed up in starched organdy and a blue sash. Meanwhile, Edward was fit to be tied when a velvet "Lord Fauntleroy" suit was given to him to wear, accessorized with a lace collar and flowing bow tie. "For once Dad was on my side. But Mamma liked it. And off I went, miserable and uncomfortable."

> The titters that greeted my appearance started an immediate brawl. But cooler heads and the lure of ice cream and cake prevented mayhem. However, there was a catch to the party. Being show kids we were expected to perform for our share of goodies. Josie flatly refused, and was all for storming out of the place. Finally, we succumbed. With very bad grace and scowling faces we went through the motions of one of our acts. Finishing a dance, Josie deliberately tripped me. I lost my balance—

crashed into the table. It toppled over on me. My new suit was a mess from the deluge of melting ice cream and gooey cake. The hostess was horrified but the kids loved it.

At that moment Dad and Mamma arrived to take us home. She took one look at me and nearly fainted. Dad chucked and gave me a sly wink of approval. Strained apologies, forced smiles. Thanks for such a lovely party.

The family returned home to find that a tragedy had struck: Madame was dead. Ned was heartbroken, crying like a baby as he knelt beside his pet.

Mamma was misty-eyed, too. First time I ever saw Josie really cry. I tried valiantly to squeeze out a tear. No go. However I did feel sorry for Dad. In his book, he had lost a member of his family. We had a funeral. Madame was laid away in style. Dad officiated. She was buried in her favorite resting place under an oleander bush.

When it was all over, Dad blew up. Blamed it all on the house. It was a damn Jonah! We were getting the hell out of there at once. He sent for the real estate man on the corner. A quick deal was consummated. The place was leased to the Kinkaids for the summer season. Packing, plans—getting rid of the chickens.

As we were ready to leave I played a farewell scene with Mabel Tidd. My first kiss. It was all right. Poor Mabel—her old man caught us. Big hassle. You'd think I had ruined the girl. Dad promised he would look into the matter. That ended it. Somehow, I think he went for it.

We should always be reverently grateful to Madame. Strange—the workings of fate. Destiny's tots and other phenomenon certainly applied to us. The death of a hen saved all our lives.

The Sedgwicks moved into a new house in the heart of the city: ten rooms for twelve dollars a month rent. Ned missed his Madame, and Edward missed Mabel.

The morning of Sunday, September 8, 1900, held ominous signs. Edward was doing duty as an altar boy at St. Patrick's early mass, with Ned and Fenie singing in the church's choir. Fenie voiced a strange feeling of premonition—she felt she was singing in that church for the last time. Others churchgoers felt apprehensive. Rumors that a major warning had been posted by the Coast Guard were met with troubled comments. Parishioners started for their homes in a quiet, subdued mood.

The Sedgwicks were hosting an oyster roast and afternoon party at their house, with games, barrels of beer, and mounds of good Southern food. The enjoyment was false and strained as anxious eyes kept looking up at the sky.

Thunderheads appeared out of the southeast. An unnatural stillness. Not a breath of air, like being in a vacuum. The children's laughing and crying sounded unreal. Parents were overly solicitous. A few big drops of rain, and the gathering broke up early.

Dad did yeoman service trying to discredit the ominous rumors that poured in from all sides. There came news of a major disturbance at New Orleans. Small vessels were swamped trying to reach port. Old seafaring men advised that we batten down. The food was carried inside. We were alone when the first heavy rain fell from a copper-colored sky. A gust of wind rattled the loose gear. Then again that terrible silence.

With estimated winds of 135 miles per hour, the Galveston Hurricane of 1900 made landfall.

By mid-afternoon it was in full fury. Blinding lightning accompanied by tremendous thunderbolts. Sheets of impenetrable rain. Water rising until the streets were impassible. Refugees staggered in from the outlying districts. Hysteria. Panic. Terrified humans already tolling great losses. Sagas of courage and heroism.

Dad pulled several women and children into our house. The men were struggling against impossible odds, fighting for their lives. Mamma found extra coverings and medicines for the injured.

Edward and Josie, about the time that Eileen was born, and the Galveston Hurricane of 1900 made landfall (courtesy E. Hutson).

Brownie, my dog, was lost. I spotted him drifting towards the rushing torrent. Instinctively I ran out to save him, and both of us nearly went under. Only Dad's tremendous strength dragged us back to safety. Brownie crawled under a bed, whining, terrified.

The building across the street collapsed with a thunderous roar. All occupants disappeared. We stared helplessly. Our house was jammed with unfortunates. All we could do was pray. Mamma bundled Eileen and held her tight. Josie clung to Dad. The house lurched, trembled, as the hurricane velocity of the wind struck us broadsides. The house next door slid off its foundations. But it braced as it shored our side—and held. The Freeds [next-door neighbors] lost a roof. They joined out with us.

Terror-stricken people stampeded in panic—wept—called on the Master for help. Dad was compelled to knock out two half-crazed men. They attempted to kill their own—put them out of their misery. Mamma tried to rouse the women to help. But they just sat, staring with unseeing eyes into space.

Night fell. The wind and waters increased. Our lower floor was flooded six feet deep. It was seawater; Dad tasted it. I heard him tell one of the saner men, another hour or so and it would be the end. A few flickering candles were our only source of light, casting eerie, ghost-like shadows. I thought of the old witch in Hillsburg. I prayed harder and louder.

The storm grew in intensity. Our front windows were now bending with the wind, the glass acting like rubber. We huddled around Dad. It looked as if this was the end. We kissed and said our goodbyes. With a crash the huge brick chimney collapsed on the roof. Maddened hysteria—frenzied screams. It was terrible!

Suddenly Dad perked up. He had heard something. The tempest was abating, the rain slackening off. The wind died down abruptly, In a measure of moments the hurricane blew itself out, as it rushed over to the mainland. Soon, there was complete silence. Only the faint splashing of water as it receded and swirled back towards the Gulf. We froze in disbelief, fearing to move. Dad pushed his way out to the wrecked front porch. Despite Mamma's frantic calls I followed him.

The overhead clouds were being cleared away by a brilliant moon. Even in this dull light we could see the terrible havoc. Mounds of debris. Rapidly receding waters. It was past midnight. We were alive—we were safe. Everyone joined in a solemn prayer of thankfulness to the Almighty. The storm was over!

With the first streaks of dawn we were outside. Watching, heartsick, the stream of battered humans struggling down the twisted street. Each had a tale more horrifying than the other. The entire beachfront, for miles, was completely gone. A Catholic orphanage was wiped out. Nuns were found with their little charges tied to them. Their last act one of heroism. Fort Crockett and the entire garrison was obliterated. The waterfront was smashed. The stories grew and grew.

The hurricane caused a great loss of life, with the death toll estimated to be 8,000 individuals. (Various records list the death toll to be anywhere between 6,000 and 12,000 deaths.) Dead bodies were everywhere. As the day wore on, Ned learned that he had lost several relatives and many friends. The mayor proclaimed a state of grave emergency. Work gangs were organized to clear away enough debris to make passage possible. Ned was sworn in as special deputy to assist the remnants of the police and fire departments. The ghouls started robbing the dead of their precious possessions. Short work was made of these criminals, as they were shot on the spot or were hanged.

The devastated city was completely cut off from the mainland. All bridges were destroyed, with most of the boats wrecked and no channel available for larger crafts to navigate. The area was without potable water and very little clean food. The Army, the Navy, and the Red Cross eventually arrived to help. Edward recollected:

> Yes, I saw all this. I saw much too much for a lad of my age. Mamma was an angel. With other women, she cooked in outdoor ovens. They boiled water. They slaved at the most menial tasks. Due to their care, the rest of the population was saved.

The second day Dad took me out to where our home had once stood. There was nothing for miles. Just a flat and barren landscape. Even the rubble had been washed out to sea. Poor little Mabel. Dad tried to locate our backyard. I knew what he was searching for. But there was no trace. September 8, 1900.

Without a home or job, the Sedgwicks once again turned to show business and participated in dozens of benefits for the flood sufferers. Josie and Edward performed in their first act together, introducing "Honeysuckle and the Bee." The city leaders erected a huge auditorium for a mammoth show, with Ned handling its production. He used the tried-and-true Native American theme and made it a huge success, raising a lot of money for the needy. Although it was several weeks of hard work, living on commissary issue. The city awarded the family medals for their generosity and humanitarian efforts.

Chapter Two

Tank Towns and Four-a-Day Vaudeville

Oil! Black gold! On January 10, 1901, at around 10:30 a.m., the Lucas Gusher at Spindletop blew. Beaumont, Texas, was in the first throes of her oil boom. There was an intense excitement as Galveston newspapers covered the story and travelers handed out bulletins about the get-rich-quick opportunities that were available.

Ned ran into an old grifter named Doc Hollings, who was working with a carnival outfit. Together they concocted a scheme to make some money. Galveston, as a city in ruin, lacked any type of business opportunities for entertainers, so the family prepared to move to search for work. Doc had a sister who ran a boarding house in the heart of Beaumont, which Edward described as a dump:

> What a town. Mud, madness, money talk, and more mud. We were all herded into one room. Two double beds and a cot. Cheap, too. Brother, what prices! Four dollars a day for that rat hole. But it was a palace compared to the hovels, tents, and hogans where others were living. Oil-crazed people poured into town by the thousands. And the mud, inches deep—everywhere. The streets were so gutted from the heavy hauling equipment that the slime and black clay was almost down to bedrock. It was horrible. But money? Oh, yes!
>
> Doc dug up an old warehouse and converted it into a theatre. Picking up three or four stock actors, we were in business. A ten, twenty, and thirty show. But our prices were two and a half top. And we got it. The pioneer west? This was much worse. Bearded brutes from the fields, drillers, truckmen, thugs, raucous and smelly. They loved our show. Weepy old melodramas: "The Convict's Daughter"; "The Golden Giant Mine"; "The Two Orphans"; and other creaky vehicles of that ilk. It was a pushover. The comedy specialties brought the howls. Mamma was thoroughly disgusted. I had my snoot way up in the air. Dad placated: We were here to quickly line our pockets and then leave. Confidentially, he loved it—Josie, too."

Four months after the excitement of the Lucas Gusher, news leaked out that the Higgins No. 1 pump was brought in at Spindletop. A wild stampede began as droves of people made their way over the muddy roads to the edge of town to see the well. Ned hired a team a team of horses to drive the family over to the site. The team soon bogged down in the deep mire and choked roads. They abandoned the buckboard and set out on foot, with Ned and Edward alternating in carrying Eileen through ankle- and sometimes calf-deep mud.

They eventually reached a spot on a small hill, just a few hundred yards away from the well. The family was cranky and hungry from their tiring trek. Ned cajoled a vendor into selling him some stale sandwiches and sour milk for the obscene price of five dollars.

Edward described the thrill of the excitement as something he would never forget. "Higgins No. 1 blew in. With a roar that could be heard for miles the cap tore loose with the rush of confined gas and oil. The black gold gushed from the casing, spouting hundred [*sic*] of feet over the top of the rig. It was terrifying and awesome to watch that geyser of deep black liquid shoot forth, flowing one hundred thousand barrels a day. We were deluged with the stuff. The crowds screamed, cheered, went berserk, to see millions of dollars fly into the air. My knees buckled, and Dad lifted me from the ground. The emotion was a bit too much."

As the workers struggled to cap the precious flow of oil, lucky investors danced about and embraced each other, acting like maniacs. Fenie became ill from all of the excitement and asked Ned to take them home. It was late when they returned to the boarding house and dropped, exhausted, into their beds.

All of the next day they listened to the bedlam of a town gone completely mad. There would be no show that night as the population of Beaumont was milling around the streets in drunken revel. Edward wrote, "From then on we coined money. Our makeshift theatre was packed and jammed at outlandish prices. More and more people poured into town every hour: Riff raff, con men, thieves, harlots. We paid an ex-sheriff twenty five dollars a night to carry the sacks of money to a hotel safe. It was mostly gold."

Tempted by the new wells that were established in the area, Doc left the group and invested in the oil business, leaving the front of the house without anyone to keep an eye on it. Ned replaced Doc with a man named Charlie Brown, making him company manager. After three weeks, Brown went oil-happy. "Everybody in the county was investing in what later proved to be the mother lode of Texas oil. Everybody, with the exception of us. We had a chance to make a killing. Two acrobats, the Heyworth brothers, invested five thousand in a lease and wanted Dad to go in with them. Oh, no. Six years later they sold out for twelve million!

"But we, too, were getting up in the world. We were now the proudly ensconced lodgers in two rooms of the big hotel."

Ned met an entrepreneur named W.W. Kyle, Sr., who was just completing the Kyle Theatre in 1900. The "opera house," which was planned for future road shows, was a combination house—the type of theatre that showed both motion pictures and vaudeville. It was the first large building on Beaumont's Orleans Street, and properly was on Liberty, with Orleans Street itself ending at the playhouse. For more than a quarter of a century it was the entertainment center of Beaumont and southeastern Texas. In its peak it had boasted the largest stage in the South, and was the largest and finest theater between New Orleans and Houston. The theatre, which seated a total of 1,700 people on its three floors, was rich in its accouterments, comfortable, and was all that a legitimate theater should be in its day.

Beaumont was fortunate in that it was located between New Orleans on the east and Houston and San Antonio on the west. The greatest actors of the time who were on the road took the coast route, eventually stopping over in Beaumont for a night or two, giving Beaumont the status of being one of the best "one-night stand" towns in the country. In years to come, famous plays such as Tom Dixon's *The Clansman* appeared on its stage. The Kyle stage was said to be the only one in the area that could handle the colossal production *Ben-Hur* without having its back removed to afford additional space. Memorable entertainers such as Lillian Russell, Julia Marlow, and Charles B. Hanford performed there. Lew Dockstader's famous minstrels were often included on the billing at the Kyle. The theatre closed in 1940, due to competition with other motion picture theaters.

Ned and Kyle went into huddles, discussing future possibilities as to how his theatre should be used once construction was completed.

Two of the group's actors quit for oil. Ned found a juvenile man of about forty and a heavy woman whom Edward described as a "washed-out, voluptuous blonde, a bit on the balmy side." He was just entering manhood and she was taking notice.

> I was just about to announce to the world "Today I am a man" when I found her looking me over. One night she coaxed me into her hotel room. She kissed me. I had never known anything like that kiss. It scared the hell out of me.
>
> Mama had missed me in the family checkup. I was trailed and caught with my siren. What a battle! Completely forgetting her refinement, she swung from the floor in a most unlady-like manner. Blonde hair flew all over the room and hall. The night man and house dick came up. Dad arrived. When he heard the story, he stood by and held the men off. Mamma went the limit. For the finale, she kicked my inamorata's rather larger posterior down the stairs and out of the hotel. It took a doctor and a few sedatives to calm her down. Dad insisted on a little private chat with me. I came out second best. But—I learned about women from her.

That ended the show, with it being closed right then and there.

Ned kept himself busy by organizing a tribe of Red Men, which was primarily comprised of members who needed a decent place to go in the grimy town. He made three times the membership dues on them. Josie and Edward were placed back in school.

In 1901 the Sedgwicks were the first act to open the Kyle Theatre in Beaumont, Texas, where they would hone their vaudeville skills.

Edward found a part-time after-school job, taking tickets for a novelty show called "The Eruption of Vesuvius." "It was a combination traction miniature and electric illusion show," Edward explained. "Good effects for that period. But the real feature of the show was a moving picture, *The Great Train Robbery*. That was really why I took the job."

Considered to be the first narrative film, *The Great Train Robbery* (1903) changed the techniques that were being used to film and edit movies. The ten-minute silent incorporated a major breakthrough in that it used parallel editing to tell its story, showing two separate lines of action or events happening continuously at identical times but in different places. In addition, there was an emphasis on location shooting which added a sense of realism to the story—all prior filming had utilized static stage-bound camera placements. Directed and photographed by Edwin S. Porter, a former cameraman who worked for Thomas Edison, it became the most popular and commercially successful film of the pre-nickelodeon era, confirming the marketability of the photoplay.

Edward was in awe of the projected story. "Several times each afternoon and night I stared fascinated at this new medium. I made mental notes for the future. I dragged the family in as my guests. Mamma thought it was quite interesting. Josie merely sniffed. Eileen stared open-mouthed, enthralled. Dad waxed prophetic: 'Moving pictures! Never last—just a silly novelty.' We had another little discussion. I was all enthusiasm—all for trying to become part of it. I saw the Edison trademark. That meant New York! Some day I'd get there. Then the power plant failed. There was no juice heavy enough to carry the load. The exhibitor pulled out with his apparatus. I was left with my dreams and plans."

The family went back to see Spindletop, which was now a forest of derricks with hundreds of wells. Ned continued to refrain from investing in the billions of barrels of oil that were being pumped.

A fortune of another kind meant big news to the Sedgwicks, as Edward explained:

> We were to open the Kyle Theatre with a temporary variety show. The town had calmed down considerably—almost back to normal living. We gathered a few good acts. Dad was master of ceremonies. Josie and I did a singing and dancing skit. One of our old sketches closed the show. But the big hit was "Baby Eileen, the Child Wonder." It was her first whack at our business. A Spanish dance—with a tambourine. She sang a little song, recited a semi-naughty poem. Just approaching three, and she slayed them. There was a sister act on the bill. I caught myself looking at the younger one with ideas. Dad also caught the look and made dire threats, which I somehow believed. But—could I help it if I had a line?
>
> My big moment arrived. Gus Hill sent one of his better road shows, "Pickings from Puck," to the Kyle for three days. Straight from the Tulane in New Orleans, it was big-time. They laid off for a day and caught our show.
>
> The company manager was having trouble with a youngster who played a bellhop. Willard Simms, of "The Paperhanger" [vaudeville sketch] fame, was the star. He cajoled Dad into letting me play the part until they could find a replacement. He countered by insisting that Josie must also have a spot. It was agreed, and I was in tenth heaven. A big musical show. Fifty people. Tripping over chorus girls. Swell scenery. I knew this was it!

Edward rehearsed the part in a few hours and prepared himself for the opening. To the delight of the audience, Josie and Edward performed a new song and cakewalk: "Georgia Camp Meeting," a hit song that was recently recorded by John Philip Sousa. Simms approved of Edward's style and wanted him to continue on the road with the show. Ned wouldn't allow it, even though Fenie offered to go along as a light character woman, playing a bit part, and in the process acting as Edward's chaperone. After pleading with him to give Edward his big chance, Ned finally allowed them to stay for two weeks. They performed in Port Arthur and Orange, Texas, and then on to Lake Charles, Louisiana. "This was big league! I hoped that Dad might relent. No, sir. He pulled us away from what, to me, meant Broadway. The show was to close in New York on the Subway Circuit. We got as far as Alexandria, Louisiana."

The family returned to perform in the Galveston area as the Sedgwick Comedy Company. The January 1, 1905, edition of *The Galveston Daily News* announced a show later that week that also included other talented performers.

> The three Sedgwick children, Dora Andres and little Rhea Nichols, the five phenomenal children performers, and Ethel Hanson, Genevieve Foster, Will Lathrop, Moss and Seymour and the two great acts, "The Miser Ghost" and "Booker Washington's Statue," will all be seen at the Sedgwick Company's show and dance at Red Men's Hall Thursday, Jan. 5.

Fenie and Ned were still very active in fraternities, with Ned an officer of the Caronkaway Tribe of Red Men and Fenie a member of the Ladies of Dingeman Hive No. 851, Ladies of the Modern Macabee. Fenie made plans to entertain with the Ladies of Dingeman later that month, performing one of her popular recitations. With over 500 in attendance, filling Cathedral Hall to capacity, others on the program sang, played instruments or performed magic.

Frustrated because he wasn't advancing quickly enough to the big stage, Edward got into a serious argument with Ned, accusing him of standing in his way. "Called him old-timey—tank actor. Wondered why he didn't slug me. Mamma tried to intervene and I yelled at her. Then I got flattened." Without delay, Edward was sent off to attend Peacock Military Academy at San Antonio. "Tuition was part paid but I must work my way through if I want to stay. So, in hock for six months, I left the family on my pilgrimage. I felt I hated my father for stifling my big chance—planned on ways to hurt him. But when I arrived at my prison, I got the works so strenuously that I forgot all about my martyrdom. Much too occupied dodging upper classmen. Bless him for this decision. It saved me from—well, whatever kids are saved from."

Edward won an academic and athletic scholarship and stayed on at the academy through the summer term. By the following year he was the hot shot of the school, putting on shows that helped him pay his own way through school. Edward often performed solo at Peacock's entertainment venues. On the school's football team the stocky Sedgwick played right guard. During his sophomore, junior, and senior years, he was recognized as the best tactician in the corps. Graduating with the rank of first lieutenant, he seriously contemplated a military life, but the lure of the stage proved the stronger, and in the end he eventually rejoined his family.

Meanwhile, the Sedgwicks, minus one, had started out on the road once more. Promoting themselves as the Four Sedgwicks they continued to play around the oil fields. Fenie felt that the seedy towns weren't an appropriate environment for Josie and Eileen to grow up in. They returned to Galveston where the girls could get proper schooling. With the money that she had carefully saved from their work in Beaumont, Fenie signed Josie up for piano lessons and enrolled Eileen in dancing school.

In late spring of 1908 the family wired an emergency message to Edward, asking him to meet up with them in Zwolle, Alabama. When he read the wire, he thought the request

Left to right: Eileen, Edward, Fenie, and Josie, circa 1905. Edward had just entered the Peacock Military Academy in San Antonio, Texas (courtesy E. Hutson).

for him to respond to the crisis was a gag of some kind. His cadet battalion was just preparing to go on a hike with the regular army, and as a cadet captain Edward was to command his company along with the real soldiers. Although he was disappointed that he had to leave school, he eagerly anticipated the reunion with the family, as it was several years since he last saw them. Having no civilian clothes, and a lack of funds to purchase any, he left for Zwolle wearing the school-issued olive drab uniform that was patterned after the army.

My family were all at the station to meet me. It was a shock from both sides. We stared at each other with mixed emotions. Somehow, I couldn't orient myself.

Josie was now a young lady. Pretty as a picture, and pert as ever. Dad looked tired and worn. The streaks of silver in Mamma's hair showed the strain she had been under in those years on the road. I gulped when I kissed her, then swept her off the ground in my arms. I was nearly six feet and I wanted her to be proud of her big strong boy. I reached for Josie to inflict the same treatment. With a sharp remark, she rudely pushed me away. No silly college "Rah Rah" boy was going to mess her up! She hadn't changed.

Eileen was another shock. All taffy and wide grins. Quite a little girl now. But she showed the proper respect for her brother in military dress. I went for her in a big way.

Then I reached for Dad's hand. A moment of silence as he looked straight and deep into my eyes. He took my hand. I couldn't resist being a smart aleck and put the pressure on hard. What a mistake. I nearly went to my knees. He still had it! Then I embraced him. He smiled happily and we were friends again.

> Zwolle was a little sawmill town in a clearing on the edge of a forest, with the stumps from cut-down pine trees still sticking out of the center of the streets. At breakfast in the wide-porched boarding house, Edward got the complete low-down on just how poorly they were doing. They were in debt due to a foolish investment promoted by a relative, who had taken everything. Again Ned was forced to put on shows for the Red Men. Edward realized the trouble they were in and that his help was desperately needed.

We went into the parlor and Josie played the piano for me. She was quite good. I sang some of our school songs. She said they were awful. I rose to the defense and our first battle was on. This was more like it—I was beginning to feel at home.

I soon learned that I was to be in the amateur show that very night. Playing the soldier lover opposite Josie's Indian princess, Little Fawn. Then we really had at it. I began throwing rhetorical ambiguity around, choice metaphors and similes bounced off the walls. Dad sat in frozen silence. Josie countered with the lowest form of slang. Mamma finally broke up this little verbal shindig. Eileen sat and squeezed a giant Teddy bear, not in the least perturbed. What was there to do? I played the part that night.

Disgusted and confused by the amateur actors, I was lousy. So was the show. There was one exception—Eileen. That kid was great. I got ideas about her right then.

Poor Dad—everything happened to him. "The Chief's Revenge" finale called for the soldier to shoot the bad Indian. Dad was this Indian—Chief Standing Mule. I read my line and pulled the prop gun. It jammed. No shot. To save the curtain I rushed in and hit him on the head with the pistol butt. I swung a bit too hard—Dad was out cold. Hastily, we improvised a curtain speech. When the show was over, he still laid there. But when he came to and realized what had happened—wow! Leaping to his feet, he started after me. I beat all printing records out of that little opera house and down the main street. Dad, in hot pursuit, called me everything in the book. It was a ludicrous situation—mad Indian chasing brave soldier. He would have beaten my head in if he had caught me. I managed to duck into the boardinghouse, upstairs to my cell, and bolted the door. I wanted no part of him in that mood.

Later on that night I heard a timid knock. The door cautiously opened, and Josie entered. Ill at ease, she came over and sat on the edge of the bed. I was all set for a brawl, but she crossed me completely. She wanted to have a confidential talk. This was my first real glimpse of her in repose. She was a woman; her negligee emphasized this fact. A darn good-looking girl. Then I received another shock. She blushed.

Then she gave me the cold facts regarding the gravity of the family situation. It was not a pretty picture. In no uncertain terms I told her we were wasting our lives, our youth. These terrible little burgs, Red Men, and amateur shows; these sort of things were Stone Age. Our place was in the east. Big time vaudeville was the answer. I called attention to the talents of Eileen. We could frame a novelty family act—a good one. I modestly told her I had a sensational idea. She went for it, and we plotted and planned a line of attack. First, some good hot letterheads, then advertising, secure a go-getter agent. It all sounded great—but how? We knew there would be opposition from Dad. I argued that somewhere along the line he had lost his grip. She blew up on that one and I had to back water quick. However, she agreed on our plans. Now—how to get money. Mamma would never dig into the shrinking "grouch bag" unless she was in on it. We had to manage this on our very own. Then Josie completely floored me. She had a bracelet that was worth quite a few dollars. We could pawn it, and use that for money. She gave it to me unhesitatingly.

Far into the night we conferred, and all in perfect harmony. I drew up a dummy letterhead and submitted it for her approval. She thought it was very clever. There, in that little stuffy room the FIVE SEDGWICKS VAUDEVILLE ARTISTS was born. I kissed her good night, and she blushed again. The die was cast.

The family still needed to fill a final obligation to the Red Men for a show that sent them to Opelousas, Louisiana. It turned out to be a fairly good-sized town, with a greater amount of larger sawmills. Edward wrote that in Opelousas, "[w]e were pleasantly surprised at the local stage-struck kids who turned up at the first call for talent. A flock of mighty nice-looking chicks strutted in. They seemed to know their way around, too. It looked like a few interesting weeks in the offing. I even caught Josie casting an appraising eye over the male stalwarts. Solicitously, I offered to take over the rehearsals for Dad. But he didn't fall for it. He just grunted that he and Mamma would be present at all gatherings. Well, you can't be ruled off for trying."

Edward and Josie schemed at every possible opportunity. They hocked the bracelet and hid the pawn ticket. They purchased a money order for the cost of the letterhead printing and sent it off, along with the layout dummy and head shots to a printer in Kansas City. They had crossed their first Rubicon.

Edward befriended an expert pool player named Adrian Jones. A New Yorker, he taught Edward pool tricks and wanted him to become his shill to knock off the players who thought they were good. They would split the take. After one trail Edward quit, as he had too much sympathy for the loser. Adrian shrugged off his decision and invited him upstairs to a gambling room.

> On our way we ran into Josie and Eileen, off on a shopping tour. When we gave her the eye she didn't seem to resent it, so I was forced to introduce them. He was all set for a nice cozy chat. She smirked coyly. I could have slugged her. When I started hustling him away, Josie glared at me and attempted to follow. Why couldn't she go along? It was a bit embarrassing, but I finally managed to shoo my sisters away. Adrian got over definitely that he had future ideas. I said nothing.
>
> Upstairs, Adrian started shooting craps. I sat in a lookout chair and watched a stud game. Several nasty glances were tossed at my uniform. Did I know it resembled the state troopers? I found out later, but at the present all was serene. Harmony reigned as the boys lost or won. My thoughts started to stray when...
>
> A pistol shot came from right under me. A player, seated in the game I was watching, gasped, hit the center of the table, then slumped to the floor. There wasn't a sound. Everyone froze. Fascinated, I stared at the small blue hole in the man's forehead, right between the eyes. He lay motionless. Suddenly there was a scream, an accusing curse from across the room. Two quick shots. Then all hell broke loose.
>
> I hit the deck—and fast. Slid under a table for cover. Crawling towards me, Adrian indicated that we make a break for the door. Strangely enough I wasn't afraid, weapons had never bothered me much. However, there was nothing heroic about me. Several more shots zinged overhead as we made the stairs. At that moment the police came charging up. They passed me up with a quick glance, but they grabbed Adrian. Struggling and yelling for me he was dragged back into the room. My uniform again. This was quite all right with me. I was getting the hell away from there.

When I hit the street I found myself slap-bang in the middle of a gambler's war! Two rival factions were fighting over some issue and were throwing plenty of slugs. I took cover back of a brick abutment of the corner building. A hasty reconnaissance, and my heart nearly stopped.

Josie and Eileen were just leaving a department store, directly in the line of fire. I screamed for them to go back, but they couldn't hear me above the din. For a moment they were badly frightened. Then Josie regained her wits. Quickly, she forced Eileen against the brick wall. She stood perfectly still, shielding her.

The firing increased. An old gentleman, coming out of the same store, was hit and crumpled to the street. He lay there, just a few feet from the girls. A gun-happy moron, brandishing a huge horse pistol, charged straight at Josie. She rammed her parasol down his throat. Dropping the gun, he staggered away.

Bullets spattered like rain as I leaped across the street. A policeman spotted me, saluted the uniform, shoved a gun in my hand and ordered me to take over. I haven't the remotest idea what I did, but it must have been the right thing. Firing a few shots over the heads of the battlers, I started toward them. Why? I still haven't the faintest idea. They ran, and the scrap ended abruptly.

I made my way to Josie and Eileen. There was lots of excitement. Two people had been killed, and several others wounded. I was some kind of a hero. Even Josie beamed at me. I gave out with an "Oh, it was nothing," but had to get into a drugstore. A pretense to get the girls a sedative—but really for me. My knees were buckling as I fought off the sickness, the seasick kind. I talked a clothing store proprietor out of a suit of civilian clothes the next day.

Later on, at rehearsal, Dad congratulated me, but there was a skeptical look in his eye. Also, there was something accusing in his manner. Guilty, I felt sure he knew something of our little plot. Mamma lectured the girls severely for going away without her. The local young ladies made a big fuss over me. Yes, it looked like a pleasant stay in Opelousas. Adrian went to jail—I never saw him again.

Fenie eventually noticed the absence of Josie's bracelet. Then Ned found the pawn ticket. With Edward wearing a new civilian outfit, things started to look suspicious. Ned questioned Edward but he refused to talk. Josie jumped to her brother's defense and turned against her dad for their first quarrel. The two siblings had decided to stick it out together. While waiting for the printed letterheads to arrive, Edward wrote his first sketch: "Jerry, the Booby Boy." "Featuring that inimitable young comedian, Ed Sedgwick. Josie read it carefully and gave her approval. It was a serio-comic little opus and its locale was a farm kitchen. Dad and Mamma played the characters, Josie and I, the younger ones. Jerry was a "silly kid" with red wig, blocked-out teeth, etc. Dad was a tramp, and Mamma, the farm wife. The whole thing was good and corny. I was eager for a try-out. Still being in wrong I didn't dare to speak to Dad about it."

The package of letterhead arrived from Kansas City and Ned intercepted it, but did not open it. He called a family gathering.

The suspense was terrific. I was sweating blood when he forced me to cut the string. I glanced at Josie's face—it was dull gray. Licking dry lips, I gulped, cut the string, and tore off the wrapping. There they were—the letterheads. Thank the good Lord the firm had done an excellent job. Dad glanced at them enigmatically. Mamma enthused slightly. Eileen loved her picture in the center.

Now what? There was a strained silence. Finally, Dad asked what it was all about. Hysterically, Josie and I started to talk at once. We told him everything. A new act. Getting into vaudeville. Going places. Get away from these jerk towns and damn amateurs. Get an agent. Dad had difficulty in quieting us. Without a word, he reached in his pocket and gave Josie her bracelet. He had redeemed it. I felt like a worm as he coolly told us he knew all about the deal. Then the lid blew off.

Misty-eyed, he said he was proud of his children who were trying to better our condition. Mind you, he did not approve of the methods. But, he would give our plan a try. The new act could get its dress rehearsal in the local show. The letterheads would become official when we started our vaudeville tour. We all gave vent to our pent-up emotions—laughed and wept. There are no reactions comparable to those of actors. I guess that's why they are actors. Delirious with joy, we hatched a million new plans with every moment.

Now, we were really and truly in vaudeville. There were a few small houses to break "Jerry" in good. Dad made some changes. I must modestly say that the act went very well. Now, to wait for answers from the floods of letters that deluged every listed agent and circuit in the land. They knew who the "Five Sedgwicks" were by now. But no answers. Dad was patient. I was going crazy. Then it came.

I called for the bulky letter at the post office and nearly broke my neck racing back to the hotel and the gang. This was it. George Greenwood, of Atlanta, was the first agent to offer us work. Enclosed were contracts for six of his vaudeville houses. They looked as big to me as if they had been for the entire Orpheum circuit. Entranced, I poured over the dates, the salary. One hundred and twenty-five dollars for the group! Mobile, Pensacola, Jacksonville, Savannah. Why, it was just a short hop from there into New York! They couldn't shut my mouth, or my boasting. Every five minutes I framed new material. Josie was just as excited as I. We had put it over.

Most of the shows were "small time vaudeville," which meant working in smaller towns, at lower pay, but doing a higher number of performances per day. The Sedgwicks were billed as the shows' headliners. There were only two other acts on the bill—a single and a double—and a two-reel film, so the family had to do four shows a day to fill it out. Edward looked at it as a good chance to rehearse, preparing for the bigger stuff. "I knocked out trying to make good. The Baby Eileen character proved sensational. We were in—there was nothing to it!"

The family's appearance in Lexington, Kentucky, was captured in a theatre's weekly promotions. An advertisement for the Hippodrome theatre appeared in the September 12, 1909, issue of *The Lexington Herald*, announcing that that week's opening act would be the Five Sedgwicks. The billing in the boxed advertisement featured:

ROSIE & EDWARD SEDGWICK.
Great Singing and Dancing Act.
Comedy Act—"A Suspicious Husband."
FITCH COOPER.
The Rube Comedian.
BABY AILEEN [sic]
Singing and Talking.
THE LADY AND THE TIGER.
Hipposcope Motion Pictures.
Orchestral Music.

The newspaper gave full coverage of what the audience could expect from the Five Sedgwicks.

Another charming production will be found in "Baby Alieen" [sic], a pretty young miss of 10 years of age, who is at once an accomplished singer with comedienne propensities. She is a star in her line and holds promise of a bright and attractive future. She will be accompanied by her parents, who always travel with her, although she faces the footlights alone and gives her turn with remarkable self-confidence and vim. She talks to the audience like one much older and carries them with her through every turn.

Next in line are "The Five Sedgwicks," who present an attractive comedy playlet, entitled "The Suspicious Husband," in which some ridiculous mix-ups are given. Both press and public have given them glowing encomiums wherever they have appeared, and the "Hipp" is fortunate in securing them for this week, which has only been made possible because of an "off week" during the summer months.

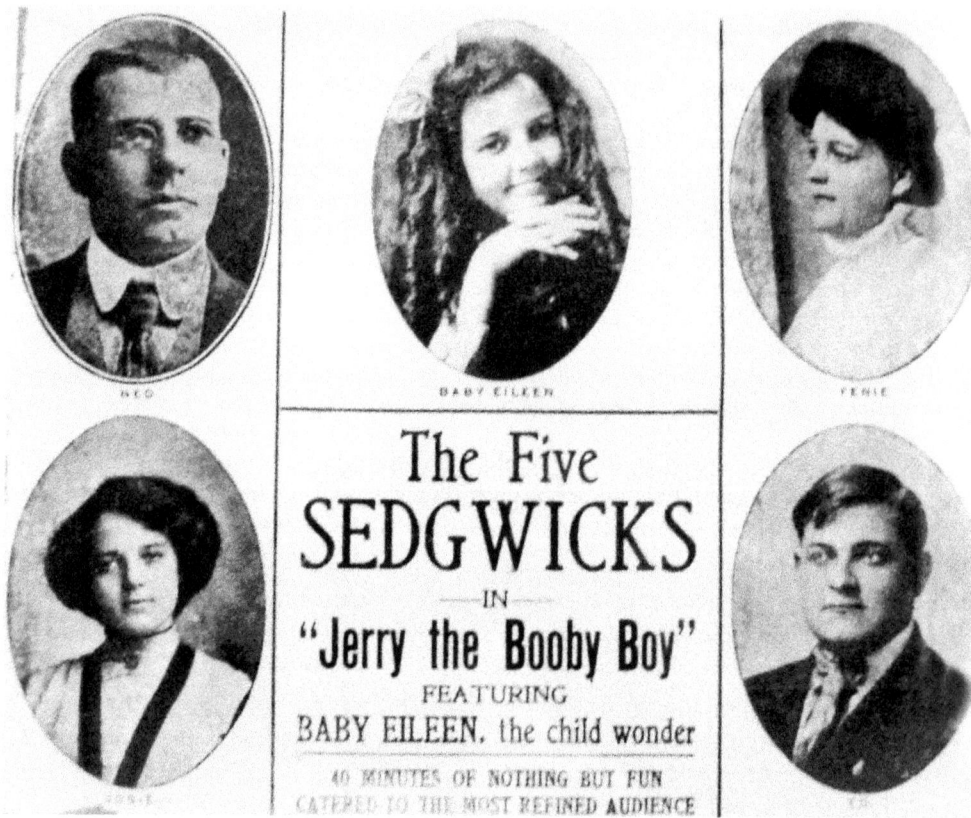

A cut from the family's letterhead, from about 1911, showing "Baby Eileen" in dyed black locks (courtesy E. Hutson).

Then there are Rosie and Edward Sedgwick in special comedy singing and dancing, admitted to be of a superior class to what is generally offered on the vaudeville stage.

Curiously, the Hippodrome promoted "Rosie" as the female half of the Sedgwicks' song-and-dance team. Perhaps Fenie was using Rosie as her stage name, as Eileen and Josie (in a subsequent article) are mentioned accurately.

The newspaper's entertainment column continued to support the Sedgwicks' appearance throughout the week. The September 13 column announced. "Charming Aileen [sic] is worth the price of admission. She is the queen of all child performers. Don't miss hearing her. Attractive and up-to-date singing and dancing by Rosie and Edward Sedgwick, and then comes the comedy playlet 'A Suspicious Husband' rendered by the Five Sedgwicks, giving pleasing and catchy sketch."

The review on the 14th reported that the show was a success: "Three performances with the sign out 'Standing Room Only' is a fair judgment of the public's opinion of the acts which are being offered at the Hipp this week.... The Five Sedgwicks presented two separate rate acts, all excellent." The column for the 15th announced more of the same: "The Hipp continues to draw crowed houses to good bill this week.... The Five Sedgwicks in three distinct acts give an example of the unusual in that all shows talent in their art. Miss Josie Sedgwick displays great versatility in two entirely different characters, and Baby Ailenne [*sic*], another Sedgwick, captivates the house." The second act on the bill, a comedy routine presented by the family, was described in the column on September 16: "The Five Sedgwicks in a comedy sketch, 'The Jealous Husband' [*sic*], develop some laughable situations and at the same time teach some valuable lessons."

The other acts featured on the bill included the return of Fitch Cooper, "the clever, comical, musical Rube," with his melodious handsaw, and Madame Lesch and her royal Bengal tiger Prince. The house's new orchestra performed special music and a motion picture closed the show, projected by the theatre's "Hipposcope." Mention was also made of an unadvertised act, Kelso and Sydney, whose "blackface caught the crowd last night and received repeated applause."

The theatre in Savannah, which was called the Orpheum, had two extra acts. Morris Green, an experienced manager who had worked with B.F. Keith, owned the theatre. "After the first show he came backstage to compliment us—told us we were to be held over. Then I received a real surprise. I had gone to school with his son, 'Blubber' Green. Blub was yachting off Tybee Island with some of the socially elite. I had no idea he was so wealthy."

Josie had also received a surprise, according to Edward: "At a matinee a huge bouquet of American Beauty roses was handed over the footlights to Josie. Her first floral tribute. We fell over each other in an attempt to read the name on the attached embossed visiting card. Mr. Alexandre Dumont, Twelve Oaks, Virginia.

"After the show Blubber came backstage, escorting a fine-looking young man. He exuded wealth and position. Mr. Alexandre Dumont was presented to us. Josie took one long, lingering look. This was it. Usually glib, she now mumbled an unintelligible word of thanks for the flowers, then dashed for her dressing room."

With more flowers and more visits backstage, the romance between Josie and Alex continued to develop. Ned, tolerant of what he called "puppy love," let the relationship run its course. "Alex had now promised his way to the front porch, sitting in the swing with Josie. He was most patient with Eileen, who insisted on hanging around. But she soon fell asleep."

An important telegram addressed to the family arrived from Chicago. "I scanned it hastily, then trembled so I could hardly hold it for Dad to read. It was from B.S. Muckenfuss, a manager of a nice-sized theater in Chicago. The contents of that wire are still stamped on my brain. 'OPEN YOU HAYMARKET CHICAGO WEEK OF 18th SALARY TWO FIFTY CONFIRM.'

"Holy smokes, that was the following week! Dad did not react. But, brother, did I go to work. I was prepared for every argument. We had been discovered! Two-a-day vaudeville. In a few weeks—New York. Maybe Hammerstein's."

Ned tried his best to reduce Edward's enthusiasm, warning him that they were taking a big chance by making the move. If they didn't do well, it would cost them their savings. Edward finally convinced Ned, and a confirmation was sent out to Chicago. From that point on, Edward's head swelled as he swore off the four-a-day small-time vaudeville shows. He lost his concentration during that afternoon's show. Ned warned him that he would cancel the Chicago shows if he didn't pay more attention to his lines.

> Mr. Green kindly allowed us to forego the Saturday show. It was a tight schedule to make a monthly morning rehearsal in Chicago. At the station, Alex and Josie said mushy goodbyes—promising to write every twenty minutes.... We were off!
>
> My heart pounded when that train pulled out for my first big city. I bragged to Dad how *I* had

> put it over. Due to *me* we were headed for the cream of show business. He finally threatened to knock my block off if I didn't shut up. I tried to talk to everyone on the train—that is, the few who would listen. Eventually, Eileen became my only audience. She and her Teddy bear. Josie was to busy writing lengthy tomes at the Pullman desk—she really had it bad.
>
> I was awake hours before the porter gave the magic word Chicago! I had the folks herded into the vestibule long before the train pulled into the Illinois Central Station."
>
> A taxi to the theatre. There I stood gaping up at the marquee. All right, so the letters were small. But there it was: The Five Sedgwicks. There were nine acts and we were down the middle of the bill. The other acts? I never saw their names—only ours. Josie had caught my excitement, and we stood there and looked and looked.

Chicago trailed only New York in vaudeville stops. Located on Madison Street near Halsted Street, the Haymarket Theatre, which first opened in 1887 as a legitimate playhouse, had seating for 2,475. Although vaudeville acts were always part of Haymarket's billing, performing alongside live theater performances, it wasn't until 1896 that the theatre exclusively became a vaudeville house.

> We had reached the big time, but I am afraid we acted very small time all during rehearsal. We had never seen such a large orchestra, nor such a large stage. Well, it was do or die. I had induced Dad to stop at the Saratoga Hotel—all the big vaudeville people stayed there. It was a bit rich for our blood and very strenuous on the grouch bag. But, again I won out. This was my big day. I strutted around the lobby. What a hick.
>
> Afternoon. Opening matinee. I was scared stiff. The other acts were going well. Then came our call. I prayed, crossed my fingers. Our introduction. We were on! The act went swell. Eileen was the big hit, and we finished to several bows. Even Dad grinned tolerantly to my ten thousandth "I told you so!"
>
> Then the house manager came backstage. He was accompanied by a sour-faced looking woman. An instinctive chill ran through me. Through some sort of mental haze I heard the manager tell Dad we were closed. Closed! The good woman was a representative of the Gerry Society. Prevention of cruelty to children. Eileen was too young to be exposed to theatrical life. We could not appear in Chicago. Sorry. There had been a mistake in allowing us to open—thought she was a midget.

Commonly referred to as "The Gerry Society," the New York Society for the Prevention of Cruelty to Children was created to prevent the exploitation of child labor. It was named after its founder, "Commodore" Elbridge T. Gerry, who devoted most of his life to this cause. It eventually became a national organization. Declaring that performers must be over 16 to work on stage, the society quickly became a thorn in the side of acts that included children. The rules that the society, as well as other local religious and social groups, tried to established were often enforced with mock arrests or fines that weren't expected to be paid. Vaudeville promoters and managers brought money into communities, so such legalities were often ignored, and only placed on the books to placate the groups. It wasn't until the advent of sound films that such laws were nationally created when the Production Code (commonly known as the Hays Code) was developed in 1930. The guideline spelled out what was and was not considered morally acceptable in the production of motion pictures for a public audience. Edward Hutson, Eileen's son, recalled his mother mentioning that the Gerry Society prevented them from performing in New York City. This, in fact, might have been part of the reason for Ned's reluctance to play the larger northern cities.

> Dad looked at me and his fists clenched threateningly. I ran for my life. He would have killed me. When I crawled up to my room I wished he had. Or, why didn't I just kill myself. Josie came in and wanted to share the blame. Who cared about sharing anything? We were disgraced. Nearly broke. In the only big city I had ever seen, I had to make a mess of things.

> Ashamed to face Mamma and Dad, I skulked out to walk somewhere—anywhere. Eventually I wound up on Michigan Boulevard. I was a pretty sick young man with a deep ache in my heart. We had flopped. Our big chance was gone. The chill winds of fall whipping around those oft-quoted corners of Chicago's windiest street meant nothing. I will never quite get over those few agonizing hours. Alone, miserable, in the midst of busy thousands. They appeared so smug, so content. I hated all of them. I—better get back to the family. A sudden strange premonition. Thoughts of the old witch from Hillsburg. I started to run. A mountain of policeman glared suspiciously. I slowed down to a walk.

The family had checked out of the Saratoga, leaving a note for Edward that they had moved to the Revere House on the North Side. The Revere House was an actor's hotel, or as Edward described it "a cheap crummy dump." Realizing that he had left his wallet and watch in the dressing room when he ran out, Edward started out to the hotel on foot. During the long hike he was held up by a robber at the North Clark Street Bridge. At first he froze in bewilderment, but then he started to laugh hysterically—what else could go wrong? Thinking he was crazy, the thug ran off. Upon entering the Revere House he collapsed into a lobby chair.

> Josie found me there later, and saw I got something to eat. She told me that Dad was not well. He had suddenly folded after all the excitement. It was an extremely emotional scene when we all gathered in Mamma's room. Dad was wonderful. Although we tried, he refused to blame anyone. It just hadn't worked out, that was all. I was years older when I left that room for my own. To save a few dollars, I was doubling up with a tramp juggler [named Nilo]. He wasn't working either. I couldn't sleep. This was my responsibility. It was up to me to do something about it.
>
> I have never quite forgiven Chicago. The next few weeks were horrible. Tramping up to agents' offices. Attempting to get work—in any kind of show business. But the waiting line was a long one. Winter was approaching faster each day. Dad was fighting to keep from becoming invalid. Pride kept us from calling for help. Josie had stopped writing to Alex, and it was hurting her down deep. Pride again. I didn't blame her. We could still hold our heads up.

Forgetting about his pride, Edward played a hunch. He had learned that Mr. Muckenfuss had children and met with his daughter, Rosalie, a girl about his age. Edward discussed their situation with her, after which she promised to do something about it. Through her connections, she was able to get the family several weeks' work in Michigan, Wisconsin, and the Dakotas. This string of cheap theatres that extended from Chicago to the Northwest, down the Pacific Coast, and finishing up in Southern California was generally known by vaudeville acts as the Death Trail.

> The weather was brutal. The first snow we had ever seen. In town after town we nearly froze to death. Split weeks all the way up to Soo. Zero was a mild day.
>
> Dad would give me an occasional chilled look and murmur something about cotton blossoms, Florida, and Texas sunshine. Eileen proved to be the best sport of us all. She never complained even when her little lips were blue with the cold. Josie was still too down in the dumps to give a hoot about anything. I was thankful to the Army for that big heavy overcoat my school had been patterned after. Mamma? She stayed in bed until show time, and ducked under the covers again as soon as it was over.
>
> Gus Sun saved us from the igloos. He offered several weeks in a much warmer clime. The weather was ten to fifteen above instead of below. But still snow—beautiful snow. Believe me, I never dream of a white Christmas. I've had too many of them. I'll take the Santa Monica smog.

They spent Christmas doing a five-a-day show at a miserable theatre in Uniontown, Pennsylvania. A baritone single on the bill was featuring nostalgic Southern songs—magnolias, cotton blossoms, sunshine—which made Edward feel so much worse about their predicament. As a bonus for doing an extra show that day, the manager sent them a meal backstage. As a Christmas dinner, it was awful. The family staggered through the day with nothing but six shows under their belts.

> Leaving the theatre, miserable and tired as we were, we planned on having a little dinner of our own. Turkey—all the trimmings. But there was no restaurant open. Not even a "greasy spoon." The town was all tucked in bed, happy and well fed. It was a disconsolate little group that gathered in the room to distribute our meager gifts. Poor little Eileen was so tired and cold she whimpered all through the presentations. Suddenly, Mamma broke. She wept like a baby. That started us all off. It was one Christmas I shall never forget. I made a feeble attempt at singing a carol and Josie hit me with a skimpy little Christmas tree. It was the signal for us all to really blow off steam—give vent to emotions that had been pent up so long.
>
> A night clerk came up to quiet us and I threw him downstairs. He called the police. An old sergeant responded. He listened, expressionless, to our tale of woe, then left without a word. In a short while he returned with a wagon. We were all hustled in and carried to the station. There we were shocked out of our stupor. The remnants of a huge Christmas dinner was reheated and served to us. The good citizens had given thought to the unfortunate prisoners. But actors? No. We ate plum pudding, drank hot coffee. Then we sang. The prisoners joined in. We were warm, temporarily content, and so very, very thankful.
>
> The human equation entered into this happy celebration. We learned that the old sergeant had a daughter. She was on the road with a musical show somewhere out west. He proudly showed us the gift she had sent him. It was in her name that he tried to give us pleasure. We blessed him and went back to the hotel. It was very late and we attempted to tiptoe past the night clerk. Much to our amazement, he grinned and mumbled a Merry Christmas!

Edward wired Mr. Green the following day. Before the day ended, Green sent a reply, letting the family know that they could play at his brother's theatre in Charleston, South Carolina. Once again they would be below the Mason Dixon line and in warmer weather.

With the Sedgwicks back in their accustomed clime, things started to quickly fall back into place. During rehearsals, Edward became enamored with a pianist who played in the theatre's four-piece combination:

> Her name was Myrtle Sanders. That afternoon, when I was on the stage, her eyes never left me. When I sang a love song to Josie, she had to pull me around toward her. Finally, she stepped on my toes and glared down at Myrt. That hurt me. At the finish of the act a huge bouquet of lovely roses was handed over the footlights. I made an attempt at nonchalance as I accepted them, and blew kisses down to Myrtle. She kept shaking her head—No! A hasty glance at the embossed card: From Alex to Josie. Her knees were a bit wobbly as she took the flowers from me and made her exit.
>
> Alex was standing in the wings, all smiles. Josie couldn't take it. Bursting into tears, she fled to her dressing room. How silly can women get? Dad shrugged. Alex gulped. But Mamma knew. In no uncertain terms she told us to go away, and followed after Josie.
>
> That was a memorable day. Each performance was the same enchanted one. Josie and Alex had come to an understanding, and were now more in love than ever. My head was in the clouds—I could think of nothing but Myrtle. I wanted to talk to Dad about this serious thing that had entered my life. He waved me off. I must confide in someone. Alex? What would he know? Eileen was the only member of the family I knew would listen. But she was taking her nap.
>
> Don't underrate this love bug—it is really deadly. Josie worked to the wings. I worked to the pit. Dad and the house manager quickly put a stop to this. A mushy French moving picture was the added attraction of the bill. They featured it between shows, holding hands. She promised she would go out with me after the show and I was in seventh heaven. Suddenly she asked me a very personal question. How old was I? I lied like a gentleman, quickly adding four years to my eighteen. She seemed a bit disappointed. I guess women are funny.

Vaudeville theatres originally used motion picture shorts in their billings as "chasers," slotted at the end of the evening to help clear the audience from the building. But as motion pictures became recognized as a standard attraction, new theatres were being built for the exclusive use of showing a program of shorts and features. The "flickers" were no longer considered a curiosity that were once regulated to the thousands of nickelodeon theatres that were already in existence.

Eileen was a rabid movie fan and each night she would watch the blow-off run after the show, from the first row. "One of us would always pick her up on the way home. The same procedure was in effect this night, with two exceptions. Josie and I were so enrapt with our companions, we left without checking. We took it for granted that Mamma and Dad would take her. They, in turn, figured she was with one of us. Later, at the hotel, Mamma got nervous. As she started her routine check she discovered that none of her children were in. Where was the baby?"

Fenie and Ned checked the theatre, which they found had already closed for the night. They then visited the local soda fountains, without any luck. Edward and Josie, both on their dates, were contacted. The parents, who were now becoming frantic and thinking that maybe Eileen was in an accident or kidnapped, called the police.

> Things were popping when I arrived at the hotel. Dad was demanding they call out the reserves. They had to restrain him from taking a punch at me. Mamma was doing her utmost to remain calm. It was now well after midnight. I was really frightened. If anything happened to that kid? Oh, Lord, please no! Josie and Alex arrived. They, too, got hell. Each one had the same alibi—we thought she was with you! Hour after hour passed. Finally, one bright young detective suggested we open up the theatre and retrace her steps.
>
> The suggestion was acted upon. The manager opened up. She was nowhere in sight. Backstage. In every dressing room. I searched the orchestra pit—pausing a moment to scent that alluring perfume that still clung around the piano.
>
> A long love-sick sigh, and I continued my search. There was no trace of my baby sister. Disgusted, I flopped down into a seat—then jumped up with a howl. I had squashed that big Teddy bear she always carried with her. I groped around the next chair—there she was, safe and sound. The poor kid had fallen asleep and slipped deep down into the chair.
>
> A hysterical reunion. Exasperated police. Dad took one look at me and the perennial chase was on. I raced from the theatre, he after me in hot pursuit. But this time there was a difference. I caught him—in my arms. He staggered and was about to fall. The days of the chase were about over for poor Dad. He gasped for breath. I gave him a whiff of spirits of ammonia that he always carried and helped him into the lobby.

The family left to play a theatre in Columbia, South Carolina, and a few smaller towns in the state. Alex and Blubber went along as prop men and general stooges, while Myrtle, who took her two weeks' vacation, played the show for them.

> The time came for Myrtle to return to her job. Madly in love, I begged her to marry me. I shall never forget the strained, haunted look that came into her eyes as she cautioned we had best wait a while. I ran to consult with Mamma. She was so understanding. Very gently she informed me that Myrtle was in her late twenties—I had just rounded nineteen. She was a grass widow, whose husband had deserted her. Manfully I rose to her defense. None of that mattered—I loved her! Mamma's smile was so kind when she said the same thing Myrtle had: Wait a while. If that was the only way I could be happy, then it would be arranged.
>
> Not satisfied, I rushed out to find her. Myrtle had gone. She had left a note which I read and re-read a hundred times. I was heartsick. I threatened to leave them all for her. Dad dryly inquired how I planned to eat in the interim. Well, he did have a point there. But—I'd show them!

At that moment Josie came in all aflame. She displayed a hunk of ice on her finger the size of a walnut. All fluttery and coy she gave out the big news. She and Alex were engaged! Dad didn't react too happily—the girl was too young. Mamma took Josie in her arms and kissed her. With a sly smile she patted the "grouch bag." She had a little something put away just for this day. Her girl was going to be beautiful at her wedding! Then women's talk—clothes, dainty under things. Alex arrived on the scene. More plans—marriage, futures. I sat in silent disgust, eating my heart out.

The Sedgwicks' next performance was scheduled for Asheville, North Carolina. They were to stay as long as they could do business and change shows. Ned had booked an independent date to play for Steve Lynch on a percentage basis. Lynch had dabbled in show business with a little picture house that was about to fold. Lynch was planning a chain of motion picture theatres and asked him if he would consider becoming his partner. Ned shook his head and said that pictures would never last—"just a novelty." The S.A. Lynch Enterprises went on to become a successful chain of theatres. Lynch retired many times a millionaire. Once again the Sedgwicks had missed out on a profitable opportunity.

The family played a string of small-time vaudeville venues in the Carolinas, Tennessee, and Virginia. Edward lost Myrtle completely, never hearing from her again. Alex was dragged to Europe by his father. He kept writing to Josie, promising he would soon come back to her.

A bulky letter arrived from Mr. Muckenfuss, enclosing contracts for the Interstate time [the Interstate vaudeville circuit]. Two-a-day vaudeville in the south and his prize Majestic house in Texas. Ordinarily I would have been up in the clouds—framing new material, new songs, heated arguments with Josie. Dad was puzzled at my indifference. But somehow I knew we would never play those houses. I don't know why—perhaps the witch of Hillsburg was tapping me on the shoulder again. The strangest feeling of insecurity possessed me. I found Josie crying softly and trembling with the same apprehensions. We tried to analyze. There was not a logical reason. We were working steady; making fairly good money. No scrapes, no family quarrels. But, just the same...

During their run of performances in Knoxville, Josie met young John Dorsey, a member of one of the prominent merchant families in town. Although she was still loyal to Alex, she went out a few times with John.

One night a huge bunch of American Beauties was handed over the footlights. The familiar embossed card. A glance toward the wings. There stood Alex, all grins. On the other side of the stage stood John Dorsey. He too was all grins—he had sent gardenias.... I figured perhaps I had better stick around. That Dumont came from temperamental French ancestors—that Dorsey looked like he could well take care of himself. It looked like business was about to pick up.

Josie was overjoyed to see Alex. But she liked John and didn't want to hurt him. She had a date with him and attempted to explain to Alex. He became a bit possessive. Resenting his attitude, she told him off and slammed into her dressing room.

Alex and John stood and glared at each other a moment or two. Then Alex made a foolish blunder. He accused John of chiseling with a married woman. We both leaped at that. John challenged this statement. Alex amended it by saying—well, practically married. I relaxed. Then a few hot words. Alex, who had obviously been drinking, made a clumsy pass. Whoa Nellie! My prospective brother-in-law was knocked for a loop by a stiff right. I had to barge in and wrestle Dorsey and he was a tough customer. Dad came out to help. Suddenly Josie, half dressed, burst out of her dressing room. There was no doubt who was headman. She flew at Dorsey like a tigress, then cradled the groggy Alex in her arms. John, puzzled and dejected, left the theatre.

About dawn we were all awakened by two shame-faced youngsters who stammered out the news. They had sneaked away. They were married! Dad and Mamma valiantly kept their poise. But it was a terrific blow to him—Josie was his heart. He fought back his tears, the imprecations on his lips. I thought it was a lousy trick to play and told them so in no uncertain terms. What about the sacrifices to garner that little trousseau Mamma had planned? All the long night hours of fine needlework? What about the act? I was on a soapbox and really held forth. Dad finally quieted me. We still had three weeks of contract to play. Alex condescendingly agreed that we should fulfill them. Damn nice of him! We were all pretty much mixed up. Dad insisted that Alex call his family, but he weakly decided it would be better if he personally related the news to them.

I felt sorry for Josie. We were booked to play Roanoke in two weeks and I knew how she was dreading it. So was I. A run down on the family did little to help my feelings. Old Pierre Dumont was a despot. Descendant of a long line of French noblemen, huge tobacco plantation owner. He ruled with a rod of iron both his family and his interests. However, Josie implicitly trusted and believed in her loved one. I wasn't so sanguine but for once kept my big mouth shut. I never mentioned more than his share. I tried to appear confident when I was with Dad and Mamma but I was inwardly prepared for anything. Funny how quickly you can become a man when the chips are down. As for my sister, I made a mental vow to hurt somebody if she got a raw deal. With all these tortuous thoughts gnawing at me we reached Roanoke.

The family was rather shocked when Alex wasn't at the train station to meet them. Upon their arrival they were informed that a carriage awaited to take them for a conference with the Dumonts.

I never put in such a miserable time. Squeezed Josie's hand all the way out. Mamma's aplomb was perfect as she held her head as high as any queen's. Dad was turning greener by the moment. Only Eileen enjoyed the ride.

We pulled into Twelve Oaks [the Dumont family's estate in a small, exclusive Roanoke suburb]. It was a magnificent place. Under any other circumstances I would have been enthralled by its beauty. But I was definitely not interested in broad acres or classic Colonial lines at this sitting. We were ushered into a beautiful paneled library. I could sense the extreme coldness of the place and I knew we were in for it.

Edward described Alex's father Pierre as perfect casting:

Small, semi-bald, piercing black eyes, and the Bourbon nose. He twirled pince-nez on the proverbial black ribbon. Accompanying him was a florid-faced, paunchy man carrying a sheaf of papers. Mrs. Dumont followed. Her face was kind, but her sad eyes told the story of her life with the old ----. She was the only human being of the lot. I was very proud of my people for the gracious manner in which they accepted the introductions.

It seemed that the paunch was a barrister, who hemmed and hawed his role to perfection. Old Pierre sized us up. He seemed to be disappointed at meeting ladies and gentlemen, both in appearance and demeanor. He looked long at Josie. You could discern the admiration he tried to keep out of his eyes. There was an element of uncertainty in his attitude as he opened proceedings. Mrs. Dumont made an effort to be friendly but was promptly squelched. I heard the crisp tones insisting that we get down to this unfortunate business as quickly as possible.

Josie interrupted the proceeding and demanded to know the whereabouts of her husband. Pierre attempted to get dictatorial, but Josie took control of the situation. Her family stood behind her, prepared as reinforcement. He admitted that Alex was ill and upstairs in his room. Pierre attempted to physically restrain her from going to Alex, but Josie spun him around and unceremoniously dropped him into a chair. Edward blocked him as Josie made her way to the stairs.

"It was a sordid picture that Josie looked in on. Alex was sprawled across his unmade bed, blind drunk. A half empty bottle of the potent absinthe was on a side table, along with several illegibly scrawled notes all addressed to her. She tried to rouse him; made every effort to reach him mentally. But it was no use. With womanly pity and love she bent over him and kissed him gently, then softly left the room."

Josie coolly stated that she was going to take Alex away with her. Pierre called attention to the impossibility of their relationship ever being a successful marriage. Josie was underage and the differences in their lifestyles were too great. It was for their good he was having it annulled.

> After a moment pause Josie questioned from her heart: Did Alex know of this plan—had he consented? Was he of sober mind and not coerced in any particular? Without a second's hesitation Mr. Dumont nodded, yes. His wife tearfully corroborated. Then Pierre became wily; the sharp trader. Naturally, she would be paid off. Shall we say—fifty thousand to sign away any...
>
> Josie's heart was in shreds but her eyes were blazing as she faced him. He cringed from that look of unutterable loathing and scorn as she waved both him and his filthy proposition aside. Tearing off her beautiful ring she tossed it on a table. He could give that to Alex for a souvenir. Dumont tried to placate. The lawyer yelled that this was a trap. We were planning to sue and disgrace the family! I shut his trap good. I would have gone further but Dad restrained me.
>
> Josie took one last lingering look at what had been her home for a short hour. As she started out, Pierre followed—urging her to reconsider. He used every tactic: He had been mistaken; she was a wonderful girl; deserved every happiness. But Josie never looked back. We followed in silence. I wanted one last poke at Mr. Paunch. He remained discreetly behind.

The family refused a carriage that was waiting to take them back to town, opting for a ride on a passing farm wagon instead. Upon their arrival in Roanoke, they were informed by the theatre manager that he had cancelled their engagement in favor of another act. However, they were to be paid for the full week.

> As we were packing to get out of town as quickly as possible, a messenger arrived at the hotel. He attempted to deliver a letter to Josie. The outlines of a bank check were clearly visible through the thin paper. The crest of the Dumonts stood out boldly. The messenger was politely told what he was to tell his master—and what he could do with the money. Pierre made several efforts to contact us before leaving. He still expected us to hold out for a larger settlement. We refused to see him. And that was that.
>
> So ended the marriage of Josie and the weak, unfortunate Alex. He also tried on occasions to contact Josie. His letters were returned unopened. A year later we heard that he had passed on. Acute alcoholism. Poor devil.

Edward, becoming increasingly restless touring with the family, was ready to break out on his own. He developed a burlesque show that was known as the Cabaret Girls, receiving credit as the musical comedy company's producer, director, and manager. Edward also volunteered to guard the U.S. border at the time of the Mexican Revolution, working both as a Texas Ranger and member of the National Guard. The Mexican conflict also helped him hone his writing skills, as he worked the wire for Associated Press and was on the staff of *The Galveston News*.

Because of Edward's absence, the family added Lee Edmunds, an experienced vaudeville performer, to their ensemble. The November 10, 1910, *Galveston Daily News* reviewed the group's performance from the previous night, which included Edmunds' routines.

Sedgwick Vaudeville Company.

> The Sedgwick Vaudeville Company presented an entire change of bill Friday evening at the Grand Opera House to a large audience. The bill was one of general excellence and the efforts of the Sedgwick family and Mr. Lee Edmunds provoked much laughter.
>
> The bill opened with a farce entitles, "The Two Senators," in which Mr. Edmunds pulls off some good Irish comedy as Murphy, the Irish senator, while Mr. Sedgwick convulsed the audience with his German dialect in his portrayal of Schultz, the German senator. His song and burlesque George

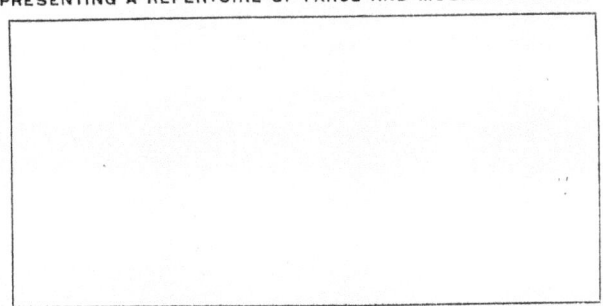

"BIG" ED SEDGWICK'S MUSICAL COMEDY CO.
PRESENTING A REPERTOIRE OF FARCE AND MUSICAL COMEDIES

New **N**ifty **N**ovel

Clean **C**lever **C**lassy

Pretty Girls
Fancy Comedy
Harmonious Singing

Elaborate Wardrobe
Complete Changes
Good Dancing

FEATURING CLEANLINESS

Edward experienced success with his repertoire company, as his signature card suggests. Due to Ned's failing health he had to close the show after three seasons (courtesy E. Hutson).

M. Cohan dance was a hit. Mrs. Sedgwick, in her interpretation of an Irish landlady, was clever. Miss Josie Sedgwick was exceptionally good in her conception of a French maid. In this act Baby Eileen scores a hit as the hotel bellboy.

Billy Ellwood, lightning cartoonist, executed a number of clever caricatures, most of them being new.

Baby Eileen, in her impersonation of a picaninny in her single act, was easily the hit of the bill. Her song, "Shaky Eyes," took well, and she responded to several encores.

The performance was brought to a close with "Fun in a Dissecting Room," a mirth-provoking farce, filled with ridiculous situations. In this piece Mr. Lee Edmunds is seen as a superstitious darky, who, in order to earn 75 cents, consents to visit a graveyard at midnight and deliver a corpse to the dissecting room of a surgeon. All members of the cast are given parts which enable them to display their versatility.

Manager Brian announced a special school children's matinee this afternoon at 3:30 and a regular performance tonight.

During the months of March and April 1913 the Sedgwicks performed around Gulfport, Mississippi, as a family of four, promoting themselves alternatively as "The Four Sedgwicks" and "The Sedgwick Tabloid Company." *The Daily Herald*, a newspaper that was published for the Gulfport area, included advertisements and reviews of their performances. Their opening show on March 4 at the Gulfport Opera House proved to be quite successful. The entertainment section of the following day's newspaper contained a positive review for their act: "The Four Sedgwicks in blackface comedy, singing and dancing, played to a large audience at the Gulfport Opera House last night and made a decided hit, as was attested by the rounds of applause given them in the rendition of 'Aunt Dinah's Baby.'"

A second review of the act, which was performed on March 21 for the reopening on the Dukate Theatre in Biloxi, noted that there was a house filled to capacity: "Expectancy was rewarded with a show of unusual merit—clean-cut comedy, excellent dancing, good singing, and moving pictures as good as money can buy." It continued,

The Four Sedgwicks were featured and their little playlet, which was really a series of loosely connected dialogs, songs and dances, was thoroughly enjoyable from start to finish. The two young girls

> have good voices, are inimitable little actresses and little Eileen Sedgwick is a graceful and captivating dancer. Mr. and Mrs. Sedgwick are as capable blackface comedians as have ever been seen in Biloxi. They strike that happy medium in negro impersonation which is the mark of true art, neither failing to properly emphasis the negro traits and dialect nor going to extremes which make the negro impersonations of so many actors ludicrous to Southerners who are thoroughly acquainted with Ethiopian peculiarities.

According to the review of the March 5 show at the Gulfport Opera House, "A large audience witnessed the performance of the Four Sedgwicks in the laughable comedy entitled 'The Dutchman's Troubles,' at the Gulfport Opera House last night. The Sedgwicks created much laughter and were heartily applauded."

Their March 27 show at Dukate's Theatre was entitled "The White Squaw," a feature that the Sedgwicks only performed at benefits, in this case the Red Men's Biloxi tribe of Hiawatha Council No. 10 Degree of Pocahontas. The following review, featured in that day's *Daily Herald,* reveals how complex their performances were becoming.

> The Sedgwick Company will present the great Indian musical song-drama at Dukate's theatre tonight assisted by several of Biloxi's best home talent. Today is Red Men's day and "The White Squaw" is being presented for their benefit. Over $1,500 worth of costumes are worn during the performance. There has never been a play of this character presented in Biloxi before and lovers of theatricals should not miss this opportunity, besides it is for a worthy cause. The local amateurs who will take part are Bernice Catchot, Hazel Matians, E. Combel and others. The New Orleans papers proclaimed this to be one of the best little plays ever put on in that city. Mrs. Sedgwick, who is a past Pocahontas of the order of Red Men, will take the part of the White Squaw, while Miss Eileen will play Little Fawn, the Indian girl, and Miss Josie will handle the part of an army lieutenant and Mr. Sedgwick will change from Pat the Mick, to the Bad Indian, Gray Wolf. Little Bernice Catchot will play the captured child. The Sedgwicks have proven their worth during their stay here and a large crowd should attend.

The reviewer noted that Josie's role was that of an army lieutenant. Josie apparently took over the roles that used to feature Edward, and with his absence she was noted in reviews as excelling in male impersonations. Eileen's character Baby Eileen was evolving to that of the "Southern Beauty." The following article, titled "EARLY CAREER, YOUNG ACTRESS—The Four Sedgwicks at Dukate's Theatre Compose Happy Family Group," appeared in *The Daily Herald* during their performances at Biloxi:

> Pretty little Eileen Sedgwick, who fills the soubrette part in most of the tabloid comedies presented by the Theatre this week, began her career on the stage when she was three years of age, and her elder sister Miss Josie was before the footlights at five. Their splendid acting and singing and dancing is the result of years of training and continual practice to a large extent of course, but without their native ability and natural fresh beauty and their enjoyment in the work, they would not have attained such an enviable reputation throughout the South where they have spent most of the years of their career.
>
> Every movement and every word of these two winsome maidens convinces the audience that Eileen is having as much fun on the stage with her jokes and songs, and that Josie is as deeply interested in the development of her impersonations as the captivated people on the floor of the house could possibly be. That is the secret of their remarkable success.
>
> These two younger girls have received many offers to join larger stock comedies and to play leading roles with some of the best theatrical aggregations in the country. Once a famous motion picture company wanted them to join its cast and to assist in making some of those sensational wild west episodes that thrill thousands every day and night. But the girls refused all of these offers because they prefer to remain with their father and mother, Mr. and Mrs. Ned Sedgwick, in their own little

independent company, free to go where they please, to play what they please, and to work out their own parts in accordance with their own ideas. On and off the stage the family is an example of felicitous good fellowship which could well be emulated by many a hearthside fathering not darkened by the many vicissitudes of life that necessarily come into a career of jumping from place to place.

The little family comedies in which this talented family are appearing at Dukate's theatre are clean, lively and as funny as could be wished for. The performances are of that wholesome nature that pleases not only the habitual theatre-goer with their originality and chicness, but the children and older people, known as stay-at-homes, as well.

It was only a matter of time before Josie and Eileen would appear in front of movie cameras. The theaters where they were performing were featuring an increasing number of reels of film per night and less live acts. In the past, movies were used to end a night of several live performances; the current trend was changing to one live act per night followed by three movies.

The Sedgwicks' schedule was booked solid. In addition to their performances at the Gulfport Opera House and Dukate's Theatre that month, they were also booked to do weekly performances at the Airdome at Laurel and the Auditorium at Hattiesburg. During each booking the family would feature a different drama playlet or comedy skit each night. In addition to the previously noted performances, "The Street Singer," "The Mixup in the Studio," "Broncho Kitty from the West," and a blackface comedy entitled "Post Office Sam" filled out their weekly billing.

After completing three successful seasons with the Cabaret Girls, Edward had to close the show, as he was once again asked to help out with the family's act. Ned was failing rapidly—the intensive schedule of constantly being on the road, and the substandard living conditions that went with it, took a great toll on him. Josie had retreated into a shell. In Hot Springs, Arkansas, the family attempted to reorganize their act. The Sedgwicks were to open a show the following week. To get away from the stressful atmosphere, Edward went for a long walk. On the way he unexpectedly met Nilo, the tramp juggler he roomed with at the Revere House in Chicago. Nilo, who was performing as a clown with the 101 Wild West Show, which was playing in town, invited Edward out to the lot.

The Miller brothers, Joe C., Zack, and George, operated the 101 Wild West Show. Owners of the 101 Ranch in Oklahoma Territory, the trio each had their own skills, which they combined into a worldwide traveling show. Their appearance in Hot Springs would have placed the timeline during the spring of 1913, as the show opened its 1913 tour in the city on April 5.

In the show's pad room, Edward was introduced to the troupers. The air was alive with excitement, and for a moment he had an impulse to blow off the family and join this show. He was introduced to Frank N. Thayer, a producer who worked for the Mutual Film Corporation. Thayer was recruiting some of the show's riders to work for him the following winter. The film he wanted them for was *The Life of General Villa* (1914), a documentary starring the Mexican revolutionary Pancho Villa.

> Thayer looked me over—said I was a good type. He advised me to go to the coast. They were hiring young comics out there. I evidently impressed him for he gave me a letter to one of the headmen at a studio. I thanked him and put the letter in my pocket.
>
> There was one particularly good-looking cowboy he had his eye on. The cowboy chatted with me when Mr. Thayer left. He certainly was a fine specimen of manhood—and could he ride! He told me to look him up personally if I ever came to California. He was going out there as soon as the

show closed. I thanked him, said goodbye to Nilo, and went out front to see the show on a ducat. Oh, yes, the cowboy's name? Tom Mix.

The opening matinee in Hot Springs was the Sedgwicks' final show together. In the middle of the act, while doing a comedy routine with Edward, Ned suddenly lurched forward, gasped, and collapsed in his arms. He was in near-critical condition by the time the doctor arrived.

I aged overnight. Now what? I knew without medical advice that Dad's acting days were over. But without working, how could we afford to keep him in a hospital? That night I framed an act for the four of us, but Mamma refused to leave him. The doctors wanted her around; she was the only thing Dad had to cling to. The Interstate time was gone for good. The Baby Eileen routine was getting a bit stone age. I took a second look at her. There would be another woman on my hands before long.

Well, I booked a dump on the other side of the tracks for the three of us. Thank the Lord we could sing. I taught the girls some barbershop harmony, and we got by.

Every time we called at the hospital Dad was worse. I played a hunch. Twisting Josie's arm till she gave out with a big smile, I forced her to take over. Get him to listen to our harmony—see if he would approve. She thought I was nuts, but it worked. It made him feel he was still headman. He rallied enough to hear our whispered tones as we stood at the foot of the bed. His eyes cleared as he criticized; gave a few suggestions. Then we dashed out into the hall and went all to pieces. How much emotion can you take?

Due to his failing health, Ned would never be able to work again. The doctor recommended that if he were moved to a semi-tropical climate, such as California, he could enjoy many years of sedentary life.

Fine! It looked like I was head of the family. California—Oh, sure! Where in the hell could I dig up that kind of money? And do what after we got there? What—of course! I thought of the 101 outfit. I had seen a picture made by the Bison 101 Company. All I had to figure out was how to get a load of coin. There was only one way.

I remembered a couple of tricks I had learned and coaxed the hotel manager to take me to a rather loose gambling house on the main street. It was do or die. It was no sinecure getting some money out of Mamma—but I succeeded. With Dad's ham bone and rabbit's foot rooting for me I stepped up to a crap table. I got hot after a while. The licks and passes were rolling for me so fast the headman came over. But they never got on to me.

When I left I had enough sugar cubes to pile the whole gang on a Limited headed for the Pacific coast. My Broadway dream still tugged at my heart but—another Rubicon was crossed.

Chapter Three

Orange Groves and Shootouts

"Sunset and Gower. A funny-looking place with overhead sheets strung on wire. This was a movie studio." Edward was hardly inspired by his initial impression of the town that was destined to become overrun with corporation-operated motion picture studios and celebrity megastars. The black and white sheets Edward referred to were reflectors used to change lighting on scenes being filmed. Studios, which lacked advanced lighting for their stages, were usually built outdoors, and took advantage of the sunlight, or the lack of it, by directing the amount of light that fell on the stage.

In 1911 the Centaur film company of New Jersey opened Nestor Studios in this neighborhood, becoming the first company to set up a permanent studio in Hollywood. The location was the converted Blondeau Tavern building and a barn situated on the corner of Sunset Boulevard and Gower Street. Universal Film Manufacturing had acquired the Christie-Nestor studio in 1912, and in a short period of time the area had become home to a collection of businesses that catered to independent film studios. The location would be nicknamed "Poverty Row" as it evolved into a home to low-budget film production companies and a marketplace for items such as "short ends" of film (unused portions of unexposed film) from the major studios, which were resold at affordable prices.

It was only 17 years earlier when B.F. Keith and E.F. Albee, the exhibitors who pioneered the continuous variety show in the 1880s, became two of the first promoters to exhibit motion pictures in a theatre. Their Union Square Theatre in New York City was the site of the first American exhibition of the Lumière Cinématographe. After obtaining the exclusive American rights to the Lumière apparatus and their film output, they presented their first showing on June 29, 1896. Their success led to other theatre openings in Philadelphia and Boston, and smaller theatres through the East and Midwest. In 1896 Keith and Albee signed a contract with Biograph Studios, which guaranteed them a fresh supply of motion pictures to show in their growing chain of theatres. In July 1905 they switched to Edison Studios as a supplier of new films. By June 1906 Keith and Albee merged their theatre chain with Frederick Freeman Proctor to form an impressive circuit.

Up until that time, the majority of the industry's films were being produced on the East Coast. The few studios that traveled to California to do location shooting enjoyed the favorable weather conditions of the area—outdoor filming could be done practically year-round, without the problem of the seasonal extremes that Chicago and New York experi-

An early outdoor motion picture stage, the type that the Sedgwicks would have experienced upon their arrival in Hollywood in 1913, just two years after the first permanent studios were set up in the area.

enced. In 1910 director D.W. Griffith and a group of Biograph's actors were sent west from their New York City studio to film a melodrama. The film, a short titled *In Old California*, was the first movie shot in Hollywood. Four years later *The Squaw Man*, starring Dustin Farnum and directed by Cecil B. DeMille, became the first feature movie filmed in Hollywood. Previous to *The Squaw Man*, all of the movies that were being shot in the Los Angeles area, from 1908 to 1913, were shorts. The period before World War I saw the Los Angeles area quickly transition from an agricultural community to the motion picture production center of the world. What was once considered a peep show curiosity, the motion picture was now on its way to becoming a major industry.

By 1911 moviegoers were showing an increased interest in motion pictures, supplanting the melodramatic theatrical stage performances as their popular choice of entertainment. Audiences soon became curious and wanted to know the names of the uncredited actors and actresses appearing in their favorite films. Florence Lawrence, who was only known to her audiences up until then as the "Biograph Girl," was the most valuable film actress of the time. As a promotional device, reports of her death in a streetcar accident were faked, after which she reemerged working for the IMP Company, now known as the "IMP Girl," and with onscreen credits. Francis X. Bushman, affectionately known to moviegoers as just "F.X.B.," became film's first true matinee idol, often appearing with Beverly Bayne as the first great romantic team in movies. This was the beginning of the star system, publicity stunts, and "moviestaritis."

The Sedgwicks' arrival in California was timely. The growing number of studios were in need of fresh talent for their productions, as the demand from moviegoers for new films was becoming insatiable. At first the Sedgwicks' parts were uncredited and their pay was low. But the work provided a fairly steady source of employment, which they supplemented with occasional vaudeville performances.

Edward described their first audition as being, for the most part, successful. "I had insisted that Josie and Eileen go with me—might be able to make a bargain deal. Eileen, wearing one of Josie's dresses, looked like a young lady. The Mr. Isadore Bernstein, my letter was addressed to, did business right away. He hired both girls on sight at thirty-five a week. Me? They were not interested in comedians at this time. They could get them at a dime a dozen."

The Sedgwicks' meeting with Bernstein was the start of Josie and Eileen's success in motion pictures, and eventually for Edward and Eileen a long-lasting relationship with Universal. Bernstein, the general manager of Universal's West Coast operations, was in the process of breaking ground for the studio's Universal City. The size of a small city, Universal City was planned to become a self-sufficient studio. The dream of "Uncle" Carl Laemmle, Universal's founder, it was created from a 230-acre San Fernando Valley ranch which was purchased for $165,000. Bernstein, who previously worked for Bison Motion Pictures, was responsible for negotiating the sale of the Taylor Ranch and getting the studio operational by 1915.

Feeling dejected, Edward gave up all hope of ever becoming successful in Hollywood:

> Over their protest I left the girls there and slunk out of the studio. Another flop. I sat on a bench under some orange trees on Hollywood Boulevard. What a hick town! A few stores, a bank, but mostly old-fashioned houses set well back among thousands of orange trees that lined this famous street. I was contemplating the gas pipe or a few feet of rope when Dad came shuffling up, leaning heavily on a cane. I gave him the good news about the girls and passed lightly over my failure. He nodded—let us get all we can. After he had rested a bit the Five Sedgwicks would go out again bigger and better than ever. I had to bite my lip.
>
> Sudden excitement on the corner. A cowboy came running out of the bank, shooting. He hopped on a horse and tore away. With the other yokels I raced over to the scene of the crime. A hidden camera was getting all this and I spotted it. Did I put on an act! I did pratt falls—made faces at the lens. This was my big chance! Then I heard my name called, and again I met my friend Tom Mix. He brought me to the director who gave me an address in Edendale. I was to report in the morning.

Allesandro Street in Edendale was the location of the Keystone Film Company. Between the years 1912 and 1917 Keystone was synonymous with comedy films. Keystone's producer and director, Mack Sennett, pioneered and defined screen comedy in his slapstick films. Sennett, who was responsible for creating the bumbling Keystone Kops, and discovering Mabel Normand, Roscoe "Fatty" Arbuckle, and Charlie Chaplin, used the streets of Edendale as backdrops for his comedies.

The bit parts were only a starting point for the Sedgwicks: Within the year they would be working with various studios and receiving onscreen credit. Looking back, Edward had realized that the family had reached success through a slightly different means, one that didn't involve vaudeville. "And so, the Five Sedgwicks were disbanded forever. This new medium, motion pictures, that Dad said was only a passing fad, brought us to the goal we had never attained before. Through this great industry we found success—romance [Edward married Rose Adams in 1913]. But that is another story.

"New York? I was sent there on location in the next few months. Broadway? It suffered miserably in comparison with *my* Hollywood Boulevard."

Although Hollywood was a brand new experience for Edward, it wasn't his first interaction with the motion picture industry. While he was developing the Cabaret Girls show, he repeatedly rejected offers from film director Romaine Fielding, who had unsuccessfully attempted to persuade him to become a photo-player and leave the stage behind. Edward was bit by the film bug when, before departing Texas for California, he had helped form the Hotex Film Manufacturing Company with King Vidor. Edward met Vidor during his final year at Peacock Military College, where Vidor (who later became famous in his own right as a director) wasn't quite as enthusiastic as Edward was about attending the military academy and left after only one year. Vidor's real passion was the moving picture. He entered into the business filming newsreel footage for Mutual Weekly and invested the money he earned filming the "newsies" into the production of a couple of comedy shorts. In September 1914 he teamed up with Edward and produced two films: *Beautiful Love*, starring Eileen, and *The Hero*, starring Eileen and Josie. In October, Vidor contracted with Sawyer, Inc., to distribute Hotex's films. Unfortunately, A.H. Sawyer, who had only distributed a handful of films in 1914, wasn't successful in the distribution trade and sold his business to the Colossus Feature Film Company. Colossus obtained Hotex's negatives in the deal and distributed the films without ever paying royalties to Vidor or Sedgwick.

It wasn't long before Romaine Fielding, along with Siegmund "Pop" Lubin, convinced Edward, Josie, and Eileen to work at Lubin's new studio. In 1902, Lubin, an experienced businessman who had entered the motion picture industry in the 1890s though the distribution and production of films, formed the Lubin Manufacturing Company. Lubin, who previously owned an optical shop, invented the Cineograph, a combined camera and projector. In 1898 Thomas Edison sued Lubin, claiming that the Cineograph infringed on copyrights that Edison held for his system. In 1909, after years of dealing with Edison in court, Lubin gave up the costly fight and became part of the Motion Picture Patents Company (MPPC). Known as the "Edison Trust," the MPPC consisted of the companies that Edison claimed were infringing on his copyrights. All members agreed to pay Edison a royalty for the use of the various patents, including one for raw film. To avoid Edison's costly suits and injunctions, many of the non-complying independent companies moved their studios to the West Coast, in the hope that the distance from Edison's New Jersey location would make it harder for the MPPC to enforce its patents. The trust, which included all the major film companies, including American Pathé, American Star, Biograph, Edison, Essanay, Kalem, Lubin, Selig, and Vitagraph, was dissolved in 1915 after a Supreme Court anti-trust decision brought the MPPC to an end when it canceled all of its patents.

Aside from owning a growing chain of East Coast movie theatres, Lubin operated several studios that were located throughout the U.S. and Europe. "Lubinville," his Philadelphia studio, was considered the industry's most state-of-the-art studio when it was completed in 1910. In 1912 Lubin had placed director Wilbert Melville in charge of a group of actresses and actors who were to travel the world making movies for the company. Due to the increasing international tension that was leading up to World War I, the group was prevented from venturing any further than the West Coast. As a result, in January 1913, Melville set up his Los Angeles studio at 4550 Pasadena Avenue, the site of a rented Colonial mansion that had a breathtaking view to film stories against.

Lubin teamed the three Sedgwick siblings with Romaine Fielding, one of the actors who traveled west with Melville. Previous to working with Lubin, Fielding was employed by the Solax Company, a studio located in Flushing, New York. Fielding had a distinctive acting style which won him the honor of being named *Moving Picture World* magazine's most popular film performer. He had a very articulate face that allowed him to play any type of personality believably. Within a year's time working under Lubin, his responsibilities expanded from playing lead and character parts to that of cinematographer, director, and screenwriter. Like his acting, Fielding's work behind the camera was expressive, as well as creative.

In 1914 Fielding had been assigned to direct a total of 14 films. One of them, *The Battle of Gettysgoat*, offered Edward his first major role. The four-reel comedy, a departure from the Western dramas Fielding was familiar with, is considered by some to be the first American feature-length comedy. The story involves two overweight boys, one weighing 350 pounds and the other 375 pounds, who leave home and enlist in the Mexican Army. Aside from directing the film, Fielding played the role of the Interchangeable Spy. The production, which was scheduled for four weeks, took ten weeks to complete due to poor weather conditions that interrupted filming—a delay that would have been a major drain on Lubin's disciplined budget.

In 1914 Eileen and Edward appeared in at least eight one- and two-reel Lubin comedies, acting alongside Fielding. Fielding also wrote and directed the shorts, titled *All for Love, The Belle of Brewerville, The German Band, On Circus Day, The Crooks, Love and Flames, Green Backs and Red Skins,* and *The Kid's Nap*. Their synopses describe them as being slapstick, and in most cases, predictably ending in havoc; they hardly seemed to be films that

Lubin teamed up the three Sedgwick siblings with director Romaine Fielding for a series of shorts, including *On Circus Day* (1914). Edward appears in the foreground with Robin Williamson. Josie appears just above Edward wearing a cowboy hat, with Eileen the second female from right (courtesy Niles Essanay Silent Film Museum).

A poster for the short *Green Backs and Red Skins* (1915), featuring Robin Williamson and Edward. Williamson would go on to direct screen comics Ben Turpin and Mack Sennett, as well as the first Laurel and Hardy comedies.

emphasized the cinematic qualities that Fielding was critically known for. Filmed at a time when the United States was being drawn into World War I, the shorts poked fun at Germans, with characters named Fritz Schultz, Helma Snitz, Hans Dinkenspiel, the Sauerkraut Twins, and Chief Hoggenheimer.

From the beginning of their time with Lubin, the Sedgwicks were receiving credit for their roles. An advertisement in the December 22, 1914, issue of the *Sheboygan Press* promoted *Love and Flames*: "A first-class Lubin Comedy written by Romaine Fielding. The cast includes E. Sedgwick, Jacob Rasmoff, Robin Williamson, Eileen Sedgwick, Romaine Fielding and Harry Kenneth. Don't miss it, and all the fun that goes with it."

Lubin was ardent about keeping a tight rein on expenses, and it was rare that he would allow a film that was four or more reels to be directed away from the Philadelphia area studios without his supervision. *The Eagle's Nest* and only three other films directed by Fielding were the exception. Released April 15, 1915, *The Eagle's Nest* showcased Fielding's trademark talent, and presented Eileen, Josie, and Edward with their first feature roles. Produced in Del Rio, Texas, it was originally filmed as an eight-reel drama but edited down to a six-reel story before it opened in theatres. Collaboratively written by Edwin Arden, Harry Chandlee, and Fielding, it was based on a play that Arden wrote and acted in back in 1887. With many of its scenes shot at the scenic "Garden of the Gods" in Colorado Springs, Colorado, it made use of hundreds of local cowboys and Native Americans who worked as extras.

A synopsis for the movie, which was included in Lubin exploitation material, explained that, as an infant, the principal character Jack Trail was the sole survivor of an Indian attack on a wagon train. The remainder of the story hinges on a deed that Jack's father had left with his friend, Geoffrey Milford (Harry Kenneth), before the family set out on their journey. Robert Blasedon (Fielding), the movie's bad guy, attempts to take control of the deed, as does Rose Milford, Geoffrey's daughter. The photoplay's comedy relief, Edward plays the part of Dibsey, a lawyer who befriends Jack Trail. By the end of the sixth reel, Jack, played by Arden, gets the deed and the love of Rose, who was played by Eileen. Robin Williamson, who played the part of Slater, would go on to direct screen comics Ben Turpin and Mack Sennett, as well as the first Laurel and Hardy comedies.

What the Lubin synopsis failed to promote as being an important feature of the film was the massacre segment, which critics had preferred to focus on instead of the rest of the story. A *Philadelphia Inquirer* reviewer described its terrifying realism:

> One watches the battle, when shown on the screen, from the side of a mountain, down on the plain, far in the distance, the long wagon train of emigrants approaches—not a detail of the early days is missing. The scene suddenly switches and one gets a glimpse of hundreds of Indians, stripped to the waist, daubed in war paint, crawling down the side of the mountain for the attack. Other Indians are racing down to the plain on fleet ponies.
>
> The emigrants hurry the wagons into a circle for the common defense and then the battle is on. The following scenes are stupendous. The warfare of the old days is reproduced with historical accuracy and it is intensely dramatic. The Indians win and the massacre follows. Only one survives—a baby, and it is this baby who forms the chief keynote of the play. Another long wagon train of emigrants sees in the distance the burning wagons and rushes to the scene and attacks the Indians. The wild ride of the second emigrant train is spectacular. Every man rides or drives at top speed. Wagons turn over, horses go down and riders are thrown, and one gets a very intimate idea of how the men of the West can ride and drive when a goal has to be reached in record time.

A critic writing for *The Dallas Morning News* praised *The Eagle's Nest* as a director's picture: "Merit, ability and talent—call it what you will—has counted, does count, and always will count in the end for success, though the end is like Tipperary, a long way off, but to that end years ago Romaine Fielding set his ideal. Many will say he has arrived with his production of *The Eagle's Nest*."

Mississippi's *The Daily Herald*'s review pointed to Josie's character as being quite intriguing. "Sierra Suze is a page out of life, a character that may not be altogether pleasing, but wholly real. In fact *The Eagle's Nest* is intended to portray history as it was actually written in the pioneer days, and it is the strict adherence to fact that makes this play an educational force, as well as a stirring, romantic story."

The Eagle's Nest was the first Lubin production released by V-L-S-E Incorporated. Four members of MPPC—the Vitagraph Company of America, Lubin Manufacturing Company, the Selig Polyscope Company and Essanay Film Manufacturing Company—formed V-L-S-E on April 13, 1915, as an alternate distribution company to MPPC's General Film Company.

Encouraged by their recent success in *The Eagle's Nest*, the Sedgwicks invested their earnings in their own movie concern, the Excel Photoplay Company, based in San Antonio, Texas. Plans for the studio's first feature film production developed in May, with Edward assigned the position of director-in-chief, and Josie and Eileen promoted as the company's leading actresses.

Their earliest attempt, a comedy titled *Bravery*, featured all three siblings. Possibly only presented locally on screen, the film was shown at the Grand Opera House on the night of September 4, 1915, accompanied by live vaudeville acts and a dramatic film feature. An advertisement in *The San Antonio Light* described the evening's lineup:

> The musical comedy which will be presented is entitled "The Vaudeville Shop," with funny big Ed Sedgwick as the comedian. Others who will be seen to good advantage are Wayne and Marshall and Josie and Eileen Sedgwick. An exceptionally good picture program will also be on today which includes the dashing romantic actor Francis X. Bushman and fascinating little Ruth Stonehouse in a beautiful romantic love drama *A Battle of Love*. Two other features will also be shown including *Bravery*, a comedy featuring the three Sedgwicks and made in San Antonio.

The Sedgwicks returned to work at Universal Film Manufacturing, the precursor of Universal Pictures. Eileen appeared in *The Mysterious Contragrav*, a two-reel science fiction film involving an invention that offsets gravitation, the scientist who invented it, and his efforts to keep the contragrav out of the hands of foreign spies. *The Mysterious Contragrav* introduced the blonde-haired, blue-eyed Eileen to the adventure genre. It also featured Marie Walcamp and William Clifford and its highlights included scenes with pilots dueling to the death in midair. A reviewer for *The Daily Herald* who watched the film at the Big Airdome theater in Laurel, Mississippi, breathlessly described its thrills: "Aviators pursuing each other while flying at sixty miles an hour, throw bombs and grenades, one of which brings aeroplane crashing to the ground. Auto runs over steep cliff into ocean while piloted by actress."[1] It was inevitable that the Sedgwicks' films would be shown at the same theaters where they had previously appeared live onstage, which was the case with *The Mysterious Contragrav* appearing at the Airdome, a theater where the Four Sedgwicks had performed vaudeville just a couple of years earlier.

Eileen's next film was the two-reel *Lone Larry*, a Western co-starring Kingsley Benedict, an actor who would reunite with her in future productions. It was filmed at Bison Motion Pictures, a studio controlled by New York Motion Picture Company, an independent production company that had merged with other independents under the umbrella of Universal Film Manufacturing. Carl Laemmle, founder of Independent Moving Pictures (IMP Studio), formed Universal on June 8, 1912, in protest of MPPC's enforcement of their patents. The companies that were part of the merger included Champion Film Company, IMP Studio, Nestor Film Company, New York Motion Picture Company, Powers Motion Picture Company, and Rex Motion Picture Company. In the upcoming years the Sedgwicks would work for several of the independent studios. As Eileen's popularity grew, Universal took advantage of her stardom by re-releasing her earlier films. *Lone Larry* was re-released in 1919 and again in 1924.

In 1916 Eileen and Edward were assigned to work with director Roy Clements in a one-reel comedy titled *His Golden Hour*. It was made by Victor Film Company for Universal. Victor, formed in 1912 by movie actress Florence Lawrence and her husband Harry Solter, was another studio that became part of the Universal Film Manufacturing Company amalgamation. Clements, an actor with years of stock company stage experience, entered moviemaking as a director at Essanay Film Manufacturing Company's West Coast studio. In December 1913 he was hired to work on the studio's successful "Snakeville Comedy" series, and after directing close to 75 of the shorts he left for Universal in September 1915. *His Golden Hour* featured actress Jane Bernoudy along with another Essanay alumni, noted comedian Victor Potel.

The careers of Clements and Potel were firmly established in Essanay's "Broncho Billy" films, a series of shorts introduced in 1907. Created by Gilbert M. "Broncho Billy" Anderson, the character of Broncho Billy is considered to be the first good guy–bad man cowboy of the movie screen—the classic outlaw with moral values. Anderson started acting in films in 1903, with one of his first roles as a bandit in Edison's *The Great Train Robbery*. In 1907, with George K. Spoor, Anderson founded Essanay (the "S" and "A" in Ess-an-ay) in Chicago, where they produced films featuring Charlie Chaplin, Ben Turpin, Francis X. Bushman, and Gloria Swanson. The Broncho Billy shorts became immensely popular and in 1911 a Snakeville Comedy series, directed by Clements, was spun off from it. Snakeville regulars included Harry Todd as Mustang Pete, Ernest Van Pelt as Hiram Clutts, and Fred Church, who played both Rawhide Bill and Coyote Simpson. The hybrid Snakeville series "Alkali Ike," which featured Augustus Carney as Alkali Ike and Anderson as Broncho Billy, proved to be just as popular. It was filmed in and around Niles, California, with Carney starring opposite his wife Margaret Joslin (the future Mrs. Harry Todd), who played Sophie Clutts. The Alkali Ike series' success produced an additional spin-off, which was created around another Snakeville denizen, Slippery Slim (Potel), who was introduced in the 1913 short *"Alkali" Ike's Homecoming*.

Feature-length films were in popular demand, and Essanay, as well as other MPPC motion picture companies, were facing tough competition from the independent companies who were now concentrating on producing them. In addition, the loss of foreign film markets, due to the disruption caused by World War I, devastated the older companies Essanay and Lubin. Essanay closed its operations in February 1916, with many of its actors signing up with Universal and other studios that were building permanent studios in the Hollywood area. Potel and his hayseed Slippery Slim character followed Carney to Universal, which had previously brought his Alkali Ike character to the studio. The studio renamed him "Universal Ike" for legal reasons.

Edward and Eileen continued their work relationship with Clements, Bernoudy, and Potel in at least nine episodes of the Snakeville-like comedies that were produced at Universal. The majority of the shorts, which slyly referred to Potel's character as "Slim," were written and directed by Clements. Released throughout 1916, the titles included *Hired, Tired and Fired* (written and directed by Jay Hunt), *Lily White of Centerville, Some Heroes, I'll Get Her First, Ain't He Grand, The Gasoline Habit, Town That Tried to Come Back, When Slim Was Home Cured, When Slim Picked a Peach*, and *Room Rent and Romance*. Potel continued Universal's Slim series for another year before joining Mack Sennett's Keystone Film Company where he became one of the original Keystone Cops. Prints of these titles are no longer extant. Influenced by the collaboration of Potel and Clements working together, one can surmise that they followed the style of Essanay's surviving Snakeville Comedy films, which are more situational than slapstick in their type of humor.

In the meantime, Josie had performed in two dramatic shorts released in January 1916 under Universal's Laemmle division. *Missy,* a two-reeler, and *Her Dream Man,* a one-reeler, were written and directed by Lynn Reynolds and featured Universal's ensemble players Myrtle Gonzales, Frank Newbury, Alfred Allen, Val Paul, William Brunton, and Fronzie Gunn.

Ben Turpin, another Essanay alumnus, crossed paths with Edward. The brush-mustachioed, cross-eyed comedian was one of Essanay's first actors and a regular in the Broncho Billy and Snakeville series. At one point Essanay unsuccessfully tried to team him with Charlie Chaplin after Chaplin traveled out to Niles from the studio's Chicago location. When Essanay's Niles studio closed, Turpin signed up with Vogue Films. Vogue, designed to compete with Universal's L-Ko and Triangle-Keystone comedies releases, was created in October 1915 as a production company affiliated with the American Film Company of Chicago and Santa Barbara to produce comedies for the Mutual Film Corporation. At Vogue, Edward acted with Turpin in his one-reelers *National Nuts* and *His Blowout,* which were released in 1916. The films also featured Paddy McGuire, a comedian who was previously a regular player in Chaplin's Essanay shorts. After working at Vogue for a year, Turpin left for Keystone, where he had his greatest success. Capitalizing on Turpin's popularity, Vogue re-released several of the films he made for them, including *His Blowout*, which was renamed *The Plumber* for its 1921 re-release.

The Sedgwicks continued to build their résumés through employment at the smaller studios in the Hollywood area. Nestor hired Eileen for a part in a one-reel situation comedy titled *Kill the Umpire*. Released in July, it starred ex-vaudevillians Eddie Lyons and Lee Moran, with Lyons directing. Just the previous year Nestor's producer, Al Christie, had teamed Lyons with Moran, which proved to be an excellent decision, as their clean-cut comedies became extremely popular. When Christie left Nestor to create his own company, he took Lyons and Moran along to fill out his star lineup. Universal lured them back to Nestor, giving them greater control of their productions and more money than Christie could offer. Considered the first successful film comedy team, Lyons and Moran's sophisticated humor would become one of Universal's biggest box-office draws of the time. Eileen followed *Kill the Umpire* with a second Lyons-Moran short, *It Sounded Like a Kiss*, directed by Louis Chaudet. Nestor released the film in December.

The role of the stocky character was a requisite in comedies of the time, with Edward having little trouble filling the part. He appeared in three late-summer releases directed by Roy Clements. *Some Medicine Man*, produced by Universal's Joker unit, was followed by *A Lucky Leap* and *He Became a Regular Fellow*, both Victor Film Company productions.

A Lucky Leap also starred Evelyn Nesbit, an actress appearing in her second film. Just ten years earlier Nesbit was in the center of a murder case known internationally as the "Crime of the Century." As a teenager she was one of the most sought-after artists' models in New York City. Charles Dana Gibson popularized Nesbit as one of his famous turn-of-the-century "Gibson Girls." When a theatrical magazine published her photo, the offers came, and within days Nesbit had joined the chorus of the hit Broadway show *Florodora*, featuring a chorus of six young girls. At the age of sixteen she was allegedly taken advantage of by 52-year-old Stanford White, America's leading architect and designer, becoming his lover. At age twenty she married Harry Thaw, the son of a coal and railroad baron. Thaw was an abusive husband and insanely jealous of Nesbit's past relationship with White. On June 25, 1906, Nesbit and Thaw ran into White while attending a performance at the Madison Square Garden's roof theatre. Thaw fired three shots at White's face, killing him instantly. His first trial ended in a hung jury. Pleading temporary insanity at his retrial, Thaw was sent to a mental institution for the criminally insane. Thaw's mother struck a deal with Nesbit: In exchange for testifying that White had raped her and that Thaw had only tried to avenge her honor, Nesbit would receive a quiet divorce and a one million dollar divorce settlement. She was granted the divorce, but Thaw's mother reneged on giving Nesbit the money. Nesbit looked to various entertainment opportunities for employment, including vaudeville. In 1915 she found work as a motion picture actress, appearing in eleven films over the years, often with her son Russell William Thaw, who she insisted was Thaw's son.

Long before the powerful studio system took hold of Hollywood and changed the way the earlier, casual moviemaking processes worked, an individual entering the industry had the opportunity to perform as a director, producer, scriptwriter, and actor—all in the same movie. Already an experienced actor and anxious to expand his skills, Edward received his first job as a scenarist, although uncredited, in Fox Film Corporation's *The Beast*, released in July 1916. (Perhaps it wasn't ironic that the title—*The Beast*—was also the nickname Harry Thaw used when referring to Stanford White.)

Edward collaborated with director Richard Stanton on the film's scenario. The storyline for *The Beast* is somewhat typical of the type of scripts written for the Western melodramas: A millionaire's daughter is separated from her father and suitor after a train wreck. She comes upon a town and is abducted by a brutish ranch hand. They encounter a band of Mexican bandits who want her jewels. Afterwards, the ranch hand apologizes to her, letting her know that he isn't really the beast he appears to be, and brings her to an area close to where her father is searching for her. Years later, after reforming himself, he is reintroduced to the girl who doesn't recognize him, being the refined person he now appears to be. Only after he attends a masquerade ball dressed as a cowboy does she recognize him, and they are reunited at last.

Edward's entry into scriptwriting paid off, as he eventually received credit as a scenarist (collaborating with Stanton) on at least nine additional Fox films. By 1920 Edward would be given the responsibility for writing Fox's first serial, *Bride 13*. By 1923 he was regularly directing films for Fox. William Fox, a pioneer in developing theater chains, formed the Fox Film Corporation in 1915 by merging two companies he had established in 1913, Greater New York Film Rental, an independent film distributor, and Fox Office Attractions Company, a production company. Although he owned a film production studio in Fort Lee, New Jersey, up until this time Fox's primary concern was film distribution. In 1917 Fox sent Sol

M. Wurtzel to Hollywood to oversee what would become the company's permanent West Coast studio.

Edward completed two fall releases for Nestor, *It's All Wrong* and *Married a Year*. *It's All Wrong* featured another actor-scenarist, Pat Rooney, who had worked with Edward in previous films. Although Rooney appeared in 22 silent and sound films, one of them an early Broncho Billy short, he was better known as a Broadway dance legend. Working in vaudeville with his wife Patricia (known as Marion Bent) and son, Percy (known as Pat Jr.), his signature act was a tap routine set to the song hit "The Daughter of Rosie O'Grady." Edward closed 1916 with a release that was directed by Roy Clements, *The Fascinating Model*, produced by the independent Powers Picture Plays studio.

Towards the end of the year Eileen appeared in two Victor releases, *It's Great to Be Married* and *A Plumber's Waterloo*. The former featured Fred Church, a Western actor with whom Eileen would work in over a dozen films. That fall Eileen appeared in two 101-Bison films, *The Quitter* and *Giant Powder*. Church also appeared in *Giant Powder*, a film directed by Henry MacRae, who would be responsible for directing Eileen in several films during the following year. Between 1912 and 1933 MacRae was responsible for directing at least 137 films, most of them silent Westerns. Throughout the '30s and '40s, after motion pictures transitioned to sound, MacRae produced many comic hero–related adventures, including Tailspin Tommy, Flash Gordon, and the Green Hornet serials and series.

In 1915 Universal had set up a three-tiered marketing system to classify its releases by budget and status. A Red Feather film was a low-budget release, a Bluebird film was a mainstream release, and a Jewel film was a high-budget feature utilizing prominent actors and actresses. Because Universal lacked its own theater network, the branding system helped theater operators and audiences differentiate the films being offered.

In 1916 Eileen appeared in two five-reel Red Feather Photoplays, *The Isle of Life* and *The Heritage of Hate*. They were low-budget Red Feather Photoplays but that didn't mean that they were second-rate dramas. *The Isle of Life* was shot on location at the Carmel Mission and the surrounding areas of Monterey, California. About 100 local fishermen and their wives were employed as extras, using Monterey's boat-filled harbor and house-lined streets to suggest its location to be Sicily. The two films were directed by Burton George, who was also responsible for directing Eileen that year in the two-reel Laemmle production *The Emerald Pin*, as well as the previously mentioned *The Quitter*.

In 1916 the newspapers were continuing to comment on the acclaimed *The Eagle's Nest*, which was still making the rounds in theaters, giving the Sedgwicks' careers an additional boost. "*The Eagle's Nest* is a remarkable picture and has been shown perhaps oftener than any other photoplay in filmdom," according to the theatrical section in *The Daily Herald*'s morning edition of August 16. Working alongside Potel, Turpin, Moran and Lyons also gave Edward and Eileen the sort of exposure that was necessary for them to get proper recognition, and introduce the two to steady paying acting jobs. The August 22 issue of the *Morning Oregonian* made mention of Eileen's rise to stardom: "One year ago Babe Sedgwick, firmly a vaudeville player with the Five Sedgwicks, was playing small parts in Universal dramas. Now she has been chosen for prominent parts in Bluebird features." Starring in a Bluebird photoplay was considered a prestigious step for Eileen. The motion picture that was being referenced was *Man and Beast*, a film that was in production, with plans to be released in June 1917.

The siblings were now working independently of each other in separate projects. Eileen

As late as 1916 Eileen was still using her "Baby Eileen" persona.

By 1917 Eileen reverted back to her natural blond hair and started to take on mature parts.

worked steadily with director Allen Curtis through 1917. In the period from 1913 to 1922 Curtis was responsible for directing, producing, and writing close to 280 films, mostly Universal comedies. With Curtis, Eileen turned out a dozen predictably titled shorts that year, including *It's Cheaper to Be Married, Good Morning Nurse, It's Cheaper to Be Single, A Bare Living, The Woman in the Case, His Family Tree, The Thousand-Dollar Drop, Flat Harmony, Swearing Off, Making Monkey Business, Not Too Thin to Fight*, and *The Paperhanger's Revenge*. Victor teamed Eileen and Curtis with comedians Milton Sims and Ralph McComas in at least sixteen films. Although the shorts might have been routine comedies, Eileen's fanbase was being built through the films' promotions. These shorts were mostly shown in smaller theaters. She was already getting top billing over Sims and McComas in the local newspaper advertisements, such as in the promotion for *His Family Tree*, which ran in the June 21 edition of the *Indiana Evening Gazette*: "Victor Comedy, Featuring the Universal Star, Eileen Sedgwick."

Good Morning Nurse was co-written by Captain Leslie Tufnell Peacocke, who was responsible for scripting countless photoplays. (The July 11, 1914, edition of *Motion Picture World* might have slightly exaggerated his skills, noting that he had produced 338 scenarios to date.) Peacocke was also experienced in directing films; in addition to the 1916 release *It's Great to Be Married*, he directed Eileen in at least three Victor comedies in 1917, including *The Honeymoon Surprise* and *The High Cost of Starving*. As with Allen, Sims, McComas, and so many other actors and directors from this period of silent movies, Peacocke's career was somewhat limited, and he dropped out of filmmaking by the early 1920s.

A poster for the release of *Man and Beast* (1917). Starring in a Bluebird photoplay was considered a prestigious step for Eileen.

Of the 23 films in which Eileen appeared in 1917, five were directed by Henry MacRae. Well-versed in the Western genre, MacRae directed her in the Bison Motion Picture titles *Dropped from the Clouds* (re-released in 1923), *Number 10*, *The Last of the Night Riders*, *Westbound*, and *Money and Mystery* and in *Man and Beast*, a five-reel Butterfly Picture which received the additional exposure that came with the exploitation of the mainstream release. Hyped as "A Most Wonderful Production" in the July 23 edition of the *Mansfield News*, the melodrama was set during a drought in South Africa.

The story centers on the von Haagen family and their refusal to share their water rights to a cattle spring with the Townsend family. While the families feud, Gretel von Haagen (Eileen) and Ned Townsend (J. Park Jones) fall in love, marry against their families' wishes, and travel to the interior of the country to start a life together. Her brother pursues the two, and is saved by Ned when confronted by a lion. Years pass before Gretel's father Carl (Harry Clifton) searches for his daughter to seek her forgiveness. He discovers that he is now a grandfather ... just as the infant wanders off into the jungle in pursuit of some monkeys. The infant is rescued from predatory wildlife by a friendly elephant and returned to his parents, with the two families reconciling by the story's end.

The film also starred Kingsley Benedict, an actor who first worked with Eileen in the 1915 short *Lone Larry*. The elephant, played by Charlie, was just one of the animals in the film that received screen credits. Universal's studio zoo supplied the animals, as it did for most of their "wild animal" pictures. The menagerie was situated on a parcel of land that was also used to film the animals, included lions, leopards, tigers, apes, monkeys, and bears, as well as performing cats and dogs.

Eileen acted in the Victor comedy *The Losing Winner*; released in February, it featured fellow vaudevillian Carter DeHaven. DeHaven often wrote, directed and acted in many of his films—a bargain for any studio who might have paid him one salary for performing three responsibilities.

Eileen teamed with Fred Church for at least four more Bison adventure films which were released throughout the year: *Jungle Treachery*, *The Lure of the Circus*, *The Lion's Lair*, and *The Temple of Terror*. The two actors were receiving equal billing in newspaper advertisements, as shown in the November 16 *Mansfield News* entertainment section: "*The Lion's Lair*, Animal Drama of merit.... Fred Church and Eileen Sedgwick."

The September 9, 1917, *Lima Sunday News* hyped Eileen's appearance in *The Lure of the Circus*: "Nothing pleases so much as to see Eileen Sedgewick [*sic*] in one of her impersonations of a circus actress in *The Lure of the Circus* at the Strand today, she will [no] doubt draw capacity houses." Eileen's first serial was also titled *Lure of the Circus*, but aside from the similarity of their titles the two productions were worlds apart. The 1917 feature was a typical Universal animal adventure, which easily could have gone in and out of theater circulation without much notice. Her role in the studio's 1918 adventure serial, however, would propel Eileen to stardom.

At the beginning of World War I, after war broke out in Europe, America believed in neutrality and saw their role as that of peace broker. But America was slowly drawn into the conflict, and by April 2, 1917, President Woodrow Wilson asked Congress for a formal declaration of war. The lack of public unity in America was a primary concern, as unanimous public support was considered to be crucial to the entire wartime effort. Wilson created the Committee on Public Information (CPI) to promote the war domestically while publicizing

American war efforts abroad. Through the CPI, the Division of Films was developed to support the war through motion pictures, with the film industry enthusiastically flooding theaters with patriotic and anti–Hun movies. Movie stars, including Charlie Chaplin, Douglas Fairbanks, and "America's Sweetheart" Mary Pickford helped finance wartime efforts by attending Liberty Bond rallies. On April 8, along with actress Marie Dressler, the three held a bond rally on Wall Street in New York City, greeting a crowd that was estimated at 30,000.

Although the U.S. Army stood at 200,000 troops, it was estimated that the Army would need to mobilize one million troops for the war. On May 18, the Selective Service Act became law, making it mandatory for American men between the ages of 21 and 29 to register for the draft. Droves of actors and motion picture industry employees registered for the war's first draft, including established stars such as Buster Keaton, and newcomers like John Gilbert. Not all workers in the Hollywood community were happy about the compulsory draft, as the May 11 issue of the *Denver Times* pointed out when it quoted popular screen actor J. Warren Kerrigan: "I am not going to war until I have to. I will go, of course, if my country needs me, but I think that first they should take the great mass of men who aren't good for anything else, or are good only for the lower grades of work. Actors, musicians, great writers, artists of every kind—isn't it a pity when people are sacrificed who are capable of such things—of adding to the beauty of the world?"

The Sedgwick family fully supported the war effort. Eileen, along with Universal actresses Violet MacMillan, Priscilla Dean, Gretchen Lederer, and Edith Roberts, donated their time to collect books, newspapers, and other reading material for the recruits who were away training at camps.

On June 5, 1917, Edward registered for the draft. As a Texas Ranger and member of the National Guard, he had received military experience when he was assigned to guard the U.S. border during the Mexican Revolution. The Mexican conflict also helped him hone his writing skills, as he worked the Associated Press wire for *The Galveston News*. However, things had changed for Edward since the time of the revolution, as he weighed in for his examination at 305 lbs. The examining officer's recommendation on Edward's draft registration card was that he was unfit for service, indicating his disqualification as being "Over Weight" and "Very Stout." The home address noted on Edward's card was "1835 Argyle, Hollywood, California," listing his occupation as "Motion Picture Actor" and his place of employment as "Morosco Film Co., 201 North Occidental Boulevard."

At the time Edward registered, he was working on *The Varmint*, a comedy being produced by the Oliver Morosco Photoplay Company. Released in August of that year by Paramount Pictures, *The Varmint* was directed by William Desmond Taylor and featured Jack Pickford, brother of Mary Pickford. Oliver Morosco, a theatrical producer once considered to be the nation's most spectacular showman, organized the studio. Although he made more than $5,000,000 from a succession of Broadway hits, Morosco experienced bad fortune and was bankrupt by 1926, due to an 18-year-long plagiarism suit over the production of Richard Walton Tully's musical play *The Bird of Paradise*.

Morosco wasn't the only one associated with *The Varmint* to experience bad luck in the years to come. On February 1, 1922, director Taylor was shot to death in his Westlake Park bungalow. The press and police named at least a dozen suspects, with accounts focusing on two popular actresses. It was determined that Mabel Normand, a leading comedian and good friend of Taylor, was the last to see him alive. Although she was never charged, her career was tarnished due to her association with Taylor's murder. Actress Mary Miles Minter's movie career also came to an end after her belongings were found in Taylor's bungalow. Taylor's murder is still unsolved and has become one of Hollywood's greatest scandals of the silent era.

In 1917 the film industry was rapidly expanding, and so were the star-related scandals. Newspaper and magazine publishers picked up on Hollywood gossip and created a profitable business out of the misfortunes of others. In addition to the Taylor murder, there were two other scandals in the early 1920s that would affect the industry, and in the process create a close scrutiny of and censorship in movies by various review boards: the 1923 drug-related death of matinee idol Wallace Reid and the 1921 rape and manslaughter trials of comedian Roscoe Arbuckle. (After two trials, he was acquitted.)

Jack Pickford also became a sad casualty of the Hollywood scene after he developed addictions to drugs, alcohol, and gambling. His first wife, actress Olive Thomas, was a heroin addict who committed suicide in 1920. By the late 1920s, with his health rapidly deteriorating, he was regarded as undependable. Battling bouts of syphilis and chronic alcoholism, Pickford died in 1933, with the cause of his death listed as "progressive multiple neuritis."

The Sedgwicks managed to keep themselves out of trouble. Edward was still happily married to Rose. Josie married William Gettinger in 1917. Gettinger, also known as William Steele (in addition to an assortment of other screen aliases), started with Bison in 1914 and continued to work steadily for 20 years as a mostly uncredited minor actor in Universal Westerns. Coincidentally, he had enlisted for service the same day as Edward, and at the

Josie was given the opportunity to act in a more dramatic role, alongside Rowland V. Lee, in Triangle's *The Maternal Spark* (1917).

same recruitment office. Josie married Gettinger after he had been selected for service—partially out of sympathy for him, thinking that he might not be returning from the battlefield.

Josie was busy establishing herself in the Western genre. That year she worked in several of Triangle Film Corporation's features, including *The Boss of the Lazy Y*, *The Devil Dodger*, *Ashes of Hope*, *One Shot Ross*, *Fighting Back*, *Indiscreet Corinne*, and *The Maternal Spark*. Two brothers, Harry and Roy Aitken, founded Triangle in 1915 and made the studio self-sufficient, handling the production and distribution of their films, as well as a chain of theaters to exhibit them in. Originally their Culver City studio planned to release prestigious films such as *Intolerance: Love's Struggle Throughout the Ages* (1916), and to feature major stars in their productions (Mary Pickford, Douglas Fairbanks, Lillian Gish, and Roscoe "Fatty" Arbuckle). But by 1917 Triangle was experiencing problems due to its rapid growth. In the process they lost three of their principal producers, which led to the studio's demise and its sale in 1918. Although Josie's films didn't match the impressive quality of the studio's earlier films, they did give her a foundation of solid acting credits. Her characters were often on the shady side: dance hall girls or "the other woman." Quite often she would play alongside up-and-coming actors such as John Gilbert and Olive Thomas. Josie worked on only one non–Triangle film that year, a Universal–Gold Seal film release titled *The Pullman Mystery*, featuring an ensemble cast of Universal players.

Continuing his success as a screen comedian, Edward appeared in two Victor comedies, *Fat and Foolish*, in which he was given top billing, and *Who Said Chicken?* He also appeared in a Yorke Film Corporation feature, *The Haunted Pajamas*, a June release. The comedy featured former stage and vaudeville actor Harold Lockwood, one of the earliest romantic actors of the silent era; he and May Allison were one of the movies' first romantic teams (23 films in 1915 and '16). *The Haunted Pajamas* also featured Carmel Myers, an actress who in due time would be ranked among the silent screen's most bewitching vamps (a sexually predatory woman who takes advantage of men for her personal gain). She appeared with Rudolph Valentino the following year in *A Society Sensation* and *All Night*. In 1925 she was seen in the epic film extravaganza *Ben-Hur: A Tale of the Christ*.

Directed by Richard Stanton, Fox's *The Yankee Way*, a September release, credited Edward as scenarist along with Ralph Spence. According to the July 31, 1926, *Motion Picture World* Spence would become the "highest-paid title writer in the world at $5/word." Edward would continue to collaborate with Spence in various film productions over the next ten years.

The years 1917 and 1918 were pivotal for the motion picture industry. The headline of a feature article in the May 27, 1917, *New York Times* announced, "Three Film Stars Get $1,000,000 a Year Each; Motion Picture Business, at Pinnacle of Success, Sees No Sign of Waning Popularity—Tax Talk Stops Boasting of Profits." The article estimated that there were 15,000 theatres in the United States, exclusive of vaudeville and other theatres in which motion pictures were shown as a part of a program that was devoted to movies. The daily attendance in those theatres was estimated to be between 12,000,000 to 17,000,000 viewers. The newspaper determined that "the general consensus of opinion among trade authorities seems to be that while the movies may have reached the zenith of their popularity they have not passed it. They are at least holding their own, and students of the industry believe they will continue to do so as long as the standard of excellence is increased." The three film stars referred to in the article's headline were Charlie Chaplin, Mary Pickford and Douglas Fairbanks, who were receiving combined earnings estimated at $3,000,000 a year. The previous year state legislators, staggered by the size of the reputed earnings of movies stars, started investigations to determine if an industry that could afford to pay out enormous salaries to their contracted actors should also be able to afford a war tax.

Nineteen seventeen's top-grossing movie was *Cleopatra*, starring the queen of film vamps, Theda Bara. Loosely based on William Shakespeare's *Antony and Cleopatra,* the film was noted for its elaborate sets and risqué costumes. Moviegoers also flocked to see Chaplin in *The Cure*, Pickford in *Rebecca of Sunnybrook Farm*, and Gloria Swanson in *Teddy at the Throttle*. Slapstick vaudevillian Buster Keaton starred in *The Butcher Boy*, his first film, which featured Roscoe Arbuckle. Keaton would go on to become a major screen comedian, competing with Chaplin for box office business. In years to come, he would work with Edward, as his director of choice, with the two forming a lifelong friendship.

In early March of 1918, cases of a mild form of influenza were being reported in the United States. By May, the influenza was spreading through Europe, most likely carried over by the military whose stateside training camps were infected with it. The influenza virus mutated into a severe form of influenza in the fall, with a final wave occurring in the spring of 1919. It has been estimated that worldwide it caused the deaths of between 30 and 50 million people, including an estimated 675,000 Americans.

The pandemic adversely affected Hollywood as movie theatres were forced to close their doors in an effort to prevent the virus from spreading among patrons. Some theatres tried to suppress the fear by announcing that their venues were healthier than most homes, as the Lyric did for their Lima, Ohio, theatre: "During the Flu epidemic no one need fear attending the Lyric. The theatre is fumigated and disinfected daily by means of mechanical ventilation. The air throughout the theatre is changed with fresh pure air every ten minutes, while the air in your own home does not change twice in an hour." The theater closures meant that studios were forced to postpone the opening of their films. Some of the smaller studios went out of business. In an effort to protect themselves from catching the virus, actors wore cotton masks when making public appearances. Theda Bara, however, felt that the hospitalized veterans she visited should have an unobstructed view of their idol's face, so she refused to wear a mask during her appearances. Harold Lockwood was one of the industry-related personnel who contracted influenza and died from it.

These were also pivotal years for the Sedgwicks. Although the family may have benefited from the reduced workforce that was caused by the war and influenza, they were also progressing on their own merit. In 1918 Eileen continued her appearances in Universal adventures and Nestor comedies. She was quickly becoming experienced in horseback riding and learning how to perform her own stunts. Her growing number of fans were beginning to know her as the "she dare-devil."

For Universal releases Eileen acted in *Hell's Crater, Quick Triggers, Trail of No Return, Roped and Tied, The Human Tiger, All for Gold*, and *Lure of the Circus*. *Quick Triggers*, written and directed by George Marshall, featured Neal Hart as the hero. Marshall had a career that covered seven decades, beginning in silent movies, successfully transitioning through the introduction of sound, and into the medium of television. He began with a Western in 1915 and ended with television shows, including episodes of *Daniel Boone, The Odd Couple* and *Here's Lucy*, Marshall also directed "The Railroad," a segment of the Academy Award–winning film *How the West Was Won* (1963).

Lure of the Circus was realistically promoted by Universal as their $100,000 serial; however, its trade advertisements claimed that the studio laid out "more than half a million dollars for the circus scenes alone." It brought Eileen into the forefront of star recognition. Eileen received the role as the result of an unfortunate event: The original leading actress, Molly Malone, underwent an emergency appendectomy during filming, and therefore appeared only in the first five chapters. Eileen's character, a bareback rider, was quickly written into the story and she became the female lead in the remaining 18 chapters. Interestingly enough, five years later there was a very similar situation in the story of Rupert Hughes' *Souls for Sale* (1923). The character that actress Eleanor Boardman portrayed in *Souls for Sale* received her first real acting role because another actress had her legs crushed while filming a circus-related movie. The similarities to *Lure of the Circus* are so strong that they appear to have been intentional and not coincidental.

The cast of *Lure of the Circus* included professional circus performers, among them two famous clowns, Roy Miller and Frank Chester. Its male lead was Eddie Polo, a trapeze artist who first worked with his brother Sam as a catchman in a trapeze act in Vienna, and then in the U.S. with Barnum & Bailey circus for 13 years. Polo, known as "the Hercules of the screen," built a reputation for his daring and strength in his previous work in the *Liberty* and *Bull's Eye* serials.

Polo's contract called for at least two stunts in each episode. In the November 23 issue of *The Moving Picture Weekly* it was explained that if it wasn't for the outbreak of the Spanish influenza temporarily shutting down production on the serial, Polo might have been in grave danger due to the stunts he performed. He had already made three 100-foot jumps into a river, leaped twice from a rapidly moving train into an automobile, and had fights

An advertisement for *Lure of The Circus* (1918). Eileen's role in the serial would propel her to stardom.

The leading male in *Lure of the Circus* (1918) was Eddie Polo, a trapeze artist who became known as "the Hercules of the screen." Eileen was offered the leading female role when the original leading actress, Molly Malone, underwent an emergency appendectomy during filming.

with mobs. During the break in filming, Polo took inventory of his injuries, totaling fifty sprains caused by the stunts. Polo believed that if it weren't for the influenza outbreak he would have had to attempt further feats while in a crippled condition which might have compromised his stunt skills and might have led to a life-threatening injury.

The December 21 *Kansas City Star* reported on Polo's local promotion for *Lure of the Circus*, in which he described his brushes with death while performing stunts. One *Lure of the Circus* incident he recalled involved a planned 35-foot leap from a pier to a boat, which ended with him striking the edge of the craft instead of landing in it. He suffered two fractured ribs, four broken fingers, and a sprained left leg. "The hard thing about making serials," he remarked, "is that to be successful each one must have more thrills than its predecessor. In *The Lure of the Circus* a burning oil derrick fell on me, I had to dive through a glass window, I had to jump through an open drawbridge in a motor car and a horse fell on me."

Its first chapter, "The Big Tent," was released in November. The February 1919 edition of *Photoplay* gave the serial a passing review.

> When is a circus not a circus but an oil well conspiracy? When it's in a Universal serial. It does seem a pity serial writers will not stick to their subjects, but must, perforce, chase the hackneyed hokum of utter and uncreditable sensation. The best part of the circus stuff, as I saw it, was a wonderful camera shot apparently made from the whiffle-trees of a run away chariot, looking up at the flying tent roof, and past the agonized face of the horrified woman driver. This was really sensational shoot-

ing, and a brand new idea. Eddie Polo is the star, and apparently, if one may judge from a brace of episodes, he will have naught but villain-whamming in the customary places to occupy his time.

Universal heavily promoted the serial as "the greatest film show on Earth." Their exploitation magazine, *The Moving Picture Weekly*, printed a letter from the manager of Detroit's Warren Theatre, who detailed the literal smashing of their box office when people who were waiting on line for hours rushed in to see the first chapter of the series. The publication also related a second case: "There are but two instances so far as the writer knows where box offices themselves have been smashed in the enthusiasm over even a serial. This is one of them. The other occurred while this same record-smashing Eddie Polo was in New York and tried to get into a theatre on Rivington Street. In their rush to see the star, the crowd pushed box office, cash, ticket seller and all two whole blocks away from the theatre." The exploitation of a serial such as *The Lure of the Circus* was necessary for the entire success of its run in a theatre. If a properly promoted business could increase their receipts on Monday, generally the slowest day of the week, from $40 to $45, that would be considered an achievement. For most serials, word of mouth was necessary to form the viewer anticipation necessary to draw crowds for future chapters. In an effort to hook an audience, some theatres showed the first chapter for free. Others gave customers the final chapter free if they collected a punched-out card that showed they saw all previous episodes.

For the Nestor division Eileen appeared in *Watch Your Watch*, *A Kitchen Hero*, *The Shifty Shoplifter*, *Passing the Bomb*, *The Butler's Blunder*, *Naked Fists*, *Oh! Man!*, *Repeating the Honeymoon*, *The Slow Express*, and *The Fickle Blacksmith*. Allen Curtis directed the majority of films.

The Nestor films were promoted as "mirth-provoking" comedies. In *Repeating the Honeymoon*, which was typical of the studio's output, Eileen and Al McKinnon play a married couple who divorce over a trivial matter although they're still in love with each other. On the night of their wedding anniversary they both get the idea to spend the night at the hotel where they honeymooned. Through a misunderstanding the hotel proprietor books the bridal suite for both of them. Eileen locks Harry out of the room, reminding him that they are divorced. Luckily a minister is rooming next door, and Harry gets him to retie their nuptial knot, with the chambermaid and proprietor standing by as witnesses.

Working for Triangle, Josie was receiving increasingly sophisticated roles. She acted in nine Triangle features released in 1918: *The Man Above the Law*, *Keith of the Border*, *Paying His Debt*, *Wolves of the Border*, *Flapjacks*, *The Poor Fish*, *Hell's End*, *Beyond the Shadows* and *Wild Life*, and also played a part in *Lure of the Circus*.

Josie worked with Roy Stewart in *Keith of the Border*, *Paying His Debt*, and *Wolves of the Border*. Stewart, an actor who was often compared to the cowboy matinee idol William S. Hart, had successfully teamed with Josie the previous year in *The Devil Dodger*, *The Boss of the Lazy Y*, and *One Shot Ross*. Based on the successful book by Randolph Parrish, *Keith of the Border* was given good reviews. The March 5 issue of *The Duluth News Tribune* included the following critique of the film's stars:

> The display of earnestness and power will convince the most skeptical that some screen fights at least are bona fide attempts at complete physical destruction, and with Roy Stewart roaming into camera range the picture is given an added individuality worth while. *Keith of the Border* sparkles with Stewart personality. It would seem that he knows the life of a border ranger well for the part fits him like a skin. Dual roles always hard to portray find Josie Sedgwick equal to the task, while

The Poor Fish (1918), a Triangle production, helped Josie build solid acting credits.

Norbert Cill's villainy is of a furious quality, giving the screen a new type of "heavy." Albert Lee, a perennial favorite, is the mother, and Pete Morrison is at his best, as sheriff, cowboy and such.

Josie was keeping good company in her films.

In the Triangle melodrama *The Man Above the Law*, Josie is tangled in a love triangle with her co-stars Jack Richardson and Claire McDowell. As a missionary schoolteacher sent West to teach religion to the Indians, Josie develops the role of an independent female. This was the type of character that she would be known for; her character takes on an additional cause to redeem the ruthless owner of a trading post who takes advantage of the natives after selling them cheap whiskey. In the process the two fall in love, but Josie's character realizes the trader must return to his Indian wife and child, who needs his support. In the end the schoolteacher is left alone as the trader and his family move further west to start a renewed life together.

William Desmond, an Irish-born stage and vaudeville actor, appeared with Josie in *Hell's End*, *Beyond the Shadows*, and *Wild Life*. In the years to follow, Desmond would become a major Western star, joining Eileen in some of her most memorable serials, including *The Riddle Rider* (1924), which spurred a successful sequel serial for Desmond.

In Beyond the Shadows Desmond plays Jean DuBois, a Canadian trapper. His parents (Graham Pettie and Alberta Lee) have a second son, Horace (Ed Brady), who they haven't seen in years. Horace, who is aligned with a dishonest fur trading company, convinces Eleanor (Josie), the daughter of a minister, to marry him. Realizing his deceitfulness, she comes to

In *Keith of the Border* (1918) Josie was in good company: Roy Stewart played the border ranger, with Norbert Cill (shown above) excelling as the villainous heavy.

her senses and rejects his offer of marriage. Jean becomes entangled with Horace's company, and at the same time falls in love with Eleanor. When Horace discovers that Jean is his brother, he promises to reform, asking Eleanor for a second chance. She agrees to give marriage a second try too, leaving Jean alone in the end.

Beyond the Shadows was filmed at Little Bear Lake near San Bernardino. Josie narrowly missed drowning in a canoe scene with Desmond. About a hundred yards from shore, Desmond paddled their canoe a bit too vigorously, capsizing it. *The Pueblo Chieftain* reported on the incident in the April 20, 1919, edition:

> "Josie can't swim," cried Director J. W. McLaughlin from the shore and Bill manfully struck out for his leading woman. Grasping her by her golden locks, Bill turned and made for shore, warning Miss Sedgwick not to struggle or he'd "knock her cold."
>
> Amid the cheers of the onlooking company, Bill made shore in safety with Miss Sedgwick. While he was receiving the praise of the other members of the company, Miss Sedgwick meekly thanked him, saying it was a most enjoyable trip. "You see," Josie murmured, "I sure dreaded that long swim with all my clothes on, Bill, and as it was your fault that we tipped over I thought it no more than fair that you do all the work. I've known how to swim since I was four years old."

The December 1918 edition of *Motion Picture Magazine* announced that Josie had severed her ties with Triangle.

Edward was given the opportunity to work on four scenarios for Fox, all of which were directed by Richard Stanton: *Stolen Honor*, *Cheating the Public*, *Rough and Ready*, and *Why I Would Not Marry*. Filmed against the snow-covered Adirondack Mountains of New York, the Western *Rough and Ready* featured Dustin Farnum's brother William, who would become one of Fox's highest paid actors during the silent era. William was well received by film critics, who alternatively called him "America's most popular actor," a "fighting lover," the

Although a stunning beauty, Josie eventually chose to portray more action-oriented roles.

"screen Samson," and a "man of action" in their reviews. Sounding overly influenced by exploitation material, the July 31 *Columbus Enquirer* praised Farnum's heroic acting style: "[His] fights before a motion picture camera are always a seven-day wonder. In *Rough and Ready*, his newest de luxe production, there is a two-handed battle forming the thrilling climax of a thrilling drama that will go down in celluloid history, because of its vivid realism."

Based on a story by Mary Murrillo and billed by Fox as a "Cinemelodrama Standard Picture," *Cheating the Public* was an ambitious socially themed movie dealing with food profiteering and the child labor problem of the time. Its promotional material hyped "the thrilling food riots, the fight between man and girl on golden stairs, the 100-mile-a-minute-race-against-death, the electric chair in operation, the fight in the jury room, the powerful scene in the court room," and emphasized "the greedy, grasping nature of the slave-driving 'Bull' Thompson, [the] factory foreman."

Edward quickly realized that not all of the films he contributed to would have the same sort of success. In the case of *Why Would I Marry*, *The Duluth News Tribune*'s dramatic critic, Marie Canel, unkindly but honestly wrote:

> This picture is melodramatic and not very convincing with scarcely a smile in the entire photoplay until almost the end, but if you prefer bitter chocolate to sweet, or coffee without sugar you may not be bored while seeing it. *Why Would I Marry* is billed as a movie "showing girls how to avoid present-day temptations," as a "modern morality play," and as a picture "which makes a profound impression." It is to be doubted whether it is any of these.
>
> The heroine's imagination seems exaggerated and you gaze at subtitles with such legends as "The Spider and the Fly," "Go to his apartment to-night and save me from disgrace," "Isn't there one decent man among you?" etc. So whether you're going to recommend the picture to the family is uncertain. But don't for one tiny minute let us give you the impression that you're going to be thrilled beyond words if you see the picture! It isn't presented cleverly enough for that.
>
> The writers of the movie began with a good idea but it was developed poorly. Evidently it was their plan to show us that the independent businesswoman is better off than a married woman. If they had worked out this idea cleverly or at least sincerely the picture would undoubtedly have a strong appeal to many. If they had shown us a woman who was a successful businesswoman, and just independent enough to enjoy being independent, and then without exaggeration showed us the "sordid lives" of her married girl friend; if they had done this and done it well the picture would have been enjoyable.

In addition, Edward appeared in three standard-fare Nestor comedies that year: *Bruin Trouble*, *Don't Flirt*, and *There and Back*. Toward the end of December 1918 he traveled to Miami with William Bache, general technical director, to scout a location for Fox's adventure movie *The Jungle Trail*. With a working title of *The Lucky Charm*, the William Farnum film was scheduled for a June 1919 release. Edward, who was now working as an assistant director to Richard Stanton, was responsible for securing property to build a Hindu village and Buddhist temple on. The locations for both were built on the Spring Garden subdivision, with each scene located on either bank of a canal. In addition, a Zulu village site was erected on the Elser estate.

Florida was attempting to draw movie companies to their state, away from the West Coast, promoting it as a perfect option for a motion picture studio location. Convenient to the majority of the movie industry's East Coast corporate headquarters, Florida offered an abundance of natural resources to film against, such as the Everglades National Park. Vicinities in the Miami area could be used to shoot jungle scenes, and its close proximity to the ocean made it desirable as well. The one drawback, however, was its sometimes oppressive humidity. Burton Mank, an old friend of Edward and Bache and the manager of Miami's Airdrome Theatre, invited the two to investigate the possibility of filming in the area. The city of Miami was hoping that the production of *The Jungle Trail* would encourage other companies to follow. It was estimated that the single production would put over $100,000 into circulation and employ close to 1,000 people from the area. At the time Fox was producing one regular feature release each week and one feature film each month. With Fox planning to increase their production to two film releases each week, the cities of Fort Lauderdale and Daytona also put in bids, vying with Miami to become the studio's new branch location for Fox.

Negatives and copies of the majority of silent films that the Sedgwicks worked on naturally decomposed or were intentionally destroyed decades ago, as in the case of *The Jungle Trail*. It becomes a challenge for contemporary researchers to attempt to determine the true feeling of a lost film's direction, photography, acting, and story when there isn't a copy available to review. Publications of the time, such as fan magazines, might have included only a story summary or a one-paragraph review, with newspapers using favorably written exploitation material sent out by a production company's publicity department.

Following are two different first-hand examples of how *The Jungle Trail* was reviewed. Appearing in the May 20, 1919, *Philadelphia Inquirer*, this review places the reader in the mind of an adventure-oriented fan, calling the feature "a spectacular affair":

The Jungle Trail ... is a story of travel and romance, and offered with spectacular stagings. In fact it is the unusual showing in the natural scenic, rather than any merit the play possesses, that will make the movie work a success, for the thrilling African jungle scenes, with their real African tribesmen, will in themselves attract and interest. One really marvels at the magnificence of the vast African fastness reproduced, and thrills and wonder mingle with the exhibits of the hunt of wild animals that habitate these parts, while the showing of the African villages is an education of the Tropics brought to Ninth and Market streets. There is lots of good material in the works, that reaches from New York to the jungle trail and interwoven is a nice romance, that through sensational, is not impossible.

Of course Farnum has his fights, and these to lovers of robust manhood are well worth while, for this popular actor's fistic prowess is among his many talents that have helped much in his work. The cast is exceptionally good, including Anna Lehr, G. Raymond Nye, who was Farnum's fistic opponent, and who is mightily clever and agile; Lyster Chambers, Anna Schaeffer, Edward Roseman, Henry Armatta, George Stone and Mrs. Sara Alexander, whose mother was a work that alone would make the play worth while.

The Duluth News Tribune's critic Marie Canel had a more critical eye. She often wrote her reviews in the form of a moviegoer named Angela writing a letter to her friend Claribel. The following "letter" appeared in the July 23, 1919, edition of *The Duluth News Tribune*:

Dear Claribel:

Here is a real man's picture that will undoubtedly prove interesting to your brother, father and everyone else except your sisters, mother and dear self. I did so like Bill Farnum in *The Man Hunter*, his last film, but somehow I'm not extremely keen about this new picture.

Don't for one tiny minute let me give you the impression that your own Bill isn't interesting and clever as usual. He is—but the story seems sort of swishy-swashy and nothing to rave about. There are a few close-ups of the star that are just about as fine ones as I've seen of Farnum—and I've seen lots. The settings are interesting and the jungle atmosphere is well maintained.

There surely are thrills in the movie and everyone who enjoys seeing lions, snakes, natives of wildest

Africa and a newly discovered race, bayonets, liquid fire (only it's not that but something similar), guns, murder and other things will witness excitement a-plenty. But it appears to me, Claribel, that we have thrills at the expense of heart interest—and don't you prefer the latter?

However, we learned one new thing in *The Jungle Trail*. There's a new but always infallible method of getting rid of the third partying the triangle. We've had him or her poisoned, shot, left on the sands of the desert, et cetera, but here it's different. What the villain does is to have his rival embark on an African hunt for a mate to some animal. Of course there's supposed to be a big price paid by a museum or society and then too the hero thinks it will improve his heart crusade with his lady fair.

But the villain thinks it out "with malice aforethought" and shows the hero what a good friend he is. Why he even furnishes Bill the guides for the expedition—but the guides are instructed to lose or kill the hero in the jungle, so it's not philanthropy plus, you know.

And that's about all we see in the movie—just the attempts to kill our hero in Africa and his subsequent revenge when he gets back to the states. The villains are the blood-and-thunder kind and not as interesting as the lovable villains who are bad one minute and good the next. The men will undoubtedly love this movie—but for the women—it may be different.

Yours forever and ever,
ANGELA.

Fortunately for Edward, the bulk of the *Jungle Trail* critiques focused on the imagery and action, as described by the first reviewer. The second reviewer, although cleverly tongue-in-cheek, concentrated on its weak scenario, which might have prevented potential ticket purchasers from going to see the film. *Lure of the Circus* author Hope Loring made a legitimate point, that female scenarists tended to write stories with detail, as opposed to the male author who "paints his dramatic picture with a broad brush and lays his colors on thickly." In an article which appeared in the March 3, 1919, *Oakland Tribune*, Loring wrote that she based her belief on her observations that the male writer lacked the characteristics to explore feminine qualities of feeling, observation, intuition, and expression. "He builds his plays on a situation—and leaves his creation to stand or fall on that scene, motif, or episode. His problem play is a thing of crude conception and blunt workmanship. There are lacking the moods of character, the influences of environment and the play of psychological undercurrents that are the essence of the proposition to woman." Regardless of the accuracy of her observations, adventure films relied on leaving nothing to the viewer's imagination.

The other 1919 releases that Edward worked on were a pair of sports-related films. Richard Stanton directed *Checkers*, based on a popular stage play by Henry M. Blossom, about a racetrack tout. Blossom had passed away just as Stanton, who himself played the main character on stage, was interpreting the play for the screen.

Writer Raymond L. Schrock collaborated with Hamilton Thompson and Edward on the scenario for *The Winning Stroke*. Schrock would go on to collaborate with Edward on many films that Edward directed at Universal. The film was based on the great Yale-Harvard varsity rowing match which took place on June 20 of that year; director Edward Dillion utilized ten cameras positioned on bridges, piers, the tops of trains, the ferry, on launches, etc., to record the event. *The Winning Stroke* was promoted as the "first big film dealing with the life of a great American university in which scenes were made 'on the spot.'"

Eileen's only performances that year were in two Universal properties, and they reunited her with Eddie Polo. *Cyclone Smith* was a series featuring Polo as adventurer Cyclone Smith. Starting in May, a string of Cyclone Smith movies were released through 1919, with Eileen appearing in six of the episodes: *A Prisoner for Life*, *A Phantom Fugitive*, *The Wild Rider*, *Cyclone Smith's Comeback*, *Cyclone Smith Plays Trumps*, and *A Pistol-Proposal*.

In *The Great Radium Mystery*, an 18-chapter serial, Eileen co-starred with Cleo Madison and Bob Reeves. It featured characters named "The Buzzard," "The Rat," and "The Hawk," and had chapters titles such as "The Fatal Ride," "Creeping Flames," "The Scalding Pit," "The Wheels of Death," and "Liquid Flames"; one can only imagine what sort of precarious situations the serial's characters faced.

Eileen was quickly becoming a popular film personality, as illustrated by the cover of the June 1917 issue of *Moving Picture Stories*.

The cover of the November 1919 issue of *The Moving Picture Weekly* publicized Eileen's performance in Universal's serial *The Great Radium Mystery*.

Josie found work at various studios, performing in *Kingdom Come* for Universal, *The She Wolf* for the Frohman Amusement Corporation, and *Jubilo* for Goldwyn Pictures Corporation. *Kingdom Come* featured Western star Hoot Gibson, a matinee idol with whom the Sedgwicks would have a lasting relationship. *The She Wolf* starred vaudevillian star and future Prohibition-era speakeasy owner Texas Guinan. She was modeled as a female version of William S. Hart but reviewers disagreed about Guinan's success at being a "good bad woman."

Jubilo featured popular Ziegfeld Follies star Will Rogers in his third film. It was based on Ben Ames Williams' serialized story "Jubilo" which ran in *The Saturday Evening Post* from June 28 to July 5. Rogers claimed that it was filmed without a script, with the cast reading their parts directly from the magazine. Although Rogers was able to interject his well-known wit into the film through the use of body language and title cards, he got mixed reviews. Josie received praise for her performance as the judge's daughter who falls for the hobo played by Rogers.

Now that the Sedgwicks' grouch bag was comfortably filled, they were at the point where they could be choosy about the type of films they worked on. Ned and Josephine were living with Josie and Eileen on the West Coast as Edward spent more time involved in movies being filmed on the East Coast. Eileen married Justin H. McCloskey, an experienced assistant director with aspirations to become a director. Josie was becoming well known through her films as a skilled horsewoman. *Motion Picture Magazine* reported that she was planning to enter the women's bucking bronco contest at the 1919 Phoenix State Fair. "We're

Shown with Pete Morrison and Hoot Gibson (left and right) in a scene from *Kingdom Come* (1919), Josie started in Westerns as a damsel in distress, but quickly became a strong female figure.

Jubilo (1919) featured Josie and Will Rogers, a popular Ziegfeld Follies star who was appearing in his third film. Josie plays a judge's daughter who falls for a hobo played by Rogers.

banking on her to 'bring home the bacon,'" they exclaimed in the December 1918 issue. The following month they reported that she was prepared to "pit her knowledge and cleverness against the famous feminine riders of our country." Footage of her participation was shot for possible use in her films, a practice that continued in succeeding years. Her marriage to William Gettinger was quickly failing. Josie's original reason to accept his proposal was based on the sympathetic notion that he wouldn't be returning from duty at the frontlines in Europe. He returned unscathed.

Note

1. *The Daily Herald*, Mississippi, June 3, 1915, p. 2.

Chapter Four

Dynamite's Daughter, the Ramblin' Kid, and the Diamond Queen

Twelve wealthy brides locked in a dungeon in a castle! Outside their prison room, the pirate captors are indulging in a drunken orgy, taking advantage of the absence of their chief to glut themselves with liquor. In the subterranean passages of the castle is a furtive figure clad in the uniform of a United States naval aviator. The aviator is taking a desperate chance to reach the girls and save them single-handed.

This description of the seventh episode of Fox's 15-part serial *Bride 13* ran in the entertainment section of the December 4, 1920, edition of *The Fort Wayne News and Sentinel*.

The concept of the serial dates back to the late 1800s when serialized novels were first published in monthly magazines so that readers would purchase the following issue in order to complete the story. Serials that utilized a "cliffhanger" device climaxed each chapter with an unexpected ending, leaving the audience in suspense, with the following chapter starting off where the previous one ended. The chapter's cliffhanger ending might have left the serial's hero in a precarious situation or learning of an eye-opening detail, with the situation resolved in the following chapter. The term "cliffhanger" is attributed to Thomas Hardy's serial novel *A Pair of Blue Eyes* (1873): At the end of chapter 21, Hardy chose to leave his protagonist Henry Knight hanging off a cliff, while waiting for Elfride Swancourt to return with help. As his grip weakens, Swancourt returns in chapter 22 with a rope made out of sheets and linens, which Knight uses to climb to safety.

The classic serial film format uses a plot device where all chapters are interconnected through characters and a common underlying plot. Its ingredients include fast action, suspense, thrills, and a charming love interest. Each chapter closes with a dramatic cliffhanger that is magnet-like in its ability to pull the moviegoer back to the theater the following week to see the succeeding chapter. In comparison, the series format is made up of episodes involving the same main characters in each film, but does not rely on a linking story thread to make it complete, such as with the Cyclone Smith series.

In 1912 Edison released the 12-chapter *What Happened to Mary?*, a serial some genre specialists regard as a serial-series hybrid. Considered to be the first of its kind in the U.S., each of its one-reel chapterplays contained a short story which utilized the same underlying plot. Starring Mary Fuller, individual chapters were released on a monthly basis to coincide

Bride 13 (1920), promoted as being filmed with the cooperation of the U.S. Navy, was the first serial done at Fox, and was one of their limited ventures into the genre.

with the appearance of the published version in *McClure's Ladies' World* magazine. The following year Selig Polyscope Company released a 13-installment serial starring Kathlyn Williams, titled *The Adventures of Kathlyn*. Each of the serial's chapters existed on their own but related to one another through incidents that loosely tied them together, with minimum regard to the overall plot.

The earlier silent series and serials, especially those filmed during the period before and after World War I, featured females in the leading roles. Pearl White and Ruth Roland, the queens of the early movie serials, defined the genre, and in the process set the standards for serial heroines and heroes, often performing their own daredevil stunts. Mentally, as well as physically, the characters portrayed by these actresses, including Helen Holmes and Ann Little, were equals to their male counterparts, and especially to their villainous antagonists.

White's 1914 serial *The Perils of Pauline*, produced by Pathé Frères, was the first film to continually make use of cliffhangers in its chapters. The 20-episode epic placed White in danger as various villains persisted in getting their hands on her inherited fortune. Unlike subsequent serials that used the cliffhanger at the ending of each episode, *The Perils of Pauline* used them just before their endings, and instead ended chapters with Pauline escaping imminent danger. One chapter literally placed her hanging over the cliff's edge of the New Jersey Palisades. *The Perils of Pauline* spawned a successful spin-off, *The Exploits of Elaine* (1914), setting the standard for all serials that followed as it ushered in the first golden age of the film serial.

As White's popularity grew, her penchant for performing her own dangerous stunts became a growing concern to the studios. They soon insisted on White making use of stunt doubles for the more difficult stunts, a fact that was kept secret from her fans until John Stevenson, her stand-in during the serial *Plunder* (1922), was killed. Stevenson leaped from the top of a bus to grab a prop string of pearls that dangled from an elevated structure. He missed his aim and fell to his death. The news quickly spread to her fans in the form of a rumor—"Pearl White was killed!"—followed by a scandal when the real story emerged, and fans found that she used a stunt man. *The Cincinnati Times Star* published an article after Stevenson's death, paying homage to the stunt double:

> Stevenson wasn't known to the public at all, but there were few people in what is known as the moving picture business to whom his name and fame were not familiar things. In perilous feats he had impersonated dozens of famous stars. When they picked the poor fellow up, crushed and dying, underneath the elevated structure at Seventy-second Street and Columbus Avenue, he wore the flapper frock and the blonde wig of Pearl White.

The article continued to explain to viewers that the real star of an adventure movie is the stunt double.

> There are dozens of men like Stevenson, who earn a living as stunt actors. They are well known among directors, their services are in constant demand, and they receive good pay. The extent in which they substitute for the stars is not realized at all by the public. Whenever you see your favorite hero fall with his favorite horse, stagger to his feet and fearlessly resume his battle against countless odds with the bandits who have sought to rob him of the paper, you can bet whatever you want that the hero was "off," probably having his fingernails manicured, when the fearless horseman fell, and that the horseman was someone whose name you'll never know, but who gets his pay because he knows how to fall with a horse and isn't afraid to do it.

Unfortunately for White, the article never mentioned the countless death-defying stunts that she personally performed in her films. By the time the first chapter of *Plunder* opened, Pathé's exploitation machine was already repairing White's reputation with moviegoers by continuing to give her the sole credit for all of her stunt work. An article in the December 10 *Charlotte Sunday Observer* overlooked Stevenson's death: "Pearl White is well-known as the peerless, fearless serial queen, and in *Plunder* she more than lives up to her title. Thrills are plentiful and none of them can be too hazardous for Pearl to take a chance with. The locations in New York City give an opportunity for unusual thrills and automobile chases through busy streets."

Ruth Roland, born to a show business family, made her stage debut at age three and a half. By the time she was eight she performed her own vaudeville act; a director for Kalem spotted her in 1909. She signed up with the studio and found popularity in their "Ruth, the Girl Detective" series. In 1915 Balboa recruited Roland and featured her in her first serial, *Who Pays?* Roland decided to utilize a stunt double, but her decision was the result of a fall from a horse which caused injury to her spine.

As an outcome of World War I the U.S. saw a rapid growth of its middle-class segment. Partially created by the country's industrialization to support the needs of the war effort, the rising class experienced an increase in their leisure time due to automation, as well as an increase in their disposable income as the country entered a period of prosperity. Up to that time, the serials' main audiences were comprised of children and viewers from a lower socio-economic class who attended each week as a means to escape their drab existence by entering a world of fantasy.

This middle-class segment of moviegoers proved to be more sophisticated than previous cinema viewers. As risqué slapstick comedies fell out of favor, dramas with developed plot settings were on the rise. The larger production companies quickly became aware of the middle class' preference for more refined and varied features and abandoned the serial genre, leaving Universal and Pathé to dominate the market. Also still in the serial biz were a few of the independents, including American, Kalem, Lubin, Mutual, Reliance, and Vitagraph. Most of these studios had little influence in the exchange business and as a result were unable to get their serials into the hands of the major urban theater managers. Instead, they were often booked by the rural and lower-end movie theaters where the offerings weren't as critical as in the huge photoplay palaces. By nature, a large percentage of the audiences that attended the smaller local theaters were children. The serial-producing studios recognized this and redirected the majority of serial productions with adolescents in mind.

By the early 1920s serials experienced a role reversal as male actors took over the part of the protagonist, with the female usually taking a subordinate role as his love interest. Following World War I the rough-and-ready female fell out of style as her movie presence shifted towards a more polite and dignified role. Ruth Roland limited her involvement in motion pictures, decreasing her output of new titles in 1920 from 44 in 1914 to only one short which was done for her own production company. Pearl White also decreased her film appearances, from 39 titles in 1914 to three in 1920, after she left Pathé in order to make features for Fox. Actors such as Hoot Gibson, Tom Mix, Eddie Polo, and William Desmond started appearing as the lead male characters. By the time of the sound era, the male serial idol became the dominant attraction.

The Sedgwicks were well-positioned to find their individual niches in the serial market. Eileen along with Josie had already appeared in their first serial, *The Lure of the Circus*. Edward was first introduced to the serial when he wrote the scenario for the aforementioned

Four. Dynamite's Daughter, Ramblin' Kid, and Diamond Queen 79

thriller *Bride 13*, one of Fox's releases for 1920. Based on a story by E. Lloyd Shelton and directed by Richard Stanton, the 15-chapter serial dealt with a band of international pirates who steal wealthy girls from the side of their groom at the ceremonies. The pirates, chased by a Secret Service agent, have a submarine to carry away the brides. Promoted as being filmed with the cooperation of the U.S. Navy, *Bride 13* was the first serial done at Fox, and one of their few ventures into the genre. The studio was one of the few major film companies to produce serials, a decision that William Fox must have rethought after *Bride 13* was released, as the chapterplay format didn't appear to be a successful endeavor for them.

Josie's big opportunity came in *Daredevil Jack*, a 15-chapter Pathé serial featuring boxer Jack Dempsey. Nicknamed the "Manassa Mauler," Dempsey held the world heavyweight title from 1919 to 1926. In 1917 his style and punching power caught the attention of manger Jack "Doc" Kearns, who recruited the pugilist. Within eighteen months under Kearns' management, Dempsey knocked out the top contenders and took the heavyweight title from Jesse Willard on July 4, 1919. Capitalizing on Dempsey's fame Kearns signed him to appear in the Pathé serial. *Daredevil Jack*'s production, however, would be postponed due to an unexpected experience.

The day after Dempsey won the championship from Willard, *New York Tribune* columnist Grantland Rice wrote an accusing editorial, convincing readers that Dempsey was a draft dodger. "If [Dempsey] had been a fighting man he would have been in khaki when at

Josie was hired to play the heroine in *Daredevil Jack* (1920), a role that was first offered to Mae West. Boxer Jack Dempsey, a world heavyweight title-holder, played Jack.

twenty-two he had no other responsibilities except to protect his own hide," Rice wrote, criticizing the champion for not joining the 50,000,000 men willing to give up their lives in battle. Dempsey had attempted to enlist when the United States entered World War I but had been turned down. Instead he was assigned to homefront duty as a shipyard worker, which gave him the opportunity to continue to accept boxing matches. After the war ended, pro–American groups accused him of getting preferential treatment during the war because of his boxing status. Although he was acquitted by the San Francisco U.S. District Court in 1920, public accusations continued, and it took him several years to overcome the humiliation associated with the "slacker" label. The felonious charges that were brought against him were part of the scrutinizing that took place during the 1920s of everything related to Hollywood. An example of the unfair incrimination appeared in the March 4, 1920, *Fort Wayne News and Sentinel*: "Jack Dempsey is starring in a movie thriller entitled *Daredevil Jack*. The prize plug-ugly sidestepped the fine opportunity the war offered and is doing his daredeviling within the safe precincts of a Los Angeles screen studio. In accepting the title role of his play this make-believe daredevil betrays pathetic want of a sense of humor." Several American Legion posts passed resolutions about Dempsey, claiming that "he couldn't properly be termed a fighter, because he failed to join in the fight which had honor rather than profit for its reward," denying that he was entitled to profit gained from moving pictures or boxing matches. Franklin D'Olier, national commander of the American Legion, had affirmed that the organization in general wouldn't take steps against Jack or his pictures, and that the retraction of resolutions passed was a matter for local posts, not the national headquarters. "Dempsey was drafted and placed in Class 4-A. Later he was reclassified, but the war ended before he was called. He did his duty. He was registered and would no doubt have done as others have done, had he been called," D'Olier stated.

Exchange managers for Pathé were forced to defend Dempsey and the upcoming *Daredevil Jack* release. E.E. Heller, the manager for the Charlotte, North Carolina, territory, released a statement characterizing the charges against Dempsey as a "malicious attack by unscrupulous enemies." Heller's statement declared Pathé's belief that "he will be vindicated as soon as he has had an opportunity to make his defense. An indictment is no proof of guilt and every man is deemed innocent until proven guilty. Our information indicates that the practical certainty that when this case comes before a jury in court where the defense may submit rebuttal, Dempsey should be acquitted on the charge alleged."

In the meantime, Robert C. Brunton, producer of *Daredevil Jack*, continued his preparations for the release of the "million-dollar serial." Dempsey only had twelve weeks free before joining a tour with the Sell-Floto Circus, so Brunton hired W.S. "Woody" Van Dyke to direct the film. Agreeing to complete what would normally take twenty-five weeks to film, Van Dyke, who had a reputation of completing shots in one take, was encouraged with a $500 bonus to complete one episode per week.

Van Dyke discovered he had a second challenge that he had to deal with: Dempsey's face wasn't camera-friendly, as years of boxing scarred and toughened his muscular features. Lon Chaney, actor and self-taught makeup artist, who later would be known as the "man of a thousand faces" for his transformed roles in *The Hunchback of Notre Dame* (1923) and *The Phantom of the Opera* (1925), was called upon to complete "straight" makeup on Dempsey, including straightening his battered nose and ears with putty, giving shape to his eyebrows, narrow eyes, and mouth, and smoothing his rough face with pancake makeup and rouge. The cover-up made the boxer appear ghoul-like. Van Dyke was forced to "go" with that look due to the restraints.

When Dempsey was signed to work on the serial, Kearns negotiated a contract: $50,000 down and 50 percent of the gross profits. At the time this was more money than any professional boxer would be rewarded after winning a match.

Josie Sedgwick was hired to play the heroine, a role which was first offered to Mae West. West had tested for the part in a love scene with Dempsey but declined due to previous vaudeville commitments. Chaney, in addition to his makeup responsibilities, played a villain in his only serial appearance. Ex-boxers Bull Montana and Spike Robinson joined Universal actors Edgar Kennedy, Carl Stockdale, and Eddie Hearn to form a group of oversized thugs. Overacting during the fight scenes, employing a careless combination of pulled and real punches, the plug-uglies toppled sets and knocked off putty noses.

The serial contained two story threads: The first one revolved around the all–American hero Jack Derring (Dempsey), whose father was framed and sent to prison, and Jack's attempt to prove his innocence. The second plot involved the campus sweetheart Gloria Billings (Josie), owner of a bracelet which, when combined with a matching bracelet, shows the location of a great underground oil lake that her father had discovered. In an amazing twist of fate, Gloria turns out to be the daughter of Leonard Billings, the man who was responsible for sending Jack's father to prison. The following synopsis for "The Ball of Death" demonstrates the writing and pacing of a typical fifteen-minute *Daredevil Jack* chapter. The bolded scene descriptions are taken from the actual title cards used in the chapter, with the summaries recounting the scenes as they appeared in the film.

> The chapter opens with Jack Derry and his teammates preparing to play a game at their college's football stadium.
>
> **The "Duke" watches proceedings.**
>
> Jack prepares to start the game off as he kicks the football, but the ball tips over before he gets the chance to. He picks up the football and notices that it feels strange. The referee feels it too, agrees that something is wrong with it and tosses it aside. Without warning it suddenly explodes. The audience runs in a panic. Jack and the referee seem indifferent about the exploding football and Jack places another ball in position for a kickoff. Duke and his gang leave upset that the plot to kill Jack was foiled.
>
> **The game goes on.**
>
> Gloria is sitting in the bleachers with her stepbrother Edgar and father Leonard. Jack makes a touchdown. His team wins the game and Jack is carried off on his teammates' shoulders. Gloria congratulates Jack.
>
> **Later the "Duke" hatches another plot to dispose of Jack.**
>
> **That Evening.**
>
> As Jack leaves the house, thugs kidnap him. They pull him aboard a boat and knock him out. He wakes up and is roughed up by the crew members. A hand is shown holding a club, which repeatedly comes down on Jack.
>
> **To Be Continued.**

In his autobiography *Dempsey*, he wrote of his experiences working with Van Dyke on *Daredevil Jack*:

Costarring with Edward Hearn (left) and Jack Dempsey in *Daredevil Jack* (1920) gave Josie the exposure and leverage she needed to work in future serials and features.

> Shooting started every morning at 6 a.m. and frequently continued well past midnight. Van Dyke arrived on the set before anyone else.
>
> I told Van Dyke not to expect much and was surprised to hear him say, "I won't." Woody had the reputation of doing only one take—he didn't give a damn what anyone else's policies were. He sure had his hands full with me; even Teddy Hayes, who was present, admitted that I was a bad ham.

Kearns' biography, which was published as a syndicated newspaper feature in 1926, described Dempsey as being "a fellow of quick, burning heart impulses." Dempsey became infatuated with Eileen after his trainer, Ted Hayes, introduced them to each other. Hayes was also attracted to Eileen, causing Dempsey to become "insanely jealous by turns." Hayes described the outcome as ending up as a "free-for-all battle one night at Fanny Ward's house."

The February 29 edition of the *Charlotte Sunday Observer* reported on Dempsey's observations of seeing himself acting onscreen for the first time while watching *Daredevil Jack* at Brunton's production studio's screening room.

> It was the champion's first look at himself as a screen actor, and he admits he experienced rather an uncanny feeling as he sat back in an armchair and watched himself rescue Josephine Sedgwick from the band of thugs that had attacked her in one of the early scenes of the picture.
>
> In this particular scene Dempsey is called upon to beat up the three thugs; but, as he is not supposed

to be a professional fighter in the picture, he was required to go through the beating up process in as amateurish a manner as he could and still get away with it. "If any one of those three had been a real fighter," said Dempsey, "he could have beaten my head off, because I went at them just as I imagined an untrained fighter would do. But it was only in the picture. If it happened in real life I would have used my hands a little differently."

Although *Daredevil Jack* received some negative publicity when it was first released due to Dempsey's draft evasion charges, the serial received decent reviews from some of the major film publications. Mainly due to Dempsey's celebrity status, the press exposure gave Josie the leverage she needed to work in future serials and features. Her positive relationship with Van Dyke allowed her the opportunity to work under his direction the following year in the serial *Double Adventure*. Van Dyke, already a successful director during the 1920s, would become well known for directing several entries in the *Thin Man* series during the 1930s and 1940s, including the original film.

Josie was once again paired with Roy Stewart in *The Lone Hand*. The Western feature, produced by Richard Kipling Enterprises for Universal, was directed by Clifford Smith. Since the scenario was so similar to numerous other Western films that were released each week, *The Lone Hand* needed to rely on its star power to become successful, with Josie and Stewart proving to be a winning couple. In this typical ranch romance, the sheriff's daughter (Josie) falls in love with Stewart, a cowboy who is framed for killing a man. The real killer, who is the deputy, plans to lynch Stewart. Josie is apprised of the deputy's plot and helps Stewart escape from jail. The crooked deputy kidnaps Josie, but in a gunfight he is killed by a stray bullet from one of his gang members. Stewart's character is cleared of the murder charge and becomes both the town's new deputy and Josie's husband.

Josie was signed to appear in the Fox Western *The Square Shooter*, a story about cattle rustling featuring the up-and-coming matinee idol Buck Jones. Jones, an ex-bronco buster who performed with the Miller Brothers 101 Ranch Wild West Show, started his film career appearing in a number of Westerns along with Tom Mix and Franklyn Farnum. By the 1930s, along with his sidekick, a horse named Silver, he was well regarded as one of the greatest of the B-Western stars.

The Square Shooter's direction was originally assigned to Charles Swickard. William Fox watched the rushes shot by Swickard and found them to be "miserable, terrible, and rotten," reassigning the Western's direction to Paul Cazeneuve.

Advance publicity for the comedy-drama announced that Josie would be playing the role of Barbara Hampton, with Jones playing Chick Crandall.

> There's a smile on the face of Buck Jones, William Fox's newest screen sensation, as he looks into the eyes of his pretty leading woman Josie Sedgwick in *The Square Shooter*, a photoplay in which the man who trained horses for four allied governments during the war demonstrates his right to the title "the one greatest horse man in the world."

Due to other commitments, Josie wasn't able to play the role of Barbara in the retakes, and was replaced by Patsy De Forest as Chick's love interest.

That same year, Eileen appeared in two independent films that were released by the States Rights Independent Exchanges. *The White Rider*, a Western adventure directed by William James Craft, teamed her with Joe Moore. Moore played the part of the White Rider, a mysterious crusader who exposes the town's recorder of deeds as an extortionist. After the White Rider foils the scheme to extort $5,000 from a landowner, Moore's character reveals his true identity and wins the heart of the landowner's daughter (Eileen). The November 24 *Mansfield News* boldly promoted the Western: "It will make you grip your seat and hold your breath with thrills and the suspense of the mystery with the special extra feature *The White Rider*. Starring Joe Moore and Eileen Sedgwick. The Best Western Picture of the Year. See wild riding down the mountain, Dare Devil stunts, Death Defying 1000 Thrills—Gripping Mystery."

Love's Battle was produced by Climax Film Corporation and once again paired Eileen with Moore. This time Moore played an ex-cowboy who has given up the range for riding the rails as a hobo. He rescues Eileen's character from a runaway horse, sparking a romance between the two. Framed for a robbery and murder, the hobo is sentenced to death. Eileen's character begs the governor for a pardon, arguing the unfairness of using circumstantial evidence in a trial. The governor receives word that the actual killer has confessed to the crime on his deathbed, saving the hobo from the gallows in the nick of time. The May 11, 1921, *Fayette Daily Democrat* promoted the film's local appearance: "On her knees she pleads with the Governor for his life, at the point of a gun she demands his freedom, but the manner in which she secured it is not only novel but surprising. A powerful Western picture."

Not all of Josie's films were career-building. The daily rushes shot for *The Square Shooter* (1920), which matched Josie with Buck Jones, were so bad that direction was reassigned for retakes. Due to other commitments Josie's role in the retakes was replaced by Patsy De Forest.

Fox assigned Edward to work on three additional titles that year. The first project, a collaboration with Max Marcin, was the scenario of *Face at Your Window*. For Marcin, the author of many Broadway stage successes, this was his first venture in the motion picture field. Directed by Richard Stanton, *Face at Your Window* dealt with foreign agitators (implied to be Russian) and their plot to take over the U.S. government. The anarchists, who are causing strife between capital and labor, invade a mythical American city which falls into their power. In 1920 the country was still riding high on the fervor created by World War I, and the threat from western powers was still real. The previous year the American Legion was founded by veterans returning from Europe, with its organization comprised of mostly young adults who were still heroes in the eyes of Americans. As the city is burning and its inhabitants are fleeing, the legionnaires, garbed in white hoods and cassocks similar to those worn by the Ku Klux Klan, make a dashing appearance, rushing to the relief of their fellow townsmen and driving the miscreants from the streets.

Edward's second collaboration was a scenario for *Sink or Swim* with Ralph Stanton. Also directed by Stanton, the Fox film gave Edward an opportunity to once again appear in front of the camera, although in a minor role. George Walsh is featured as the hero of this comedy, Dick Mason, who is arrested for protecting the honor of a girl in a cabaret (Enid Markey). To keep him out of trouble, his wealthy father sends him to Europe, along with his two buddies, to tend to a cattle concession. While aboard the Europe-bound ship he comes face to face with the girl from the cabaret. Later he discovers that she was traveling incognito and that she is the princess of the principality where the concession is located. Dick helps her thwart a conspiracy against the principality. Princess Alexia renounces her title and becomes his bride, moving with him back to the U.S. to live happily ever after. The story's theme is very similar to that of *Tin Hats*, a film that Edward would direct for Metro-Goldwyn-Mayer in 1926. Throughout his career Edward was very successful in reworking past scenarios into new feature productions.

Fox, very impressed with Edward's work, gave him the opportunity to direct their next serial, *Fantomas*, a 20-chapter thriller released at the end of the year. It was based on the famous Fantomas novels by French authors Marcel Allain and Pierre Souvestre; Edward also collaborated on the scenario. Horace G. Plimpton Jr. (AKA Horace Plympton) handled the photography.

The Fantomas books had already been translated into 13 languages, with over 30,000,000 copies of the books sold. Gaumont Studios had previously produced five stories in serial format in 1913–14, each of them three to six chapters long and directed by Louis Feuillade. The Fox production was the first American appearance for the anti-hero. The stories revolved around Fantomas (Edward Roseman), an arch-criminal willing to go straight if the police give him an unconditional pardon. Instead, the authorities will accept nothing but an unconditional surrender. Enraged by their refusal, he terrorizes the city, harassing the police and civilians. Determined to bring Fantomas to justice is Detective Dixon (John Willard).

It was originally planned as a 15-chapter Fox Photo-Play Masterpiece serial; Fox promoted the fact that so much material was filmed that William Fox decided to increase it to run 20 chapters. The serial's run in a local theater was announced in a gripping review appearing in the March 30 issue of the *Port Arthur News*: "Burning bridges with failing railroad trains; high dives—the divers being fully dressed; wild railroad trains smashing into each

Fantomas (1920) was based on the famous Fantomas novels by the French authors Marcel Allain and Pierre Souvestre. Edward directed and also collaborated in writing the scenario for the serial's 20 episodes. The role of Fantomas was played by Edward Roseman, with Edna Murphy playing the female lead.

other, while in the box car of one are the heroine, Miss Edna Murphy, and her sweetheart, Johnnie Walker; auto chases; motorcycle in flames; fights between the police and gangsters that look as if they were taken from real life."

Josie kicked off her 1921 releases with *Double Adventure*, a 15-chapter serial directed by W.S. Van Dyke and written by Jack Cunningham. It featured Charles Hutchison, publicized by Pathé as "The Thrill-A-Minute Stunt King." Previous to signing with Pathé, Hutchison broke both of his wrists while performing a stunt in his successful adventure film *Hurricane*, forcing him to resort to using stunt doubles in *Double Adventure*. Edith Thornton, Hutchison's wife, was scheduled to co-star in the serial but one side of her face was still temporarily paralyzed from a *Hurricane* stunt in which she and Hutchison rode a motorcycle down the side of a road's rough embankment.

Josie accepted the female lead, a millionaire's grandniece targeted for kidnapping. The millionaire is murdered and Hutchison's character, a newspaper reporter who is a dead ringer for the millionaire's son, is charged. Hutchison works with the authorities to break the case and reveal the true criminals, in the process winning the affection of the grandniece. The

Eileen starred in *The Diamond Queen* (1921), an 18-chapter jungle serial that was loosely based on Jacques Futrelle's novel *The Diamond Master*.

story was typical Western melodrama but Hutchison's character proved popular enough for the production of several "Hutch" action films distributed by Pathé and other exhibitors.

Beginning in March that year, Eileen appeared in nine releases directed by Edward A. Kull. One of Eileen's most ambitious projects to date was Universal's *The Diamond Queen*, an 18-chapter jungle serial loosely based on a novel by Jacques Futrelle, *The Diamond Master*. The serial's plot centered on a philanthropic millionaire's attempt to break a diamond cartel's power by flooding the market with artificial diamonds that he is able to produce with his diamond-making machine. When he refuses to bow to their unjust demands, the unscrupulous combine of enormously wealthy financiers bring the millionaire to ruin and eventually suicide. His daughter (Eileen) resolves to avenge his death and is led to Africa where she experiences adventures amongst cannibals, becoming a queen of the tribe herself.

Eileen followed *The Diamond Queen* with a second serial for Universal, *The Terror Trail*. The 18-episode serial, directed by Kull, had an international theme dealing with a "recent case to be found only in the hidden archives of secret diplomats." George Larkin, a serial actor, appeared opposite Eileen as her masculine interest.

The entertainment columns were reporting on details surrounding Eileen's next big serial, *The Clutch of the Octopus*. The 18-part serial was set to be directed by Kull and Craft; it was written by George Plympton from historical accounts of Henry M. Stanley's expedition

A poster for the 17th episode of *The Diamond Queen* (1921). Known to her immediate friends as "Babe," Universal gave Eileen a new nickname: "The Girl Without a Double," as she performed many of her own stunts.

Eileen appeared on the cover of the April 1921 issue of *True Story* magazine, a non-movie related publication. With success Eileen Sedgwick became a household name.

into Africa for the rescue of Dr. David Livingston. An embellished romantic sub-theme was written to include Eileen as the young reporter assisting Stanley. However, the role of the female reporter in the jungle adventure, which was re-titled *With Stanley in Africa* when released, went to Louise Lorraine, an up-and-coming actress of the adventure genre who appeared in her first serial, *Elmo the Fearless* (1920), acting opposite Elmo Lincoln. The following year she signed with Universal to a long-term contract, acting in eleven serials.

The serial heroines of the 1920s, including Eileen, Lorraine, and Allene Ray, appeared to be anomalies in the male-driven serial market. Refusing to idly sit by as the hero's love interest, they took full command of nerve-wracking situations in their films. These slightly built actresses (Eileen and Ray were 5'3", with Lorraine measuring 5'1") all had a natural athletic ability to perform their own stunts, often refusing the use of a double. In each chapter they rivaled the skills of their predecessors—Pearl White and Ruth Roland—while challenging the skills of their male counterparts Eddie Polo and William Desmond.

Eileen was known to her friends as "Babe"; Universal gave her a new nickname: "The Girl Without a Double." The studio's exploitation department crafted a release intended to be published in daily newspapers which commented on the attributes that made Eileen successful with thrill-seeking theatergoers:

> Not only have picture producers failed to find a girl whose unusual type of beauty parallels that of Miss Sedgwick, but they have been unable to find a girl who will take the physical risks the star does in the hazardous production of Universal serials.
>
> Working absolutely without a "double" and not availing herself of "trick" photography to cover up a hesitancy to risk her life, Miss Sedgwick does hair-raising feats of skill and daring throughout the entire eighteen episodes of her forthcoming serial, tentatively called *The Terror Trail*.

In a cliffhanging scene in *The Terror Trail* (1921) Eileen hangs from a fire escape high above the ground. As she climbs the ladder it detaches from the fire escape and falls downward toward the street as the episode ends.

> In her forthcoming serial Miss Sedgwick is given the best opportunity of her career to display her dramatic as well as athletic ability. Her role is forced to weird circumstances to match her wits against the combined forces of several groups of master criminals.

An identical press release was used for *The Diamond Queen*, substituting the serial's name and the number of episodes appearing in the chapterplay. The content of the promotional material didn't stretch Eileen's skills too far, as legitimate reviews of her films corroborated the studio's spin. The April 2, 1921, *Hamilton Evening Journal* contained a review of the serial's first episode, in which Eileen performs a dangerous stunt:

> Eileen Sedgwick, daring star of *The Diamond Queen*, is an expert motorist. Her ability to handle the wheel came to her in good stead in the first episode of *The Diamond Queen*. Here, racing against death in a high-powered car, she sees a child directly in the road in front of her, while another motor car is fast approaching from the opposite direction. At the risk of her life, to save the child as well as the driver of the approaching car, the daring star deliberately turns her machine into a fence at the side of the road. She crashes through it with terrific speed. Miss Sedgwick staunchly refused to have a skilled double perform this hazardous stunt. Excitement ran high in the company during the filming of the danger-fraught incident.

The mechanics of the stunt Eileen performed in *The Terror Trail* (1921) shows that trick photography was used. The building set was filmed on Court Hill overlooking the south end of the former Hill Street Tunnel in Los Angeles.

The *Fort Covington Sun* printed a *Diamond Queen* review in its November 17, 1921, issue describing one of Eileen's stunts:

> Thrills by no means have been neglected in the development of the realistic and logical story. In the first episode there is one of the most perilous stunts ever performed by a serial player. Eileen Sedgwick, the star of the serial, walks a frail plank connecting two buildings, eleven stories above the ground. She is seen to stumble and pitch downward toward the street as the episode ends. Some thrill!

Eileen appeared in three additional summer release for Universal: *The Heart of Arizona*, *The Girl in the Saddle*, and *The Shadow of Suspicion*. The Westerns co-starred Scott Pembroke, Albert J. Smith, and Stanley Fitz, who were drawn from Universal's pool of actors.

For a July release, Fox reunited Edward with Edna Murphy and Johnnie Walker in *Live Wires*, a romantic adventure which Edward directed and wrote. Pleased with Murphy and Walker's previous appearances in *Over the Hill to the Poorhouse* (1920), the studio decided to co-star the two in the feature.

Western Hearts, a September release produced by Cliff Smith Productions, featured Josie. In this Western directed by Clifford Smith, Josie is cast as an Eastern girl who falls for a ranch foreman (Art Straton). A complicated love story entangles the two with another ranch hand and the ranch owner's daughter. In the end the rival ranch hand is apprehended for rustling cattle from the ranch. "Those who remember Buffalo Bill and his sweetheart of the plains will have a pleasant awakening when they see how the modern cowgirl and cowboys make love in *Western Hearts*," commented the *Daily Olympian* (June 29, 1922). Written by Alan James, the scenario proved that a Western melodrama could actually be treated as a sophisticated story. The *Daily Olympian* continued, "[C]owboys and cowgirls and some of the best horses ever shown in a Western drama are seen galore in the picturization of *Western Hearts*."

Bar Nothing, an October release directed by Edward for Fox, featured Buck Jones. Ruth Renick played Jones's romantic interest in a story that pits his character against crooked cattlemen who try to discredit him. A review in the *Duluth News Tribune*'s October 23 edition commented on the energy generated by Jones in the silent Western:

> There are action, adventure, horseplay, exciting fights and thrilling rescues without letup, from the time the hero makes his appearance in a cloud of dust to the final closeout when he has vanquished the villain and won the heroine. Buck has a way of impressing one that he is not merely a screen actor, for instance, in one big scene Buck and a villain of the story plunge through a window of a speeding train during a fierce fight and when they land they are still at it, although both experienced an awful jolt, that's real Buck Jones action. And when there's hard-riding horses or gunplay around, Buck wants to know about it.

Eileen wrapped up her 1921 film appearances with four November releases, all directed by Kull. The Universal Westerns included *A Woman's Wit, Arrest Norma MacGregor, Dream Girl*, and *A Battle of Wits*. Her roles were becoming more complex, as is the case of her character in *Arrest Norma MacGregor*. The story, which takes place in Vancouver, has circumstantial evidence linking Eileen to the murder of a well-known broker and clubman. The action centers around her need to prove her innocence.

Josie appeared in a supporting role in *Duke of Chimney Butte*, a December release, and the first Metro Pictures Corporation-related production for the Sedgwicks. Richard A. Rowland founded Metro in 1915, with Louis B. Mayer joining soon after. Through their partnership they formed Solax Studios, a film distribution operation. Mayer left the company in 1918 to form his own company, leaving Rowland to continue to produce films at Metro's New York City, Fort Lee, and Los Angeles locations. In 1920 Marcus Loew acquired the studio as a source of films for his theater chain, eventually merging it with his Goldwyn Picture Corporation to form MGM. Edward would eventually have a lucrative career working with MGM, directing star-studded films for the studio starting in late 1926 and taking him into the golden years of the great studio system.

Directed by Frank Borzage, *Duke of Chimney Butte* was based on George Washington Ogden's novel of the same name. Staring Fred Stone, a famous musical comedy stage star, the cowboy melodrama also featured Vola Vale. As a ranch owner Vale's character finds little relief in trying to manage cattle on her spread despite the constant raids of rustlers. Stone's character comes to the rescue, breaks up the gang, and captures the love of the ranch owner.

Edward has often been credited with discovering cowboy star Tom Mix, a claim that is far from the truth. Back in 1913, when Edward first met Mix, Mix's resume included over 30 films, and by 1921 it contained at least 230 titles. Mix started off his career as a Western performer in 1906, working in a series of Wild West shows, including a position with Will A. Dickey's Circle D Ranch. The Circle D Ranch supplied Selig Pictures with "cowboys" and "Indians," including Mix. In 1910 Selig hired him to acquire and train horses needed for their Westerns, and within a short time he was regularly appearing in their films. His relationship with Selig continued for seven years, during which time he was also given the opportunity to direct and write. Making an average of two films a week, "Tom Mix" quickly became a household name, as well as a profitable marketing property. His popularity soon eclipsed that of William S. Hart's as the favorite cowboy matinee idol. In 1917 Mix left Selig and signed with Fox, where he worked until 1928, producing five to ten titles per year. Mix's popularity was due to his humorous spin on the traditional Western hero, as well as his skilled stunt riding, accomplished marksmanship, and his talented sidekick, Tony the Horse. As king of the cowboys, Mix's persona successfully transitioned into sound films and a radio show.

Credit can, however, be given to Edward for effectively directing Mix in his first non-cowboy feature, *The Rough Diamond*. Written by Edward, Mix, and Ralph Spence, the story has Mix playing the part of a daring and dashing cavalier to the tune of a romantic story that sends him adventuring across the seas into the broil of a political revolution in a Latin republic—just because the eyes of "the most beautiful girl in the world" beckoned.

Edward has often been credited with discovering Tom Mix, a fact that is far from the truth, as Mix had already appeared in 30 films when they first met. By 1921 his resume contained at least 230 titles. Credit, however, can be given to Edward for effectively directing Mix, shown with Eva Novak, in his first non-cowboy feature, *The Rough Diamond* (1921).

The December 4, 1921, *Dallas Morning News*, and other publications, approved of Mix's departure from his past character portrayals:

> Like a modern D'Artagnan, reckless and romantic, finding nothing an insurmountable obstacle in his path as he makes his daring and dashing campaign for a woman's heart and hand—that is the new role in which his admirers will greet him.
>
> Called upon to abandon his famous and familiar cowboy outfit, away from plains and ranches, exchanging them all, with the exception of his horse Tony, for ships and shoes and palms and revolutions, Mix makes the transition with an ease and power that proclaim him a finished and singularly versatile actor. Never before has he had an opportunity to play on the emotions such as he has in his present production.

Eileen appeared in five Universal Westerns released in the early part of 1922: *The Night Attack, The Open Wire, False Brands, Judgment* and *The Wolf Pack*. *The Open Wire* and *The Night Attack* were directed by Edward A. Kull and written by George H. Plympton. In the former, Eileen is given a top-billed role portraying a girl reporter who experiences difficulties in getting an important story into the hands of her newspaper.

The remaining three films were directed by William James Craft and featured Joe Moore. *False Brands* promoted Eileen as "the type of Western girl born of the courage and spirit which won the West." The story sweeps from a peaceful Midwest college to the wildest regions of Wyoming when a young man (Moore) is sent to look after his father's interests on a ranch. The usual romance, this time between Moore and Eileen, enters into the story.

In *Judgment* Moore portrays a locksmith who robs a safe to get money for the medical operation needed by his crippled brother. He is caught in the process of cracking open the safe by the leader of a gang and is blackmailed because he refuses to join them. The gang leader turns him over to authorities, but he's saved from prosecution by the man whose safe he opened: the physician who operated on his brother. Eileen plays the part of a gang member who helps Moore redeem himself, and together with his brother start a new life together. *Judgment* had a title change to *The Problem Eternal* when it reappeared in theaters in 1923.

The Wolf Pack was promoted as "a startling sensational story of the frozen fighting north" and "a smashing tale of the strong lawless men of the great rugged wilderness and their lumber camps." Moore, who played the part of a much-loved and -honored mounted policeman, is ordered to find a lawless lumberjack who has kidnapped Eileen. A positive review in the January 14, 1922, *Evening News* reported that the "startling events that follow and the capturing of the daring outlaw brings a romance to the screen abounding in thrills and fights."

Edward reunited with Tom Mix in another atypical Western for Fox. Co-authored by Mix and Ralph Spence, *Chasing the Moon* featured Mix dressed in civilian clothes rather than his traditional western outfit. As an idle millionaire, he is convinced he has taken a slow-acting poison through a cut in his skin. After finding out that the poison will kill him within 30 days, he starts a search for the scientist who has the antidote. His nonstop adventure takes him from America to Russia and then to Spain, as he hops from his horse Tony, to an automobile, and then to a motorboat, an ocean liner, an airplane, a train, and finally an old wagon. All the while he is chased by bandits as well as his girlfriend (Eva Novak), who is desperate to tell him that he wasn't poisoned after all, and if he takes the antidote without being poisoned he will die!

Four. Dynamite's Daughter, Ramblin' Kid, and Diamond Queen   95

Returning to Universal, Edward directed *The Bearcat*. The film would be his first Hoot Gibson–related title, and the first of 20 films he would work on with Gibson over the next four years. Similarly to how Edward changed Tom Mix's persona, he provided Gibson's character with a broadened dimension. Based on an F.R. Buckley story which appeared in *Western*

Edward directed *The Bearcat* (1922), his first Hoot Gibson–related title, and the first of 20 films he would work on with Gibson over the next four years. The film featured Gibson, shown with Lillian Rich, as a two-gun "bad man," a diversion from his well-known heroic image.

Magazine, the film featured Gibson as a two-gun "bad man," a switch from his well-known heroic image. Nicknamed "The Singin' Kid" by the townsfolk, Gibson's character was in the habit of boasting in the form of songs just how terrible his reputation was. After two weeks in town, Gibson is charged with killing a man. The sheriff (Charles French) figures out that the reason for Gibson's boasting about his own meanness was due to getting "a pretty rotten deal from a woman at some time in his life." He decides that Gibson must truly be a pretty fair person at heart and that if he shot someone, it was for a legitimate reason. Reviews favorably commented on Gibson's new characterization as "The Singing Kid."

As a teenager Gibson worked with horses on a ranch where his bronco-busting experience would lead him to rodeo competitions. He started his film career in 1910 when he and another upcoming star, Tom Mix, were hired as uncredited stunt doubles in a Western short titled *Pride of the Range*. At first Gibson didn't take his film career as seriously as competing in rodeos. In 1912 he won the all-around championship at the famous Pendleton Round-Up in Pendleton, Oregon, and the steer-roping World Championship at the Calgary Stampede. He eventually discovered that acting was a profitable occupation, and by the end of 1921 he had already appeared in 108 known titles, filming an additional 190 titles in the following 38 years. From the 1920s through the 1940s, Gibson became a major matinee idol, placing second to Mix in generating successful box office receipts for Western films. Ironically, after 50 years in filmmaking, his final film appearance was an uncredited role in *Ocean's Eleven* (1960).

Edward also found success in Western films. The next title he directed was *Boomerang Justice* with George Larkin, a Russell Productions distributed by States Rights Independent Exchanges. The film's exploitation material capitalized on Edward's previous achievement working with successful cowboy stars. "This is the super-dreadnaught of outdoor features and it was made under the personal supervision of Edward Sedgwick, the famous director who 'shouted through the megaphone' at Tom Mix in *Chasing the Moon*, Hoot Gibson in *The Bear Cat* [sic] and Buck Jones in *Bar Nothing*. Oh boy, don't miss this one! Star cast."

An advertisement in the September 27 *Idaho Daily Statesman* captured the thrills of the film in its description:

> What You Will See—
> A hero saves the girl from a conspiring half-breed.
> A daring rescue of a pretty heroine, who is headed over
>   the brink of a ghastly chasm.
> A leap from a second story to the top of a racing horse.
> A jump from a forty-foot embankment into a passing
>   automobile below going at forty miles an hour.
> AND THAT ISN'T ALL! The above are just a few of
>   the exciting happenings in the first three reels.

Edward's next Universal assignment was the melodramatic comedy *Do and Dare*, an October release featuring Mix. It was based on a story by Marion Brooks; Edward wrote the scenario for the film, and he and Ralph Spence wrote the titles. Mix plays cowboy Henry Boone, son of famed scout Kit Carson Boone. Intrigued with the idea of going on an adventure of his own, he accepts an invitation to deliver a military message to a revolutionary leader in a South American republic. His plane is forced to make an emergency landing right in the middle of the town that is swarming with Federalist soldiers. He is taken into custody, but escapes and ends up in an officer's uniform, fighting for the revolution and the heart of a beautiful senorita.

Mix was adamant that his fans knew he performed all of the stunts in *Do and Dare* without the assistance of a stunt double, as he pointed out in a December 10, 1922, *Philadelphia Inquirer* article. "I don't have to fake. I am putting real-life adventure into my pictures. Any good actor can fake his stunts and make a fairly good show—but faking isn't real life. I want to be honest with my audiences. I want them to believe that the incidents that happen on the screen before them have been the actual adventures of some real person and not the flighty work of an imaginative mind." The forty-nine scars covering Mix's body proved that he was responsible for his own hair-breadth escapes.

Josie stared in *Crimson Clue,* a Western released by Clark-Cornelius Corporation, a distributor who handled less than three dozen titles between 1920 and 1923. Jack Richardson, the male lead, was a prolific actor whose career spanned fifty years and 550 films, beginning as a silent film actor in 1911 when he was signed by the Thanhouser Company and continuing to several appearances on television. This was a rarity with actors who started their film careers as early as Richardson did, as most resigned from work by the 1920s.

The Sedgwicks finished up 1922 with each sibling participating in minor assignments. Edward directed *The Flaming Hour,* a Universal drama featuring Frank Mayo as a hot-headed husband and Helen Ferguson as his wife. The story's theme shows what type of damage a quick temper can do in business, marriage, and friendly associations. Written by Lillian Chester, with its scenario created by her husband George Randolph Chester, it was cooked up with Mayo in mind. Mayo started with Vitagraph in 1911 and continually worked in films until 1949, appearing in over 315 titles.

Josie appeared in *Eastern Heart,* a Western promoted as "A love story of old told in the 20th Century Way," while Eileen acted in *A Woman's Vengeance,* a Universal drama.

Nineteen twenty-three turned out to be a prolific year for the Sedgwicks. Their combined releases, including feature films and serials, were to outnumber that of any previous year or one to follow: Edward would direct ten films, Eileen would appear in five, and Josie in three. These films would feature prominent actors such as Jackie Coogan and Douglas MacClean.

That year Ruth Roland decided not to renew her contract with her studio. While performing in her films, Roland, an astute businesswoman, built a sizable fortune in real estate investments, which allowed her to comfortably retire from acting. She returned to the stage, performing in vaudeville, and acted in an occasional film over the succeeding years. As Roland stepped out of the limelight, the timing was right for Eileen to take the reins as a leading action film actress, becoming Universal's "Queen of the Serials." Although Eileen only had five releases in 1923, two of them were major serials: *In the Days of Daniel Boone,* a June release, and *Beasts of Paradise,* an October release.

For the 15-episode serial *In the Days of Daniel Boone* Eileen once again had the opportunity to work with action film director William James Craft. Playing the role of Susan Boone, Eileen was joined by Charles Brinley as Daniel Boone, Jack Mower as Jack Gordon and Duke Lee as George Washington.

Following the success of *In the Days of Buffalo Bill* and *The Oregon Trail, In the Days of Daniel Boone* was Universal's newest "thrills-from-history" serial. Although its publicists claimed that schools could accept the serial as "a new departure in injecting history into the thrill-craving minds of America's youth," the drama slightly altered history, placing Daniel Boone and his daughter at the center of the French and Indian War as they attempt to establish a frontier colony. Historic details aside, the serial contained a realistic reenactment of General Edward Braddock's attack and his defeat at the onset of the French and Indian War of 1755.

As with any of Universal's serials, the challenge presented by *In the Days of Daniel Boone* was to get viewers of the previous episode to return for subsequent chapters. The studio stressed exploitation on the local level, with each local exchange staffed by a specialist who was responsible for guaranteeing the success of the serial's run at a theater. For *In the Days of Daniel Boone* the tried-and-true punch-ticket promotion was utilized in various ways. The Star Theater in Lawrence, Massachusetts, decided to print 2,000 cards with the fifteen dates the serial would play, with an additional 3,000 printed for theatergoers who requested them after seeing the first episode. In exchange, at the end of the serial's run, the holder of a completely punched card would receive an Indian war bonnet. The promotion was a success. The Empire in Rahway, New Jersey, decided to approach the situation through the organization of a Daniel Boone club, which in the end realized a 400 percent increase in serial ticket sales for the theater. Thousands of punch cards were distributed, offering the moviegoer a ticket for a Daniel Boone Outing after it was completely punched. The 800

For the 15-episode serial *In the Days of Daniel Boone* (1923) Eileen once again had the opportunity to work with action film director William James Craft. Playing the role of Susan Boone, Eileen was joined by Jack Mower as Jack Gordon (shown), Charles Brinley as Daniel Boone, and Duke Lee as George Washington.

***In the Days of Daniel Boone* (1923) was one of Universal's "thrills-from-history" serials. Eileen appears with Charles Brinley in one of the film's harrowing scenes.**

members who appeared on opening day also received a Daniel Boone pin. The New Mission and New Fillmore theaters in San Francisco arranged a successful promotion with the San Francisco *Call,* inviting all children to view the first episode as guests of the newspaper. In addition, the Anglo-California bank presented a Daniel Boone essay contest at the end of the final episode, offering $500 in deposits as prizes.[1]

Sometimes the promotion of a film meant that an actor might need to stick his or her neck out to drum up business. In the case of Eileen's follow-up serial for 1923, *Beasts of Paradise,* she took the matter of booking the film at two theaters into her own hands. The January 10, 1924, *Billings Gazette* described her experience working briefly as an exchange salesman:

> Miss Sedgwick approached the manager of the Los Angeles Universal exchange several days ago. "How do I arrange to have theaters buy the new chapterplay?" she inquired.
>
> "Oh," said the manager. "You give me their names, and I'll send a salesman around, and—"
>
> "No—you don't understand," said the actress. "You see, I have already sold them the picture—but I want to give the order to someone."
>
> The amazed exchange manager handed her the necessary blanks. "I'll be back tomorrow with the manager's signature," she promised. And she kept her promise.
>
> "You see, I met them at a party, and told them about the picture—and they said if I'd come and see them about it personally they'd book it."

Directed by Craft, *Beasts of Paradise* was written by Carl Krusada, a writer who scripted stories for two of Ruth Roland's serial releases the previous year. Once again Eileen was featured alongside the valiant William Desmond in what Universal hyped as "An Absorbing Thriller of Savage Beasts and Gallant Men!" The exhibition material gave an adrenalin-filled description that was written for use in newspaper advertisements:

> The Thriller That Tops Them All!
>
> You've seen some exciting chapterplays. Wait until you see this. It's one continuous, rapid-fire succession of great big spectacular thrills that will hold you spellbound and leave you breathless!
>
> Breath-taking fights with cannibals, white marauders and mutinous sailors in a search for sunken treasures in a beast-infested jungle isle! Hair-breadth escapes from volcanic eruption, roaring tidal waves and terrific typhoons! Don't miss the most thrilling and spectacular chapterplay of love, romance and adventure ever filmed.

Although Eileen performed the majority of the stunt work in *Beasts of Paradise* herself, there were rare occasions when Paul Malvern, an actor and professional stunt man, stepped in to execute the most life-threatening routines for her.

The serial also starred Joe Bonomo, a barrel-chested body builder promoted as "The Hercules of the Screen." Bonomo, the son of a candy maker whose best selling product was Bonomo Turkish Taffy, was a contemporary of the famous muscleman Charles Atlas. In addition to playing the role of "Big Jim," he had stood in for Desmond's character during hazardous stunts. In his autobiography *Strongman*, Bonomo describes a risky *Beasts of Paradise* stunt that went awry:

> There was a scene in which Bill and Eileen were cornered on a passenger steamer named the *Yale*, that plied between Los Angeles and San Diego. As a gang of murderous seamen closed in on them they were to leap over the rail and swim for their lives. The stunt had one leap from the top deck to the water below; we had to do a quick water sprint to avoid being cut to ribbons by the vessel's twin-screw propellers. That meant we had to land in the water without being knocked unconscious and, despite the clothing that would hamper us, we had to clear the stern of the moving vessel by a good safe margin. After that it was a full mile and a half to shore, through a rough breakwater, but we were told not to worry about that as we would be picked up by a rescue boat.
>
> We donned our costumes, which duplicated those of Bill and the girl ... the time arrived and over the rail we went. We struck out at a fast clip and cleared the propellers okay, then started to look around for the rescue boat ... but no boat was in sight. However, we were both strong swimmers and, struggling out of our costumes down to the swim trunks we were wearing underneath, we finally made it to shore through that breakwater ... but it was close. We came out on a rocky beach somewhere in the neighborhood of Wilmington. After limping a painful mile in our bare feet, over sharp rocks, we reached a road and luckily an empty taxi came along and picked us up. We taxied back to the studio, a matter of a good 25 miles....
>
> The studio was delighted to see us safe and sound. We said, "Where was the rescue boat that was supposed to pick us up?" They said that at the last moment they discovered they had gone overboard on expenditures so they canceled the boat. They knew we both could swim so they weren't worried. Then they congratulated us on the stunt, which was a photographic success, but regretted there was no provision in the budget for paying our taxi fare. After all, taking that taxi wasn't in the script ... that was *our* idea.

While shooting a sea sequence for *Beasts of Paradise*, the entire cast and crew experienced a harrowing adventure on the open sea. A four-masted schooner named *John Brown* was chartered to shoot on. A tugboat towed the schooner fifteen miles out from Balboa into the Pacific every morning, stayed with the company during the day, and then towed them back in the evening. On the final day of shooting the tug burned out a bearing on the way out. The skipper decided he'd return to port, have the necessary repairs made, and come back late in the afternoon to tow the schooner back in. While the tug was being repaired, a sudden violent squall took control of the schooner, which was under full sail. Understaffed with only a captain and one seaman, the ship was hopelessly blown off course. An article in the August 11 *Lincoln State Journal* reported on the experience:

MOVIE ACTORS BECALMED
William Desmond, Ailene [*sic*] Sedgwick
and Others Drift for Two
Days Without Food.

SAN PEDRO, Cal., Aug 11. William Desmond, Ailene Sedgwick and eight other motion picture actors are recovering today from the effects of drifting two days without food in a becalmed sailing vessel.

The company had taken an eight-day voyage for the purpose of filming scenes on Santa Cruz Island. On their return trip the wind failed and the tugboat which accompanied them developed trouble.

The food supply soon became exhausted and they were compelled to live on fish caught over the side of the boat. The water supply was also running low when they were picked up by the steamboat *Marcella*, which had been sent out to search for them after motion picture officials became alarmed Friday when the company was seventy-two hours overdue.

Eileen was featured in *Beasts of Paradise* (1923), a chapter play that Universal hyped as "An Absorbing Thriller of Savage Beasts and Gallant Men!"

In his biography Joe Bonomo recalled the distressing incident. As the storm blew in, the inexperienced passengers frantically attempted to get the sails folded in an effort to control the direction the ship was sailing.

> An alert cameraman was getting some fine shots, but that was small comfort as we skidded about the decks. It was well into the night when the storm subsided, and as beautiful a girl as Eileen "Babe" Sedgwick was a sorry looking heroine when the sea finally calmed. Except for Ruth Royce, the captain and myself, every soul on the *John Brown* was deathly ill with seasickness—not excepting the "mate." Everywhere you looked were those gray-faced, green-eyed "zombies," hanging over the rails and wishing they were dead. What a mess!

As the seasickness subsided, the appetites of the twenty-eight passengers were aroused. The studio box lunches packed for the outing were eaten earlier in the day, with only a pound of coffee, a few boxes of crackers and canned soup left in the galley.

The following morning Craft announced that until the tug arrived, the company would use the time to film additional footage. Bonomo climbed the rigging to stage a fight scene. As he stood at the end of a yardarm, kicking a villain in the face, he lost his footing and slipped, falling backwards into the water.

> Because of the shortage of skilled seamen, it took more than an hour to turn the ship about and pick me up. You can picture my terrors, in that shark-infested ocean, without even a knife to protect myself. All I could do was swim around, making as little splash as I could, peering through the water hoping to spot one of the monsters before he struck. I might be able to kick him on his sensitive nose, if I were quick enough. So I watched and I watched and I watched, constantly turning to cover all sides of possible attack. But for some saintly reason the sharks still weren't biting. At last the ship passed close enough for a line to be tossed to me, and I was pulled out. And would you believe it? Just as I was being dragged out of the water, a gray fin sliced the surface and a shark snapped at me. In two seconds, I was halfway up the rope. After that I *really* hated sharks—especially sneaky ones!

A second squall struck the schooner, rocking and tossing the ship worse than before. The company became seasick again. With the last of the crackers eaten for breakfast, the passengers attempted to get some rest as they waited for help. On the third day they found themselves in the midst of a school of tuna. Managing to pull some aboard, Bonomo cooked them up, feeding the famished cast and crew.

It took another day before they were spotted by one of the search planes that Universal had sent out to look for them. Within an hour they were picked up and transferred to a Coast Guard cutter.

Edward's initial release of that year was *The First Degree*, a melodrama in which he directed Frank Mayo and Sylvia Breamer in the story of a man who was sent to prison on false charges. For February release he directed Tom Mix in *Romance Land*, their fourth film together. The Western comedy presented Mix in the role of a twentieth century Ivanhoe.

Of the ten films that Edward directed in 1923, eight of them were Hoot Gibson productions. *The Gentleman from America*, a February release for Universal, featured Gibson, Tom O'Brien and Louise Lorraine. The movie also included a little-known actor in an uncredited role, Boris Karloff, who would become famous for his horror roles in the next decade. The cinematographer was Virgil Miller, with whom Edward would have a productive working relationship (22 films from 1923 to 1926).

Under Edward's supervision, Gibson's vehicles were becoming special productions with

Four. Dynamite's Daughter, Ramblin' Kid, and Diamond Queen   103

elaborate settings and unusual stories, a switch from Gibson's previous cowboy films. *The Gentleman from America* focused on an American soldier's adventure in Paris.

Single Handed, with a working title of *Heads Up*, was a March release for Universal, with Edward directing and collaborating on the story with George C. Hull. Staring Gibson and Elinor Field, it included a part for Josie's estranged husband William Gettinger, who was now going by the name of William Steele. Steele, who was broken-hearted and often visited Josie and her family after their separation, would appear in several of the films that Edward directed for Gibson. Edward may have hired Steele for minor roles in the Westerns out of sympathy.

Dead Game, an April release directed by Edward, featured Gibson as Katy' Did, a young cowboy of the West who knows all about men and horses, but was in for trouble when women were concerned. Laura La Plante, an up-and-coming Universal actress who was making a success in serials and comedies, was featured as Gibson's "girl" in her first leading role in a five-reel production.

Shootin' for Love, a June release, and *Out of Luck*, a July release, both reteamed Edward with Gibson and La Plante. The stories revolved around Gibson being involved in an arm of the military. In *Shootin' for Love* he plays a young man returning from overseas service

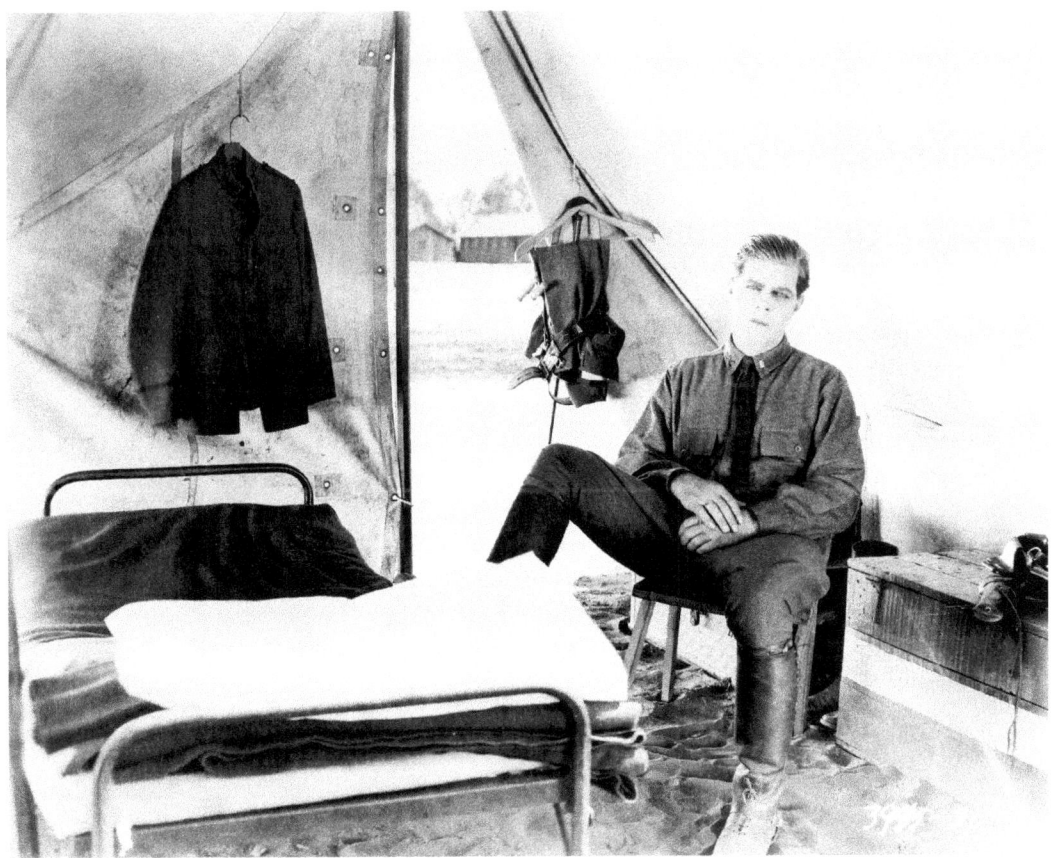

Edward and Hoot Gibson collaborated on *Blinky* (1923). The Western comedy paired Gibson with Esther Ralston, one of the highest-paid serial and Western actresses of the time.

with the American Expeditionary Forces, a victim of shell shock. In *Out of Luck* he plays a sailor in the Navy. Although the scenarios took Gibson off of the plains, in each film he was still given the opportunity to perform the horsemanship that won him the distinction of being the "world's greatest cowboy."

Edward and Gibson collaborated on *Blinky*, an August Universal release. The Western comedy paired Gibson with Esther Ralston, then one of the highest-paid serial and Western actresses. Nicknamed for his eyeglasses, Gibson played the part of Blinky, the son of an old Indian fighter. Through influence Blinky is given an army commission and sent to a cavalry camp on the Mexican border, ignorant of even the rudiments of his new job. The unlikely hero is captured by rumrunners; escapes; trails kidnappers who captured the daughter of the camp commander; and finally wins the girl; and makes good as a real, honest-to-goodness soldier.

The Ramblin' Kid, also known by its working title *The Long, Long Trail*, was released by Universal in October. Directed by Edward, the Western comedy once more teamed Gibson with La Plante. Based on Earl Wayland Bowman's book of the same name, *The Ramblin' Kid* features Gibson as a much misunderstood hero; he wins the girl, loses her because she thinks he's drunk when really he has been drugged, and in the end wins her all over again.

In their final collaboration of 1923, Edward directed *The Thrill Chaser* for Hoot Gibson Productions. A comedy featuring Gibson, James Neill and Billie Dove, *The Thrill Chaser* was a burlesque on Hollywood that was obviously influenced by the popular book *Merton of the Movies*, written the previous year by Harry Leon Wilson. Focusing on a talentless actor who stumbles into a successful career as a comedian, *Merton of the Movies* influenced at least five additional 1923 movies which had a similar premise: Rupert Hughes' drama *Souls for Sale* (1923), James Cruze's parody *Hollywood* (1923), *Mary of the Movies* (1923), *Hazel from Hollywood* (1923), and *Night Life in Hollywood* (1922). (Cruze would direct the first film version of *Merton of the Movies* the following year.) In addition, the films were similar in that they featured a number of famous actors and directors making cameo appearances. They also attempted to mend the damage that was caused by years of Hollywood scandals by placing a positive spin on the capital of the film industry

In *The Thrill Chaser*, Gibson's character enters Universal City and reports to the casting department where he casually asks for a job at $3,000 a week. Offered a job as an extra at $3 a day, he accepts but insists that he won't rescue any maidens, perform on horseback, or do any "thrill stuff" around trains for less than $1,000 a week. Gibson once again trades in his cowboy garb, this time for the limited dress of a Roman guard. It's not long before the amateur catches his spear in a rope that is attached to a set, and pulls the set down in front of real-life director Hobart Henley who is using it in his movie *The Last Days of Pompeii*.

Not used to camera techniques, Gibson's character proceeds to wander onto everyone's set in front of cameras, humorously ruining emotional scenes that are being filmed. Directors King Baggot and Edward Sedgwick are shown at their task of directing players, including Universal actors Mary Philbin, Norman Kerry, Laura La Plante and Reginald Denny.

Eileen was featured in three Westerns made for Stanford Productions: *Making Good*, *When Law Comes to Hades*, and *Scarred Hands*. *Making Good*, a February release, featured Eileen with Pete Morrison, who plays a college-cowboy, in a five-reel Western story. Promoted as "a drama of the days of '49," *When Law Comes to Hades*, a September release, casts Eileen with Noah Beery, nephew of superstar Wallace Beery.

Scarred Hands, also released in September, was helmed by Poverty Row director Clifford Smith. Featured alongside Eileen, Smith plays the rightful owner of valuable oil-rich lands. His character, Tom Stephen, is challenged by a villain who conspires to take over the property, as well as his fiancée Jane Wheeler (Eileen). The villain plots to blow up an oil well in the presence of Jane; Tom stops him and wins the girl.

Josie's 1923 film appearances were limited to only three features: *Daddy, The Sunshine Trail* and *Michael O'Halloran*. She didn't get top billing, but the productions were of a higher quality and featured popular actors in the lead roles, giving the films greater distribution potential and possible box office success. The roles presented Josie with a wide range of dramatic characters, ones that gave her opportunities to act beyond the stereotypical action heroine.

Daddy, released in March to excellent reviews, featured the child megastar Jackie Coogan. Coogan, who began his acting career as an infant appearing in vaudeville and film, was discovered by Charlie Chaplin during a performance at a Los Angeles vaudeville theater. Chaplin cast him as his sidekick in *The Kid* (1921), a movie that was very successful, making Coogan a popular child star and giving him opportunities to appear in future feature roles, including *Oliver Twist* the following year. At the time he made *Daddy*, Coogan was one of the highest paid stars in Hollywood.

Produced by independent Sol Lesser and directed by E. Mason Hopper, the Jackie Coogan Production was written by Jackie's parents, Lilian and Jack Coogan, Sr. In *Daddy* he plays the part of Jackie Savelli, the casualty of a failed marriage. Helene Savelli (Josie) accuses her husband Paul Savelli (Arthur Edmund Carewe) of being unfaithful, and takes their son Jackie to live with her on the farm of an aged couple, the Holdens. Helene dies shortly thereafter and Jackie runs away from the Holdens after they are forced to move off their farm and into the poorhouse. Jackie's genius for the violin brings him in contact with a sidewalk musician named Cesare Gallo (Cesare Gravina). Incredibly, Gallo turns out to be the former teacher of the now world-famous violinist Paul Savelli, who naturally turns out to be Jackie's long-lost father. Paul returns to America to perform a concert, but doesn't recognize his former teacher or his grown-up son when they approach him. Before he dies, Gallo reunites the father with his son and restores the farm to the Holdens.

In the Western comedy *The Sunshine Trail*, an April release for Thomas H. Ince Corporation, Josie supported Douglas MacLean and Edith Roberts. MacLean, known for his smile and winsome mannerisms, was one of the greatest exponents of good cheer on the screen.

Michael O'Halloran, a seven-reel June release for Gene Stratton-Porter Productions, was directed by James Leo Meehan. The film was based on Gene Stratton-Porter's novel of the same name. The novelist with her daughter, Jeanette Helen Porter, organized a company to adapt eight of her most popular novels to be produced by the Thomas H. Ince Studios.

In an interview appearing in the December 12, 1922, *Duluth New Tribune*, Porter stressed the importance of giving her novels true reproductions on the screen. "In my first personally produced picture *Michael O'Halloran*, we have adhered strictly to the spirit, the theme and the characters of the original story. And I personally selected each actor because in my mind, he, or she, most closely resembled the character of the book. We did not look for stars, nor did we seek pretty faces. We tried to find competent actors who could put the breath of life into the people of the book." Josie, in the important role of Leslie Winton, supported actress Virginia True Boardman as Michael O'Halloran and Ethelyn Irving as Lily Peaches in the sentimental drama.

The story follows Michael O'Halloran, an orphaned newsboy, who finds a crippled little orphaned girl whom he calls Lily Peaches, taking her in as his "family." Michael and Peaches find their way to the home of a kind-hearted farmer who helps in Lily's recovery. In a secondary story thread, contrasting examples of life amid riches and poverty, Michael helps mend the marriage of the Milturns, a wealthy couple.

The Sedgwicks were approaching their tenth anniversary working in the motion picture business. In the short period of time since the siblings first appeared in front of a camera, they adapted to an industry that was rapidly evolving—one that experienced a sophistication of direction, scenarios, acting, lighting, scenery, and film technology, a growing pressure from censors, and a change in the content and type of stories moviegoers preferred to view.

As the United States transitioned from a war-wary country to one renewed by a peacetime economy, it became the wealthiest nation on Earth, giving birth to a culture of consumerism. Popular culture thrived on the picture show, with fans emulating the dress, behaviors, and language of their favorite film stars. By the early 1920s the use of actors and actresses for the endorsement of products in print advertisements and in-store point-of-purchase displays was a commonplace marketing concept. Everyone knew that Mary Pickford used Pompeian cosmetic products as her "yard-long" promotional posters revealed; that Ruth Roland enjoyed chewing Adams California Fruit Gum as the magazine ads quoted; and that Rudolph Valentino smoked stogies from boxes of cigars that featured illustrations of the heartthrob.

By the mid–1920s the siblings' efforts were regularly being discussed in articles and film reviews in movie-related publications, right alongside tributes to Harold Lloyd, Lillian Gish, Richard Barthelmess, and Gloria Swanson. Eileen's image was already appearing in photo spreads and on the covers of movie magazines. Illustrations of the fair-haired daredevil also graced the covers of publications that were unrelated to the film industry, including housekeeping magazines. Eileen had become internationally known; the press picked up on a story that Abul Harajabub of Quetta, East India, a widower with a large estate and eight children, sent Eileen a letter of proposal after seeing one of her films.

It wasn't long before advertisers realized that Eileen's image was marketable. "Well-Known Actress Tells How She Keeps Her Complexion Beautiful," headlined Eileen's testimonial letter to the Derwille and Liska Company, which appeared in newspapers nationwide. "I have been using your toilet preparations Derwille and Liska cold cream and am more than pleased with results. So much so, that I have discontinued the use of other preparations I have used for years." The letter accompanied a tightly cropped photograph of Eileen's radiant face. The Gibson Mandolin Guitar Company used an image of her strumming a mandolin in a magazine advertisement to promote the sale of their instruments.

Eileen and Josie's likenesses, along with those of other popular film stars, appeared on trading cards that were included in packages of tobacco and candy. In addition, they appeared on cards offered in complete sets that were sold through advertisements appearing in movie fan magazines. Larger-sized picture souvenirs, including postcards and exhibit cards, were also available for admirers of the attractive and talented sisters.

The Sedgwicks' ability to adapt to the motion picture industry's progression was honed during their vaudeville days, back when they found it necessary to alter their program's content as they traveled from city to city, rotating the acts in their run of shows within a week's performance to keep their appearances fresh. The experience gave them the ability to be flexible enough to survive the fluid demands of the film industry. Within the next ten years they would experience new challenges, including the advent of sound in films, the development and demands of the great studio system, and competition with a new breed of actors and directors.

Note

1. Kalton C. Lahue, *Bound and Gagged: Story of the Silent Serials*, New York: Castle Books, pages 103–34.

CHAPTER FIVE

The Saddle Hawk, Lightnin' the Police Dog and Leo the Lion

The "Popular Player Contest" appearing in the October 1913 issue of *The Motion Picture Story Magazine* tallied up results for the 100 actors appearing in the publication's annual poll. Readers cast over seven million votes, with the first place honors going to Romaine Fielding (1,311,018 votes), second to Earle Williams (739,895), third to J. Warren Kerrigan (531,966), fourth to Carlyle Blackwell (296,684), fifth to Francis X. Bushman (252,750), sixth to G. M. Anderson (217,069), and seventh to Arthur Johnson (209,800). Actresses were judged in a separate category, with Alice Joyce taking first place (462,380) and Muriel Ostriche placing second (212,276). The list included a diverse selection of film personalities; placing Mary Pickford at #15 (130,592), Pearl White at #24 (82,209), Ruth Roland at #31 (61,780), Mabel Normand at #51 (25,527), and True Boardman at position #100 (4,982). Many of the dramatic actors appearing on the list had transitioned to the silver screen after successful careers on the theatrical stage.

Five years later, a poll in the October 1918 *Motion Picture Magazine* listed 142 actors who were voted into the magazine's "Motion Picture Hall of Fame," with the top four chosen stars listed as Mary Pickford in the #1 spot (127,832), Marguerite Clark at #2 (107,563), Douglas Fairbanks at #3 (101,068), and Harold Lockwood at #4 (99,049). The remaining names listed in the top ten selections included, in descending order, William S. Hart, Wallace Reid, Pearl White, Anita Stewart, Francis X. Bushman, and Theda Bara. Charlie Chaplin was listed at #17 (55,577) and Lillian Gish at #69 (22,006), with Roscoe Arbuckle finishing up the list at #142 (12,014). Mingled in between the names of these well-known personalities were actors and actresses of all statures. Throughout the magazine, the publisher gave the lesser-known movie stars as much coverage in articles and interviews as they did for the popular ones. This was the general trend in the majority of fan-oriented magazines of the time.

Preceding World War I, movie theaters were changing their daily programs an average of five times a week. By the early 1920s they were booking films for longer periods of time, turning over their offerings only three and a half times a week, with ten percent of them promoting a film for an entire week.[1] Naturally, the quick turnaround gave moviegoers little time to discover through word-of-mouth or printed reviews if a current offering was good or not. Therefore, theater owners often relied on the drawing power of the actors appearing in a film's limited engagement to help fill seats.

Over a short span of years the matinee idols of the past were being replaced by Hollywood's new superstars. As moviegoers' tastes changed during the postwar years, actors who were popular in the teens often found themselves being replaced by actors who had once supported them. The overwrought telegraphic performance style of acting used by the "scenery chewers" was being replaced by a more realistic method used by the up-and-coming actors. By the mid–1920s the publisher of *Motion Picture Magazine* promoted no more than a handful of the top stars in their pages, a list that consistently included the industry's top moneymakers: Mary Pickford, Douglas Fairbanks, Gloria Swanson, Charlie Chaplin, Rudolph Valentino, Norma Shearer, Lillian Gish, and Dorothy Gish. There was little attention given to actors working with independent studios.

When it came to promoting their actors and films, independent studios such as Universal were unable to compete with the expensive hyperactive publicity campaigns that larger studios developed to promote their big features and major stars. Universal, responsible for launching the careers of such actors as Harry Carey and Mae Murray, producer Irving Thalberg, and director John Ford, found it difficult enough to support the salaries of their workers once they became recognized as having talent.

Major studios also began using vertical integration strategies, an effort that would have been impossible for independents to attempt to incorporate. The vertical integration system came into use by the early 1920s when companies started to take control of the production, distribution, and exhibition of their own films. Adolph Zukor of Famous Players pioneered the concept when he joined forces with the Paramount Publix circuit. The fallout caused by the monopolizing system left Universal squeezed out of the major cities, forced to deal with the smaller rural theaters and the few big city showcases they partnered with to show their first-run films.

Actor-studio alliances were just as important as the relationship that studios had with theaters: The actor relied on the studio to promote their films properly and the studios relied on the actor to create the interest needed for theaters to book their films and produce a profit. Edward and Hoot Gibson proved to be a successful combination and were assigned to complete seven additional Universal-Gibson collaborations that were scheduled to be released throughout 1924. Edward knew Gibson's audience well and was becoming skilled at presenting Gibson's playfully humorous personality without making it appear too slapstick, but with just the right amount of hokum. It was a perfect coordination of motion picture director and star.

Richard Schayer and Raymond L. Schrock were responsible for the scenarios of the majority of the features, taking Gibson's typical cowboy character off of the ranch and placing him into unlikely situations that made the stories anything but a typical Gibson Western. So far Gibson's character was transformed from cowboy to cavalry troop of the United States Army, gob in the navy, shell-shocked doughboy returning home from war, and a movie fan who aspired to become a Hollywood star. It was important to keep Gibson's horsemanship an essential part in each of the productions, as his fans expected him to perform on his mare in every movie. Universal welcomed the change of scenery, as the films not only attracted Gibson's Western fans but also those who might not have paid to watch him in a Western.

Hook and Ladder brought Edward and Gibson together for a January release. Gibson traded in his cowboy duds for fireman gear, portraying a cowpoke who joined the fire department on an impulse. He regrets his decision the first time he starts to climb a ladder on the training tower. Gibson's character eventually gets mixed up in politics. Through his romance with the fire chief's pretty daughter (Mildred June), he incurs the antagonism of a ward heeler.

In *Ride for Your Life*, a February release, Gibson worked with Edward and Laura La Plante. The previous year La Plante was awarded the title of WAMPAS Baby Star, an annual honor bestowed upon thirteen lucky up-and-coming actresses whom the Western Association of Motion Picture Advertisers believed to be on the verge of movie stardom. *Ride for Your Life*, based on a story by Johnston McCulley, the creator of Zorro, placed Gibson back on the plains as a cowboy. La Plante is pursued by a devious saloon owner who holds the deed to a ranch owned by a murdered friend of Gibson. Predictably, Gibson and La Plante sparked the required romance that was a necessary element in his films.

40-Horse Hawkins, an April release, teamed Gibson with Ann Cornwell (as his love interest) and Helen Holmes, the "thrill-a-minute" actress who was once a major star in her own serial, *The Hazards of Helen*. In this lighthearted comedy, Gibson's character falls in love with an ingénue (Cornwell) and follows her to New York where he gets a job as a "supe"

Hook and Ladder (1924) brought Edward and Hoot Gibson together again, with Gibson trading in his cowboy duds for fireman gear. In this photograph stuntman Al Wilson makes a leap for Gibson.

in a Broadway production. Ironically, it is the same production in which she stars, although he doesn't know it. Although Gibson finds himself in a strange environment, he ends up saving the show and finds the girl he loves. In addition to directing the film, Edward also made a return to acting, portraying the stage manager. It was most likely a position that he relished, as it would have finally taken him to his lifelong dream of appearing on a Broadway stage.

For June release, Edward directed Gibson in *Broadway or Bust*. Introduced as a "poor cowhand" who craves to see Broadway, Gibson's character discovers radium deposits on his ranch and sells them for a million dollars. Along with a pal (played by King Zany), Gibson follows his girl (Ruth Dwyer) to New York City. They obtain accommodations at high-rate Fritz Hotel for themselves and their saddle horses. (The hotel was intentionally named Fritz after William S. Hart's famous horse.) The way the horse situation is handled, with twin-bed stalls on the fifth floor, is enough to convince anyone that they aren't quite ready for big city life.

Edward and Gibson's August release for Universal, *The Sawdust Trail*, was adapted from the *Saturday Evening Post* story "Courtin Calamity" by William Dudley Palley. The Western featured Josie in the role of Calamity June. Gibson played a college boy from the East who pretends to be a semi-invalid to avoid going to work in his father's factory. In an outfit reversal, he soon trades in his college cut clothes for that of a Wild West show worker, which is where his father sends him for his health and a job. To prove his manhood, he sets about courting Calamity June, one of the riders and a man-hater. In the end he wins the girl, welcoming the rough-and-ready circus lady into the bosom of his illustrious Eastern family.

Speaking to the press about her part as the hard-boiled rider, Josie made it a point to mention that in one scene she needed to show her character's feminine side and produce tears on demand, which she remarked was no cinch. She commented that in order for an actor to produce tears for movies, it is necessary to have the proper facilities, otherwise it's an impossible task. This was a very rare case in which Josie portrayed a sensitive attribute. In most of her films, Josie's appearance was

The Sawdust Trail (1924), which was directed by Edward, offered Josie the role of a hard-boiled Wild West show rider and man-hater. Hoot Gibson played the part of a college boy who wins her heart.

somewhat androgynous, with her square jawline and absence of makeup, and dressed in traditional no-nonsense working cowgirl attire—unlike Eileen who often wore more femininely designed cowgirl attire and noticeable makeup.

Hit and Run, an August release, placed Gibson in the ballpark for a sports genre film. The comedy-drama co-starred Michael Donlin, an outfielder turned actor who played on various Major League Baseball teams, including the 1905 World Series–winning Giants. Donlin played Red McCarthy, a baseball scout who finds himself in the middle of a Western desert when he leaves his train after an argument with the team's manager. Near the railroad tracks, a baseball game is underway, and the batting talent of Swat Anderson (Gibson) stuns McCarthy. Swat is signed up and quickly moves up from the minor to major leagues, eventually falling in love with McCarthy's sister Joan (Marian Harlan). Swat rescues Joan from the hands of the team's crooked treasurer who becomes jealous of the couple's growing relationship. This was the first of several baseball-themed and sports-related movies directed by Edward, a huge baseball fan.

Based on a novel by pulp magazine writer Henry Herbert Knibb, *The Ridin' Kid from Powder River* was Edward and Gibson's final collaboration for 1924, and more or less a typical Gibson feature. Gibson's character, Bud Watkins, tracks down the man who killed his father when he was a child. The Western also starred Gertrude Astor as "Kansas" Lou, Gladys

Shown with love interest Marian Harlan, Hoot Gibson was placed in the ballpark for *Hit and Run* (1924), a sports genre film that was directed by Edward.

The Ridin' Kid from Powder River (1924), directed by Edward, was more or less a typical Gibson western.

Hulette as "Miss," Tully Marshall as "The Spider" and Fred Humes as "The Scorpion." The part of "Lightnin'" Bill Smith was played by William Steele.

Aside from appearing in *The Sawdust Trail*, Josie's only other appearance in 1924 was in a March release: She played the role of a chorus girl in *The White Moth*, a Maurice Tourneur production for First National. Although her part in the romantic drama had limited screen time, it was a welcome opportunity, as it meant she would be working with the all-star cast of Barbara La Marr, Conway Tearle, Charles de Rochefort, and Ben Lyon.

Tourneur, a French director who had become a major innovator of the narrative film after arriving in the United States, directed the critically acclaimed movie. He was credited with bringing "stylization" to the screen through his mastery of costumes, set design, and lighting. In its July 14, 1924, entertainment section, *The Washington Post* described a scene in *The White Moth*.

> Miss La Marr is beautiful in the succession of gorgeous costumes which she graces in this production. The introduction of a mammoth scene depicting the Bal des Artistes permits her to baffle the male mind with the intricacies of her adornments.

Based on a magazine story by Izola Forrester, *The White Moth* follows the story of an America dancer, Mona Reid (La Marr). Mona is rescued by Gonzalo Montrez (de Roche), who prevents her from jumping into the Seine. Gonzalo, known as "The Volcano," helps her become a famous dancer. Known as "The White Moth," from one of the characters she depicts on the stage, Mona becomes the rage of Paris. Although Gonzalo desires her, she wins the love of a young American, Douglas Vantine (Lyon), who is already engaged to Gwen (Edna Murphy). His older brother Robert (Tearle) successfully terminates his brother's infatuation by marring Mona. In the end Ninon (Josie), a dancer who is jealous of Gonzalo's infatuation for Mona, shoots and kills Gonzalo.

The 1924 edition of *Film Year Book* noted that Universal had a bright outlook for serials that year. According to E.J. Smith, the serial department was busier than ever due to a growing demand for additional productions.

> I attribute this to Universal's drive during the past twelve months for more perfect serials. Following a reorganization of the serial production department at Universal City, we are concentrating on the making of super-serials—serials embodying all the punch, thrills and excitement of the old styled chaptered pictures, while attaining the story value, the finish in production and the class of acting, setting and direction accorded expensive feature productions.
>
> Universal has found the fifteen-chapter serial to be the ideal length. Our 1924 schedule embraces a series of high-class serials made by expert directors and popular stars. The outstanding feature in

The Riddle Rider (1924), a 15-chapter serial released by Universal, featured Eileen as a young heiress who desperately attempts to defend her property from the "bad guys." William Desmond plays the "Riddle Rider" who, incognito in a cape and mustache, avenges the wrongs inflicted by the villains.

our 1924 plans is the fact our forthcoming serials will be handled in production just as careful as our Jewels Super Serials demand super treatments. And the public wants nothing but super serials.

Eileen's only appearance in 1924 was her leading role in *The Riddle Rider*, a 15-chapter Universal serial released that November. William Desmond, as the "Riddle Rider," played the part of an editor of a small-town newspaper who battles a faction intent on grabbing his community's oil-rich lands. Eileen played a young heiress and the editor's romantic interest, who desperately attempts to defend her property from the bad guys. Her courageous attempt appears futile, until the Riddle Rider comes to her assistance. As the Riddle Rider, the newspaperman donned a costume comprised of a long flowing cape and well-groomed whiskers—not much of a costume, but enough to send a crowded theater into frenzy as they encouraged the crusader as he rode to the rescue.

Directed by William James Craft, the serial co-starred Helen Holmes and Yakima Canutt. Originally a rodeo cowboy, Canutt became a legendary Hollywood stuntman, doubling for major stars including John Wayne and Clark Gable, and today is considered to be a pioneer in the field. The serial proved to be profitable for Universal and in 1927 Desmond appeared in a successful sequel, *The Return of the Riddle Rider*, with Lola Todd as his love interest.

Serials and series, which were once favored by adults and featured the likes of Pearl White and Ruth Roland, were now receiving a large portion of their box office receipts from children who frequented the small neighborhood theaters. The serial stars, however, retained celebrity status in the movie magazines, especially Tom Mix and Hoot Gibson, who were successfully realigned to attract the adolescent market. The genre's marketplace was shrinking and by 1925 many of the small companies that produced serials had left the competition. That year Universal only produced four serials, with Pathé completing five.

Exhibition material for *The Hurricane Kid* (1925), starring Hoot Gibson and directed by Edward, surrounds the Bligh Theater.

Taking into consideration the reduction in Universal's serial production, the studio was doing quite well, reporting that their gross earnings for 1925 totaled $24,823,526. Universal claimed that it was the best year in the company's history, with net earnings available for dividends amounting to $1,925,506 for the year ending November 7, 1925.[2]

Part of Universal's success was due to their Hoot Gibson franchise. Edward and Gibson worked on *The Hurricane Kid*, a January "White List" release. Gibson, in the title role, falls in loves with Joan Landon (Marion Nixon). But Joan only has eyes for Lafe Baxter, the foreman (William Steele). Once the Hurricane Kid reveals that Lafe is a crook, Joan changes her feelings about him. Promoted as "The Sweetest Girl in Hollywood," Nixon was honored the previous year as a WAMPAS Baby Star. She was loaned to Universal by Fox, where they changed the spelling of her first name from Marian to Marion, and gave her Gibson as her new leading man.

Josie and Eileen's innate fearlessness made them adroit horsewoman, providing realism as cowgirls onscreen. In the November 1925 *Movie Weekly*, an article titled "Ladies of Peril," by Hal K. Wells, described the actresses of the day who filled the position of the female protagonist in Westerns.

> They hold a unique and exclusive niche in the screen work of the Film Colony.
> They are the Western heroines, the beauties in distress to whose aid rush such heroes as Jack Hoxie, Fred Thomson, Hoot Gibson, or Harry Carey. They are girls whose favor the range-riding, hard-

In the November 1925 issue of *Movie Weekly* magazine an article titled "Ladies of Peril," by Hal K. Wells, had positioned Josie as a "real cowgirl" and the "queen of all Western movie heroines."

shooting heroes of the silversheet perform prodigies of valor. It is in their defense that cowboy stars come "smokin' and a ridin' high," on galloping broncos and with six-guns flashing fire.

The most thrilling of Western pictures without a heroine would be as incomplete and disappointing as strawberry shortcake without the strawberries. But, even as the Western heroes are heroes above the ordinary, so must be their heroines be worthy of their prowess by being heroines equally unusual.

Wells called Josie as a "real cowgirl" and the "queen of all Western movie heroines":

> Josie is one of the greatest equestriennes in pictures, and is also the only one who is a full-fledged Western star in her own right. If there is anything in the outdoors line that she can't do, the chances are it can't be done. She's an expert with the lariat, the rifle, and the revolver. Last year she was the Queen of the Pendleton Roundup, one of the real frontier classics of the West. She is the idol of half the cowpunchers this side of the Mississippi, and is equally beloved by all the children on the Universal lot. Possessed of a flashing smile and a warm friendly handclasp, she has the knack of being a pal to everyone.

The board of directors of the Pendleton Round-Up, an annual rodeo held in Pendleton, Oregon, invited Josie to participate in their 1924 event as Rodeo Queen. Pendleton's rodeo queen, introduced in the 1910s as part of the round-up's grand entry activities, included cowgirls from diverse backgrounds, with daughters of local businessmen and ranchers often riding trick horses or competing with bucking horses and bulls in the event. Traditionally, the queen and her court were selected from Pendleton's community, making it a local event. In an effort to stimulate national interest in the rodeo, the directors decided it was necessary to glamorize the queen's position by inviting personalities from outside the vicinity to participate. The board's first choice couldn't have been made easier by the fact that Josie would be in town during the round-up to shoot footage to be used in the movie *Let 'Er Buck*. ("Let 'er buck" is a call used when a cowboy is about to mount an "outlaw" horse that is considered too wild to handle. The slogan is used to this day by the Pendleton Round-Up.)

The plan was a success, as Josie's appearance was reported in newspapers throughout the United States. The press also made a point to report that Josie broke with Pendleton's tradition of choosing young women as the queen's maids of honor; she selected two husky male "cowpunchers" from the unit of Universal ranch riders who had previous round-up experience. Josie was now able to add the title of Rodeo Queen to her list of current nicknames: "Ridin' Queen of the West," "the Queen of Female Western Stars," and "the Peril-Proof Horsewoman."

As a previous rodeo competitor, Gibson was already a personality in Pendleton. Along with his second wife Helen Johnson, they rode in Pendleton's round-up events long before they started acting careers. In 1912 Gibson had won the title of "World's All-Around Champion Cowboy," so it was fitting that he should be the star of a movie that incorporated the event.

On September 19, the opening day of the 1924 Pendleton Round-Up, the attending crowd of 25,000 spectators was caught in a pouring rain as a sudden gale descended upon the town. Wild horses and steers became unmanageable, with one blindfolded horse breaking loose and leaping into the bleachers. A 60-foot tower, set up in the big arena for filming the activities of the contestants, was blown down by the strong wind. Buddy Harris, assistant cameraman, descended from the platform on which he had been grinding a camera for three

Josie was invited to participate as Rodeo Queen in the 1924 Pendleton Round-Up, an annual rodeo held in Pendleton, Oregon. The film *Let 'Er Buck* (1925), which also starred Hoot Gibson, used footage that was shot of the roundup.

hours just three *minutes* before the accident occurred. Harris climbed down to confer with Edward, and while they were talking the sudden rush of wind hurled the platform into the arena. No one was injured by the crashing timbers, but the camera was smashed and the footage in the camera was ruined.

Released in March as a "White List" production, the movie, inspired by Charles Wellington Furlong's 1921 "Let 'Er Buck: The Passing of the Old West," was written by Edward and Raymond L. Schrock with the filming of the Pendleton Round-Up in mind. In addition to Josie, the supporting players included Marian Nixon in the leading feminine role, G. Raymond Nye, Charles K. French, Fred Humes and William Steele.

A ranch hand, Bob Carson (Gibson), falls in love with a wealthy Texan ranch owner's daughter, Jacqueline McCall (Nixon). Jacqueline's cousin Jim Ralston becomes upset over their romance and challenges Bob to a gun duel. Shots are exchanged and Jim pretends to be shot. Thinking he killed Jim, Bob runs away, hitching a ride on a freight train headed to Pendleton, Oregon. Arriving just in time for the Pendleton Round-Up, he meets Mabel Thompson (Josie), a ranch owner looking for a rider who can handle the bronco she wants to enter in the competition. Bob proves that he can ride the horse. Members of the McCall ranch show up to participate in the round-up, including Jim. Jacqueline asks Bob to ride for her father's ranch in the rodeo, but Bob feels obligated to ride for Mabel, who has supported him through his despair. The night before the rodeo, Jim and his men kidnap Bob to keep him out of the chariot race, but he escapes in time to drive Mabel's team to a narrow win. The impressive chariot race included in the rodeo was seemingly inspired by Metro-Goldwyn-Mayer's epic film *Ben-Hur: A Tale of the Christ*, which was released at the end of the year.

The Saddle Hawk, a second March "White List" release, took advantage of the cast, crew, and Universal ranch riders that were already located in Oregon for the filming of *Let 'Er Buck*. With a working title of *The Lone Outlaw*, the story focused on the conflict between cattle ranchers and sheepmen in Oregon, where some of the biggest beef cattle ranches in the county were located. In addition to directing the movie, Edward collaborated with Schrock on writing the story. Gibson's character, Ben Johnson, is a ragged sheep herder who hates sheep. His employer Vasquez (Tote Du Crow) gives him the responsibility of escorting Rena Newhall (Marion Nixon) to her father's ranch. Buck Brent (Frank Campeau), an outlaw who has sworn vengeance on Rena's father for sending him to jail years before, has Zach Marlin (Nye) kidnap Rena. Posing as an outlaw, Ben infiltrates Buck's gang, which is rustling cattle from the ranch of Jim Newhall, Rena's father (French). Ben lets himself get captured so that he can warn Jim of Zach's plan. Buck rejoins the gang, but is soon exposed. Just as the gang is about to kill Ben, a posse led by Jim raids Buck's camp. Buck and his gang are captured, but Zach escapes, taking Rena with him. Ben captures Zach and wins Rena's love. Josie appeared in the role of Mercedes with William Steele as Steve Kern.

Eileen appeared in *Dangerous Odds*, an April release from Independent Pictures. Jesse J. Goldburg, a pioneer producer who worked with a number of early film companies, organized Independent as an outlet for low-priced Westerns which were distributed through the Film Booking Offices of America. Directed by William James Craft and written by Goldburg, the typical B Western starred Eileen, Bill Cody, Milton J. Fahrney, Claude Payton, Monte Collins, Al Hallett, Dick la Reno, and Artie Ortego. Cody played a farmer battling a gang of greedy cattle ranchers, led by Payton. They frame Cody for murder but Cody proves his innocence, and Payton, along with his dubious sidekick (Ortego), is sent off to prison. Eileen appears as the romantic interest, with Fahrney as her father, and la Reno as the sheriff.

The Fighting Ranger, a Universal adventure serial, featured Eileen, Jack Dougherty and

Al Wilson. With the first chapter premiering in May, Universal heavily promoted the serial by making available to local newspapers a print version of the chapters to tie into the episodes appearing in theaters each week. Curiously, the total number of chapters varies: Universal trade magazines promoted eighteen chapters, handouts for local theaters listed a total of fifteen two-reel episodes, and prepared exploitation advertisements for use in newspapers noted twelve chapters.

Fred J. McConnell and George W. Pyper wrote the story that appeared in print, with the scenario for the screen version supervised by McConnell. Directed by Jay Marchant, the plot revolves around a once-prosperous cattleman, John Marshall (William Welsh), who shot an influential politician in self-defense. Hiding from the law in the mountains on his ranch with his daughter Mary (Eileen), William has left his sprawling ranch in the hands of his ranch hand "Topez" Taggart (Bud Osborne). Forest ranger Terence O'Rourke (Jack Dougherty) experiences engine trouble with his plane as he is flying over the mountains, and parachutes to the vicinity of the Marshalls. He is injured, and Mary tends to his recovery. They find out that Terence was sent by his superiors to help William prove that he has been framed by Topaz—the ranch hand discovered a source of wealth on the ranch and schemed to take possession of it from William however he had to.

The December 1925 issue of *Movie Monthly* magazine featured a front cover illustration of Eileen by Leo Kober.

An exhibitor's advertisement from Universal, running in the May 31 *Dallas Morning Star*, summed up the excitement and romance include in the action series:

THE FIGHTING RANGER
A Thrilling Adventure Chapter Play of Western Plains and Skies!
There isn't an idle moment in this thrill-crammed Western. Smashing action from the word go—sustained and exciting to the very last episode. It's chock full of daring, packed with wild riding and hair-raising aviation stunts, with a story that keeps you on your toes all the time. Just the sort of

picture your whole family deserves to see—clean, exciting, a treat and a delight. There's a whale of a love story that throbs its way straight to your heart, and twelve whole episodes to work you into a salvo of applause.

JACK DOUGHERTY

See him fight, make love, ride like a frantic fury—with all the gallant fire that has made him the favorite of all Western fans.

EILEEN SEDGWICK

The charming, beautiful heroine of numerous Westerns, whose surprising daring and reckless indifference to danger keeps you in constant suspense.

AL WILSON

The highest paid stunt aviator in the world here performs his most breathless, death-defying acts of courage.

As the serial format came to be known as a children's genre, censorship groups began to pay more attention to serials and their effects on young viewers. By having the advertisement emphasize "Just the sort of picture your whole family deserves to see," Universal assured families that it was appropriate viewing material for all ages. It also called attention to the

The Fighting Ranger (1925), a Universal adventure serial, featured Eileen together with Al Wilson (shown) and Jack Dougherty.

romantic aspect of the story, letting adults know that it wasn't just another typical kids' serial, but would also be of interest to a mature audience.

Both of *The Fighting Ranger*'s leading male stars would experience tragic deaths. Dougherty married actress Barbara La Marr in 1923, becoming her fifth husband. Although his marriage to the famous actress gave his career a boost, La Marr's sensationalized death from an apparent drug overdose in 1926 would eventually destroy his reputation. Reduced to playing supporting roles, Dougherty committed suicide in May 1938.

Wilson would die from injuries sustained in an accident that occurred at the 1932 Cleveland Air Races. A feature of the show was a mock dogfight between Wilson's modified 1910 Curtiss Pusher biplane and stunt pilot John Miller's autogiro. At the end of their show, Miller landed in the area in front of the viewing stand, with Wilson making one final pass over Miller. As the biplane passed over the autogiro, it entered the downdraft of the still turning blades, striking them before crashing to the ground.

Queen of the Round-Up, a June Mustang Western release, featured Josie in her first of twelve Universal Westerns. The story was written exclusively for her by Edward. Ernst Laemmle, who directed the two-reel film, would also direct several other low-budget Westerns that Josie participated in, including *Ropin' Venus*, *A Battle of Wits*, *The Fighting Schoolmarm*, *The Best Man*, and *Dynamite's Daughter*. As Carl Laemmle's nephew, he and other family members readily found employment at "Uncle Carl"'s Universal. Others in the *Queen of the Round-Up* cast included Edmund Cobb, Charles Bennett, Edward Kimball and Calvert Carter.

Ropin' Venus, Josie's second Universal short, was released in July. The story was written by Isadore Bernstein, the man responsible for introducing the Sedgwicks to Hollywood, back when he was working as the general manager of Universal's West Coast operations. The film's story was typical of a Mustang two-reel Western comedy-drama: Jerry Ramsdell (Josie), daughter of the sheriff, sets out to apprehend cattle rustlers. She captures Eugene Slade (Edward Cecil) just as he gives his gang an "all clear" signal. Jerry is captured by the gang but soon escapes from their hideout. She signals her father, who arrives with his posse and rounds up the gang. Bob Wallace played the romantic interest.

A Battle of Wits (the same title as Eileen's 1921 short, but a different story) was released in July, with its scenario and story written by George Morgan. *The Fighting Schoolmarm* and *The Best Man* were both released in August, with scenarios and stories by Isadore Bernstein. Edward scripted *Dynamite's Daughter*, Josie's final release for August.

Josie appeared in two of Universal's Blue Streak series. Universal used their Blue Streak brand name to promote the studio's B category stars, including the likes of Jack Hoxie, Pete Morison, and Art Acord, in five-reel Westerns. Although Josie reluctantly acted in the low-budget productions, as opposed to working on the higher budgeted films that she did with Hoot Gibson, she was now receiving top billing. Directed by John B. O'Brien, *The Outlaw's Daughter*, #12 in the Blue Streak Western series, was released in September. Josie played Flora Dale, a bandit's daughter who upon her father's death assumes leadership of his band of outlaws. When she confronts the suspected killer of her father, mine manager Jim King (Edward Hearn), she cannot bring herself to kill him. Outlaw Slim Cole (Robert Walker) shoots at Jim. Flora throws herself in front of the gun to shield Jim and is wounded.

Jim's mother nurses Flora back to health, and she and Jim try to teach her to lead a good Christian life. After Flora is well, she reunites with the bandits and plans to rob the mine safe, but at the last moment has a change of heart. She returns to the gang's headquarters to steal the papers incriminating her as the leader of the gang. The gang members catch her and accuse her of double-crossing them. During a fight between bandits and the miners at the King mine, Flora saves Jim's life, knocking Cole to his death from a suspended ore bucket.

The February 12, 1927, *Fort Covington Sun* reported on *The Outlaw's Daughter* when it was scheduled to play at the local theater:

> This as a rip-roaring western melodrama of an unusual type—starring one of the world's most famous horsewomen, Josie Sedgwick, in her first picture of feature length. It is a story of a girl leader of a band of outlaws out for revenge for the death of her father—replete with thrills—action—suspense—daredevil stunts—wild riding—and a terrific climax!

Hoot Gibson appeared in *Spook Ranch,* a September Jewel release for Universal. Directed by Ernst Laemmle, the haunted house–themed story was co-written by Edward and Raymond L. Schrock. After breaking a dinner plate over the head of a Chinese cook, Bill Bangs (Gibson) is sentenced by the sheriff (Frank Rice) to investigate a "haunted" ranch. The "spooks" turn out to be a gang of outlaws who have kidnapped a girl named Elvira (Helen Ferguson).

Josie appeared in a November release, *Daring Days*, Blue Streak Western series #17, directed by John B. O'Brien from a story by George C. Hull. Employed in the "want ad"

Josie reluctantly acted in low-budget productions, but *The Outlaw's Daughter* (1925), a Universal Blue Streak film, gave her top billing in her first feature film. Edward Hearn played her love interest.

department of a San Francisco newspaper, Eve Underhill (Josie) spots an advertisement for a female mayor in the town of Eden, Arizona. As she travels down a desert road, the stagecoach she is riding in is held up by two bandits from Catamount, Eden's rival town. The stagecoach horses take fright and dash wildly down the road with the driver lying unconscious. The March 26 *Fort Covington Sun* describes the action that is incorporated into this scene as Eve mounts one of the bandit's horses and starts off in pursuit of the flying team:

> It is a great ride and an exciting moment as the little star urges her horse on after the swaying coach and the flying horses. Finally she overtakes the runaway, and from the saddle succeeds in pulling the team and bringing it to a halt. In this one scene alone Miss Sedgwick again shows that she is the greatest equestrienne in pictures.

Eve rides victoriously into Eden where she is made the mayor. A romance develops between her and Catamount Carson (Edward Hearn), mayor of Catamount. His evil cousin Ambrose Carson (Ben Corbett) is encouraging a dispute between the two towns over water rights. Catamount hunts down Ambrose and, during a fight at the rim of a canyon, they both tumble over the edge. Ambrose falls to his death but Catamount is saved as Eve lassoes his foot.

Josie appeared in *Daring Days* (1925), a Blue Streak Western. Looking rather masculine, as her fine lines were becoming harder looking with age, she comforts actress Zama Zamoria.

Edward's most important assignment in 1925 was Universal's *The Phantom of the Opera*. A melodramatic horror story based on Gaston Leroux's 1910 French novel, *Le Fantôme de l'Opera*, it has become a cinematic enigma. Today's film scholars consider the Universal Super Jewel production one of the top silent films of its genre, but when it was first released critics weren't receptive. Its production history began in 1924, with Rupert Julian directing the first version, which was the closest to the original novel, in which Erik, the Phantom, climactically dies of a broken heart at his organ.

Carl Laemmle had conceived the million dollar prestige feature as a follow-up to *The Hunchback of Notre Dame*, Universal's box office hit from the previous year. But in Julian's hands it quickly turned into a nightmare. Julian, an actor stereotypically known for his portrayal of Kaiser Wilhelm in several World War I–era films, had become a temperamental director, and according to many, in the case of *The Phantom of the Opera*, an unskilled one as well. Julian's direction was totally unexpressive, as the pacing of the scenes was listless and the actors reverted to the emoting style of the past. Where imaginative camera angles should have been used against the elaborately designed sets to frame the story, uninspired shots were filmed.

Julian's disagreeable personality hampered Lon Chaney's portrayal of Erik, straining their relationship to the point where each refused to speak directly with the other, communicating only through a second party. Chaney had the support of cast and crew members in his feelings towards the incompetent director. In fact, Chaney was responsible for many of the dramatic scenes that turned out to be successful, working around Julian to get them filmed, as was the case with the unmasking of the Phantom by his protégée Christine Daaé (Mary Philbin).

Phantom was previewed at a limited viewing in Los Angeles on January 7 and 26, 1925, using a score prepared by Joseph Carl Breil. It got a dismal reaction from its audience, causing its January release to be cancelled. After reviewing the audiences' critiques, Laemmle realized that a common complaint concerned the handling of the romance thread, which needed further development, and that comedy relief needed to be added to offset the seriousness of the romance. The audiences also felt that Erik's death from heartbreak was too sympathetic a punishment for a murderer. When Julian was told that he would need to reshoot a large segment of the film, he walked out on Universal.

Laemmle had transferred the project to the hands of the general manager of Universal City, John Wray. Wray became overwhelmed with the idea of unraveling the mess, so Laemmle instead placed Raymond L. Schrock in charge of saving the troubled production. Schrock, now general manager of Universal City, suggested to Laemmle that Edward should be assigned the task of directing new material that would be edited into Julian's footage in an effort to bring energy to the failed movie. Schrock based his recommendation on his previous work experience with Edward, and was convinced that his success with Gibson's action movies proved that the director would help fix the mess. This was an honor for Edward, as he knew the feature was Laemmle's #1 priority for 1925.

Edward worked with Schrock and the production's original screenwriter Elliot Clawson on writing two new subplots. With the assistance of cameraman Virgil Miller, Edward fleshed out the romantic thread which introduced the Russian Count Ruboff (Ward Crane), who would duel with Vicomte Raoul de Chagny (Norman Kerry) for Christine's affection. The comedy relief footage that Edward filmed featured a romantic romp between comedian

Edward's involvement in the overhauling of Universal's *The Phantom of the Opera* (1925) gave him the influence to move on to the next level in the film industry.

Chester Conklin as Raoul's orderly and Vola Vale as Christine's maid. A new ending followed the Phantom as he is being chased through the streets along the Seine River by a mob. The revised version was previewed on April 26 in San Francisco, and once again was panned.

Laemmle assigned Lois Weber and Maurice Pivar to reedit Edward's version. In the process they cut out most of his material, with the exception of the chase scene. The third version premiered on September 6 at the Astor Theater in New York City and on October 17 in Hollywood. Universal had a full organ installed at the Astor which accompanied a score by Eugene Conte, arranged with the appropriate Faust cues.

The original 22-reel version of *The Phantom of the Opera* was finally reduced to a more watchable 11-reel feature. Due to the continuous editing that was done, even after its release, it is unknown if a copy of this premiere version exits. The storyline of a recently reconstructed version, which appears to be complete, appears as follows.

As the opera house changes management, the current owners are warned of a Phantom who haunts the building and its five levels of basements. The catacombs were used for prisons and torture cambers during France's second revolution. The ghost who haunts the opera house, the Phantom lives in the maze of catacombs that it was built upon. In reality the Phantom is Erik, a gifted musician who is an escapee from a mental institution. As a child he was tortured during the revolution—thus he wears a mask to cover his facial disfigurement.

From behind the walls of her dressing room, Erik instructs his protégée Christine Daaé, the young understudy to the opera house's prima donna Carlotta (Virginia Pearson). Hearing the Phantom's encouragement, the naive Christine thinks that the Phantom is the god of music, who her father said would one day appear to her.

In a note to Charlotte, the Phantom strongly recommends that the prima donna feign illness so that Christine can appear as the principal soloist. Infuriated, Charlotte ignores his warning. As a result, during her performance, the theater's immense chandelier is dropped onto the audience.

When the lights are turned back on, Vicomte Raoul de Chagny, Christine's fiancé, discovers that she is missing; the Phantom abducted her to his subterranean hideout. Promising her fame, the Phantom asks a return favor from her, that she never remove his mask. Thinking that she is asleep in a bedroom that he has prepared for her, he plays "Don Juan Triumphant" on the organ. Christine awakes to the music, quietly walks up behind him, and takes off his mask to reveal his hideously disfigured face.

Confessing his love for her, Erik promises Christine success and says he will release her only if she does not reveal to anyone what she has seen. She agrees. But once released, Christine meets Raoul at the Bal Masque de l'Opera and confides to him all of the Phantom's secrets. Erik, disguised in a flowing red robe and a death's head mask, listens in on their conversation. In a rage, he kidnaps Christine once again. Raoul and Ledoux of the secret police find a secret passage behind a mirror in Christine's dressing room and race to her rescue. In their effort they become trapped in one torture chamber after another. Raoul's brother Comte Philip de Chagny (Arthur Edmund Carewe) comes to free them from a locked room that is quickly filling up with water.

Erik escapes to the streets above and is chased by an angry crowd. The mob captures him as he reaches the Seine River, beating him to death and throwing his lifeless body into the river. Christine and Raoul are reunited and marry.

The Phantom of the Opera finally found success in its public release. Tie-in merchandising also proved to be profitable. In addition to color-tinted film sequences, Technicolor was also utilized. The Phantom's crimson garments, vividly captured in a Technicolor segment filmed for the Bal Masque sequence, influenced a cosmetic company to produce a shade of lipstick named "Phantom Red," supposedly designed "especially for Mary Philbin," and a shoe manufacturer sold women's shoes dyed a bright red.

Once sound was introduced into motion pictures, Universal decided to release a sound version of *The Phantom of the Opera* in 1929. Utilizing the new Western Electric sound-on-disc process, Ernest Laemmle re-shot almost half of the picture in sound, using additional dialogue written by Sedgwick and Chaney, with some scenes done in two-tone Technicolor. The remainder was redubbed with sound effects. A fully synchronized original score by David Broekman and Sam A. Perry was added. With the exception of Chaney, who was now working at MGM, the original cast members provided their own voices for the sound version. Ernest's solution to the absence of Erik's voice was to add a "third person" dialogue to shots of the Phantom's shadow. The result was an 89-minute sound version which was 35 percent talkie.

Advertisements for the sound version now utilized images of Chaney made up as the Phantom, unlike the previous versions, which intentionally didn't use photos of Erik's face in promotions, in order to keep his deformity a surprise. *Phantom*'s cost approached $1 million, $50,000 of which was spent on retakes. In the end, it turned out to be a box office hit, grossing over $2 million.

Lorraine of the Lions, a Jewel "White List" production, was directed by Edward for Universal as an October release. It's likely that its story, written by Isadore Bernstein and Carl Krusada, was influenced by National Film Corporation's *Tarzan of the Apes* (1918). In 1916 National purchased the Tarzan story from Edgar Rice Burroughs and filmed it as a three-hour movie. It starred Elmo Lincoln as Tarzan and Enid Markey as Jane Porter. Bernstein was responsible for editing it down to a 73-minute running time for general release.

The story opens with a circus being transported on a boat. The vessel is damaged by a storm and ends up shipwrecked on a remote island. The only survivors are the circus owner's daughter and the animals who now inhabit the jungle. Lorraine was played by Patsy Ruth Miller, a WAMPAS Baby Star of 1922, who had found success at Universal the previous year in the role of Esmeralda in *The Hunchback of Notre Dame*. Lorraine wins the friendships of the animals, especially that of a protective gorilla named Bimi (Fred Humes). Don Mackay (Norman Kerry) rescues Lorraine and returns her to civilization, where she is made over. A love story between Lorraine and Don ensues. As a young actor, Walter Brennan makes his first film appearance (uncredited). He went on to become a well-known character actor.

Edward directed *Two-Fisted Jones*, a Blue Streak Western which was released in December. The five-reeler featured Jack Hoxie, an actor who had previously performed in Poverty Row oaters but was now in the runner-up position to Universal's top cowboy star, Hoot Gibson. Kathryn McGuire, a 1922 WAMPAS Baby Star, who had some previous success as Buster Keaton's leading lady in his 1924 films *Sherlock Jr.*, and *The Navigator*, was the leading lady. William Steele also made an appearance, playing the role of Hank Gage. The story finds Jack Wilbur (Hoxie) on the trail of a wanted man. The trail leads Jack to the ranch of Mary Mortimer (McGuire). Bart Wilson (Harry Todd), a devious banker, is about to take possession of the ranch from Mary. When Jack catches the outlaw, he ironically turns out to be the banker, who is trying to rob Kathryn of her ranch.

Around this time, Edward teamed with Henry R. Cohen to write several songs. In 1925 they published "You Told Me to Go," with Edward penning the lyrics and Cohen scoring the music for the sentimental fox trot. Abe Lyman, a popular bandleader from the 1920s to the 1940s, collaborated with them on the arrangements. Lyman's brother Mike had opened the Sunset, a Los Angeles nightclub frequented by movie stars, including Charlie Chaplin, Mary Pickford, Buster Keaton, Harold Lloyd and Norma Talmadge. The venue closed when actors were required to sign contracts stating they were not to be seen in public entertaining at clubs.

Lyman's nine-piece band became a success after performing at his brother's nightspot, and he appeared in films with his band in the 1930s. He helped promote "You Told Me to Go" by appearing with his band members on the front cover of the song's sheet music. Two other versions of the sheet music were also published, one with a photo of the Little Playmates, featuring the heavyweights William Haynes, Howard Kaiser and Tony Lehmann, and one with a photo of Al Moore and his U.S. Jazz Band.

The song had some success, being recorded by several different artists, including Carl Fenton's Orchestra, Ben Selvin and His Orchestra, Fred Rich and His Hotel Astor Orchestra, Roger Wolfe Kahn and His Hotel Biltmore Orchestra with Franklyn Baur on vocals, and Bailey's Lucky Seven with Arthur Fields on vocals.

A second song hit for Edward and Cohen that year was "On the Oregon Trail." The appearance of George Olsen and his band in a photograph appearing on the front cover of the song's sheet music helped promote the tune. Olsen and his band were a popular Broadway act, appearing in 1923's hit musical *Kid Boots* starring Eddie Cantor and *Ziegfeld Follies of 1924*. The Golden Gate Orchestra, AKA the California Ramblers, featuring jazz artists Red Nichols, Jimmy Dorsey, and Tommy Dorsey, recorded the song that year.

In 1926, it was twenty years ago that Carl Laemmle opened the White Front Theatre on Milwaukee Avenue in Chicago. Within a few months he was operating four theaters. This anniversary coincided with the industry's thirtieth anniversary, celebrated on April 27. In 1896 the moving picture as a theater-shown form of amusement was first introduced as an added attraction on the variety bill of the Koster & Bialey Music Hall, located at Broadway at 34th Street in New York City. The program's selection included the American Mutoscope Company's film of serpentine dancer Annabelle Moore performing and a brief view of waves breaking at Manhattan Beach.

The studio's celebration was somewhat marred due to several defections from its talent pool. In March, Louis B. Mayer, MGM vice-president in charge of production, announced that Edward had signed a contract with his studio. At the time of Edward's departure from Universal he was being paid $1,250 weekly; other directors in his salary range included Ralph Ince, George B. Seitz, Harry Beaumont, Emmett Flynn, and William K. Howard.[3] Although Edward's responsibilities were increasing, Universal felt that his salary was not negotiable. Lon Chaney, Irving Thalberg, and directors Tod Browning, Erich von Stroheim, and Clarence Brown also left for MGM. Edward was preparing to join the ranks of some of the industry's top talent, including directors such as Fred Niblo, Rex Ingram and his old friend King Vidor. Universal continued to promote Edward's films as if he was still working for them. The June 12, 1926, *Reel Journal* announced that Edward was on Universal's "Greater

White List" of directors who were selected for the studio's 1926–27 programs. It was noted that he was scheduled to direct Courtney Ryley Cooper's "The Trail of the Tiger" and Richard Barry's "The Big Gun."

Just as Edward's career was moving forward at full speed, Josie's was winding down. The injuries that Josie sustained while performing her own stunts were affecting the 32-year-old's health. After fulfilling her commitment to appear in the Mustang shorts, she decided to retire from acting.

Josie appeared in six Mustang two-reel Westerns which were released throughout the year: *Montana of the Range, Queen of the Hills, Mountain Molly O', Outlaw Love, The Little Warrior*, and *Jim Hood's Ghost*. All were written by William A. Berke, credited as William Lester, and directed by John B. O'Brien. The oaters featured character actors well-known for portraying cowboys, including Curley Baldwin, John Elliott, Earl Metcalfe, Joe Rickson, Floyd Shackelford, Jack Trent, Duke R. Lee, Jack Padjan, Tex Young, Edward Hearn and the versatile African American actor Noble Johnson.

Taking a break from acting, Josie volunteered at the Red Cross' relief tents, which were set up in Santa Barbara's de la Guerra Plaza after an early morning earthquake ravaged the seaside village on June 29, 1925. Along with other Universal stars, including Laura La Plante, Josie helped to hand out rations at the makeshift canteen.

Under Western Skies, an Edward Sedgwick-Universal-Jewel production, was a February release that Edward wrote and directed. The cast featured Norman Kerry as Robert Erskine and Anne Cornwall as Ella Parkhurst, with Ward Crane, George Fawcett, Kathleen Key, Eddie Gribbon, Harry Todd, Charles K. French, William Steele, Hans Joby, and Artie Ortego filling out its supporting cast. In the story, Robert, son of a prosperous New York banker, falls in love with Ella, daughter of an Oregon rancher. The Parkhurst ranch, where Robert works as a ranch hand, is facing financial trouble and may lose their crops due to a group of Eastern bankers who refuse to extend credit to the farmers in Oregon. Ironically, Robert's father is leading the group of financiers. Robert's father will only help the farmers if Robert wins the steeplechase event in the upcoming Pendleton Round-Up. Robert enters his stallion, a horse he tamed after catching it in a wild horse roundup, and wins the obstacle race, rescuing the farms and winning Ella's fidelity.

A portion of the movie was filmed during the Pendleton Round-Up, with additional footage shot in New York City and Universal City. In one scene Kerry sustained groin and rib injuries when the cinch broke on a wild horse and the animal knocked him unconscious. The horse continued to charge against Edward, knocking him over, along with a camera.

Eileen and William Desmond appeared in Universal's *The Winking Idol*, a February release. Francis Ford, who entered filmmaking as an actor in 1909 and appeared in almost 300 movies by 1926, directed the ten-episode serial. Francis was the older brother and mentor of John Ford, another actor-turned-director, but one who was destined to become an Oscar-winning and influential director of American film.

The Winking Idol was taken from a story that author Charles Van Loan was working on at the time of his death. Universal had purchased the rights to this and several other Van Loan stories. The mystery involved an image which was the key to a gold cache that was hidden by a group of Indians. The serial opened with a back-story: A villain kills one man and frames another in an attempt to secure possession of a small piece of the image that would help him locate the gold. Years later, the son of the murdered man, Dave Ledbetter

(Desmond) and the daughter of the imprisoned man, Jean Wilson (Eileen), took up the quest to recover the treasure.

The supporting cast included Jack Richardson as heavy Crawford Lange and Grace Cunard as Thora Lange, with comedian Syd Saylor added for comedic relief. Bert Sutch, playing a character part, was previously an assistant director with D.W. Griffith for nine years.

The *Santa Cruz Evening News* reported on the daily progress of the filming for *The Winking Idol*. A company of 35 cast and crew members arrived at Boulder Creek on Sunday, July 12, 1925, to film the thriller, with plans to stay at least three weeks. Boulder Creek brimmed with film people, as Fox was also making use of the town for a production. Taking advantage of the situation, the town planned a "Movie Dance" at Middleton's Hall in honor of both companies.

On July 16 the company was filming at the George Nord Ranch on Bear Creek, having just completed scenes at the Bear Creek mill, with plans to shoot additional exterior footage at Big Basin Park. Known for his action films, Ford directed the stunts that were seen in the serial. On July 18 the filming of one scene on Boulder Creek, only a short distance from Alpine Inn where the company was staying, required a stunt man to dive 50 feet into the creek. Albert Malone, a Boulder Creek resident, doubled for Helen Broneau who was playing the role of an Indian girl. With a temperature of 102 in the shade, it didn't take much persuasion by Ford to get Malone to take a fifty-foot dive from a tree limb into the creek to rescue the heroine in the canoe. The July 21 *Santa Cruz Morning Sentinel* described the thrilling scene, but ignored the fact that a stunt double was used in the jump:

> A good many spectators were present along Boulder Creek last Friday and witnessed a thrilling scene in the making of a movie. It was a spectacular dive from a high bank into the creek made by Miss Helen Broneau. William Desmond was in a canoe below, supposedly wounded and unconscious. Beside him was Eileen Sedgwick, attempting to steer the boat with a broken paddle. As it swung into the rapids just above the dam, the girl figure above, clad as an Indian maiden, dove from her pinnacle into space. There was a splash and then she came up, grabbed the canoe as it neared the dam and towed it to shore. It was an act which made the spectators gasp and one which should make a thrilling scene on the silver screen when shown.

Several other scenes were filmed along the dam and the creek below the dam that day. As with most of the outdoor filming, a large crowd of locals gathered there to watch. The newspaper also reported that a few days later, somewhere along a railroad spur track not far from the Boulder Creek station, an upcoming action sequence required the blowing-up of a boxcar.

The Flaming Frontier, also known as *The Indians Are Coming*, was promoted as Universal's major production for 1926. With a superior cast selected from the studio's large contract roster and an estimated budget of $400,000, this was turning out to be the most important project Edward had handled to date. Scheduled for April release, the Western was directed by Edward and based on an original story he wrote to commemorate the fiftieth anniversary of the battle of Little Big Horn. Raymond L. Schrock and Charles Kenyon worked on the adaptation of the story, originally titled "The Pony Express," with Edward J. Montagne developing the scenario.

According to Carl Laemmle, the idea to produce *The Flaming Frontier* came to him in response to a question he asked readers of his Universal column appearing in *The Saturday*

With a superior cast and an estimated budget of $400,000 *The Flaming Frontier* **(1926) was turning out to be the most important project Edward had handled to date.**

Evening Post and *Photoplay Magazine*: What type of story did they want to see on the silver screen? Responders requested Laemmle produce "some glorious epic of American history." The battle at Little Big Horn was a perfect choice. The film was promoted as being three pictures in one, taking the viewer from a romance which formed at "Flirtation Lane," West Point, to political intrigue in Washington, and on to the sensational Indian fighting on America's last frontier. The story's climax came with Lt. Colonel George Armstrong Custer's memorable battle with a combined force of Lakota–Northern Cheyenne warriors at the Little Big Horn.

The film begins with Bob Langdon (Hoot Gibson), a Pony Express rider, receiving an appointment to West Point. His friend Custer (Dustin Farnum) uses his influence with Senator Stanwood (George Fawcett) to get Bob admitted to the military school. At the academy, Bob meets Stanwood and is introduced to the senator's son Lawrence (Harold Goodwin) and his daughter Betty (Anne Cornwall). As an outcome of a life-threatening situation, Bob and Betty take an immediate romantic interest in each other.

As the white man's settlements push further Westward, Indians become increasingly restless. In the footsteps of the settlers followed ruthless profiteers who, led by crooked Indian agent Sam Belden (Ward Crane), joined with politicians in Washington to sell whiskey and arms to the Native Americans. Attempting to bring peace in the West, Custer faces resistance from the profiteers who attempt to disgrace him before President Ulysses S. Grant (Walter Rodgers).

In retaliation for the senator aiding Custer, the plotters drag his son Lawrence into a West Point scandal that involves Sam's vamp daughter Lucretia Belden (Kathleen Key). In an effort to shield the senator and his son from scandal, Bob takes the blame for defiling Lucretia and is expelled. He decides to return West to join Custer's command.

On June 25, 1876, Custer and his Seventh United States Cavalry set out to attack the Indians massed on the Little Big Horn. The Sioux braves, aided by the renegade whites and numbering over 3,000, united under Chief Sitting Bull for an attack on the troops. Realizing he was misled about their numbers by one of Sam's henchmen, Custer sends Bob through the Indian lines with orders for Major Reno and his reinforcements to come to the rescue. Also included in the message is a confession that Lawrence made to Custer describing the true details of the scandal with Lucretia, proving Bob's innocence. Reno refuses to sacrifice his men to the amassed Indians, leaving Custer and his command of 263 soldiers and attached personnel of the U.S. Army to be massacred.

The dishonest agent, Sam, has taken the senator's daughter prisoner. In retribution for the massacre, Bob leads an uprising among the settlers against the profiteers and rescues Betty. Custer's death is avenged as Sam is killed in the confrontation.

The film's promotional material have conflicting total numbers for the number of Indians used in the battle sequences—between several hundred to over 5,000 actors—with many real Native Americans representing a number of tribes from across the country. In addition, hundreds of actors portrayed the doomed troopers.

As a director Edward already had a reputation for being a stickler when it came to shooting historical scenes, making sure that they were created as accurately as possible. Retired Colonel George S. Bryam, a West Point graduate (class of 1885), was hired to supervise the military aspects of the film, even in the battle scenes.

Among the Indians used in the battle scenes, were descendants of Indians who took part in Custer's massacre, with many wearing the clothes that their ancestors wore into battle, handed down from them to sons and grandsons. Some of the Indians were descendants of chieftains, although not all of the Sioux lineage. Chief Tall Pine was a Sioux, as well as Chief Standing Bear, the son of one of Sitting Bull's great war chiefs. Chief Big Tree and Chief White Feather descended from a long line of Iroquois chieftains. Big Tree had posed for the Indian equestrian statue "The End of the Trail," made by James Frazier for the San Francisco Exposition.

In researching Lieutenant Colonel John G. Frémont's daring triumph against the Mexican leader Pico, Edward was surprised to find that the location where Frémont camped on January 12, 1847, was now covered by the grand entrance to Universal City's administration buildings and stages. Half-heartedly Edward asked Laemmle if he wouldn't mind moving the administration building to accommodate the filming.

The scene being filmed had Frémont preparing to face Pico, who was approaching from the south with a numerically superior army. The lieutenant colonel resorted to cutting down trees and making their trunks look like cannons. Facing what he thought was a formidable line of artillery, Pico accepted defeat. In an adobe house which once stood a few feet from where the entrance to the administration building was built, Pico signed the treaty of Cahuenga.

For one *Flaming Frontier* segment it was necessary to build, at a great expense, the town of Crane City—a frontier settlement and a rendezvous point for all of the bad characters selling rifles and alcohol to the Indians—and then burn it down after only a few days of shooting. After spending time scouting around the Pendleton, Oregon, area for a suitable site surrounded by hills and a running river, Switzler Island, a location 50 miles north of Pendleton on the Columbia River, was selected.

The actors, who had already spent several months filming around the Pendleton area, along with laborers and building material, were transported by truck to the location. The first 25 miles of the trip took them over paved roads, which quickly degenerated as the procession passed through marshes. For several days a corduroy road of heavy planks was laid, a quarter of a mile at a time, with the used planks brought forward for an additional quarter mile and reused until the destination was reached. After reaching a selected point on the river opposite the island, Edward's technical advisor swam out to the island, explored it, swam back and reported it suitable for filming. Ferries were then built and the entire party and supplies were transported across the river.

After bunkhouses were assembled for the cast and crew's lodging, the town was quickly built. The razing of the buildings was one of the film's spectacles, with Bob Langdon leading his men into the town to destroy it. As its townspeople fled the burning buildings to escape the flames, they swam across the river to the opposite shore to escape the cavalrymen. Fort Hays, Custer's outpost, was recreated on the back lot in the San Fernando Valley.

Promoted by Universal as "A Spectacular Thrilling Epic of the Glorious West," the Edward Sedgwick–Universal–Super Jewel production premiered at B.S. Moss' Colony Theatre in New York City at a Saturday midnight showing on April 3, 1926. Special gold invitations were printed and delivered to leading stage and screen actors, directors, producers, and prominent government and military officials. In addition, gold souvenir coins, decorated with an Indian head on the front and the name of the film on the reverse side, were distributed to viewers. The entire front of the theater was covered by an immense sign, with cutouts of Custer and his troops in mortal combat adorning the marquee and the lobby. Positioned in the lobby was Chief Red Eagle with several Indian braves and buglers from the 71st Regiment Armory, who announced each performance for the length of the film's run at the theater.

The guest of honor at the premiere was a survivor of the Little Big Horn battle, Brigadier-General Edward S. Godfrey, who provided a "stirring moment" when he rose to take a bow. Godfrey and his troops were assigned the task of supervising the identification and burial of the dead, as they were some of the first to arrive at the site and see the aftermath of the massacre.

Dr. Hugo Riesenfeld wrote the arrangement for the showing, claiming that it was "the most inspiring screen production for which he ever wrote a musical score." According to an article appearing in the April 10 *Motion Picture News*, Riesenfeld researched the U.S. Army and the Indians of 1876 when writing his arrangements. In his performance he made use of a "frontier horn," an instrument used by Indians of the period to reproduces the sound of a brave's war cry. He purportedly used the same horn that Chief Gall took into battle at Little Big Horn.

Theater owners were asked to promote the film in exciting ways, with all types of means used to encourage ticket sales for the potential blockbuster. The manager of the Gilloz

Theater in Springfield, Missouri, arranged a street exploitation stunt to promote the film, with braves dressed in war bonnets riding horseback around the busy street in front of the theater and appearing on stage before its premiere showing. As part of Universal's national advance campaign, local publicity representatives were encouraged to invite state officials to viewings. In return the officials would send in their comments on the film. The representatives would then uses their "positive comments" in local campaigns that would praise the film's historical and patriotic qualities to educators and parents.

The Flaming Frontier received an enthusiastic reception in Sheridan, Oklahoma, one of the three official locations that commemorated the battle that year. The June 23 *Sheridan Post* reported, "Forty Chieftains and Scores of Tribes Reported Mobilized at 'Little Big Horn.'" In a published story, Universal's exploitation representative Charles R. Lounsbury interviewed a Sioux named Red Horse, who related how he struck with his tomahawk the last coup on Custer before the officer, realizing his company's defeat, took his own life.

For the most part, critics gave the film excellent reviews for its spectacular action sequences, with most complaints focused on the lackluster acting of its lead actors, including Gibson. The cast was culled from Universal's large contract roster, with Farnum emerging from a semi-retirement to play Custer. In addition to the previously mentioned actors, Eddie Gribbon, Harry Todd, Noble Johnson, Charles K. French, William Steele, Ed Wilson, and Joe Bonomo appeared.

The majority of the film is believed to be lost. Surviving stock footage of attacks on a wagon train were used in the serial *The Indians Are Coming* (1930). Possibly unintentionally, the serial, directed by Henry MacRae and starring Tim McCoy, Allene Ray, Edmund Cobb and Francis Ford, used *The Flaming Frontier*'s working title.

Eileen and William Desmond found themselves together again appearing in a serial titled *Strings of Steel*. Henry MacRae directed the ten-chapter serial, with its first chapter released at the end of June. The romantic adventure takes place in 1878, shortly after the invention of the telephone by Alexander Graham Bell. The story concerns the problems associated with the rapid growth of the telephone industry, with most of its scenes taking place in New York City's Bowery, back when it was the center of political power.

Eileen portrays Gloria Van Norton, a young lady from a wealthy family. She insists in finding her own way in the world and takes a job at the American Speaking Telephone Company as their first female telephone operator. It is there that she meets and falls in love with Ned Brown (Desmond), a young engineer who has a fearless enthusiasm for expanding the lines of the new company into hostile territory.

In defending Gloria's honor, Ned gets in a fight with the office manager, Albert J. Smith (Peter Allen), and is forced to leave the company. He finds work at American's leading competitor, the Bell Company. In the process of expanding the number of towns that subscribe to Bell's services, Ned faces a ruthless and unscrupulous gang from American who seeks to break the Bell Company and secure a monopoly. Ned proves himself a hero as he ruins the plans that American is perpetrating in order to steal contracts from Bell, and in the end he marries Gloria as his reward.

The stars are supported by Arthur Morrison as Jim Hogan, George Ovey as Willie Gray, Grace Cunard as Bowery Belle, and Alphonse Martell as Alexander Graham Bell. Stuntman Max Marx was killed when a rope snapped while he was performing a stunt.

Strings of Steel (1926) reunited Eileen and William Desmond in a story that concerns the problems associated with the rapid growth of the telephone industry. The two are shown on the cover of a photoplay book.

Eileen clearly understood the drawback of being a popular cowgirl of the silver screen: It would eventually stereotype her as a Western star. By 1926 she became restless working at Universal, so she left in search of studios that would give her more diverse and challenging roles. Looking towards the independent companies for employment, Eileen found work at Chesterfield Motion Pictures. Although Chesterfield, a fairly new film company, was only able to offer her roles in three Westerns, the low-budget films at least gave her top billing and ultimately the opportunity to play more of a variety of roles. Alan James, also known by Alvin J. Neitz, directed her three five-reel features. *Beyond All Odds*, a June release distributed by Transfax Film Productions, cast Eileen as Betty Mason, who avenges the death of her brother and the abduction of her fiancé George Baker (Karl Silvera) by killing the villains responsible for both crimes.

Thundering Speed, an August release distributed by States Rights Independent Exchanges, featured Eileen as a woman involved in a legal hassle over water rights which was instigated by a villain's scheming. With the support of a United States marshal she regains her property rights. *The Web* featured Eileen, Barney Furey, Jack Richardson, and Eddie Barry. Promoted as "the girl of the West," Eileen played Mary Anderson in this Western. In danger of being trampled by cattle, Mary's brother is rescued in the nick of time by a stranger (Furey), who is introduced as the mysterious Spider. A gang robs a stagecoach and kills Mary's father in the process. Two of the bandits are arrested, along with the Spider. They soon escape from the jailhouse. The bandits are aware that Mary's father had money, and when she discovers where he buried it they prepare to steal it from her. The Spider comes to her rescue, with the sheriff's men showing up to arrest the gang. The Spider is revealed to be a state marshal who in the end falls in love with Mary.

The Sagebrush Lady, an October feature release, starred Eileen and a cast of Chesterfield players. Rancher Paula Loring (Eileen) is threatened by a gang of cattle rustlers. The leader of the gang is her neighbor Tom Doyle (Jack Richardson), who is secretly scheming to marry Paula. Henry Hayden (Eddie Barry), a government agent, arrives in town disguised as a drifter. Henry is suspected of being a holdup man and soon faces the possibility of being lynched. Paula rescues Henry, lying that he is her fiancé. Henry returns the favor and comes to Paula's assistance when Tom's henchman (Ben Corbett) attempts to kidnap her. After the cattle-rustling gang is broken up, Hayden and Paula agree to marry. William Steele also appears as Sherriff Martin.

A November release for Chesterfield, *Lure of the West*, featured Eileen, Les Bates, Ray Childs, Dutch Maley, Alfred Hewston, Elsie Bower and Karl Silvera. An old medicine show salesman arrives in town with his daughters. The saloon owner hires one of the quack's daughters (Eileen) as an entertainer at his establishment. As the saloon owner plans to take advantage of the girl, the hero of the story is introduced and rescues her from the vile barkeep.

The "dog as an action hero" concept was developed in the 1920s by independent producers Samuel Sax, Nat Levine and Duke Worne. Primarily created for the children's market, the adventure-oriented genre usually featured a German shepherd who would heroically race to the rescue and save the day. One early canine star was the world-famous Rin-Tin-Tin, a German shepherd who premiered in the 1922 adventure *Man from Hell's River*. Rin-Tin-Tin was discovered during World War I at a bombed-out dog kennel in Lorraine, France, by U.S. Air Corporal Lee Duncan and his battalion. Duncan brought the dog back to the U.S.

and trained him to perform to cue in front of movie cameras. The Rin-Tin-Tin franchise proved to be a great success story, literally pulling Warner Bros. out of Poverty Row status, and in the process creating a formidable competitor to the matinee cowboy.

Some of the silent movie dogs that followed in Rin-Tin-Tin's tracks included Peter the Great, Fang the Marvel Dog, Thunder the Wonder Dog (a.k.a. Thunder the Marvel Dog), Silver Streak, Wolfheart, Napoleon the Dog, Champion and Ranger. Strongheart, who appeared in films before Rin-Tin-Tin, was another German shepherd who was highly merchandised during the silent era. Trained as a police dog in World War I Germany, he was transported to the U.S. by director Laurence Trimble and his wife, writer Jane Murfin. Strongheart's film debut was in *The Silent Call* (1921), and although he only "acted" in a limited number of films, his appearance in Jack London's *White Fang* (1925) made him very popular. Strongheart and Rin-Tin-Tin's colorful real-life stories of being rescued from postwar Germany influenced *Black Lightning* (1924), a Samuel Sax production starring Thunder and Clara Bow. The twist in *Black Lightning*'s story has the dog rescuing Ray Chambers, a World War I veteran played by Harold Austin, from the front line in France, instead of the war hero rescuing the dog.

In a rushed effort to get exhibitors to sign up for their new offering of canine adventures for the 1926 season, Standard Film Exchange of Kansas City prematurely ran an advertisement promoting "Lightnin' the Super Dog" in the August 1, 1925, *Reel Journal*, a southwest trade publication. Announcing that Jesse J. Goldburg would be presenting the dog "in a series of Big Timber Productions, each with a separate and distinct cash value and each a gem of motion picture artistry and action," the advertisement implied that eight titles would be available for exhibition: *His Master's Voice, Lightnin' Strikes, The Forest King, Flaming Timber, The Danger Call, Pal o' the Redwoods, The Silent Hero,* and *Crimson Fangs*. A followup advertisement in the August 15 *Reel Journal* promoted the "Super Dog" series with a cast that included Stuart Holmes and Alice Calhoun, noting that the first episode, *Lightnin' Strikes*, was to be released on September 1.

The 1926 *Film Yearbook* included an announcement from independent producer Hans Tiesler about his upcoming releases, listing twelve two-reel "International Detective Stories" featuring Eileen Sedgwick and Lightnin' the Great. The advertisement promoted Tenneck Film Corporation as the series' distributor, calling them the "World Distributors of High Class Films." By the time the Lightnin' action thrillers were released, the series was being promoted as a Sava Films presentation, with SUN Pictures Corporation being the distributor. The German shepherd was eventually promoted to Lightnin' the Police Dog.

Of the eight titles that Goldburg advertised, only *Lightnin' Strikes* was produced as a Lightnin' episode. Considering the fact that *His Master's Voice* ended up as a Thunder release and *The Silent Hero* a Napoleon release, it's possible that the dogs used in Goldburg's list of films could have been interchanged. If extant footage were available to research the titles, one might be able to determine if any of the dogs appeared in the various films using different aliases. This suggestion becomes obvious when comparing the locations of both companies involved in producing the films; the address listed for Tenneck was the same location as Chesterfield, both of which were located in the heart of New York City's Times Square district at 1540 Broadway. Chesterfield, the distributor of Joe Rock's "Fearless, the Dog Detective" series, advertised the Fearless series as twelve two-reel Van Pelt Productions. It's possible that Rock, a well-known comedy producer who previously directed Stan Laurel's two-reelers

Lightnin' the Police Dog received top billing for the first three Lightnin' films, including *Honor* (1926).

Presenter Sam Efrus then realized who the real star of the Lightnin' films was, changing the credits to give Eileen the top billing, as shown on the poster for *Vengeance* (1926).

for Film Booking Offices of America, could have conveniently used the same dog in his films that was used for the Lightnin' series.

Eileen appeared in six of the series' twelve episodes, which were directed by Hans Tiesler, William Curran, and Alan James: *Fangs, Honor, Vengeance, Lightnin' Strikes, Lightnin' Wins* and *Lightnin' Flashes*. Presenter Sam Efrus, a producer of low-budget films, gave Lightnin' top billing on promotional material for the first three films that Eileen appeared in, before he realized who the real star of the films was; he changed the credits from "Lightnin' the Police Dog with Eileen Sedgwick" to "Eileen Sedgwick with Lightnin' the Police Dog." James Vincent produced the canine's solo Lightnin' episodes, including *Claws, Rage, Speed, Instinct* and *Blitz*. Tom London appeared in the majority of the episodes as Eileen's male lead, with Frank Lackteen as the classic villain.

Lightnin' Wins, an October release, cast Eileen alongside Gary Cooper as the male lead. The supporting cast included Lackteen, Zalla Zarana and Walter Maly. Although it was a low-budget two-reeler, this was a breakthrough film for Cooper, as he previously only had minor roles in films. His next role was in Samuel Goldwyn's *The Winning of Barbara Worth* (1926), which gave him the recognition that he needed to become a major star. By 1938 Cooper was the highest paid movie star, making $370,214. According to a report released

In *Lightnin' Wins* (1926) Gary Cooper was cast against Eileen as the film's leading man. Previous to this role Cooper had only played minor parts (courtesy Edward Hutson).

by the Treasury to the House Ways and Means Committee, Ronald Colman followed Cooper with $362,500, Claudette Colbert with $350,833, and Mae West with $323,333. Charlie Chaplin was "only" making $125,000, and Edward Sedgwick $40,000.

The Spider's Net, a feature-length version of the Lightnin' films, edited together the two-reel episodes into one detective mystery. Distributed by Goodwill Pictures in 1927, with a story written and directed by James, the feature's cast included Eileen, Lightnin', Cooper, Lackteen, London, Robert Walker, Harry Semels, Wilbur McGaugh, William Lowery and Hal Water.

Eileen was reunited with Fred Church in the thriller *Temple of Terror*, an independent film produced by Fred Balshofer Productions. A decade earlier, the two had appeared in *The Temple of Terror*, a similarly titled short. In an effort to reestablish himself in the film business, Church had renamed himself Montana Bill. Balshofer, who directed the thriller, had first directed Edward in 1917's *The Haunted Pajamas*. He started his career in the motion picture industry in 1909 as a cameraman for Bison Motion Pictures.

The Runaway Express, a December Universal Jewel release, was loosely based on Frank H. Spearman's popular 1910 short story "The Nerve of Foley." Directed by Edward, the railroad-themed thriller featured Jack Dougherty as Joseph Foley, Tom O'Brien as Sandy

Edward directed *The Runaway Express* (1926), which featured Blanche Mehaffey and Jack Dougherty. The scenario was loosely based on Frank H. Spearman's popular short story from 1910, titled "The Nerve of Foley."

McPherson, and Blanche Mehaffey as Nora Kelly, with supporting roles played by Charles K. French, William Steele, Harry Todd, Madge Hunt and Syd Saylor.

In the film's story Joseph is given a job as the Limited's engineer. Sandy, who unsuccessfully competed for the job, knocks him unconscious in an effort to get the position. Planning on robbing the gold shipment on the train, Blackie, Sandy's outlaw brother, drugs the engineer, not realizing that it's Sandy who has taken Joseph's position at the throttle. Passengers aboard the train include Joseph's mother and girlfriend Nora. Without an engineer at its brakes, the train is headed towards a washed-out stretch of tracks. Foley regains consciousness and, without a minute to spare, races on his horse to catch up with the runaway train, jumping aboard at the last minute to halt the train, saving it from a catastrophe.

Edward's big break came with the November release *Tin Hats*, his first directorial assignment for MGM. The studio promoted the film as the sequel to their highly successful World War I film from the previous year, *The Big Parade*, starring John Gilbert and Renée Adorée. Directed by King Vidor, *The Big Parade* tells the story of an idle rich young man who is sent to France to fight for America in World War I, the relationship he has with two working class men as they go to battle, and the French girl he falls in love with and returns for after the war is over. Aside from *Tin Hats*, the precedent-setting dramatic film influenced a string of comedies in 1926, which included *What Price Glory*, *Behind the Front* and its follow-up *We're in the Navy Now*.

It's very possible that Vidor put in a good word for Edward, as the studio placed their trust in Edward for the highly publicized film. He was given all the perks that came with working on an MGM film: set decorations supervised by Cedric Gibbons, costumes designed by André-ani, exhibition material illustrated by renowned artist John Held, Jr., and a notable cast that included Conrad Nagel and Claire Windsor. Edward even secured an uncredited part for Eileen.

Edward wrote the story for *Tin Hats*, a comedy that sounded very similar to an adventure story he wrote with Ralph Spence in 1920, Fox's *Sink or Swim*. Spence, coincidentally, or maybe not coincidentally, did the titles for *Tin Hats*. The story begins with buddies Jack Benson (Nagel), "Dutch" Krausmeyer (Bert Roach), and "Lefty" Mooney (George Cooper) preparing to go overseas to fight for their country. After traveling to Europe by boat, they end their journey "somewhere in France," in a trench on the front lines. At zero hour, just as they are about to go over the top, the lieutenant receives a letter notifying his troops that the Armistice has commenced. Upset that they didn't have a chance to fight as doughboys and collect war souvenirs to show off to their friends and families back home, they go in search for medals and weapons that might have been left behind by the enemy. While they are visiting a photographer to get pictures taken of them wearing prop medals and holding German helmets, they become separated from their unit. Grabbing bicycles from the front of the photographer's shop, they ride in search of their division. A passing car that splashed mud on them comes to a stop as it gets a flat tire. Jack takes an interest in the passenger, Elsa von Bergen (Windsor), who tells him that she loathes all Americans as they killed her father and brother in the war.

As is the case with many other films produced during this period, *Tin Hats* is assumed to be lost. The following description from *Tin Hats*' continuity script gives the reader a fair impression of how Edward would have set up the scene where Jack introduces himself to Elsa—an ambitious, and most likely dizzying tracking shot.

Edward's big break at MGM came with the directorial assignment of *Tin Hats* (1926). Starring Conrad Nagel, it also featured Eileen in a bit part (third and fourth from left).

SCENE 220: PANNING SHOT OF ELSA, FROM JACK'S ANGLE.

The camera likes the position of Jack on the bicycle, and moves around Elsa in the car in a complete circle, keeping the focus on her, so that we see her from every angle continuously. When the camera has gone around her completely, it comes to a stop and then moves up in a direct line towards her until we have a semi–close-up of her in profile to the camera, the impression of the scene being that Jack has ridden in a complete circle around the car, has then dismounted from the bicycle, and has advanced to the running board of the car.

The chauffeur fixes the flat and Elsa drives off, leaving the trio behind. They continue to follow the road and unknowingly cross the border into Germany, ending up in a small town. As they arrive, the war-wary villagers think that they are members of the Army of Occupation that is supposed to take charge of the town, so they are given a royal welcome. Jack recognizes Elsa in a tavern and finds out that she is an aristocrat on her way to a castle she has inherited from her uncle. He gets an idea on how to keep her in the town, and lies that no one can leave the town while the Army of Occupation is stationed there. Jack courts Elsa while Lefty and Dutch enjoy the tavern's food, beer, and women, including a barmaid named Frieda (Eileen).

The trio decides to investigate the castle, which they find to be haunted. In reality, the spooks who are hiding behind secret panels, or are dressed in coats of armor, are Elsa's servants, who fear that the soldiers intend to harm her. Before Elsa realizes who the ghosts are, a melee breaks out between the servants and doughboys. As the trio prepares to exit the castle, they enter its great hall, coming face to face with their sergeant (Tom O'Brien), who places them under arrest.

Jack, Lefty and Dutch are charged with being "Absent without leave," "Stealing French property, v.z. three bicycles," "Occupying the village of Schlossheim without due authority," and "Violating the armistice by invading the castle Schwarzzimmer." Locked in a cell at the brigade headquarters, they fear a court-martial and time at Leavenworth. An orderly opens the brigade's door and Elsa enters, followed by a crowd of Germans. As they pour into the room, she makes a plea for them, insisting that they have established friendly relations in the occupied territory.

In the final scene, Lefty and Dutch are on a transport headed to America. Jack and Elsa are at the rail looking at the Statue of Liberty.

SCENE 642: That's the only girl you'll ever have to be jealous of.

FADE OUT

THE END.

With his successful MGM directorial debut completed, Edward had crossed another Rubicon. The studio was entering its Golden Age, which had commenced with its epic production of *Ben-Hur* (1925). As MGM's head, Louis B. Mayer had stated his vision earlier in his career: to promote great talent and stories in his films, without sparing the expense to make them great. This certainly was an arrangement that Edward liked.

Nagel worked with Edward on a second MGM, *There You Are!*, based on F. Hugh Herbert's play of the same name. Nagel played downtrodden bookkeeper George Fenwick, who falls in love with his employer's daughter Joan Randolph (Edith Roberts). Through a chain of events George gets involved in a kidnapping scare and captures a bandit, becoming a hero and gaining Joan's affection and promise of marriage.

The Times-Picayune gave Edward a rave review: "Farce is a form hard to handle on the screen, but the director, Edward Sedgwick, did his job swiftly and fearlessly. He romped through his picture holding a high tempo, building up novel situations and getting the best out of his players. There are chuckles enough in the result."

Nagel was part of the group of film industry members, which included Windsor, Mary Pickford, Douglas Fairbanks, Harold Lloyd, Richard Barthelmess, Jack Holt, and Milton Sills, who founded the Academy of Motion Picture Arts and Sciences (AMPAS) on May 11, 1927. In 1932 and 1933 Nagel served as president of the professional honorary organization that is dedicated to the advancement of the arts and sciences of motion pictures. He was also a founding member of the film actors' labor union, the Screen Actors Guild. In 1927, Nagel starred alongside Lon Chaney, Marceline Day, Henry B. Walthall and Polly Moran in the much-talked-about lost horror classic *London After Midnight*, directed by Tod Browning.

Although MGM's directors were allowed a certain amount of creativity, an entire production would have been closely scrutinized by a producer. Edward was already growing accustomed to the industry-wide changes that were happening, as the major studios were implementing rules and regulations which were being supervised by a fairly inflexible system.

The jack-of-all-trades director was a thing of the past. This was just one of the challenges that the Sedgwicks would face as the motion picture industry was entering a new era.

Notes

1. *Big U: Universal in the Silent Days*, I.G. Edmonds, Cranbury, NJ: A.S. Barnes, 1977.
2. *The Reel Journal*, March 6, 1926, page 4.
3. *An Evening's Entertainment: The Age of the Silent Feature Picture 1915–1928*, Richard Koszarski, Berkeley, CA: 1994, University of California Press, pages 211–213.

CHAPTER SIX

The Rise of the Almighty Studio System and the Fall of the Silent Film

Towards the end of the 1920s, the industry's "Big Five" motion picture studios—MGM, Paramount, RKO, Fox, and Warner Bros.—coalesced into a powerful force that was to be known as the studio system. With a factory-like structure in place, the studios operated under a central producer system that closely supervised all productions. The system was developed as a means of delivering a steady and timely supply of quality feature films, a way to keep production costs under control, and as an assurance that all films conformed to a studio's style. As part of the process, the pre-production, production and post-production staffs were responsible for reporting their work status to a producer, who would then report to a top producer team. In such a system, a central producer at a West Coast facility would usually report directly to the executive team located at a studio's East Coast business headquarters so that they could efficiently monitor the filming and editing process.

MGM's formation was one of the industry's driving forces that compartmentalized the responsibilities of the industry's employees. The studio, which would become known for its glamorous and sophisticated films, was a conglomerate of several companies acquired by Marcus Loew, owner of the Loew's Incorporated theater chain. Loew purchased Metro Pictures Corporation in 1920 as a means of integrating his company into the motion picture marketplace. Metro possessed a nationwide distribution network and a working studio in Los Angeles that would be able to produce the quantity of titles that Loew's theaters required to stay competitive. Although the acquisition of Metro's exchanges helped create the international network that Loew's sought, Metro could not deliver the quality or quantity of films that this new setup demanded.

Spurred on by 1923's industry-wide recession, Loew was prepared to sell Metro's studio to concentrate on the distribution side of his company, leaving himself without a ready supply of motion pictures. By chance, Goldwyn Pictures, a similarly integrated company, went up for sale in 1924. Owned by Joe Godsol, Goldwyn's strength was its huge Culver City production studio. The forty-acre studio, originally built for Thomas Ince's Triangle Pictures, included a large office building, stages, bungalows, processing and editing labs, and the necessary shops required to dress actors and stages. In addition, the offer included contracted actors, directors, cinematographers, and other skilled workers. The purchase of the Culver

City studio would complete Loew's aggressive plan by creating a merger that would utilize Goldwyn's motion picture output, Metro's exchange network and Loew's theater chain.

Loew placed Nicholas Schenck, his chief lieutenant and the person responsible for film bookings for his New York theaters, in charge of pursuing the Goldwyn deal. In the meantime, Robert Rubin, a top executive who came to work for Loew's through the Metro merger, was placed in charge of recruiting a manager who could efficiently run Goldwyn's Culver City studio and produce the first-class films that Loew insisted upon showing in his theaters.

Rubin's choice to fill the executive position was producer Louis B. Mayer. Mayer, who had already worked for Metro, was now owner of Louis B. Mayer Pictures, which he opened in 1918. Rubin was impressed by Mayer's record as a successful independent producer, and upon his recommendation, Loew hired Mayer as vice-president and made him the head of California studio operations. Mayer brought along his two aides Harry Rapf and Irving Thalberg, who were already valuable production executives. In the spring of 1924 Loew acquired Mayer Pictures, merging it with Metro-Goldwyn to form Metro-Goldwyn-Mayer.

Working at smaller studios, Josie and Eileen would experience the effects of the studio system, but their experiences would pale in comparison to the shift of power that Edward was experiencing working for MGM under Mayer's management. Whereas the director of Hollywood's pioneer days could insert himself into every aspect of filmmaking—producing, writing and editing—under the control of Mayer, Edward was now only responsible for directing and was held responsible for doing so by his producer. But for Edward, the opportunity to direct at a studio like MGM was exactly what he wanted.

A landmark year for the major studios, 1927 marked the beginning of what was to become the "Golden Age of Hollywood," a period which would span three decades. MGM, soon to be known as the studio that had "more stars than there are in Heaven," excelled at the box office throughout this era, creating the Hollywood star system with its top actors and actresses. MGM employed an efficient publicity department, operated by over 100 employees, which was responsible for sustaining the wholesome images of the idols that the public obsessed over though the fan magazines. The studio collaborated with the press in keeping any of the actors' transgressions out of print; in exchange the publications were given access to MGM's top stars.

At the time MGM's roster included Greta Garbo, Ronald Colman, Lillian Gish, and Wallace Beery; with Ramon Novarro, Viola Dana, Jackie Coogan, Buster Keaton, and Monte Blue acquired from Metro; Mae Murray, Blanche Sweet, Aileen Pringle, Eleanor Boardman, Mae Busch, John Gilbert, Conrad Nagel, and Marion Davies from Goldwyn; and Lon Chaney, Renée Adorée, Norma Shearer, Huntley Gordon, and Hedda Hopper from Mayer. One of the holdovers from Goldwyn was William Haines, an actor who was on his way to becoming a top-five box-office star. Along with actress Eleanor Boardman, Haines had entered the industry by winning an acting contract in Goldwyn's "New Faces" contest of 1922. By 1926 he had already acted in twenty-six films, with most of his performances going unnoticed, as they were minor parts or a background extra. At MGM he was found to have a flair for playing the part of an arrogant young adult whose large ego held him back from achieving success.

Starting with his first hit, *Brown of Harvard* (1926), a football-themed film, Haines was typically cast as an athlete who competed with a rival student for the coveted title and the affection of the girl, in this case played respectively by Francis X. Bushman Jr., and Mary Brian. *Photoplay*'s July edition described *Brown of Harvard* as a "flip and lively" film of college life, agreeing that Haines was ideally cast as Tom Brown. "He makes the football team and gets scratched in his first big game. The only girl drops him. But Tom wisecracks on until Doolittle [Jack Pickford], having run through the rain to tell him of his second chance on the football team, dies of pneumonia." MGM discovered the formula to be a profitable one and stuck to it for a number of Haines' movies: young wisecracking hero realizes his shortcomings, redeems himself, gets the girl at the end.

Several of these stories included a hero-worship thread which wove in subtle homosexual relationships between Haines' character and his roomies or bunkmates (Doolittle in *Brown of Harvard*) who was the only one on campus or in camp who truly believed in him. Although the scenarios only hinted at the relationships, ones that would have been taboo for MGM to present in detail on-screen, in reality Haines was gay. This worried Mayer, as he always promoted his movies as being wholesome entertainment. Mayer was concerned that if Haines' sexual orientation was made public, people might boycott the features. Haines refused to hide his preference as Mayer had asked him to, and eventually left acting to form a successful interior decorating business that catered to Hollywood clientele.

Following *Brown of Harvard*, Haines' success became apparent in *Tell It to the Marines* (1926), a film that featured a dominant role for Lon Chaney. Although *Photoplay* described Haines' appearance in *Brown of Harvard* as that of a wisecracker, an acting trait that appeared to be a natural one, it was *Tell It to the Marines* that cemented that image for him. Haines was the embodiment of the free-spirited youth who came of age during the 1920s; the children who grew up deprived and repressed during the years of the Great War when all made enormous sacrifices.

On the success of the leatherneck comedy, MGM quickly teamed Haines with Edward on three consecutive features, the first of which was *Slide, Kelly, Slide*, released in March 1927. In addition to Haines, the light comedy's top-notch cast was comprised of petite Sally O'Neil as the tomboyish Mary Munson, Harry Carey as a veteran Yankees catcher and Mary's sympathetic father, Tom "Pop" Munson, and Karl Dane as the lanky pitcher Swede Hansen. Frank Coghlan, Jr., played Mickey Martin, an orphaned child and New York Yankees fan who follows them around as their unofficial water boy. "An Edward Sedgwick Production," the baseball-themed film also featured a mix of major league baseball celebrities who all played themselves: Mike Donlin, Tony Lazzeri, Taylor Douthit, Chick Hafey, and brothers Emil and Bob Meusel.

The story unfolds as the New York Yankees are training at their winter camp in Florida. Jim "No Hit" Kelly (Haines), a talented pitcher without any major league experience, is one of the rookies expected to arrive by train. As he disembarks he immediately takes an interest in Mary Munson. Mary could easily be mistaken to be a boy, as she is dressed in a very masculine sports sweater and is wearing her short hair parted in a man's style. Kelly makes a move on her with a "Hello, cutie!"—leaving one to wonder if Kelly had determined her sexual vagueness before making his remark.

Upon meeting his teammates, Kelly turns up his smartaleck personality, boasting about his pitching skills. Rooming with Swede, he befriends Mickey after he finds out that the boy is homeless. It soon becomes apparent that Mickey worships Kelly as the team's hero. In the process, Kelly is encouraged by the kid to become a better man.

Kelly gets a swelled head as fans become ecstatic over his pitches during a no-hit game against the Cleveland Indians, with the Yankees winning the game. After Kelly refuses to slide home on a close play and is called "out!" the team's manager (Donlin) reprimands him for not taking his advice on the slide. Kelly insists that his pitching is all that the team needs to rely on to win a game. After going out on a bender, he returns to the hotel in an inebriated state. He berates his team, and especially Pop Munson, letting them know in no uncertain terms that they'd be nowhere without his pitching.

Kelly realizes that he has let his team down with his behavior, and thinking that they would perform better without him he returns to New York after being suspended indefinitely. However, the team decides they need him after all and they set out to look for him when they return to the Bronx to play against the St. Louis Cardinals in the final game of the World Series. In search of Kelly, Mickey rides his bicycle down the busy streets and is hit by a car. Kelly is found and he returns to pitch in the game, a bit raggedly though as he has lost his desire to play. The ninth inning score is St. Louis 1–New York 0. Mickey is released from the hospital and arrives at the game just in time to cheer Kelly on, with Kelly regaining his spirit when he sees the bandaged boy in the crowd. With the score now tied, Kelly, in a last effort, slides into home plate and the Yankees win.

For Edward, an ardent baseball fan, this was another heavensent directorial assignment. He previously directed Hoot Gibson's baseball film *Hit and Run* in 1924, which also featured Donlin. Some of the footage seen in *Slide, Kelly, Slide* was filmed at the World Series of the previous year, when the Cardinals played the Yankees at Yankee Stadium, with many of the game highlights used throughout the movie. During the summer following *Slide, Kelly, Slide*'s release, Bob Meusel became a key member of the 1927 New York Yankees, which added to the film's appeal as it continued to make its rounds in the theaters throughout that year. Considered by baseball enthusiasts to be one of the greatest teams ever, the 1927 Yankees lineup, nicknamed "Murderer's Row," defeated the Pittsburgh Pirates in the World Series.

Eileen placed an uncredited part in *Slide, Kelly, Slide*, giving her limited screen time. However, what started out as a minor role unexpectedly found Eileen mentioned nationally in the entertainment columns of newspapers, with the headline "FISTS TOO HEAVY, SAYS EXTRA." Playing an overenthusiastic fan seated in the bleachers, with Bronx-accented intertitles ("Pretty fieldin', Saint Looo-oo-ie! Good-bye, Noo Yawk!"), her character taunted Kelly as he pitched. Eileen was instructed to throw herself into the part by crushing the hat and messing up the hair of a nearby spectator. In her exuberance Eileen accidentally punched actor Basil Webb in the nose, teeth, and one eye. In June, three months after *Slide, Kelly, Slide*'s release, Webb, supported by the United States Fidelity and Guaranty Company, took his case before the State Industrial Accident Commission to ask for compensation. Although in one scene it did appear that Eileen's character gave the spectator at least one good whack on his head with her hand, it was unlikely that there were any real injuries sustained as she would have been skilled in the art of throwing fake punches, a staple routine used in action films.

Karl Dane, an actor who had recently found stardom in his role in King Vidor's huge hit *The Big Parade* (1925), was tentatively teamed with Eileen for a comedy release titled *Red Pants*. Although Eileen and Dane didn't appear together onscreen in *Slide, Kelly, Slide*, their off-screen chemistry must have proved to be successful enough for MGM to develop a feature starring the two of them. The 1927 *Film Daily Year Book* included an advertisement for Edward, announcing that he was now working for MGM and would be responsible for directing five films: *There You Are*, *Tin Hats*, *Slide, Kelly, Slide*, *Red Pants* and *The West Pointer*. Although *The West Pointer* would be released in 1928 as *West Point*, *Red Pants* was shelved.

Haines and Edward's second collaboration *Spring Fever* was released in October and was another hit for Haines. Contrary to what Elinor Glyn had to say in her article in the March 1927 *Photoplay* about Haines not having "It" (Clara Bow, John Gilbert, Greta Garbo, Pola Negri, Douglas Fairbanks, and Gary Cooper had "It"), the movie proved to be his biggest success to date.

The drama also featured another up-and-coming star, Joan Crawford. She wasn't yet getting the top billing but the industry and moviegoers were quickly taking notice of her. Just a few years earlier, in 1925, Crawford had arrived in Hollywood as a motivated chorus girl, with aspirations of making it big in the movies. She had previously worked alongside Haines in *Sally, Irene and Mary* (1925), an opportunity that started their lifelong friendship. Additional support was given by George K. Arthur as Eustace Tewksbury, George Fawcett as Mr. Waters, Bert Woodruff as Pop Kelly, Eileen Percy as Martha Lomsdom, and Lee Moran as Oscar.

In *Spring Fever* Haines plays Jack Kelly, a shipping clerk whose only ambition in life is to play golf. (In real life Haines loathed golf, as he hated most of the sports that he pretended to excel at in his movies.) His boss, Mr. Waters, is so impressed with his golf swing that in exchange for golfing lessons he gets Jack a two-week guest membership at the prestigious Oakmont Country Club.

As Jack arrives at the club he sets his eyes on young member Allie Montestar (Crawford). He immediately comes on to her, but a bit too coarsely, resulting in Allie putting a bit of distance between them. On the golf course Allie warms up to him as he attempts to give her instructions. Her boyfriend, the club's current champion, is jealous.

The other club members are impressed with Jack's game and favor him to win the trophy in their upcoming golf tournament. During the tournament Jack's boss, Mr. Waters, becomes excited with Jack's performance and starts to introduce himself to spectators as Jack's uncle. Jack wins the tournament as he breaks the course record for all 18 holes.

To Jack's dismay, his father, a laborer at the same factory where Jack works, shows up after the tournament to congratulate his son. Jack becomes upset with him as he is reminded that it's time to go back home as his vacation is over. Jack refuses to leave and insists that somehow he will get the money he needs to live the country club lifestyle that he is becoming used to. He will marry for money!

Jack is about to propose to Allie when she tells him that her father has lost all his money. Now *she* must marry a man for *his* money. Jack attempts to confess to her his true status in society, but instead runs off with her to elope.

After registering at a posh hotel as Mr. and Mrs. Jack Kelly, he comes to his senses, realizing that he can hardly afford the $22 per day room charge. Jack gets his nerve back and confesses to her that he was lying about his social position and being wealthy. Heartbroken, Jack leaves her to find someone else who could afford to support the lifestyle she demands.

Mr. Waters, who turns out to be Allie's uncle, visits her at the hotel room. They discuss the fact that they were testing Jack's love for Allie, and determined that he actually loved her for herself, and not for the money that he once thought she had—the money that she still had—as she tricked him into believing that she was penniless. The movie almost predictably ends with Jack winning a $10,000 golf tournament prize and the love of Allie, as she cheers him on from the back row of a crowd of spectators.

Although Edward's previous credentials more than qualified him to be chosen to direct *Spring Fever*, his camera direction for the film didn't appear to be anything more elaborate then a standard use of long, medium and close-up shots. The success of *Spring Fever* didn't rely upon its technical direction, but instead upon the direction of the relationship that was forming between the film's two main characters as portrayed by Haines and Crawford. It was apparent that the actors had onscreen chemistry but it was up to Edward to get them to perform for the camera as if their romantic relationship was a natural one. He succeeded.

West Point, Edward and Haines' third collaboration, premiered in New York City on December 31. The story was filmed over a period of about five weeks at the United States Military Academy and aboard the famous steamer *De Witt Clinton*, with the cast and crew rooming at the Thayer Hotel in Highland Falls, New York. Overall, *West Point* was the most ambitious Haines movie up till that time. As with his preceding films, there were touches in the scenario which previously proved to be successful: the proliferation of Haines' wisecracks and one-liners throughout the story; he flirts with and manages to offend a pretty

It was apparent that William Haines and Joan Crawford's chemistry worked well onscreen, so MGM placed them back under Edward's direction for *West Point* (1927).

young girl; through the compassion of a close friend he overcomes his personal flaws, helping him to triumph at an important sporting event; the girl falls head-over-heels for him after he redeems himself.

Haines, appearing as West Point candidate Brice Wayne, arrives at the military institute carrying his luggage: a suitcase, a set of golf clubs, and a ukulele. Wisecracking from the get-go, his first intertitle reads, "Wire the Academy that General Nuisance is arriving! Have a flock of Colonels meet me!" Before he disembarks the ferry that is transporting him to West Point, Brice ogles charming Betty Channing (Crawford), the daughter of the owner of the West Point Hotel. Although he is an irritation to Betty, she is secretly interested in him.

At the academy he's billeted with a slightly built cadet named "Tex" McNeil (William Bakewell). Tex takes an instant liking to his new roommate, to a point of hero worship, with Brice reciprocating by taking a protective interest in him.

It's soon October and the academy's football season is underway. The press takes notice of Brice's athletic ability, with headlines exclaiming, "Brice Wayne's Brilliant Playing Boots Army Half Back to Big Lead Among Eastern Point Scores." As his head grows larger, his smartaleck attitude gets worse, with Betty lecturing him that he has no respect for anyone. Although she still admires him, she lets him know in no uncertain terms that they have absolutely nothing in common.

When Brice arrives late for practice, Coach Towers (Major Raymond G. Moses) orders him sidelined. A member of the press approaches Brice and asks why he's sitting on the bench. Brice's reply ends up a headline in the next day's newspaper: "Brice Wayne, Star Army Player, Decries Coach's Favoritism Among Football Players." The coach approaches him, asking him if he had anything to do with the content of the article, to which Brice replies, "To hell with the Corps!" Fearing that Brice would be shunned by West Pointers for life, Tex pleads for him to apologize. In a building rage Brice strikes Tex on his face, knocking him across the room into a row of lockers. Running after Brice, Tex trips down a flight of stairs, causing additional injury. Tex approaches the football team and tries to explain that, although Brice doesn't show it, he actually has a great deal of team spirit. In the excitement of getting them to listen to his explanation, Tex passes out due to a concussion. The Honor Committee that was planning to silence Brice decides to postpone the action until after Tex recovers. Brice mails a letter of resignation to the superintendent before visiting Tex in the hospital. After asking Tex for his forgiveness, he is convinced not to resign from West Point— but the letter has already been delivered.

On the morning of the big Army-Navy game, Brice meets with the superintendent. He pleads for a second chance and is given his resignation back after the superintendent is convinced that he truly does have school spirit. The superintendent orders him to join the rest of the cadets who are already on their way to the match. He apologizes to the coach and is allowed to sit on the sideline to watch the game. The final quarter's score is 0–3 in favor of Navy. With only five minutes left in the game, the coach sends Brice in to replace an injured player, ordering, "I want a touchdown, understand?" Brice repeatedly gets possession of the ball, driving it closer and closer to the Army goal line. With the clock running down he injures his right arm but ignoring the pain, makes the game's decisive goal, ending the match at Navy 3, Army 6. At the goal post he apologizes to his team just before he passes out from the pain.

After the graduation ceremony, Brice approaches Betty, this time as a perfect gentleman. The two embrace and kiss as Tex plays a minstrel song on the ukulele.

West Point ads presented Haines as a sheik on campus, with advertisements running the ad lines, "His ideas of Field Maneuvers weren't military, they meant a petting party! While the other 'kadets' studies War, he studied Love." What was different in this film was that the love interest aspect of *West Point* had less weight than it did in *Slide, Kelly, Slide* and *Spring Fever*. The first part of the movie is full of extreme wisecracking, which Haines performs flawlessly, creating the type of arrogant character that one quickly grows to hate. As the story unfolds, Brice's remarks get nastier and are no longer funny, seeming to become almost pathetic as he uses them to hide his emotional issues. The second half of the film becomes a story of Brice's coming of age, as he learns through teamwork and caring for others that that the world doesn't revolve around him. His attraction to Betty becomes secondary to the story's greater arc.

Crawford played a supporting character, but within the next few years she would go on to acting in more demanding films for MGM. She was already getting the same kind of exposure as the best of their stars. After the success of *West Point*, Crawford's facsimile signature and an image of her, dressed in a negligee, appeared in advertisements for Lux Toilet Soap, with Crawford confessing, "I have tried innumerable French soaps—but never have I had anything like Lux Toilet Soap for keeping my skin fresh and smooth. 'Studio skin' is the all-important asset for a star." In the ad, Edward is quoted as saying, "People open their hearts instantly to the appealing loveliness of exquisite skin and every star knows how essential it is to have beautiful smooth skin. No makeup can fake it in the glare of a close-up."

Edward's direction for *West Point* was more advanced than the work he did for *Slide, Kelly, Slide* and *Spring Fever*. The scenes flowed tightly from one to the other, with an excellent use of varying angles of the same scene. Considering all of the Western adventure films he directed, Edward must have been very comfortable shooting the film's outdoor scenes. There were many open space shots created for *West Point*, such as the cadets in training and the Army-Navy football game, which Edward handled capably. His *West Point* crew included assistant director Edward Brophy, who previously appeared in *Spring Fever* as an uncredited actor and would later appear as a character actor in several movies that Edward directed. Brophy started his career in movies in 1919 in small parts, switching to behind-the-scenes work for job security.

Irving Thalberg, Louis B. Mayer's second-in-command, would have been the chief of production during the writing, filming and editing of the movies Edward worked on. Thalberg's relationship with Mayer began in 1923 when Metro recruited him from Universal where he was working as a production supervisor. Nicknamed "the Boy Wonder" for the mature decision-making skill he possessed at such a young age, Thalberg had a nose for marketable story properties. His perfectionism and dedication to his job were responsible for producing the type of quality features that the public demanded, and the better theater owners insisted on showing.

Edward was next assigned to direct *The Bugle Call*, an action melodrama that took place at a frontier cavalry post in the Great Plains during the 1870s. Written by C. Gardner Sullivan, the story featured child actor Jackie Coogan as Billy Randolph, a young bugler mourning the death of his mother. His father Capt. Randolph (Herbert Rawlinson) has now married Alice Tremayne (Claire Windsor), who as his stepmother attempts to fill the void left in the boy's heart. The cast is filled out with Tom O'Brien as cavalry sergeant Doolan, Harry Todd as Corp. Jansen, and Nelson McDowell and Sarah Padden as a frontier husband-and-wife team.

Despite the fact that *The Bugle Call* was profitable for MGM, Coogan was experiencing the beginning of his career's decline, with fewer adolescent parts available for the 13-year-old. When he had appeared with Josie in *Daddy* back in 1923, he was one of the highest paid players in Hollywood. But now he had outgrown the roles that utilized his trademark pageboy haircut, oversized overalls, and cap—jobs that helped him amass an estimated $4 million. Unfortunately, the money he earned as a child actor, the money which would have allowed Coogan to live a life of luxury while being unemployed between acting assignments, was being spent on extravagances by his mother Lilian and stepfather Arthur Bernstein. He attempted to sue them in 1935, but due to the absence of written laws that protected the earnings of child actors, he failed to get any of the money back. At the end of the trial Coogan only received $126,000 after his legal expenses were paid.

Aside from the uncredited part in *Slide, Kelly, Slide*, Eileen's only other screen appearances for 1927 were in a compilation feature of the Lightnin' series, titled *The Spider's Net*, the drama *When Danger Calls*, and a re-released oater with Joe Moore, re-titled *The Price of Youth*. She was in a situation similar to Coogan's in that she was finding a decrease in the

Edward was guaranteed the use of MGM's star-studded contract players for future projects, including Jackie Coogan for *The Bugle Call* (1927).

available opportunities to play the type of roles that she was experienced in playing. By now the part of the female action hero was practically nonexistent, with the serial and series format finding little if any support in the movie magazines. Although Eileen had a good deal of experience playing dramatic roles, she realized that she was typecast as a serial queen and would need to change her image. Her attempt to do so through the Lightnin' series didn't give her the big boost that she was hoping for, as it did for Gary Cooper. She also found that she was competing with newer actresses who were filling the challenging dramatic roles that she was interested in receiving—causing her to think that maybe, at 30, she should consider retiring from motion pictures altogether.

In an effort to reinvent herself, Eileen took the exotic-sounding stage name of Gretel Yoltz. Although the name change was leaked to the public through the press, it likely fooled many, and may have even helped her get a role in *A Girl in Every Port,* a film that many contemporary critics recognize as a significant American film.

According to Eileen she went to interview with Howard Hawks concerning a part in the film. She recollected in the April 1928 issue of *Photoplay* that Hawks said, "I want a girl like Eileen Sedgwick, only not so heavy." "What's your name?" he asked her. Eileen responded, "Gretel Yoltz." (She thought that Hawks was kidding and gave him the first name that she could think of—that of a former maid.) "Gretel" got the part. Still thinking that Hawks was joking, Eileen kidded him about not realizing who she really was. He seemed amused, but seriously advised her to keep the new name.

Written and directed by Hawks, *A Girl in Every Port* was released on February 26, 1928. Hawks started his motion picture career as a property man for Famous Players–Lasky. He had a strong desire to direct but he wasn't given the opportunity to do so until he was asked to work at Fox. *A Girl in Every Port,* his fifth directorial assignment for Fox, was destined to become a film of great importance as it broke new ground with its evolved style of direction. During the silent era, however, American critics panned his films, stating that they were uninspiring and showed a lack of artistic ambition. Criticized as a commercial director, Hawks was said to lack originality. While *A Girl in Every Port* performed well at the box office in the United States, it became extremely popular in the overseas market, especially in France. French film critics viewed Hawks as a distinctive filmmaker who was instrumental in changing the look and feel of the way movies were presented. Whereas American critics tended to view Hawks' films as nothing more than a combination of learned techniques that he picked up working in Hollywood, the French celebrated the subtleties that made his films superior. Jean-George Auriol, editor of *La Revue du Cinéma,* critiqued *A Girl in Every Port* for the December 1928 issue, pointing out that as an innovator of a new school of directing, Hawks could be distinguished from other directors by the following qualities: "[H]is simplifying style, the way he composes films through violent cuts, the astonishing seductiveness of his images." Decades later, in retrospect, the film would be recognized as the earliest appearance of contemporary cinema, with Hawks having the honor of becoming the first American auteur director.

Hawks came up with the concept for *A Girl in Every Port* as a follow-up to Fox's 1926 box office hit *What Price Glory?,* changing the main characters from doughboys to merchant seamen. The story was based on the exploits of sailors Spike Madden (Victor McLaglen) and Salami (changed to Bill in some versions due to its sexual connotation) (Robert Armstrong), and how their competition for the same women at foreign ports created a profound friendship between the two. The team would go on to became infamous in ports the world over: "As time went on, sailors spoke of them together—like Tom and Jerry—Rock and Rye."

The film opens with Spike sailing his tramp steamer into the port of Amsterdam and looking forward to his next romance, noting in his black book that he hasn't seen her in over four years. As he greets her at her doorstep, he is taken aback to see that she now has three young children and a husband. Walking away in dismay, he makes eye contact with a smiling Dutch girl (Eileen). The two ride off on a tandem bicycle into the windmill-covered countryside, taking a spill as they awkwardly pedal down a dirt road. While they romantically cuddle on the side of the road, Spike notices that she's wearing a bracelet with an anchor-in-heart charm dangling from it. Infuriated, he demands to know where she got it. "Ach! Mine heart goes pitty-pat ven I think of such a sailor!" she responds with eyes aflutter. "I'm tired of finding his heart and anchor mark on my women!" Spike says as he stomps away in frustration.

Eileen's onscreen appearance lasts for slightly over two minutes—just long enough for the audience to notice her presence as she helps to set up the story's theme. Although Auriol briefly praised Eileen's role in his review—"I will take my turn at mentioning the beauty of the little Dutch girl"—he failed to credit the girl in Holland to either "Gretel Yolz" or "Eileen Sedgwick," as he did with Maria Alba's role as the "little Argentinean." It's likely that Auriol experienced a disconnect between Eileen's new name and her onscreen appearance, dressed in a Dutch bonnet and a pair of long blonde braids. Without a doubt, Auriol would have recognized her true name if it was listed in the credits, as her films were regularly shown in Europe. In a way, the result would have been the effect Eileen was originally hoping for: giving her a new identity. On the other hand, the plan might not have gone exactly as expected, as it seemed that many reviewers dismissed Gretel Yoltz as an unknown actress, without giving her credit similar to Auriol, and focusing only on the names of the recognizable actresses, as minor as their parts were. To make matters worse, *The New York Times'* Mordaunt Hall totally ignored Eileen's role in his February 20 review—a role which is second to that of the film's leading actress—giving credit to actresses who have less prominent screen time: "Maria Casajuana is a girl in Buenos Aires. The Panama beauties are impersonated by Natalie Joyce, Dorothy Mathews and Elena Jurado. Sally Rand is the Bombay charmer and Natalie Kingston is the joy of the South Seas." It is clear that Hall, too, failed to recognize that Gretel Yoltz was Eileen Sedgwick.

Spike eventually meets up with Salami in Central America, as the two start a fight over the attention of a girl. After being thrown into prison for their barroom brawl, Spike notices an indentation on his jaw where Salami punched him, an anchor-in-heart design which matches the ring on Salami's finger ... the same design that he's been noticing on the bracelets and garters of the girls that he's been romancing. He suddenly realizes that he has caught up with the sailor who has been beating him to the clinch. Spike is able to bail himself out but Salami doesn't have enough cash to do so. Spike, who admires Salami and his style, offers to pay for his freedom. As the two leave the prison, walking down a dark street looking for trouble, they accidently fall off a pier into the water. Salami saves Spike, who can't swim, evening their score. They decide to sign up as shipmates for life, with the two forming a close friendship as they sail the seas.

Halfway through the story the film's female protagonist is introduced. Marie, the girl

In an attempt to reinvent her image Eileen took on the stage name of Gretel Yoltz. She had fooled Howard Hawk when she screen tested for his film *A Girl in Every Port* **(1928)—he told her to keep the new name and gave her a part in the film as one of the girls in Holland.**

in France, played by Louise Brooks, is also known as Mademoiselle Godiva. She's a performer in a high-dive act at a carnival. Spike immediately falls in love with her and they soon discuss plans for a lifetime together. He entrusts her with his savings, money to be spent on acquiring the farm of his dreams. When he tell Salami about his plans, Salami prepares to sail on alone—the two separated by a woman.

Upon meeting Marie, Salami immediately recognizes her as Tessie, a girl he once had a relationship with when she was part of an act at Coney Island. Marie, who's hiding a small anchor-in-heart tattoo under an armband, is still in love with Salami and lets him know that she's only interested in Spike for his money. Concerned for Spike's well-being, Salami wants to have nothing to do Marie, and warns her, "That big ox means more to me than any woman."

Spike learns that Marie went to visit Salami, and breaks down after he sees the tattoo on her arm. Intent on killing Salami, he finds him in the middle of a barroom fight. Salami convinces Spike that he didn't double-cross him, and in fact was trying to warn him that she was a gold-digger. Realizing the truth of the situation, Spike says to Salami, "There ain't nothing ever going to come between us again, is there?"

A Girl in Every Port presented a glimpse into Hawks's early thematic developments, subjects that would dominate his later films. One of his recurring themes was the buddy team-up. Although the gimmick was previously featured in films such as *What Price Glory*, the tight-knit relationship was never before explored to the extent as it was in *A Girl in Every Port*. Spike and Salami's rivalry forms a masculine relationship which develops into an emotional attachment. The fact that they try to outwit each other to get the same girl only deepens their camaraderie, with no resentment on the loser's part. In later films the gold-digger role of Marie was developed into the "female buddy" theme, what would later be known as the "Hawksian woman," a female whose behaviors made her a near-equal to her male counterpart.

Brooks gave a performance as Marie that created a charisma which mesmerized filmgoers of the silent era, one that intrigues contemporary viewers even today. Her performance immediately caught the attention of German director G.W. Pabst, who cast her the following year in *Pandora's Box*. Today considered to be a classic, *Pandora's Box* featured Brooks in a role which was sought by many European actresses.

Hawks went on to direct numerous box-office successes covering multiple genres, including *The Dawn Patrol* (1930), *Scarface* (1932), *Twentieth Century* (1934), *Bringing Up Baby* (1938), *Only Angels Have Wings* (1939), *His Girl Friday* (1940), *Sergeant York* (1941), *Ball of Fire* (1941), *Air Force* (1943), *To Have and Have Not* (1944), *The Big Sleep* (1946), *Red River* (1948), *I Was a Male War Bride* (1949), *Monkey Business* (1952), *Gentlemen Prefer Blondes* (1953), *Land of the Pharaohs* (1955), *Rio Bravo* (1959), *Hatari!* (1962), *Man's Favorite Sport?* (1964), and *El Dorado* (1966). Today his style is widely acknowledged as being pioneering, one which over the years has become an influence for numerous directors.

Eileen's next feature, *White Flame*, was released in March by I.H. Adam, an independent production company, and starred Mahlon Hamilton and William V. Mong. Unfortunately the drama was distributed by Biltmore Pictures, a small company which was lacking in all areas, including exhibition skills.

Hot Heels, a May release for Universal, was another success for Eileen as Gretel Yoltz. Reunited with director William James Craft, Eileen played the part of Fannie, supporting Patsy Ruth Miller and Glenn Tryon in a parody of horse racing melodramas of the past. Miller, who previously worked with Edward in *Lorraine of the Lions* (1925) and was now recognized as a successful comedienne, was paired with Tryon for a series of four dance-filled features, *Hot Heels* being their third together. Supporting roles were filled by James Bradbury, Sr., as Mr. Fitch, Lloyd Whitlock as Manager Carter, and Walter Brennan.

In *Hot Heels*, Miller and Tryon played Patsy Jones and Glenn Seth Higgins, a song-

and-dance vaudeville team stranded in Havana, a tank town populated by devious characters. Acting on a hot tip, Glenn bets their entire savings on a "sure win" at the track, "Hot Heels," a horse that's been fixed to lose. The jockey, played by real-life rider Tod Sloan, is unable to ride Hot Heels, as he's been roughed up by the villains who are betting against Hot Heels. Glenn, obviously not fit to be a jockey, miraculously wins the race.

Eileen followed Miller to Tiffany-Stahl Productions for a July release titled *Beautiful but Dumb*. Formed as Tiffany Productions by actress Mae Murray, the studio was renamed Tiffany-Stahl Productions after director John M. Stahl took controlling interest in 1927. In *Beautiful but Dumb*, Janet Brady (Miller) is a stenographer in love with her inattentive boss. Mae (Eileen) encourages her to develop sex appeal by exchanging her "masculine" clothes for more feminine dresses. Janet completes her transformation by removing her glasses and acting dumb, a move that makes her boss notice her. Additional players included Charles Byer as James Conroy, George E. Stone as Tad, Shirley Palmer as Beth, William Irving as Ward, and Harvey Clark as Broadwell. Although the inexpensive melodrama wasn't a major box office success, it gave Eileen an opportunity to act in an adult-oriented production.

Eileen's next film role was in *The Vanishing West*, a ten-episode Western serial produced by Mascot, a recently created production company created by Nat Levine, former personal secretary to Marcus Loew. Directed by Richard Thorpe, the appropriately titled serial rounded up a star-studded cast of once-popular Western actors, including Bob Burns, Yakima Canutt, Fred Church, Jack Dougherty, William Fairbanks, Helen Gibson, Leo Maloney, and Jack Perrin. As an homage to her past, Eileen was credited as Eileen Sedgwick.

Perrin played the part of Jack Marvin, a man unjustly accused of a crime. A fugitive from justice, he is in jeopardy of losing the guardianship of his son Wally Lee Marvin (played by child actor Mickey Bennett) to a devious uncle who is after the family's fortune. By the end of the series Jack is proven innocent and reunited with his son, and in the process is able to keep the fortune out of scheming hands.

Up until 1927 the technology of incorporating sound dialogue into motion pictures was still in its developmental stage, with most studios limiting the exhibition of sound films to novelty shorts. On August 6, 1926, Warner Bros. had premiered *Don Juan*, a nearly three-hour-long film that utilized a synchronized sound system throughout. Recognized as the first sound feature, the movie was shot as a normal silent film with a soundtrack added later. Its soundtrack included a musical score and sound effects, but no recorded dialogue.

On October 6, 1927, Warner Bros. premiered *The Jazz Singer* with Al Jolson, one of America's top music entertainers. The film's soundtrack, mostly relying on its score and effects, included limited sections of dialogue and musical performances. Although it wasn't the first to utilize live sound recorded during filming, the inclusion of Jolson's personality was enough to make it the first successful "talkie." *The Jazz Singer* was highly profitable, earning a total of $2.625 million in the U.S. and overseas markets. Its success was enough of a reason for the motion picture industry to invest in sound movies.

In *Yellow Contraband*, Eileen had the Sedgwick family's first sound film experience. Released by Pathé in October, the drama utilized the sound-on-disc technology which utilized prerecorded discs cued-up to the film projector. The two technologies that existed at the time were sound-on-disc and sound-on-film, with the latter technology chosen by the industry after that equipment was perfected. Although the sound-on-disc technology was

Yellow Contraband (1928) featured Eileen in the Sedgwicks' first sound film experience. Leo Maloney (middle), who also played a dual role in the drama, directed the Pathé film, which utilized the sound-on-disc technology.

less expensive, sound-on-film kept dialogue in registration with moving images. The process of soundproofing studios to record sound-on-film and the converting of theaters to incorporate adequate sound systems was expensive, which is one of the reasons why a studio like Pathé would have been slower in embracing the sound-on-film technology.

The *Yellow Contraband* director was Leo Maloney, who in addition to directing played the dual roles of Leo McMahon and Blackie Harris. Recently appearing with Eileen in *The Vanishing West*, Maloney had an extensive motion picture career before he died from alcohol abuse in 1929: He acted in over 160 films and directed 48 films from 1911, when he first entered the industry. Maloney directed and produced *Overland Bound* (1929), the first independently made sound Western, just before his death. Edward A. Kull, who had directed Eileen in eleven action films in the early 1920s, was the cinematographer. Kull easily shifted between working as director and cinematographer in Westerns.

The storyline revolves around Internal Revenue agent Leo's attempt to seize a shipment of heroin being transported across the Canadian border by Chicago gangster Blackie Harris. Leo, who bears a strong likeness to Blackie, disguises himself as the gangster and intercepts the heroin. Blackie manages to regain possession of the heroin and ships it back to Chicago.

Leo, with the help of his girlfriend Mazie (Eileen), who's disguised as a gun moll, infiltrates the gangsters' hideout, breaks up the drug ring, and confiscates the "yellow contraband."

The supporting cast included Noble Johnson as Li Wong Foo, Tom London as Drag Conners, Joe Rickson as Pierre Dufresne, Bob Burns as the sheriff, Vester Pegg as Dude McClain, Walter Patterson as Ice-house Joe, Bill Patton as Rawhide, and playing dope runners, Bud Osborne, Frank Ellis, and Tom B. Forman.

The entertainment section of the May 1, 1927, *Oakland Tribune* reported that Josie was coming out of retirement to appear in *The Trail of '98*, MGM's epic tale of the 1898 Alaskan gold rush:

> ACTRESS RETURNS AFTER RECOVERY FROM HURTS
>
> A slim, animated girl about whose face appeared a familiar look, walked briskly onto the Metro lot the other day carrying a well-worn makeup kit. She headed for the set where they are making *The Trail of '98*. Many stopped to glance at her. Several spoke.
>
> "Who is that?" others asked.
>
> Presently it became noised about that "Josie Sedgwick is back!"

By 1925 the many injuries that Josie incurred during the filming of her mostly horse-related stunts (including one that was diagnosed as a near-fatal injury to her spine) were taking a toll on her body. Starting in 1917, while attempting a running dismount in *One Shot Ross*, she broke both ankles. That same year she dislocated both ankles, sprained both knees, and literally had her shoulder wrapped around her neck when a horse fell on her in *The Boss of the Lazy Y*. Nineteen twenty-five proved to be the most hazardous year of all, with injuries forcing her to quit acting: Josie was thrown from a stagecoach in *Daring Days*, tearing one of her kneecaps loose. She then cracked five ribs when her pony fell in *Dynamite's Daughter*. To top the list that year, a tree was dropped upon her in *The Outlaw's Daughter*. As a result of the final injury she was unable to walk for some time.

Old-timers who signed on to work on the film warmly welcomed Josie back to the industry, with newcomers becoming curious about her past. The film's impressive cast featured Dolores del Rio, Ralph Forbes, Karl Dane, Harry Carey, Tully Marshall, George Cooper, and about 2,000 extras, including Josie, whose appearance was uncredited. As the love interest Carey leaves behind when he is overcome by the lust for gold, Josie's part as a dance hall girl is very minor.

Clarence Brown, experiencing success in directing John Gilbert and Greta Garbo in the sensual drama *Flesh and the Devil* (1926), was assigned to direct and produce *The Trail of '98*. The film was released with much fanfare on March 20, 1928, at New York City's Astor Theater. William Axt composed an original score for it. Extensive roadshow publicity was planned, as it was expected to be one of MGM's most important releases of 1928. With cinematography by John Seitz, the motion picture was originally presented in theaters using an experimental widescreen process called "Fanthom Screen." Utilizing an adjustable lens to enhance the spectacular sequences, the process allowed the enlargement and reduction of the projected image size to take place without the need of a projector change-over. It also involved moving the screen towards the audience on rollers. The March 24 *Motion Picture News* described the use of the effect for four of the sequences: "a breath-taking snowslide; the running of the rapids in frail boats; the Chilkoot Pass stuff, with big panorama shots; and the burning of Dawson City. For the snowshoe sequence, the screen is suddenly enlarged to twice normal size, and moved down to the curtain-line. The effect is, of course, electrifying and carries a big punch. The same method is used with the running of the rapids, a remarkable spectacle."

Based on Robert W. Service's novel *The Trail of '98—A Northland Romance*, the story recreates the discovery of gold in the Klondike and the fever created as news of it spread across the continent—uprooting families and their lives as they headed west in search of a fortune. This exposes the dark side of humanity as a mad lust for gold is unleashed. The film focuses on four men and the bad luck that follows their discovery of a vein of gold: Samuel Foote, known as "The Worm," played by George Cooper; Lars Petersen, a Michigan lumberman who leaves his wife behind, played by Karl Dane; Salvation Jim from the deserts of Nevada, played by Tully Marshall; and a young adventurer named Larry, played by Ralph Forbes.

Berna (Dolores del Rio) and her blind grandfather Henry Kelland (Cesare Gravina) follow the Bukleys (Emily Fitzroy and Tenen Holtz) from Dawson City to the Klondike area where they plan to set up a restaurant. Henry is among the many who die during the long journey. Finding the existence too harsh, the Bukleys return to Dawson City, leaving Berna behind with her boyfriend Larry. Berna attempts to convince Larry to return, but he insists on trying to locate gold one last time.

The four men eventually discover gold. Lars and Jim return to file a claim, leaving Larry and "The Worm" behind to guard their find. "The Worm" and Larry struggle with one another in an effort to survive, with "The Worm" losing his life. Larry returns to find that Berna is now a dance hall prostitute working for a known murderer, Jack Locasto (Harry Carey). After Jack is burned to death in a saloon fire, Berna, Larry, Lars, and Jim attempt to redeem their greed-filled lives.

Uncredited stunt performers included Lou Costello, who doubled for Dolores del Rio in a window-jumping scene, Joe Bonomo, Gordon Carveth, Harvey Parry, Bob Rose, and Ray Thompson. The gold rush scenes were shot near Denver at an altitude of 11,600 feet and in temperatures down to minus 60, with additional scenes done in Alaska. On June 29, 1927, while filming stunts for a white water rapids scene on the Copper River in the Abercrombie Canyon near Cordova, Alaska, three participants drowned, including Thompson, who had fallen into the water (with F.H. Daughters of Spokane, Washington) from one of the many small crafts carrying stuntmen and cameramen. In a failed effort to save them, Joseph Bautin of Juneau, Alaska, jumped in and drowned. In all, six men lost their lives during the process of filming the story. News of the accidents must have been disturbing for Josie, who knew firsthand that stunt work was indeed a dangerous profession.

Just as Eileen and Josie were thinking of permanently retiring from the film industry, Edward was hitting his stride directing comedies. Of the 48 features MGM released in 1927, one quarter of them were comedies, putting Edward in an excellent position as he was recognized as a seasoned comedian of the stage and film. King Vidor acknowledged Edward's directorial style in *Show People,* released in November 1928. Loosely based on the career of Gloria Swanson, the comedy satirized Hollywood as it followed Marion Davies as Peggy Pepper on her rise to stardom. The film featured cameos made by real-life celebrities, including Charles Chaplin, Mary Pickford, John Gilbert, Douglas Fairbanks, William S. Hart, Mae Murray, Leatrice Joy, Norma Talmadge, and Elinor Glyn. As Edward was preoccupied filming *The Cameraman*, actor Harry Gribbon was given the responsibility of satirizing Edward as an overtly enthusiastic comedy director named Jim.

Edward directed George K. Arthur (left) and Karl Dane in *Circus Rookies* (1928), one of the several MGM comedies features that the duo teamed up in.

Edward was assigned to write and direct *Circus Rookies*, a March release featuring the team of Karl Dane and George K. Arthur. With the working title of *Monkey Business*, the comedy used the big top as its background. Dane and Arthur were previously teamed in *Rookies* (1927), a MGM comedy in which the elongated Dane played a tough sergeant and pint-sized Arthur a bumbling recruit. The combination proved to be a box office success, with MGM following it up with *Baby Mine* in 1927, and *Detectives*, *Circus Rookies*, *Brotherly Love*, and *All at Sea* in 1928. As in each of their features the two characters were antagonists who fed off of one another, as is the case in *Circus Rookies* where Dane plays odd-job worker Oscar Thrust and Arthur circus press agent Francis Byrd. Dane is given the job of training a rebellious gorilla, which leads to the two participating in a mad chase with the wild ape over the tops of a speeding circus train. The supporting cast included a list of names familiar to Edward: Louise Lorraine as La Belle the trapeze star and Francis's love interest, Sydney Jarvis as Mr. Magoo the circus owner, and Fred Humes as Bimbo the gorilla.

Of the five Kane-Arthur features that followed *Rookies*, only *Circus Rookies* found similar success. MGM lost interest in the pair but they continued to appear as a team in a series of slapstick shorts released during 1930 and 1931. These were directed by Lewis Foster for Larry Darmour Productions.

MGM acquired Buster Keaton through the merger with Metro, filling in their star comedian position in their roster of contract actors. Under the working title of *Snap Shots*, his first assignment for MGM was *The Cameraman*, a film which Edward directed. Edward and Keaton had similar backgrounds and much in common. The Sedgwick and Keaton families, numbering five members each, both made a life of performing on the vaudeville circuit. The families belonged to the White Rats of America, a union organized by vaudeville comedians who demanded from theater owners better salaries and working conditions. They also experienced similar hardships during lean times, and had similar experiences dealing with the wrath of the Gerry Society, which barred them from performing in the legitimate vaudeville houses in New York City and other northern towns.

Born to parents who were medicine show performers, Keaton ventured into vaudeville at the age of nine months when he allegedly made his first appearance onstage after he unexpectedly crawled from the wings during his parents' performance, upstaging them while amusing the audience. It wasn't long before his parents, Joe and Myra, incorporated him into their act, which would be known from then on as "The Three Keatons." When the family finally had their big chance to appear on Tony Pastor's stage in New York City, the four-year-old Keaton was sidelined due to the Gerry Society's presence. The family was forced to play smaller towns where the Gerry Society wasn't in force.

Buster Keaton's first assignment for MGM was *The Cameraman* (1928), a film which Edward was given the responsibility of directing.

When he was twenty-two Keaton was signed to appear on Broadway in *The Passing Show of 1917*. But before the musical opened, he broke his contract with the Shubert brothers to appear in films with Roscoe "Fatty" Arbuckle, a former Keystone comedian whom he had recently met. Arbuckle was now a partner with entertainment entrepreneur Joseph M. Schenck, working at Comique Studios in New York City. In a matter of months Keaton became Arbuckle's assistant director and head writer. Unlike other film comedians who simply transferred their vaudeville routines to film, Keaton developed a sophisticated style of humor, which he physically integrated with his surroundings. His subtle, almost nonexistent facial expressions gave him the soubriquet "The Great Stone Face."

Schenck, Nicholas's older brother, promoted Keaton to head Arbuckle's unit when Arbuckle moved to features. Once Keaton married Natalie Talmadge, the sister of Schenck's wife Norma, their business relationship became very supportive. His two-reeler shorts, which were being released every other month during the early 1920s, quickly established him as a popular film comedian. Keaton was soon promoted to starring in his own feature films. By 1928 he had directed twenty-nine of the films that he appeared in. Until then, Keaton had worked as an independent artist, with the majority of his films produced by Schenck and released through studios such as First National, Metro and United Artists. Although critically acclaimed today, Keaton's films from the late 1920s proved to be commercial failures, including *The General* (1927), which now is considered to be one of silent comedy's greatest feature films.

At Schenck's advice, Keaton gave up his failing production company and signed on to work for MGM—a decision he considered to be the worst of his career. Contemporaries, including Charlie Chaplin and Harold Lloyd, advised him against doing so. In giving in to the studio system, he lost most of his creative responsibility, as he was assigned a production supervisor and a team of screenwriters who developed his scripts for him. Similar to Edward's experience as a jack-of-all-trades director, Keaton suddenly discovered that the independent comic filmmaker, who wrote, directed and starred in his own films, was a concept of the past.

The responsibility of introducing Keaton to MGM's bureaucratic machine, through the direction of *The Cameraman*, was left in Edward's hands. By now Edward was well experienced working in a micromanaged position, following directives from an organized team of producers and scriptwriters. Although he was capable of directing films without comprehensive instructions for camera direction, he learned that it was wiser to follow orders when necessary, and acquiesce to the powers that be, than to try to buck the corporate system. For Keaton, however, it was a rough transition. From the start, he complained of the size of the staff that was dedicated to writing the film's script. Records indicate there were only five writers assigned to creating the *Cameraman* story but Keaton remembered closer to twenty-two, plus any executive who thought he could write a gag. "They complicated our simple plot with everything they could think of—gangsters, Salvation Army street bands, Tammany Hall politicians, longshoremen, and lady gem thieves," Buster recollected. After eight months, a story was finally completed.

In May 1928, MGM sent Edward, Keaton and a crew to New York City to film scenes on location. The company realized that they would need to be inconspicuous when shooting Keaton on the streets of Manhattan, but they weren't prepared for the havoc that would follow once the star was recognized by his fans. A trolley driver who spotted Keaton as they

The Cameraman featured Keaton (center) as a struggling tintype photographer who falls head-over-heels for a secretary at the MGM newsreel office, played by Marceline Day.

were filming a scene on 23rd Street at Fifth Avenue shouted out his name. The alert to pedestrians in the area immediately triggered a traffic jam which stretched for three blocks, with the gathering crowd disrupting the filming. The crew decided to move downtown to the Battery area to continue shooting scenes, but again Keaton was recognized by passersby.

Edward and Keaton returned to their Ambassador Hotel rooms to sort things out. Edward phoned Irving Thalberg to let him know that things weren't working out as planned; they would be able to shoot a few exteriors on the streets of the city, but the other scenes would need to be shot back at the studio.

Keaton complained to Thalberg that, except for the basic storyline—the plot he had originally suggested—the script was the problem. He pleaded with Thalberg to toss out the script and let him film it the way he was used to—off the cuff. Thalberg gave him the permission to create the simple comedy that he wanted. With a portion of the script salvaged, Keaton was free to improvise the rest.

Additionally, Keaton voiced his concern that Edward was rushing him, which was only slightly bending the truth. Edward, who was responsible for delivering a scheduled amount of exposed film to the studio each day, found Keaton's work methods time-consuming. Tension grew between the two, as Keaton would consume valuable production time to work through unprepared material before the camera could start rolling. Edward eventually came to the conclusion that although Keaton's work style was painstakingly slow, its results were worth it. He realized that the only way he could keep filming on schedule was by giving Keaton a certain amount of freedom in directing his own scenes and giving him the assistance he needed to do so. Their directorial collaboration formed the basis of a lifelong career and friendship.

Released on September 22, *The Cameraman* proved that despite MGM's bureaucratic rules, Edward and Keaton could overcome the obstacles and create a film that would one day be critically acclaimed as one of the best comedy features of the late silent era. To MGM the film's box office success only proved that their assembly line production process was working, overlooking the fact that it was Keaton's ability to visualize and direct the production on the fly that helped make it successful. In 1953 a friend of Keaton asked to have a private screening of the film. To his surprise, Keaton was told by MGM that their print could no longer be run through a projector as it was in poor shape: For the past 25 years, it had been presented as an example of the perfect comedy, and a required training film for up-and-coming comedians.

The story features Keaton as Luke Shannon, a struggling tintype photographer. Luke falls head-over-heels for Sally Richards (Marceline Day), a secretary at the MGM newsreel office. After finding out that her company will buy any film that is newsworthy, he trades in his still camera and savings for an antique motion picture camera. Luke is prepared to film anything that will get the attention of the newsreel office, as well as that of Sally. Harold Stagg (Harold Goodwin) is another employee at the office who is interested in Sally, and he becomes intent in foiling Luke in getting both the job and the girl.

One of Luke's efforts takes him to Yankee Stadium to cover a Yankees game, but he finds out that the team is playing in St. Louis. In one of *The Cameraman*'s most memorable moments, Luke takes advantage of the empty ballpark by setting up his camera on the playing field and pantomiming players of both teams, including a catcher, pitcher and a batter who swats a homer. Edward's direction of this segment captures Keaton's brilliant talent, alternating cuts with long, medium and close-up shots to give moviegoers an in-the-stadium seat experience. This would be one of Edward's final opportunities to film wide-open spaces, as the direction of filming was about to move into soundproofed studios which were necessary to record early sound on film.

In an attempt to impress the company with his photographic skill, Luke presents his footage to the studio, only to discover during the viewing that his exposed film is composed of a mess of unusable double-exposed images, including scenes of battleships cruising down busy city streets.

The next morning he takes Sally on a date to the municipal swimming pool. In another one of Keaton's unforgettable sequences, he ends up sharing his cramped changing room with a heavily built man (Edward Brophy). The two simultaneously attempt to change into their swimsuits, with Luke ending up in the other man's huge outfit. Predictably, Luke loses the suit after taking a high dive into the pool, forcing him to steal an old-fashioned pair of bloomers off of an unsuspecting lady. Brophy, a property master for Keaton's MGM production unit, was cast by Keaton in larger parts in two of his talkies, and by 1934, Brophy abandoned the production end of the movies altogether and was acting full-time.

Early Monday morning Luke visits the newsroom, once again hoping for a chance at becoming an official cameraman. Sally passes along to him a tip that was phoned in: a Tong

Edward borrowed the Roy camera that Keaton used in *The Cameraman* from the Selig company—Selig used it in making the first picture filmed in the Los Angeles area. Today, film critics often include *The Cameraman* in their Top Ten lists of the all-time best films produced.

War is about to erupt during a celebration that is winding its way down the streets of Chinatown. In his rush to film the incident, Luke runs into an organ grinder and his monkey. Thinking that the monkey has been squashed to death, he is left to dispose of the animal. The monkey, played by Josephine, is only unconscious, and once revived is equally featured with Keaton in the film. Upon returning to the office he sadly discovers that the film broke in the camera just as he had started to film the brawl.

In a final attempt to prove his skills, Luke decides to film the Westport Yacht Regatta. While setting up his camera he discovers the unexposed film that he took of the Tong War—Josephine had playfully exchanged the cartridge in the camera after the skirmish. Harold recklessly speeds by in a motorboat which is carrying him and Sally. Harold makes a sharp turn and he and Sally go overboard. Luke springs to the rescue, pulling an unconscious Sally to the shore. As he runs to a nearby pharmacy for first aid supplies, she revives. Harold takes the credit for saving her life.

The next day, after submitting his Tong War material to the newsreel office, Luke despondently trades in his movie camera for his old tintype camera. In the meantime, the film is being screened at the office, with the boss concluding that it's the best camerawork he's seen in years. The fight footage is followed by coverage of the Westport Yacht Regatta, and surprisingly shows Luke saving Sally: The monkey cranked the camera during the entire rescue, proving that Luke was the true hero. Sally runs out to the street to find Luke as ticker tape for a Charles Lindbergh parade falls all around them.

The Cameraman's opening credits gave equal billing to the two: "A Buster Keaton Production, Directed by Edward Sedgwick." The film's success pulled Keaton out of his box office slump and confirmed that Edward was an accomplished comedy director. Keaton felt confident that if MGM gave him his own unit, he would be able to work more effectively. In his autobiography, written over thirty years later, Keaton remembered begging Thalberg, "Give me Eddie Sedgwick to direct, two or three writers, my own prop man, electrician, wardrobe woman, and a few technicians, and I will guarantee to deliver pictures as good or better than *The Cameraman*." Keaton believed that by working with his own crew, who would be used to his working style, he would be able to continue to improvise the on-the-fly routines he had successfully performed in his previous films, all the while keeping the cameras rolling.

Thalberg's reply wasn't the answer Keaton was hoping for; like everyone else working for MGM, Keaton would need to strictly adhere to the studio's preapproved shooting scripts, production schedules and budgets. He was reminded that Mayer dictated that MGM's actors would no longer have the support of their own mini-studios which utilized their choice of directors, scriptwriters, supporting players, and film editors, and that all aspects of filmmaking would now be supervised by their superiors. Nor would he be able to perform the more dangerous stunts in his films. Keaton's days of creative independence were over.

Skeptical that theatergoers would accept talkies, MGM was the last of the major studios to embrace sound technology. Although they found themselves in a bit of a rush to catch up with the others who were already releasing sound features, they successfully transitioned to the new format by 1929. MGM had decided that the studio would initially concentrate on adding sound dialogue to dramas and musicals but not comedies, which they didn't perceive to be as profitable as the other genres.

For the silent film actor, the emergence of sound might have appeared intimidating, as dialogue skills were not a previous requirement in motion pictures. Edward and Keaton, both having years of dialogue experience growing up on vaudeville stages, felt confident working with the new medium. The two, prepared for the challenges that their first talkie would offer, were disappointed after finding out that their next collaboration, *Spite Marriage*, would have a soundtrack limited to a synchronized score and sound effects.

Spite Marriage's preapproved script was delivered in time for filming to commence on November 13. A couple of weeks into production, on November 28, filming was briefly halted due to a case of mild influenza that struck the film colony. The epidemic sent Edward and Keaton to their beds, along with actors Clara Bow, John Gilbert, Lois Wilson, Monte Blue, Richard Barthelmess, Mary Philbin, Loretta Young, Shally Phipps, Jean Arthur, Ruth Taylor, William Haines, and director F.W. Murnau. *Spite Marriage* completed filming on December 24 and was released in theaters on April 6, 1929.

In this romantic comedy Keaton plays pants presser Elmer, a dedicated fan of stage actress Trilby Drew (Dorothy Sebastian). Arriving each evening at the theater to see her in

Carolina, the Civil War melodrama she's starring in, Elmer falls in love with her from his front row center seat. Trilby, who is aware of his presence at each performance, is amused by his interest in her.

After 35 performances Elmer finally gets up enough nerve to go backstage to bring her flowers. He loses his courage outside of her dressing room door and the stage manager must deliver the flowers to Trilby. Elmer meets an actor who has a bit part that enables the actor to steal a kiss from Trilby's character after she faints. In a stroke of luck, a detective enters the theater looking for the actor, who is a wanted man. The actor flees, leaving Elmer with his Union soldier's sword and rifle. Elmer has the opportunity to play a part that he had only dreamed of playing. After applying a fake beard and eyebrows—in a scene which provides Keaton a chance to make a mockery of the art of applying stage makeup—Elmer proceeds to transform the evening's performance of *Carolina* into a burlesque, as he misses his queues and knocks down scenery. When it's time for him to kiss Trilby, he is unable to gather up the courage. By now the show's manager is furious about how he's transformed the play into a comedy and chases him from the stage. Elmer sneaks into the dressing room, removes the facial hair and makeup, puts on his tuxedo and quickly blends into the crowd that is searching for him.

Trilby's fiancé, actor Lionel Benmore (Edward Earle), jilts her in favor of society blonde Ethyl Norcrosse (Leila Hyams). After finding out that Lionel and Ethyl are engaged, Trilby

For Keaton *Spite Marriage* (1929) was the beginning of the departure from the type of movie that he was used to doing on his own. But for Edward this was the beginning of the sort of comedic dramas that he would become well known for.

spitefully marries Elmer. After the wedding ceremony the two celebrate at a nightclub where, coincidentally, Lionel and Ethyl are sitting at a table, amorously preoccupied with each other. Livid at the sight of the couple, Trilby proceeds to get drunk on champagne. Elmer must get her back to the hotel where they are spending their honeymoon—in separate rooms. Keaton and Sebastian perform an amusing scene together as Elmer unsuccessfully attempts to place an unconscious and rubbery Trilby in bed.

The following morning Trilby's manager and Lionel visit her with a warning that her career will be damaged if fans find out that she's married to a dry cleaner. Trilby walks out on Elmer, leaving the manager to break the bad news to him. Brokenhearted, Elmer leaves the hotel, punching Lionel on his way out. A police officer who's alerted to the commotion chases him down the street. In what seems to be a perfect escape, Elmer hops onto a passing car. But the car is being driven by a robber who's having a shootout with the police car that is following him. The robber joins his bootlegging gang at the dock and they force Elmer to join them because he can identify and finger them.

That evening Elmer escapes the criminals by falling overboard, and is picked up by a private yacht. The following day he's put to work as a crew member, assigned to varnish the mast. Looking down from the mast he discovers that Trilby and Lionel are on board, so he asks to work below deck. There's a fire in the engine room and in the rush to abandon ship, Lionel knocks Trilby unconscious and leaves her behind. Elmer, the only crew member to stay behind, bravely extinguishes the fire.

The next day Trilby wakes, realizing the situation. The bootleggers approach the yacht and decide to appropriate the boat for their purposes. Elmer hides Trilby below and single-handedly saves the day by knocking out the gang members one by one.

After they hand over the gang to the law, Elmer escorts Trilby home. Just as Elmer is about to return to the cab, she grabs him and they go in to her hotel together. Elmer, who had bravely defended her, is her true love.

For Keaton, *Spite Marriage* was the beginning of the departure from the type of movie that he was used to doing on his own. But for Edward, this was the beginning of the sort of comedic dramas that he would become well known for. He already found success working with William Haines, so it was only fitting that he would be once again teamed with the popular actor in what would be their fourth collaboration and the first talkie for both. Promoted with the working title of *The Gob* and released as *Navy Blues*, the comedy also reunited Edward with Karl Dane and featured Anita Page, an up-and-coming actress.

Filming commenced on January 31, 1929, and, as was the case with future MGM films that Edward worked on, within a month's time he was removed from his directorial duties to work on another production. The responsibility was then given to Clarence Brown, who received the final credit upon its release on December 20. Of the footage that Edward directed, a majority of it took place aboard a destroyer.

Haines demonstrated that his voice was okay for talking pictures and proved that his characterizations could be just as arrogant as a talkie star as they were in his silent films. In *Navy Blues* Haines portrayed gob Jack Kelly, who is stationed on a destroyer. Upon the arrival of a new transfer named Sven "Swede" Swanson (Dane), Jack proceeds to make the sailor's life miserable. He receives a wallop from "Swede" in exchange. The two, of course, go on to become best buddies.

The men of the destroyer receive a high efficiency rating and as a reward they're invited to a dinner given by the Ladies' Uplift Society. Thinking that it would be anything but uplifting, the crew members are convinced otherwise upon their arrival. Jack meets Alice Brown (Page) and the two instantly fall for each other.

Jack insists on taking Alice home, and upon entering her house they find that her parents haven't yet returned from the theatre. When the parents arrive, Jack hides in the kitchen, making a mess of things. Once he is discovered, Alice's parents become upset with the fact that their daughter is dating a sailor, so her mother throws him out with Alice following him. Alice is without money for a hotel room so Jack goes out to search for "Swede," who he hopes will lend him money she can use to pay for a place to stay. They become separated and Alice assumes that she has been abandoned by Jack. In need of money, she finds a job as an escort at a nightclub.

After returning from a tour of duty, Jack discovers where she's been working. With "Swede"'s assistance he busts up the club in an attempt to rescue her. In the course of a few minutes "Swede" knocks out two dozen men with his mighty fists.

Kelly rescues Alice and eventually convinces her that he didn't ditch her. The two are reunited, and before he returns to his ship Kelly promises to her that he doesn't have a girl in every port.

Although *Navy Blues* was a mediocre movie, it received acceptable reviews, partially

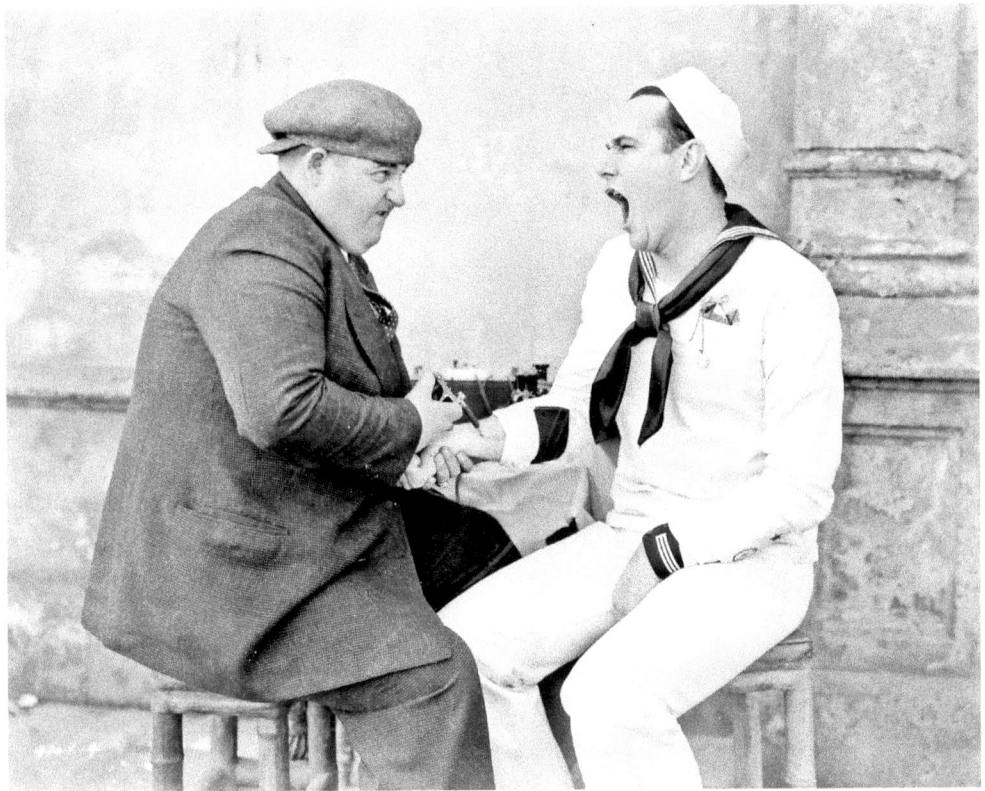

Navy Blues (1929) reunited Edward (left) with William Haines (right) and Karl Dane, and featured Anita Page, an upcoming actress. Within a month's time MGM removed Edward from his directorial duties to work on another production, with Clarence Brown receiving the final credit.

due to the fact that Haines was now a top-five box office attraction. The star's favorable status guaranteed that the film would receive proper circulation.

By the end of the 1920s Edward was living contentedly with Rose and daughter Mary. They took up residence at the Castle Apartments, a brand new first-class high-rise complex at 1919 North Argyle Avenue in Los Angeles. Although it was a long distance from his dream of living and working on Broadway, Edward was now a successful director for a major studio, proving to his father that he was wrong about motion pictures being a passing fad.

The remainder of the Sedgwick family continued living comfortably as a tightly knit group, residing at their modest home at 1930 Canyon Drive in Beverly Hills. With her days as a serial queen over, Eileen was establishing a new life as a socialite, happily dating Clarence Hutson, a real estate dealer for Syndicate Mortgage. Eileen's previous marriage to Justin H. McCloskey ended in 1924 on the grounds that he was a "terrible driver," referring to his reckless use of the family automobile. According to Eileen, McCloskey took the rebuke so much to heart that he went away and never returned. On January 31, 1929, Eileen and Clarence filed their notice of intent to wed at Los Angeles' city hall, with Eileen stating that she was only 26 instead of 30, and Clarence giving his age as 33 instead of 35. After their marriage, Clarence moved in with the Sedgwicks.

Chapter Seven

The Business of Laughter During the Depression Years

The fall of 1929 was a disastrous time for millions of people, as they experienced bankruptcy after paper fortunes had evaporated and the bottom fell out of the global economy. It was the beginning of the Great Depression, caused in part by the wild speculation in the stock market after the depression that followed World War I had eased. With sixteen million Americans out of work at its peak, every aspect of the American economy was affected. Fortunately, the motion picture industry escaped the dramatic losses that ruined other industries, partly because Depression era Americans found going to the movies a solace from misery, with between 60 and 80 million people attending shows once a week or more. They wanted escapist entertainment, which Hollywood was more than able to supply.

In addition to the loss of revenue due to the depressed economy, movie theater exhibitors had the additional expense of installing sound systems, which was necessary to stay competitive. Many independent theaters, especially the ones that survived on a small profit margin, were unable to afford to upgrade to the new technology.

Having no theater chain of its own, Universal Pictures relied heavily on booking their offerings in these independent theaters that were generally in the smaller markets (suburbs and rural areas). The absence of sound theaters in these small towns gave Universal and other serial producers little motivation to rush talkie sequences into their adventures. Taking advantage of the lack of sound technology, Universal re-released several of Josie's silent Westerns in 1930 to the unwired theaters, including *The Best Man*, *Dynamite's Daughter*, *Queen of the Roundup*, and *The Ropin' Venus*. Universal realized that they wouldn't see an increase in profits if they continued using this type of strategy, so to compensate for the theaters that were able to install sound systems they found it necessary to produce synchronized soundtracks to accompany their silent offerings.

Eileen's final acting role, a minor one compared to her past efforts, was in a Universal serial titled *The Jade Box*. It was distributed in two versions: as a silent, to take advantage of the still unwired theaters, and with a synchronized mono soundtrack, which included talking sequences, sound effects, and a music score which was recycled from the serial *Tarzan the Tiger* and written by Sam Perry. Filmed in 1929 and released the following year, the ten-episode adventure was produced by Henry MacRae and directed by Ray Taylor. The cast brought together actors from previous serials that Eileen appeared in, including Jack Perrin playing the part of Jack Lamar, Louise Lorraine as Helen Morgan, and Francis Ford as Martin Morgan.

The adventure revolves around a struggle for the possession of a jade box which John Lamar obtained during a trip to Asia. The mysterious box contains a vial which holds the secret of invisibility. When John's friend Martin Morgan discovers what is contained in the box he steals it from John, planning to use the mysterious power for his own scheme. Oriental cultists searching for the box catch up with John and abduct him. When they find out that Martin is in possession of the secret, they become determined to get the box from him.

Meanwhile, John's son Jack has just become engaged to Martin's daughter Helen. The cult sends a message to Jack and Helen, letting them know that Jack's father is in the "Land of the Shadow" and won't return until the box is returned to its rightful owners. Determined to abuse the power of invisibility, Morgan attempts to foil Jack's search for his father in the Middle East. In true serial style, the story neatly wraps up with Jack locating his father and the box back where it belongs.

To celebrate and at the same time exploit the advent of the talkie, one of MGM's top priorities was to do a musical; at one point they considered producing a musical version of *Tin Hats*, Edward's hit movie from 1926. As a solution to the growing demand for spectacular features, MGM produced *The Hollywood Revue of 1929*, a two-strip Technicolor musical featuring their major contract players.

With the exception of Lon Chaney, Greta Garbo, and Ramon Novarro, the lineup of MGM's all-star performers included George K. Arthur, Lionel Barrymore, Jack Benny, Joan Crawford, Karl Dane, Marion Davies, Marie Dressler, Cliff Edwards, John Gilbert, William Haines, Charles King, Laurel and Hardy, Gwen Lee, Bessie Love, Polly Moran, Conrad Nagel, Anita Page, Norma Shearer, Natacha Nattova and Company, the Albertina Rasch Ballet, and the Rounders.

Buster Keaton was showcased in a dance segment inspired by the Princess Rajah dance that he created during his service in World War I, and later performed on film in a short. Revising the setting to King Neptune's palace, Keaton emerges from a huge scallop shell, gyrates across the stage, and ends his performance in a cartwheel.

The Hollywood Revue of 1929 was promoted as an all-talking revue with Keaton being the only actor who remains silent during the finale. As the entire cast appears on stage singing "Singin' in the Rain," Keaton stands in line with the others, looking befuddled. Up until this time Keaton was still considered to be a silent star. It's possible that MGM was being careful not to introduce his voice until he had the right opportunity to do so—in a showcase feature of his own.

Free and Easy presented Keaton with that opportunity. MGM planned an all-out effort for his talkie premiere. Following other studios who were inserting musical segments into every major sound feature, MGM decided to include musical numbers prepared by Roy Turk and Fred Ahlert, and ensemble numbers directed by Sammy Lee. Edward, now regarded a specialist at directing comedic features, was again assigned to direct for Keaton.

In this backstage musical, Keaton, as Elmer Butt, was cast opposite Anita Page as Elvira Plunkett. The film also featured comedienne Trixie Friganza as Elvira's stage mother Ma Plunkett, up-and-coming actor Robert Montgomery as Larry Mitchell, a popular actor who takes an interest in Elvira, and cameo appearances by Fred Niblo, Lionel Barrymore, William

Free and Easy (1930) was Buster Keaton's first sound film. In this backstage musical Keaton (right) was cast with Anita Page, Trixie Friganza (shown), and Robert Montgomery. A critic's legitimate complaint panned Keaton as "trying to imitate a standard musical comedy clown" which is "no longer Buster Keaton and no longer funny."

Haines, Dorothy Sebastian, Karl Dane, Jackie Coogan, Cecil B. DeMille and Joseph Farnham.

The storyline: Elvira, the beauty queen from Gopher City, Kansas, wins a grand prize trip to Hollywood, and instead of finding work as an actress finds a proposal of marriage. Following a twist on the *Merton of the Movies* theme, Elmer, acting as Elvira's manager, runs amok on the set as he attempts to get her a role in a movie.

Larry, a caddish movie star, attempts to take advantage of the naive Elvira, but Elmer and Ma come to her rescue. Knocked out by Ma, Larry comes to and realizes that he was a jerk for making inappropriate moves on such a sweet girl. Larry apologizes to Elmer for the way he treated Elvira and asks him if he can forgive him. The two become friends once they realize they knew each other as kids in Kansas. In exchange for bringing Larry to his senses, the actor gets Elmer a screen test for a comic opera that he is appearing in.

Elmer is found to have a natural talent for comedy and receives the role of King. In a search for his Queen, he's put through merciless physical abuse as actress after actress knocks him about as part of their screen test with him. Finally, with the director becoming frustrated in the search to find the appropriate talent to fill the part, Ma Plunkett tries out, knocking the wind out of Elmer and winning the role. Dressed in a baggy clown-like costume with facial makeup, Keaton, playing Elmer as King, seems out of place singing and dancing with Ma Plunkett, with the number quickly becoming a slapstick routine. During a break, Elmer tries to propose to Elvira, but he's too bashful to get the words out. In his attempt to woo Elvira she confuses what he is saying, mistakenly thinking that Larry is the one who wants to marry her. Later, she tells Larry that she forgives him; he proposes to her.

Larry promises Elmer that he will get him a contract as a comedian. Excited about the opportunity, Elmer feels that the time is right to propose to Elvira. Summing up the courage to ask her for her hand in marriage, he is interrupted as Larry and Elvira announce their engagement.

Elmer performs his final number heartbroken, with his true emotions disguised under his Pagliacci-like makeup.

The movie opened in April to mixed reviews. Louella O. Parsons, entertainment columnist for the *Los Angeles Examiner*, wrote, "The merriest, gayest, meatiest movie Buster Keaton ever made opened at Loew's State yesterday. So well proportioned are the laughs, so beautifully distributed in the romance and so subtly planted is the final pathos that we vote *Free and Easy* not only Buster's best achievement, but also one of MGM's most complete talkies."

Unfavorable reviews, such as the one written by Robert E. Sherwood, critic for *Film Daily*, panned the Great Stone Face: "Buster Keaton, trying to imitate a standard musical comedy clown, is no longer Buster Keaton and no longer funny."

Sherwood was correct in pointing out that the type of character Keaton was playing had changed. His previous films focused on the clever ways his characters overcame obstacles. Keaton's roles were now being reduced to that of a slapstick comedian who relied on verbal gags. The film's ending is also very unlike Keaton's other features, in that his unrequited love remains unrequited, with his competitor getting the girl at the story's conclusion.

Historically, as a Keaton feature, it pales in comparison to his silent efforts, but as a comedy that was geared towards a Depression era audience, *Free and Easy* proved to be successful. MGM invested nearly a half-million dollars in it, turning it into one of the studio's biggest moneymakers that year. The film, along with Mayer's conservative formula, helped MGM survive the first year of the Depression, with the studio realizing a growth in profits of $15 million in 1930 from $12 million in 1929. In his autobiography Keaton recollected of its box office success, "Louis B. Mayer was so pleased by the large earning of *Free and Easy* that he rewarded me with a $10,000 bonus and a three-month vacation with pay. Adding my $3,000 a week salary for thirteen weeks, the bonus, I suppose, actually amounted to $49,000."

For his talkie premiere, Keaton's enunciation sounded natural and animated enough to match his character. After years on the vaudeville stage he was well-prepared for this moment. Keaton had a following overseas for his silent movies, and now that sound was a part of his features MGM needed to produce a Spanish-speaking version, in which Keaton phonetically spoke his part in Spanish. Working alongside Salvador de Alberich, Edward directed Keaton in the Spanish-speaking *Free and Easy*, titled *Estrellados*. Featuring Raquel Torres as Elvira, Don Alvarado as Larry Mitchell and María Calvo as La Mama, the version was released to the foreign market in August.

It was apparent that Keaton was no longer in charge of his productions. Finding it harder to get any sort of artistic control of his films, he became anxious as he was assigned to work on one stylistically boring feature after another. As a frustrated producer Keaton would sulk around the set, often forgetting his lines during filming. Edward, who was recognized by MGM for his unerring sense of comedy, also found himself becoming weighed down each time he was assigned to a new Keaton film. The importance of Keaton's success or failure directly impacted Edward's career. It was becoming Edward's responsibility to make sure that Keaton performed the way the studio expected.

For his next directorial assignment Edward was asked to work with Keaton in *Doughboys,* a remake of Wallace Beery's World War I wartime comedy *Behind the Front* (1926). Publicized as *Forward March, The Big Shot* and *War Babies* during its production, *Doughboys* was released in August of that year.

Keaton is cast as Elmer Julius Stuyvesant, Jr., a millionaire's son who enlists in the army and experiences nonsensical adventures as he attempts to be a soldier. To impress Mary, a shop girl who has his heart, Elmer unwillingly registers for the army. Played by Hoot Gibson's current wife Sally Eilers, Mary says that she hasn't any interest in him.

At camp Elmer is trained by a hardboiled officer named Sergeant Brophy (Edward Brophy). Brophy becomes Elmer's adversary as he attempts to date Mary, who has joined the army to help the troops. Elmer becomes jealous of Brophy's advances and confronts Mary to let her know how he feels, with the two separating on bad terms.

After being trained, Elmer's unit is sent overseas and directly into battle at the front line. During a mission Elmer stumbles into a trench of exhausted Germans. He discovers that one of the officers is Gustave (Arnold Korff), his German butler from back home. Old friends, the two get reacquainted. Upon leaving, Elmer asks if he can take one of their pistols as a souvenir—which they carelessly wrap for him in a highly confidential map of the German lines.

Elmer is again reunited with Mary after she travels to Europe to find him to let him know she is sorry for the way she acted towards him. Thinking that they're being helpful, they decide to drive an unattended ambulance full of wounded soldiers to the field hospital. When a German plane opens fire on the vehicle, they discover that they are driving a truck full of ammunition. Narrowly escaping the truck being blown to pieces, they run to an abandoned house for shelter. The plane drops a bomb through the roof of the house but it's a dud. The two don't want to take any chances being in the same building as the unexploded ordnance so they take cover in a bomb crater.

Exhausted, they fall asleep, only to be awoken by a group of German soldiers. Ready to surrender, Elmer is approached by Gustave, who tells him that the war is over. The butler quickly returns to his master's side.

Back in the States, Elmer's army buddies have become his associates and he is now happily married to Mary.

The level of *Doughboys* noticeably slipped from previous Edward-Keaton collaborations. Although the crew included most of the same workers from *Spite Marriage,* in comparison the film appears compromised in many areas. The editing appears rushed, with scenes abruptly cutting from one to the other. The majority of the gags written for *Doughboys* would have been throw-aways in any of Keaton's classic films, with their levels seeming to be more appropriate for one of Hal Roach's Laurel and Hardy shorts than a Keaton showcase.

There's little attention given to costuming, as the wardrobes appear contemporary to the early 1930s instead of those of the World War I era. But even more apparent is the inap-

Director King Vidor (left), one of Edward's oldest friends, visits with Edward (center) and Keaton on the set of *Doughboys* (1930).

propriate age level of the main characters, who in real life might have been recruits in their late teens or early twenties. Keaton was now in his mid-thirties and hardly looked like a young man, with lines forming around his eyes. The remainder of the cast was comprised of aging talent, including Frank Mayo as Capt. Scott, William Steele as Lt. Randolph and character actors Victor Potel as Svendenburg and Pitzy Katz as Abie Cohn.

In 1930, as many studios were writing off the musical genre which required a substantial investment in time and money, comedy teams were becoming popular, with the Marx Brothers (*Animal Crackers*), Bert Wheeler and Robert Woolsey (*Hook, Line and Sinker*), and the Three Stooges (*Soup to Nuts*) all making successful debuts. Following this trend for *Dough-*

boys, Keaton was paired with novelty singer Cliff "Ukulele Ike" Edwards, a major vaudeville and Broadway star during the 1920s. He played the ukulele and sang in a scat-like style which he called "effin." Keaton is often moved out of the frame of action as constant attention is given to Edwards' in-your-face character Nescopeck. In subsequent films Keaton would be matched with other comedians who were meant to support his ongoing portrayal of the Elmer character.

The music is a highlight of the movie. Its several songs are credited to Edward, Howard Johnson and Joseph Meyers. Edward was given an uncredited role as an army cook which gave him the opportunity to perform with Keaton and Edwards in a scat style number. In the musical interlude Edwards as Nescopeck plays the ukulele with a pair of drumsticks while Keaton as Elmer holds it and performs the chord changes. The cook is disgusted with Nescopeck's slow-tempo crooning and is about to hack the ukulele with his bayonet. But just in time Nescopeck speeds up the tempo and turns the song into a red-hot number. The cook joins in, grabbing his rifle to use as an imaginary bass violin, using his bayonet as a bow, while he vocalizes the sound of the instrument. Sergeant Brophy breaks up the impromptu session. The scene, which was filmed in a single take, is one of the film's highlights.

Keaton increasingly relied on his growing friendship with Edward to get his suggestions noticed. For *Doughboys* this gave him the opportunity to interject some of his own war experiences into the storyline. A dance number, in which Elmer and his buddies dress in drag, was a version of a burlesque number Keaton created during his time spent in France performing with a group of soldiers who were known as "The Sunshine Players."

Salvador de Alberich again collaborated with Edward for the Spanish version, *De Frente, Marchen*. The alternate cast included Conchita Montenegro, Romualdo Tirado Juan de Landa, Martin Garralaga, Rosita Grana, Francisco Madrid, Lolita Méndez, Gabry Rivas and Hans von Morhart.

An uncredited script supervisor named Ebba Havez assisted Edward on *Doughboys*. Ebba (née Ahl), the widowed wife of Jean C. Havez, started her career in the entertainment industry as a vaudeville singer and dancer, using the stage name Doris Vernon. In 1917 Jean Havez had formed a vaudeville combination, which included Ebba (performing vocals) and harpist Isabel White.

Before marrying Ebba, Havez was married to Cecil Cunningham, an actress who eventually found a limited popularity during the 1930s and 1940s. Their marriage lasted between 1915 and 1917, ending with Cunningham requesting a divorce from Havez on the grounds that he was a lazy man, and Havez complaining that she was a hard-headed Irishwoman. Havez soon married Ebba, with their marriage lasting until his death in 1925.

The rotund Jean, an unsung hero of the silent era, became a celebrated lyricist of many popular songs during the earlier part of the century, including "Everybody Works but Father," a 1905 hit sensation for which he wrote both the lyrics and music. For a time his name was synonymous with the New York City theater scene, as he wrote for Broadway and vaudeville musicals and comedies, working alongside such talents as Lew Dockstader and Marie Dressler.

Finding work as a gagman for Comique Film Corporation, Havez's creativity expanded from Broadway to the motion picture industry as he started to write scenarios with similar success. He and Herbert Warren collaborated on scenarios used for Arbuckle and Keaton shorts filmed at Comique's Bronx studio. One of Havez's earliest scenarios was for *Oh, Doctor!* (1917), Keaton's sixth short.

During 1921 Havez moved to the Harold Lloyd writing staff at the Hal Roach Studios. With Sam Taylor and Harley M. Walker, he contributed to the screenplay of *The Goat* (1921), *A Sailor-Made Man* (1921) and *Grandma's Boy* (1922), and co-wrote the story and screenplay of *Doctor Jack* (1922). Havez was responsible for coming up with Lloyd's famous clock-hanging scenario used in *Safety Last* (1923).

Havez moved over to the Keaton Studio and worked on *Three Ages* (1923), collaborating with Joseph Mitchell, an ex-vaudevillian, and Clyde Bruckman, a past colleague at Comique. The combination of talent formed a skilled scenario department. Keaton's fondness for baseball rubbed off on his entire crew: If there was ever a creative block in the process of working out a gag, the cast and crew would break for a game, with Havez officiating as umpire. Havez also worked on the scenarios for Keaton's *Our Hospitality* (1923), *Sherlock, Jr.* (1924), *The Navigator* (1924), and *Seven Chances* (1925), contributing many of their famous gags.

In January 1925 Havez returned to Harold Lloyd, contributing to *The Freshman* (1925). Havez didn't have the opportunity to see the work he did for this film, as he died of acute pulmonary edema on February 12, 1925.

Through his Keaton connection, Edward was introduced to the thin, blonde-haired, blue-eyed scenarist Ebba. He and Ebba worked well as a team, with the two forming a close bond that led to future collaborations and eventually to their marriage in 1932.

After renegotiating a long-term contract with MGM, Edward was assigned to direct *Remote Control*, a November release starring William Haines. Once again, Edward's work went unbilled, as directorial responsibility went through the hands of three others, with the final credit going to Nick Grinde and Malcolm St. Clair. Haines, who also signed a new contract with MGM, was featured in the comedy, which was based on the play of the same name.

The story involved fast-talking radio announcer William Judd "Bill" Brennan (Haines), the one-man staff of a nearly defunct radio station. Bill discovers that rival broadcaster Professor Leonard T. Kruger (John Miljan) is a fake on-air clairvoyant using code to communicate by remote control with his criminal gang. Bill foils Kruger before he can send a code to gangland members over the airwaves.

The leading female role and Bill's romantic interest is Marion Ferguson, played by Mary Doran. Singer Charles King plays Samuel "Sam" Ferguson, her brother and the station owner. King's part gave him the opportunity to sing the film's hit song "Just a Little Closer," written by Joe Meyer.

Despite the serious nature of the plot, the film was promoted as a comedy. Given the opportunity to perform on-air impersonations of radio celebrities, Haines' role was mostly that of a straight man to someone else's jokes. Although his fans continued to support him at the box office, critics took notice that with *Remote Control* he was losing his drawing power. Ticket sales bore them out, as they were less than half of what one of his pictures would have brought in just a year before.

Presented with one weak script after another, Edward was frustrated by the lack of creativity in MGM's assembly-line productions. He was a consummate director who took pleasure in bringing life to the characters in a script. In an interview published in *La Vanguardia*, Edward described directing as an art similar to drawing caricatures in comic strip panels. Edward explained that the comic strip artist illustrated each panel box with diverse points of view, expressing funny incidents by means of a simple look or gesture. In directing a film,

Edward would visualize these types of illustrations, corresponding them to the perspective of the movie camera. But with his direction already dictated to him at MGM, there would be little chance for him to apply his visions to an already prepared script.

Edward also feared the possibility that, because of his experience and patience working with difficult stars, he would be saddled with actors whose careers were waning, as was the case working with Keaton and Haines. As deduced, the studio assigned Edward with Keaton, teaming them up for *Parlor, Bedroom and Bath*, a February 1931 release. Due to his commitment directing *Remote Control*, Edward was unavailable to direct Keaton's previous film, *Sidewalks of New York*, which was poorly received. For *Parlor, Bedroom and Bath* Keaton demanded that Edward direct the comedy.

Wood Soanes, an *Oakland Tribune* entertainment columnist, reported on Edward and Keaton's work relationship as he experienced it during a planning session for *Parlor, Bedroom and Bath*.

> On a battered sofa in Edward Sedgwick's workroom, that worthy was sprawled with one garterless sock flopping about a shoe exposing a length of thick calf. Opposite Sedgwick, and constantly endangered by flying hooves as Sedgwick shifted his mountain of flesh, was [Enoch O.] Van Pelt, bespectacled, sober and serious-minded.

Buster Keaton (driving) demanded that Edward be assigned to direct *Parlor, Bedroom and Bath* (1931), as he was the only person who seemed to understand his ideas and visions and attempted to implement them into a production.

On the far side of the room, behind a fumed oak desk, sat Keaton, coatless, with his shirt open at the neck. Every so often he pawed Sedgwick's desk in search of a pencil to illustrate a point. Having found it, he proceeded to dismantle the desk drawers in a frenzied hunt for scratch paper, and when he did have all of the tools at hand, he forgot what he wanted them for and hurled them into the waste basket.

All the while Sedgwick, who has directed countless successful comedies without over-exerting himself, protested mildly and with quaint profanity. Van Pelt scratched away with his pencil and Keaton guffawed. It was an animated but seemingly purposeless conference but the next day Keaton was hard at work on the scenes of *Parlor, Bedroom and Bath*, in which he has Charlotte Greenwood for a comedy aide.

Written with hints of pre–Code sexual innuendo, the *Parlor, Bedroom and Bath* script by Charles W. Bell and Mark Swan appeared to be a promising one. Jeffrey Haywood (Reginald Denny) wants to marry Virginia Embrey (Sally Eilers). But Virginia won't marry until her older sister Angelica (Dorothy Christy) gets married first, as she doesn't want Angelica to appear to be an old maid. Angelica is taking her time finding a husband, who she insists must be a great lover. Out of frustration to get married to Virginia, Jeffrey determines to find a match for Angelica.

Reginald Irving (Keaton) passes Angelica's house as he tacks advertisements to telephone poles. He becomes preoccupied when he notices a bathing suit–clad Angelica diving into her pool. Jeffrey accidentally hits Reginald with his car, knocking him unconscious. After bringing Reginald into the house, Jeffrey senses an opportunity and spreads the rumor that Reginald is a great lover and a great outdoorsman. To further the plan to get Angelica interested in him, and to make her jealous, Jeffrey hires women to bust into the house in pursuit of Reginald, all pretending to be his previous lovers.

Jeffrey's next plan is to get Reginald to a hotel where he will meet a woman who will pretend to be his lover. Angelica will then enter the room just as they are in an impassioned embrace, with the thought that she would finally see Reginald as the virile type of man she has been searching for. Jeffrey tells Reginald what he's to say and do once he meets the friend at the hotel.

In the meantime, Nita Leslie (Joan Peers) is trying to get the romantic attention of her husband Frederick (Walter Merrill), who is always leaving her for business assignments. Nita devises a way to get Frederick's attention: fake an affair with the he-man Reginald. Thinking that Nita is Jeffrey's actress, Reginald takes her to dinner.

Mayhem ensues, as Reginald, following Jeffrey's advice, appears too romantic for Nita's plan. Just as she locks herself in the bedroom, Jeffrey's friend Polly Hathaway (Charlotte Greenwood) arrives to run through the routine that she and Reginald are to perform for Angelica's arrival. The Amazonian-sized Polly swings the confused Reginald around the room.

Just after Polly leaves to change her clothes, Leila Crofton (Natalie Moorhead) arrives to rescue her friend Nita. Reginald, who is now falling into the character that Jeffery has trained him to be, practices his amorous routine on Leila. Just as they are in a passionate embrace, an infuriated Frederick and Angelica arrive. A mad chase through the hotel begins, with Frederick trying to shoot Reginald for stealing his wife. Reginald finally confronts Angelica alone in the room and gives her the romantic routine as the movie fades to black.

The cast was supplemented by two familiar faces who were already regulars in Keaton's films, Cliff Edwards as a bellhop and Edward Brophy as a detective. A portion of the filming

Employees of MGM nicknamed Columbia Pictures Corporation's Poverty Row studio on Gower Street "Siberia," as actors who flexed their muscles a bit too much, or a director who shot a scene differently from the way he had been instructed, were sent there for a film or two. In 1931 Edward was loaned to Columbia to direct *A Dangerous Affair*, starring (left to right) Jack Holt, Susan Fleming, Sally Blane, and Ralph Graves.

was done on location at Keaton's Beverly Hills villa—a source of Keaton's financial stress. Keaton's anxiety was becoming obvious, as he appeared rather gaunt in the close-ups, showing the combined toll of his troubling marriage, financial difficulties, distress due to a lack of ownership in his productions, and the beginning of his problem with alcohol.

Keaton's features were profitable in the foreign-language market. Although there wasn't a Spanish version produced this time, there would be German (*Casanova Wider*) and French (*Buster Se Marie*) editions, which meant that *Parlor* had to be shot three separate times. For *Parlor, Bedroom and Bath* Edward Brophy directed both the German and French editions.

In 1931 Edward's work was limited to only two releases, *A Dangerous Affair* and *Maker of Men*, both second-rate features produced by Columbia. Founded in 1919 as Cohn-Brandt-Cohn Film Sales by brothers Harry and Jack Cohn and Joe Brandt, Columbia began by producing low-budget films in a leased studio on Hollywood's Gower Street. By the 1930s Columbia was producing moderately budgeted features and short subjects, which often featured stars and directors on loan from other studios. Employees of MGM nicknamed the Poverty Row studio "Siberia" as Mayer had an unwritten policy of punishing actors who flexed their muscles a bit too much for his comfort, or a director who shot a scene differently from the way he had been instructed, by sending them to Columbia for a film or two.

A Dangerous Affair featured Jack Holt and Ralph Graves, two seasoned actors who were paired by Columbia in several action movies during the late 1920s and early 1930s. Similar to the Sedgwicks, the two had started their careers acting in films during Hollywood's formative years.

In *A Dangerous Affair*, Holt played Police Lieutenant McHenry while Graves portrayed the role of crime reporter Wally Cook. Friendly rivals, the two are employed in the sleepy Long Island town of Havenhurst. Wally stages a burglary for the fun of it and writes lurid stories about the "ghost gang" behind the crime. The action begins once the necklace that was to have been returned to the rightful owner disappears. The story progresses from a comedy to a melodrama after two corpses and a haunted house are added, with fourteen suspects rounded up in the excitement.

Edward's second Columbia Film, *Maker of Men*, was a gridiron drama. He shared writing credit with Howard J. Green—a bonus, as Edward was no longer able to write for the films he directed at MGM. Edward directed cleverly, building the scenario into a sentimental father-and-son story.

With a working title of *Yellow*, the story featured Holt as Western University's aging varsity football Coach Dudley, who needs to win the season in order to keep his job. His son Bob (Richard Cromwell) is on the team but his heart isn't in football as his father dreamed it would be. Bob's fumble costs W.U. the game and word gets around about how bad he is, but Coach knows his son has a fighting spirit inside him. Bob admits that he doesn't have the courage to play football. Coach lets him turn in his uniform after he costs W.U. another game. Bob feels that he never was a son to his dad, but just another football player. He leaves home, telling his father that he's overcome his fears.

It's two years later and Coach refuses to correspond with his son. In the meantime Bob has entered Monroe University, W.U.'s rival, and is a player on the football team. Bob begs his coach to put him in the game against W.U.—this is the game that his dad's career depends on. Bob makes the only touchdown in the first half of the game.

Coach Dudley encourages his players to take out his son. Monroe ties the score in the final quarter, with five minutes to go. With seconds left before the game ends, Bob scores another touchdown, injuring his leg in the process. Coach comes to visit him in the locker room and is proud of his son.

Maker of Men also featured Joan Marsh as Dorothy, Natalie Moorhead as Mrs. Rhodes, Joe Sawyer as Bennett the Monroe coach, John Wayne as the W.U. quarterback, and an uncredited Buster Crabbe as a football player.

Harry Cohn, head of Columbia, was interested in changing the studio's product from low-budget westerns and comedies to sophisticated movies. Cohn was especially interested in promoting young contract player John Wayne, who had the debonair qualities he was looking for in his films. Wayne's films were starting to get recognition from critics, with an increasing fanbase forming after the successful release of *The Big Trail* (1930).

But instead of placing Wayne in important roles, Cohn reduced his parts to that of a supporting player. Apparently, rumors were spreading around the studio that Wayne was in the habit of getting drunk on the set and was fond of fooling around with Columbia's actresses. This was far from the truth, as it turned out that a starlet in *Arizona* (1931) was promoting the idea that Wayne was interested in her—this being part of the starlet's scheme to make her paramour, Cohn, jealous.

Although the accusations were false, Cohn wasn't satisfied until he took out his revenge on Wayne by casting him in small roles in westerns that featured matinee idols Buck Jones and Tim McCoy. After Wayne completed his responsibilities in the mediocre oaters, Cohn gave him a minor part in *Maker of Men*: His character Dusty appears about 35 minutes into the movie as the quarterback for W.U.'s losing team. This must have been a humiliating part for Wayne, as he previously played college football for the USC Trojans.

As in the previous year, Edward's direction work in 1932 was limited, with only three features released that year. *The Passionate Plumber* was a remake of a 1928 comedy featuring Marion Davies titled *Her Cardboard Lover*. Released by MGM in February, *The Passionate Plumber* again found Keaton doing a take on his doltish character Elmer. This time the story places Elmer E. Tuttle, an American, in Paris as a plumber who fixes the plumbing of wealthy socialites.

For *The Passionate Plumber* MGM teamed Keaton with a comic piano player named Jimmy Durante. Durante, who had just signed a five-year contract, came to the studio with a fanbase from his Broadway performances and radio shows. Playing the role of Julius J. McCracken, Durante's approach was in-your-face, a contrast to Keaton's milquetoast Elmer—a style which came close to reducing Keaton's character to that of second banana.

Julius, a French-speaking chauffeur with a Bronx accent, uses Elmer's service to repair his employer's shower fixture. Socialite Patricia Alden (Irene Purcelle), the owner of the house, is in the breakup phase of a relationship with her Spanish boyfriend Tony Lagorce (Gilbert Roland). Tony turns out to be married, and although Patricia is still in love with him she wants to have nothing to do with a married man.

Elmer is pulled into the relationship as Tony catches him in Patricia's bathroom dressed in only a towel—the outcome of Julius turning on the water before Elmer was done fixing the shower. Tony, jealous of Elmer, challenges him to a duel.

The next day as the two prepare to raise their pistols, a hunter fires his rifle at a bird. They each think the other has shot their pistol first, with Tony fainting and Elmer knocking himself unconscious as he runs into a tree. Patricia runs to each, thinking that they are both dead. As she comforts Elmer, he falls in love with her.

Tony is also seeing Nina Estrados (Mona Maris), who is jealous that Tony is married. When Nina and Patricia show up at a casino that he is visiting, he manages to keep them apart. Neither Patricia nor Nina is aware that Tony is using each of them as the wife in his story; being the cad that he is, he doesn't want to get into a serious relationship with either of them.

Elmer sneaks into the casino in an effort to speak to General Bouschay (August Tollaire) about selling the army a patented pistol-flashlight combination that he invented. He meets Patricia and Tony and, in a scheme to make Tony even more jealous, she plays up the story that Elmer is her real lover. To top off the act, she exits the casino with Elmer. Once at her apartment she demands that Elmer leave. When she sees Tony parked in front of her building she attempts to leave with him but can't, as Elmer is sitting outside of her room.

Albine, Patricia's maid (Polly Moran), announces that her Aunt Charlotte (Maude Eburne) has stopped by to keep an eye on her. As there's no time to get Keaton out of the bedroom, Patricia jumps into her bed, with Keaton pretending to be her physician. In one of his funnier scenes in *Passionate Plumber* Keaton uses a steel toolbox full of plumbing tools as his doctor bag, substituting a plunger and pliers for a stethoscope.

By now Elmer realizes that Patricia isn't interested in him. Patricia escapes Elmer and Aunt Charlotte to go to Tony's apartment. Elmer calls Tony to come to Patricia's apartment, as he wants to tell him that she's been lying about having an affair with him. Just as he gets off of the phone, Nina arrives and demands to meet with Tony's wife Patricia. The situation gets further complicated as Tony arrives and Patricia returns home.

Once Patricia and Nina find out that Tony was using the two of them for his pleasure, and had no interest in having a serious relationship with either, they both start hurling all sorts of breakable items at him, with Elmer supplying them dinner plates as ammunition. After they throw their last plate Tony runs for the door. Nina chases after him, confessing, "Can't you see how much I love you?" Patricia announces the same to Elmer, as does Julius to Albine.

Although Keaton's stone-face performance was a nice contrast to Durante's high emotional level, the general direction of the film was lacking, with scenes appearing to be dragged-out and humorless. Edward co-directed the French-language version of *The Passionate Plumber* with Claude Autant-Lara, utilizing the principal actors from the English version.

Edward's next project was a flying film for the Caddo Company, *Sky Devils*. When selected by producer Howard Hughes to direct *Sky Devils*, a World War I comedy, Edward jumped at the opportunity to work with the Academy Award winner: Hughes had won the first ever Oscar for Best Director of a Comedy Picture for *Two Arabian Knights* (1928) and nominations for *The Racket* (1928), *Hell's Angels* (1930), and *The Front Page* (1931). Hughes, an aircraft fanatic, was praised for his hard work on the filming and aircraft sequences in *Hell's Angels*, garnering him a nomination for Best Cinematography.

Released by United Artists in March, *Sky Devils* was a combination of *Hell's Angels*, an epic World War I war film, and *Two Arabian Knights*, a comedy that follows an American soldier and his detested sergeant to the front lines. Under the working title of *Sky Hogs*, a team of top writers, including Robert Benchley, Carroll Graham, Garrett Graham, James A. Starr, A. Edward Sutherland, and Ebba Havez wrote the continuity and dialogue for the film, which was based on a story by Edward. Al Boasberg, famous humorist, was eventually hired to liven up the dialogue. The addition of an original Alfred Newman score and choreography by Busby Berkeley made the film proposal sound very promising.

Surplus aerial footage shot for *Hell's Angels* was used to supplement new scenes to be filmed and supervised by J.B. Alexander, chief of aeronautics. Half a dozen authentic-type ships, including French and U.S. training and fighting planes, were obtained and reconditioned for flying sequences which were filmed at March Field in Riverside.

Production started in the middle of May 1931 and by the second week of June Edward had resigned from his directorial responsibilities. After returning home for a break from shooting ocean scenes at San Pedro, he announced that he did not believe in the storyline. The completion of *Sky Devils* was placed in the hands of Thomas Buckingham, with the final directorial credit going to A. Edward Sutherland. Hughes had promised that he would give Edward another assignment soon, but that never happened.

The entire production seemed to have been in too much of a chaotic state for Edward's liking. Hughes originally signed actor Louis Wolheim for the leading role of Sergeant Hogan.

But Wolheim's tragic and untimely death changed that plan. Hughes had a difficult time finding an actor who could fill the role that was written for Wolheim. With the exception of signing a promising young actor borrowed from Fox, Spencer Tracy, for the leading role of Wilkie, the principal roles weren't filled until just before filming started. After weeks of search in which dozens of actors were given screen tests, Caddo announced that Sidney Toler had finally been selected for the role of Hogan, but by the time of filming he was replaced with William "Stage" Boyd. Other parts were also reassigned. Lola Lane was signed to play the feminine lead Mary, but by the start of production Ann Dvorak was in the role. The part of Fifi, originally promised to Renee Marvelle, was given to Yola d'Avril. George Cooper was cast as Wilkie's sidekick Mitchell.

Two inexperienced Coney Island lifeguards, Wilkie and Mitchell, are drafted into the cavalry unit of the army and assigned to clean up after horses. In an attempt to desert to South America they mistakenly stow away on a troop transport taking air corps cadets to the war zone. While in France, Wilkie and Hogan form an unlikely alliance as they both vie for Mary, an American dancer entertaining the troops. Mary and Wilkie fall for each other as Hogan insists on making a move on her. After their night out on the town, Wilkie and Hogan are charged with being absent without leave, with military police searching the town for them. Wilkie, Hogan and Mary are arrested.

Breaking out of the brig, the three attempt to escape by plane. During their flight they accidentally drop the plane's bombs on a major German munitions dump. Word gets back to the base and they suddenly become heroes. The Germans capture them once they make it across the enemy's line. Mitchell flies a plane to where they are being held and single-handedly rescues the group. They take off in one of the German planes, and as they pass over their commanding headquarters they accidentally drop a bomb on the building as the four make their escape to freedom.

As with Edward's work on *Sky Devils*, Ebba's contribution went uncredited, which might have worked out for the best; considering the amount of talent that was utilized in writing the script, it turned out to be a B story. Although *Sky Devils* might be thought of as a forgettable comedy, at the time it did get decent reviews, and more importantly called attention to promising actors Tracy and Dvorak, who would move on to bigger projects.

Josie's return to the silver screen was in *Son of Oklahoma*, a Western that would mark the end of her acting career. Released in July by Poverty Row's Sono Art-World Wide Pictures, the Trem Carr production was her introduction to sound films, proving that she was qualified to appear in talkies if she had decided to continue. With a career as a stuntwoman in her past, the 38-year-old Josie was looking much older than her age, making her a perfect choice for matriarchal roles. Playing the part of "Shotgun" Mary Clayton, Josie was cast as the mother of Dan Clayton (Bob Steele).

Steele, son of the film's director Robert North Bradbury, was born Robert Adrian Bradbury. After performing with his twin brother Bill in their family's vaudeville act, the two did their first movie work in a series of shorts that were directed by their father. After a long career as a cowboy star, Steele crossed over to television, becoming a popular guest star on the majority of the western series during the 1950s and '60s. One of his most familiar roles was in the 1965 series *F Troop*, the cantankerous Trooper Duffy.

Filmed against the harsh landscape of the Mojave Desert near Palmdale, California, *Son of Oklahoma* opens as John Clayton (Robert E. Homans), his wife Mary (Josie) and their three-year-old son Dan are camping out in the desert. Outlaw Ray Brent (Earl Dwire) wakes Mary and demands that she leave John for him, with the threat that he will kill her husband if she doesn't. Fearing for John's life, Mary complies and Ray allows her to take her son with them. Mary leaves John a note saying that she left with Ray because of the threat on his life—a note that John would never see due to Dan playfully grabbing it and stuffing it in his overalls. Before they depart, Ray empties the bullets from the rifle of the sleeping Dan. As they ride away Dan crawls to the back of the wagon and falls out, unnoticed, into the scrub.

Manuel Verdugo (Julian Rivero) finds the boy in the desert, sitting in the dirt playing with a large nugget of gold. Apparently Dan discovered the site of a vein of gold that Manuel has been searching for. Manuel, unable to file a claim because he isn't a citizen, must keep the find a secret. After being unsuccessful in finding Dan's parents in town, he brings the boy home to live with his wife Margarita and their daughter Anita, who is about the same age as Dan.

Looking for Dan, Ray retraces the trail they took, returning to the campsite. John wakes up and is confronted by Ray, who cold-bloodedly shoots him as he tries to defend himself with his empty rifle. Ray returns to Mary and tells her that John is out of their life forever, as he was killed in their shootout. When Ray turns his back on her, Mary rides off with the team of horses, leaving the outlaw behind in the desert.

Seventeen years later, Anita (Carmen Laroux) is returning from attending school abroad in Spain, with plans of marrying Dan. Manuel intends to give the gold mine to Anita and Dan as a wedding present, so that Dan can legally file a claim on it. Mary, now known as "Shotgun Mary," is the owner of a saloon located in a town near the desert where her husband was killed. Over the years Mary has made a reputation for herself, running saloons across the west, in hopes that one day Ray would walk through the door and she would get her revenge on him. To her surprise Ray enters the bar. Now a member of a gang intent on filing a claim on Manuel's hidden gold mine, Ray tells her that he'll help her find the boy if in return she helps him get possession of the unclaimed vein.

Dan enters the bar to make a purchase. Knowing that Dan is the son of Manuel, Mary and Brent follow him out into the desert. Josie gets Dan's attention by pretending to be lost. He takes her to the mine to get some shade and to recover. Dan explains to her that Manuel discovered the vein of gold when he found him (Dan) in the desert. He still has the note that was found on him and shows it to her. Mary doesn't let on that she's his mother, telling him that Mary Clayton died a long time ago and that Ray Brent killed his father.

Dan goes off to meet Anita, who's arriving by stagecoach—the same stage that Brent and his gang are planning to rob. The stage stops in a pass so that passengers can get some water from a spring, with Anita waiting in the coach. A gang member commandeers the stage and takes off with Anita and the $40,000. Dan attempts to rescue her, jumping onto the coach, but he's knocked off and the gang member gets away.

In town, Ray frames Dan as the robber. Just as Dan is about to be apprehended by a posse, Mary disrupts the group with a blast from her shotgun, giving Dan an opportunity to escape.

Ray's gang kidnaps Manuel, threatening him with hanging if he doesn't tell them the location of the hidden mine. Manuel escapes with his life and Dan catches up with Ray. The two draw their guns on each other, with Dan wounding Ray. John, now a marshal, arrives at the scene and is reunited with Mary. Everyone is surprised to find that John is still alive; he was only wounded when Ray had left him for dead years ago. Ray draws his gun on the two and shoots Mary, grazing her in the shoulder. John returns fire, killing the outlaw. Dan goes to get water for Mary from the pack on his horse, and when he returns he overhears them talking about him being their long-lost son, and that he must never know the truth. Dan tells them that he overheard their conversation and the three are happily reunited.

Son of Oklahoma has all the ingredients of a classic B Western, with its story giving Josie ample opportunity to use her dialogue skills. She also had the chance to use her musical skills in one brief scene where she plays a piano. After years of performing in action films, for Josie *Son of Oklahoma* was the perfect film for her to retire from show business with.

MGM scheduled *Speak Easily*, Edward's next Keaton film, as an August release. Filmed during May and June, the comedy once again featured Durante as Keaton's second banana. This time Keaton's character, scatterbrained Potts College professor Timoleon Zanders Post, learns from a letter that he has inherited the huge sum of $750,000 and decides to go out and enjoy life, searching for adventure and companionship. His assistant Jenkins (Sidney Bracey), in order to motivate the professor to leave his routine job to experience an adventure with the hope of finding companionship, wrote the phony letter of inheritance.

On his train ride to New York City, Professor Post meets a troupe of entertainers traveling from town to town presenting their lackluster musical to tiny audiences. James "Jimmy" Dodge (Jimmy Durante) is the glue keeping the amateur group together, alternating between actor and piano player. One of the leggy dancers, Pansy Peets (Ruth Selwyn) takes an interest in the professor.

Professor Post misses his train connection and is forced to travel into town to find lodging. He enters an opera house where the amateurish dance troupe is practicing. The sheriff says he will be confiscating the dancers' luggage unless an outstanding hotel bill is paid. Believing that he is rich, Professor Post volunteers to pay the invoice, using money from his savings that he withdrew before his trip. In exchange for getting them out of trouble, Jimmy offers the professor control of the musical. The professor accepts the offer, replying that he has the money to take the show to Broadway.

Arriving in New York City, Professor Post is having trouble getting the attention of a producer to support the musical. Finally, a stage director (Sidney Toler) offers to run the production just as long as he is given the freedom to build it up the way he feels it should be presented. A vamping dancer named Eleanor Espere (Thelma Todd) tries out for the musical. When she mentions to the professor that she once worked at a speakeasy, he corrects her, saying that what she means to say is "speak easily." Jimmy decides to have that serve as the title of the musical production. Once Eleanor finds out that Professor Post is wealthy, she starts to make moves on him and trying to get him to pay the monthly rent on her stylish apartment. Inviting the professor up to her apartment on the pretense of meeting her brother, she proceeds to get him drunk. Professor Post passes out and wakes up the next morning in her bedroom.

Jimmy learns that the professor's inheritance was a fake, and that requests are being made for payments for the costume and scenery used in the musical. Professor Post needs to hide out on opening night, as a bill collector will be appearing to serve him an injunction and close down the production.

Back at the apartment, Professor Post can't remember what happened the previous night. When Eleanor's brother shows up, he insists that she was taken advantage of by the professor. This is a scam to force the "wealthy" professor to marry her. Jimmy arrives just in time and sneaks Professor Post out a window, telling him that he will have to lie low in New Jersey.

Opening night appears to be a success, with a full house anticipating the new musical. The collector shows up backstage, as does Professor Post, who insists the taxi driver didn't know how to get to New Jersey. Jimmy attempts to keep the professor hidden until the show is over.

After finding out that Professor Post didn't intentionally plan to spend the night at Eleanor's, and that he isn't in love with her, Pansy gives him a kiss. Surprised, he loses his balance and steps backwards onto the stage as the performance is just beginning. The professor sets off a chain reaction, knocking over dancers and scenery. The musical quickly becomes a comedy—and a successful one at that. Just as the collector catches up with Professor Post to serve him papers, investor comes backstage and offers the professor a $100,000 partnership. In the end, the production is a success and, to Eleanor's dismay, Professor Post and Pansy are in love.

Although Keaton's contract gave him consultation rights for the story and direction of his films, the final decision wasn't his to make. The production system, which already took away his individuality, was now destroying any of the remaining creative confidence that he had. If Keaton had complied with MGM's requests, or if the studio gave in slightly to Keaton's concerns, the outcome of the situation would have likely been different. Using his talent, he might have been able to ingeniously adapt the dopey characters that he was assigned into memorable ones.

The MGM films that Edward and Keaton worked on seemed second-rate compared to their previous efforts, but their collaborations were well-promoted by the studio, making them commercially profitable. The November 11 *Dallas Morning News* gave *Speak Easily* a thumbs-up review: "The action of the film is rowdy, robust and boisterous, particularly during the final sequences. Action is slowed up somewhat by the dialogue in the early parts, but when words are forgotten and the comedy goes into slapstick, *Speak Easily* becomes hilarious." The potential for a hit was there and Keaton could have easily made the best of the situation. Durante's acting in *Speak Easily* presented the audience with the appearance that he was having fun with his character, especially during his performance of a couple of novelty songs.

Keaton's lack of interest in his films was becoming obvious. Combined with his personal life, which was complicated by his divorce to Natalie that year, Keaton depended on alcohol to help him get through each day. He was soon finding it harder to come to work sober and on some days difficult to come to work altogether. Like the previous productions Keaton did for MGM, the studio threw good money into *Speak Easily*. As Keaton's situation grew more and more intolerable, MGM became concerned with the mounting costs which were generated by his poor performances that were causing filming delays.

Keaton's condition was also affecting the way MGM reviewed Edward's work. It became Edward's responsibility to make sure that all productions were running smoothly, and that meant he was responsible for making sure Keaton showed up at the studio on time and sober. Keaton was certainly placing a strain on their relationship, as it was becoming a major effort on Edward's part to get both punctuality and sobriety from his friend.

Edward "Ned" W. Sedgwick died in 1932 at the age of 64. The proud patriarch of the Five Sedgwicks had been proven wrong when he remarked to Edward that silent films were a passing fad, with each of his children building their livelihoods around the entertainment medium.

As a director, Edward's final collaboration with Keaton was *What! No Beer?*, released by MGM in February 1933. Filmed in December 1932 and January 1933, *What! No Beer?* premiered on the eve of the repeal of the prohibition of alcohol in the United States. Ratified on January 16, 1919, and going into effect on January 16, 1920, the Eighteenth Amendment to the Constitution banned the sale, manufacturing, and transportation of alcohol for consumption. The month after the release of *What! No Beer?*, on March 23, President Franklin Roosevelt signed into law the Cullen-Harrison Act, an amendment to the Eighteenth Amendment, known as the Volstead Act, permitting the production and sale of specific kinds of alcoholic beverages. On December 5, 1933, the Twenty-First Amendment was ratified, repealing the Eighteenth Amendment.

Keaton plays Elmer J. Butts, a taxidermist, with Durante playing his sidekick, barber Jimmy Potts. With Prohibition being repealed, Elmer and Jimmy anticipate getting a jump-start on slaking the public's thirst for beer. Using Elmer's lifetime savings of $10,000 they

What! No Beer? (1932) premiered on the eve of the repeal of the prohibition of alcohol in the United States. Edward directed Buster Keaton and Jimmy Durante in their third team-up together. This would be the last time Edward would direct Keaton.

reopen a bankrupt brewery. Immediately beginning operations, they produce their first vat of beer, with Elmer slipping and sliding on the spilled suds in true slapstick style.

The police become aware of the sudden activity at the old brewery and raid it. Elmer and Jimmy are arrested on charges of manufacturing, possession and intent to distribute beer in the dry town. However, the chemist at police headquarters is unable to prove that the beverage contains any alcohol. The two feel that they're a failure. Jimmy eventually discovers what went wrong in the brewing process but keeps it a secret from Elmer, convincing him that they will continue their business making near beer, when in reality they are making real beer.

The town's mob faction knows that the end of the Prohibition is the end of their bootleg liquor business, so they need to take control of the production of beer in the neighborhood. Gangster Spike Moran (Edward Brophy) complains to Elmer that he is undercutting his (Spike's) beer prices, with Elmer thinking they are talking about near beer. Spike offers to pay Elmer $50,000 to get in on their business, with a contract to deliver 1,000 barrels a day. Spike gives Elmer $10,000 as a retainer, which Jimmy later tucks away in a pocket of his overcoat pocket for safekeeping.

Elmer becomes interested in Hortense (Phyllis Barry), the girlfriend of mobster Butch Lorado (John Miljan). Sent to find out who's backing Elmer and Jimmy's operation, she feigns a sprained ankle as she falls getting out of her car and then "faints" as Elmer carries her into his office. Elmer accidentally soaks her with water as he tries to resuscitate her. He gives her Jimmy's overcoat to cover up with as she takes off her wet dress.

Back at Butch's place, Hortense tells him that Spike is backing the brewery. As she takes off the overcoat, the wad of money falls out, with Butch thinking that Spike is paying her. He becomes jealous after finding out that she isn't wearing a dress underneath the coat.

Elmer goes to deliver Spike the first shipment of what he still thinks is near beer. Butch plans to sabotage Spike's shipment and sends his gang out to riddle the delivery with bullets. As Elmer climbs a hill, the truck gets a flat tire. The barrels of beer start rolling out of the back, chasing Elmer down the street. The gang arrives and is soon overtaken by the out-of-control barrels.

Elmer makes it back to the brewery and is told by Jimmy that the beer is real. He alerts him that they will need to get out of town, as Butch's gang will soon be upon them. The headline on the newspaper announces that the War on Beer is over. Spike's gang has been wiped out. Jimmy starts to celebrate as Butch arrives, threatening him with bullets if he doesn't produce 50,000 barrels of beer a day for him.

The police discover that the brewery was producing real beer all along and plan to raid the operations. Meanwhile, Hortense, who has been falling for Elmer, tells him to escape before the brewery is raided. Elmer sneaks out in a barrel, rolled off the loading dock. He rides away in a car announcing to the townsfolk that free beer is being given away at the brewery. The people race to the brewery, emptying out the vat before the police can arrive. The people wipe out Butch's gang as the brewery is mobbed.

In the end Elmer becomes famous as he opens a free-admission beer garden. In the final scene Jimmy goes out of character, looks into the camera and tells the film audience, "It's your turn, folks. It won't be long."

In his review of *What! No Beer?* Jerry Hoffman, critic for *Los Angeles Examiner*, pointed out that it didn't pretend to be anything but an out-and-out slapstick comedy: "Made for laughing purposes only, it succeeds. Jimmy and Buster are a hilarious team whose combined efforts would be even better with less forced comedy."

If Keaton had tried to play the part better, the now stereotyped role of Elmer in *What! No Beer!* could have grown to be a popular role for him. For Keaton it was slightly ironic that he appeared in a film about alcohol at the time he was experiencing an alcohol-related crisis. Finding alcohol wasn't a great problem, as the Volstead Act did little to enforce the law during the Depression years, making it easy for him to feed his addiction.

Durante took charge of the film in his role as Jimmy. It was obvious that he was no longer the second banana to Keaton, but now the first fiddle. Like Keaton, Durante was unsuccessful in getting MGM to give him better movie roles. But unlike Keaton, Durante's career didn't stall at that point, as he was still able to leverage his talent as a radio and Broadway star.

Edward's weight was a cause of stress. Similar to Keaton's use of alcohol as a crutch, Edward was using food. One reporter made the observation that Edward's resemblance to the late Roscoe Arbuckle was growing every day. It became commonplace to see him walking around the set with the assistance of a cane for support.

He was also experiencing marital trouble, and was now separated from Rose. In July, Rose filed for a divorce in Reno, Nevada, taking custody of their daughter Mary. By the end

Edward and Ebba Havez were married on August 31, 1932. Ebba was previously married to Jean Havez, a scriptwriter who had worked with Buster Keaton in the 1920s.

of the following month, on August 31, Edward and Ebba Havez were married. The September 10 *Los Angeles Examiner* reported on their intimate wedding:

> The marriage of Mrs. Ebba Havez and Edward Sedgwick, whose romance had its inception through their mutual interest in screen activities—she as a writer and he as a motion picture director—was solemnized at the home of Mrs. Josephine Sedgwick, mother of the bridegroom, last Sunday afternoon.
>
> The bride, attired in a gray satin afternoon grown with a small gray hat to match and a moleskin cape, was attended by Miss Josie Sedgwick, who wore a maroon sheer crepe suit with a small black hat. Clarence Hutson officiated as best man.
>
> Only relatives and close friends attended the ceremony, but in the evening there was a reception.

Aside from their personal relationship, Edward and Ebba also formed a professional one. Recently, the two had worked on *Horseplay*, a Universal comedy released in June, in which Edward directed and Ebba collaborated on the scenario with Clarence Marks, Dale Van Every and H.M. Walker.

With the working title of *Tin Pants*, *Horseplay* teamed comedians Slim Summerville as Slim Perkins and Andy Devine as Andy. Summerville had started his film career as one of Mack Sennett's Keystone Kops. The lanky actor made an easy transition to sound, appearing both in comedies and dramas. In the early 1930s he acted in a series of feature-length comedies opposite Zasu Pitts, an actress known for her trademark wailing voice and fluttering hands. Devine, a stout actor with a raspy voice, also started his career in silent films. When he entered sound films it was feared that his unique voice, caused by a childhood injury, would hamper his ability to get any sort of speaking roles. Devine found that he was able to use his voice to his advantage, as it made him an increasingly popular comic.

In *Horseplay* Slim and Andy, owners of a barren Montana ranch, discover radium on their land and become wealthy. Slim is in love with Angelica Wayne (Leila Hyams) but her father, an English rancher, is against her courting the redneck. In order to keep her away from Slim she is sent to England to live with her blue-blooded relatives. Slim and Andy travel to London, along with Cynthia Ann, their white horse, to find Angelica. The men and their horse get into all sorts of trouble, and even manage to expose the real identity of a phony nobleman who is wanted by the law. As an example of the broad type of comedy that is presented in the movie, one scene finds Slim at a medieval costume party given at an old castle near Sherwood Forest. Ants find their way under Slim's armor, which can only be removed by a blacksmith.

Additional cast members included May Beatty as the Duchess, Una O'Connor as Clementia, Torrence as Uncle Percy, and Cornelius Keefe as Philip Marley. Lucille Lund a Northwestern university co-ed who was recently crowned "The All American Girl" in a contest conducted by Universal Pictures and *College Humor* magazine, appears as Iris. She would go on to become one of Universal's queens.

Working on Universal's lots was somewhat more casual than working at MGM's conservative studio. Edward appreciated the break. The October 2 *Edwardsville Intelligencer* reported on the type of mischief that ensued on the set:

> Can you imagine Andy Devine masquerading as Zasu Pitts? I couldn't until I saw him doing it the other day. Andy and Slim Summerville now are being co-starred in *Tin Pants*. It's Slim's first picture since the series he made with Zasu and he was bemoaning the fact that she was absent. An hour later, Andy appeared on the act wearing a blue dress—the only color ever worn by Zasu—and fluttering

Edward directed and Ebba Havez collaborated on writing the scenario for *Horseplay* (1932), a comedy that teamed up character actors Slim Summerville and Andy Devine (courtesy Niles Essany Silent Film Museum).

his hands in the well-known Pitts manner. The last seen of the pair was when they rounded a corner of the stage at top speed, Andy having his skirts gathered well above his knees and Slim right behind him.

Edward's last release for 1933 was *Saturday's Million*. The gridiron drama, released by Universal in October, featured Robert Young as campus football hero Jim Fowler. Young, who had only appeared in a dozen films or so, was already a promising young actor with a growing fan following.

The film returns to the fictitious Western University that Edward used in Columbia's *Maker of Men*. From a serialized story written by Falkland Lucian Cary for *The Saturday Evening Post*, it follows the final game of Jim's college career. Jim proves to be the best ball carrier W.U. ever had, a success that also has a negative effect on him, as he's become tired of the attention from fans and reporters. He believes that the only friends he has were made through the admiration that people have for him on the playing field, not off of it. For this reason Jim distances himself from his well-to-do girlfriend Joan Chandler (Leila Hyams). Instead he seeks out Marie (Mary Doran), the one person he believes cares nothing about football or his participation in the sport.

Jim also plays the sport through the racket angle, with his roommate Andy Jones (Andy Devine) in charge of collecting the bets. In a conversation with his team's captain Alan Barry

(Johnny Mack Brown), he says that he deserves some of the big bucks that the university and its coaches are making off of the team's ticket receipts. The team's coach (Joe Sawyer) is concerned about Jim's lackluster playing and expresses his fear to two of his old football buddies, Jim's father Ezra (Grant Mitchell) and June's father (Richard Tucker).

On the night before the final game, Jim starts drinking at home. Marie later tells him that he can't play in tomorrow's game against State. She explains that the owner of the inn where she works, Felix (Paul Porcasi), has bet $6,000 on State. When he refuses her request, Felix enters the room and tells Jim that Marie is actually his wife, and that they are planning to let the press know of the illicit romance if he doesn't comply. Furious about being blackmailed, Jim starts a fight with Felix and breaks his own hand. Andy and Jim's father arrive and break up the fight before any additional damage is done.

The next day, the team doctor (Paul Hurst) resets Jim's hand, telling him that it needs to be put in a cast. Jim asks the doctor to just bandage it so that he can play the game. The coach calls Jim aside and complains about his haggard appearance. He asks about his bandaged hand, to which Jim replies that it's bandaged so that he can get a better grip on the ball. He wishes Jim good luck in the game and shakes his broken hand; Jim refrains from showing any pain until he is by himself.

During the game Jim's hand keeps getting banged by State's players. The opposing team eventually realizes that W.U.'s star player is nursing his hand and makes plans to take him out of the game. By halftime the game is still scoreless, with Jim preventing a touchdown for State just six inches from their goal during the third quarter. By the final quarter Jim is in excruciating pain, but is determined to make good by winning the game. He manages to make a field goal, but State scores a touchdown, pushing ahead of W.U. by three points. With one minute to go, Jim tries to make a final score but drops the ball, with State defeating W.U.

The Sedgwicks had arrived in Hollywood over twenty years earlier. Eileen and Josie were now both retired from motion pictures. Perceived as an old-timer, Edward was no longer a director of choice, making only $40,000 annually.

Jim, realizing that he let his team down, expresses his grief to the team members. They think that he played the best game of his college career, with the coach saying that it was the best game he ever saw played. The team members were sorry that they played so poorly and were unable to support Jim, who made numerous outstanding plays. Jim realizes what a chump he's been. He confesses his love to Joan and lets her know he was wrong about everything.

Additional supporting cast included Mary Carlisle, as Thelma Springer, Andy's girlfriend, Herbert Corthell as Baldy, and William Kent as Sam.

Edward was now 41 years old, Josie 39, and Eileen 34. The Sedgwicks were aging with Hollywood. According to a 1938 report released by the Treasury to the House Ways and Means Committee, Gary Cooper was the highest-paid movie star, making $370,214, followed by Ronald Colman with $362,500, Claudette Colbert with $350,833, and Mae West with $323,333. Once a major box office draw, Charlie Chaplin was listed making only $125,000, with Edward Sedgwick far down the list with $40,000.

Twenty years ago when the family first arrived in town, movie studios were barely more than outdoor stages covered with tents. Within a matter of years the town became the mecca for moviemakers, filling up the surrounding area with sophisticated and sprawling studios. In twenty years the Sedgwicks all made a name for themselves—a fame that could easily be fleeting as an endless stream of wannabe actresses and directors continued to appear on the Hollywood scene.

CHAPTER EIGHT

A Hollywood in Transition and the Fate of the Silent Idol

Although signs of economic restoration were evident as early as 1934, the United States didn't fully recover from the Great Depression until the start of World War II. The mass unemployment caused by the Depression and competition from radio adversely affected box office receipts, forcing the film industry to close the doors to a third of its movie theaters, and studios to trim salaries and production costs. While most members of the movie industry rode out the financial chaos with great losses, MGM and Universal managed to keep their debts to a minimum by operating within their means.

During this period, Hollywood's image was in a state of flux. Many of the silent era stars found their popularity waning, making way for young exciting faces such as James Cagney, Fred Astaire, Clark Gable, Jean Harlow and Shirley Temple. For some of Hollywood's perennial silent film stars, especially those who worked at MGM, the 1930s proved to be disastrous years. This was the case with Buster Keaton. In 1935, after resigning himself to working in short comedies at independent studios, Keaton finally entered a mental hospital.

John Gilbert's inability to adapt his exaggerated pantomime style of silent movie acting for the more natural technique seen in sound films required ended his career on a low note when his contract with MGM ran out in 1933. After a decline in quality roles, Gilbert succumbed to alcoholism, dying of a heart attack on January 9, 1936.

Karl Dane's acting roles had grown smaller with the advent of sound films and he too lost his contract at MGM. After experiencing much bad luck, Dane suffered a nervous breakdown. On April 14, 1934, he committed suicide by shooting himself with a revolver.

William Haines, whose popularity was already on the decline, was released from his contract after he refused to end his homosexual relationship with his companion, Jimmie Shields. Louis B. Mayer had requested that Haines put the kibosh on the friendship, fearing that the public might boycott MGM's films once the connection was made public. Fortunately for Haines, after he left show biz, he became independently productive as an interior designer.

Like Keaton, Edward was also perceived as an old-timer by MGM. He publicly acknowledged this, as he lamented the end of the days when film comedians were developed on the studio's sets. "Practically every good comedian in the world has already had a fling at pictures," he told the *Dallas Morning Star*. Comedians like W.C Fields, Jimmy Durante, Charles Chaplin, Harry Langdon, Ned Sparks, Charles Ray and Buster Keaton came from vaudeville to the stage. George Burns and Gracie Allen came from radio. Edward was concerned that it was a long time since the screen had developed a comedy star from its own ranks. "These comedians mentioned are all sympathetic school exemplars. The purely gag comedians will last as long as their stories are good. But where will our future comedians come from?"

Edward was fortunate to have formed lasting bonds at Universal before he made his move to MGM in the late 1920s. Universal, who recognized Edward as a veteran comedy director, assigned him to *The Poor Rich*, a comedy released in February 1934. Edward, his wife, Ebba, and Dale Van Every worked on the screenplay. Infused with clever dialogue, it was a screwball-style comedy full of top-rate humor.

Universal supplied Edward with some of Hollywood's most talented character actors. Heading the list was Edward Everett Horton, a theatrically trained actor known for his nervous characterizations. He made his debut onstage in 1906, transitioned to silent and then sound films, and continued appearing in comedic roles and providing cartoon character voices on TV into the 1960s. As Albert Stuyvesant Spottiswood, Horton was paired with Edna May Oliver, an equally talented comedienne.

Other character actors that filled out *The Poor Rich*'s credits became staples in many of the movies from that era. Thelma Todd became a leading comedienne, working alongside the likes of Zasu Pitts, Stan Laurel, and Oliver Hardy in comedy shorts and feature-length movies. Edward Brophy, as the gruff Inspector Mike Flannigan, had appeared in 14 films directed by Edward, growing into a fine character actor in the process and filling his diverse roles effectively. John Miljan had a skill for playing nasty villains. Ward Bond, appearing as a motor cop, would eventually gain fame as Major Seth Adams in the popular television Western series *Wagon Train* (1957–1961). The uncredited part of the coroner was played by Walter Brennan who became one of the most recognized character actors after bridging the gap to stardom by eventually winning three Oscars for Best Supporting Actor and portraying his memorable character Grandpa Amos McCoy on the television series *The Real McCoys* (1957–1963).

The Poor Rich follows two cousins (Horton and Oliver) who had squandered their inheritances. They coincidentally return at the same time to their childhood estate, Spottiswood Manor, only to find it vacant and in a deplorable condition. Realizing they are both penniless, they devise a plan for Albert to marry into the wealthy Fetherstone family. Lady and Lord Fetherstone (Una O'Connor and E.E. Clive), along with their daughter Gwendolyn (Todd), are planning to visit Harriet at Spottiswood Manor in a few days. The Fetherstones have also hit hard times and were hoping to marry Gwendolyn into the "wealthy" Spottiswood family.

Albert and Harriet need a cook, maid and butler. Andy Crumm (Andy Devine), a local who is stuck at the estate due to his malfunctioning auto, is assigned the job of cook. Deputy Sheriff Tom Hopkins (Grant Mitchell) arrives at the house to issue an attachment to confiscate the furniture, but instead is assigned the part of the butler. Grace Hunter (Leila Hyams), a saleswoman for the Wellware Aluminum Company, calls on the household to sell her merchandise, only to be recruited as the maid.

Prince Abdul Hamidshan (Miljan), a con artist who had a scandalous relationship with

Harriet, is thrown into the mix. Inspector Flannigan arrives at the house in search of the prince. Just as the group of Spottiswoods and Fetherstones enter the prince's bedroom, his body falls out of the closet. At that point nearly half of the cast are set up as red herrings. Mistaken for being murdered, the prince eventually regains consciousness and Flannigan arrests him and hauls him out of the house. Albert and Grace marry and turn the mansion into a successful chicken restaurant.

Edward followed *The Poor Rich* with a mediocre direction assignment for Universal, titled *I'll Tell the World*. Released in April, the drama featured Lee Tracy as Stanley Brown, a foreign correspondent for United Press. With a reputation as being one of Hollywood's troublemakers, Tracy had a tendency to play Walter Winchell–type newspaper reporters, a role he had mastered on-stage as Hildy Johnson, the fast-talking newspaperman in Broadway's classic *The Front Page*. Considered the "poor man's Clark Gable" at Columbia and Universal, Roger Pryor was featured as William S. Briggs, a reporter from a competing news service. (Pryor had replaced Tracy as Hildy on Broadway in *The Front Page*.)

Stanley Brown's love interest in the story was Jane Hamilton (Gloria Stuart). Stuart, one of the WAMPAS Baby Stars of 1932, never had much of a recognized film career until she became the oldest person ever to be nominated for an Academy Award, for her performance in *Titanic* (1997) playing the part of a 100-year-old survivor recalling her experience on the ship.

Stanley is assigned to report on why Grand Duke Ferdinand (Alec B. Francis) was visiting America. As he arrives at the steamboat pier to watch the grand duke's departure back to Europe, a bomb goes off outside his taxi. Stanley's editor demands that Stanley follow the royal to Europe to find out why someone would want to assassinate him.

Upon arriving in France, Stanley follows the grand duke to Vichy, where he is scheduled to attend a birthday dinner. Disguised as an elderly man in a wheelchair, Stanley pretends to be at the grand duke's hotel to get treatment from the restorative water springs. Briggs, who arrived at the hotel to cover the same assignment, notices Stanley and sees through his disguise. Stanley wheels his chair away, colliding with a bicyclist. The bike rider turns out to be Jane Hamilton, a visitor from Baltimore. Realizing that Stanley is in disguise, she pretends that her ankle has been sprained in the accident. Stanley wheels her in his chair to the hotel.

"Jane" is actually the Princess Royal Helen. Grand Duke Ferdinand's trip to the United States was a covert mission to bring her back to their country so that she may lead its citizens as their queen. (As Jane Hamilton, the princess was secretly attending school in the United States.) The reason for the secrecy was due to the threat of terrorists who were opposed to having Helen's family back in power.

Count Strumsky (Lawrence Grant) turns out to be the leader of the opposition party, planning to assassinate the entire royal family. Helen and her family are in grave danger and must escape. Stanley, who is in love with Helen, helps sneak her and her family out. The movie ends with Stanley getting the final scoop on the story.

Edward's next project was an April release for Paramount Pictures titled *Here Comes the Groom*. Unlike *I'll Tell the World*, the musical comedy turned out to be a polished B movie. It featured Jack Haley, an entertainer who established his career on the vaudeville stage before moving on to Broadway and movies. Haley's one outstanding role would become the endearing Tin Woodsman in the 1939 version of *The Wizard of Oz*—a role that was originally going to Buddy Ebsen who suffered an allergic reaction to the makeup used.

Eight. A Hollywood in Transition and the Fate of the Silent Idol   203

Edward directed *I'll Tell the World* (1934) for Universal. The drama featured Lee Tracy (left) as a foreign correspondent and Gloria Stuart as his royal-blooded love interest.

Edward does a wonderful job in getting Haley to mug it up as Mike Scanlon, an unemployed piccolo player who has married into a family of criminals. His wife Angry (Isabel Jewell) walks out on him because he is unwilling to lead a life of crime. Getting his courage up, Mike decides to rob a neighborhood poker game. As he is about to make his move, two other crooks step into the room and beat him to the loot. The players think that he is one of the crooks, chasing him out of the house as they call for help.

The authorities track him to a train station, where he boards a train and hides in a compartment reserved by socialite Patricia Randolph (Patricia Ellis) and her new husband Marvin Hale (Lawrence Gray), who is known to his fans as "The Masked Crooner." Patricia has never seen Marvin unmasked, so when she discovers Mike in her room she believes it is Marvin *sans* his mask.

Just as the train leaves the station, Patricia receives a letter from Marvin, stating that their marriage was a mistake. Mike is forced to confess that he is the burglar that the authorities are looking for and that he is only trying to make good for his wife Angry. He prevents Patricia from giving him up by pointing out that they are both in the same situation: in love with someone who isn't interested. Patricia gets an idea to get even with Marvin and tells Mike that he needs to stay with her for at least five days.

They arrive at their destination as husband and wife and are able to outwit Detective Weaver (Sidney Toler), who is waiting for the burglar to disembark. Mike is introduced to Patricia's father George Randolph (E.H. Calvert) and her Aunt Annabelle Widden (Mary Boland). Standing beside them is the guy Patricia is really crazy about, Jim Hatfield (Neil Hamilton). When they arrive at the Randolphs' estate, Mike runs into Angry. She explains that she is posing as a maid while she cases the house.

In one ridiculous skit Mike is forced to mimic Marvin Hale, singing along in front of onlookers as Marvin is broadcasting live on the radio; Haley performs the scene amusingly. Fearing that he may have to mimic Marvin on the radio again, he puts the radio on a moving truck that is parked outside. He is unaware that Angry hid Aunt Annabelle's $10,000 pearl necklace in it.

Patricia asks Angry to return the necklace, which is now heading to the moving company's storage facility. After racing downtown they find the necklace and return it to Aunt Annabelle. Mike and Angry's identities are revealed, and as they are about to be arrested Aunt Annabelle comes to their defense, telling the officer that the whole situation was a misunderstanding. Realizing that her niece's true love is Jim, she gives Patricia the necklace as a gift.

In the end Angry and Mike come clean, with Mike finding a job in an orchestra as a piccolo player. He plays only the two notes at the end of the concert.

Here Comes the Groom featured additional small-scale talent, including Mary Boland, who would become well known in her roles as light-headed society widows. Neil Hamilton, who rose to stardom under the guidance of D.W. Griffith, would reestablish his fame at the end of his career playing the role of Police Commissioner Gordon on the campy television series *Batman* (1966–1968). Appearing in the minor role of the Randolphs' butler, British-born Arthur Treacher, known as Hollywood's perfect butler, was a top-notch character actor who already proved his talent in several Shirley Temple films.

Although the industry considered Edward a comedy director, he still enjoyed working on an occasional thriller. In the sports-related murder mystery *Death on the Diamond*, a September release, Edward had a second opportunity to direct Robert Young, now a noticeable rising star. MGM had originally cast Franchot Tone, another newcomer, in the part of hot-shot pitcher Larry Kelly, but decided to use Young instead. Madge Evans, as Frances Clark, the team's secretary and manager's daughter, played Young's love interest. Evans, who had

Eight. A Hollywood in Transition and the Fate of the Silent Idol 205

Jack Haley (second from left) starred in *Here Comes the Groom* (1934), a musical comedy that Edward helped turn into a polished B movie. The supporting cast also included (left to right surrounding Haley) Mary Boland, Neil Hamilton and Patricia Ellis.

started her career as a child in silent films, worked up until the late 1930s, and then after taking a break from acting did some television in the early 1950s.

The whodunit teamed Nat Pendleton, as pitcher "Truck" Hogan, with Ted Healy, as umpire Terrence "Crawfish" O'Toole, for comedy relief. While in vaudeville, Ted Healy had founded an act known as "Ted Healy & His Stooges." After accepting an offer from Columbia, the Stooges part of the act eventually found greater fame onscreen as the Three Stooges. Meanwhile, Healy played character roles in dramas and light comedies at MGM. He was often teamed with the athletic Pendleton, who also appeared in various films that Edward directed.

Mickey Rooney, already known for the Mickey McGuire comedy shorts he made from 1927 to 1934, was now breaking into feature films, making a brief appearance in *Death on the Diamond* as Mickey the batboy.

The scenario was based on a book by Cortland Fitzsimmons, a story that was also serialized in newspapers as part of the film's exploitation campaign. The thriller opens at the St. Louis Cardinals training camp, where the struggling team is in the race for the pennant. The manager, Pop Clark (David Landau) has hocked everything possible to keep the franchise in his control. Things look up when Larry Kelly, a wiseguy pitcher from a Texas league, arrives.

The secondary story involves gamblers betting on the Cardinals' defeat, with odds at

20–1. The head of the gambling ring, Joe Karnes (C. Henry Gordon), worries when Larry becomes a pitching sensation. It becomes apparent that the gamblers are attempting to prevent the team from winning when Mickey discovers that the players' gloves have been doped up with alcohol. After Larry pitches a no-hit game, the infuriated gamblers fire at the taxi he's in, running the car into a ditch. Although the star pitcher survives with only a few sprains, he must sit out a game. Next a Cardinal is shot in the heart as he rounds the bases. Police Sgt. Grogan (Edward Brophy) takes over the investigation to determine who's responsible for the shooting incidents related to the first place team.

The Cardinals are determined to defy the killer by continuing their schedule. Before the next game begins, a player is strangled in the locker room. When the pitcher can't be located, a search begins, with the dead player found stuffed in a locker—falling out in a similarly surprising way as Prince Abdul did when he dropped out of the closet in *The Poor Rich*. Truck is next on the list as he dies from poison-tainted mustard spread on a hot dog.

Larry is added to the game roster; if he plays, it's a sure thing that the team will win the pennant. Frances is concerned that he will be the next fatality and confesses her love for him.

Jimmie Downey (Paul Kelly), a newspaper reporter covering the murders, knocks out a man who is attempting to drop a bomb disguised as a watch into the pocket of a player's

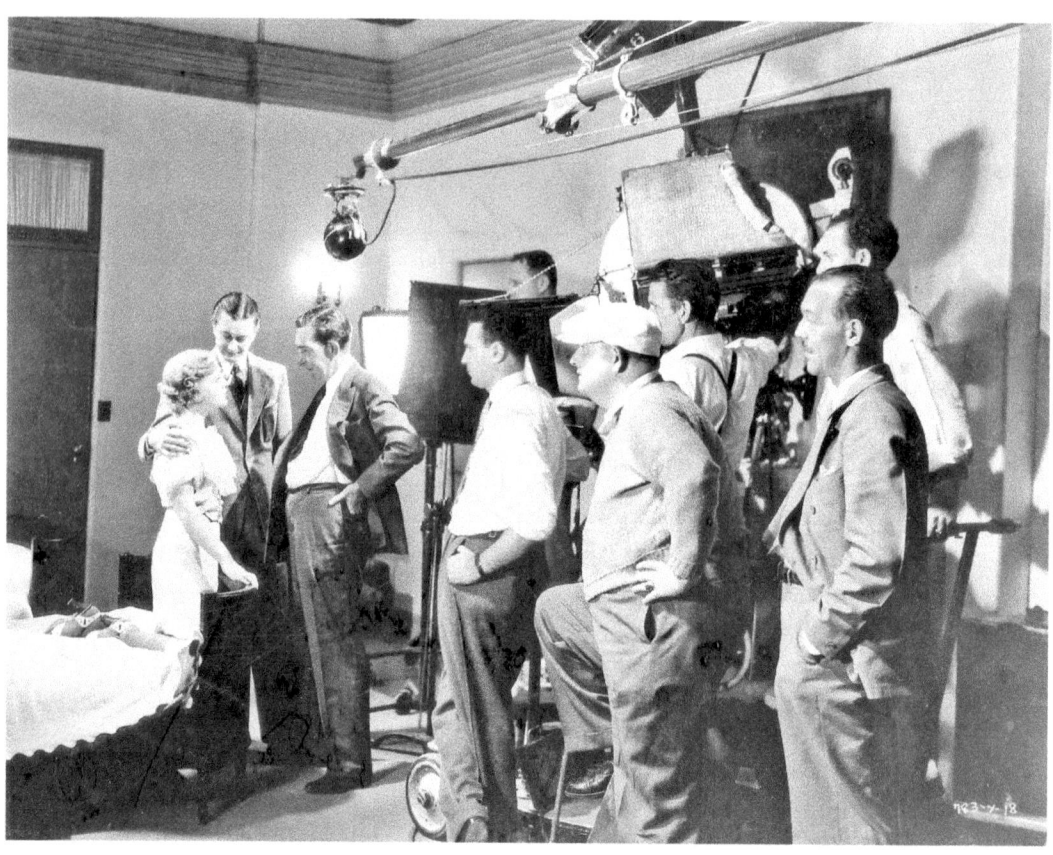

In the sports-related murder mystery *Death on the Diamond* (1934) Edward had a second opportunity to direct Robert Young, now a noticeable rising star. Edward is shown giving direction to Young, Madge Evans, and David Landau.

uniform. The murderer turns out to be Mr. Patterson the groundskeeper (DeWitt Jennings). Patterson, a former player, was once in the running to become the team's manager, but because of his gambling problem he was kicked off of the team. The game continues and Larry wins the pennant for his team ... and Frances for himself.

Edward's next job was directing and producing the Paramount mystery *Father Brown, Detective*, a December release. It was originally assigned to Al Werker, but Werker requested to be relieved of direction duties because he felt it wasn't his type of picture.

Based on G.K. Chesterton's Father Brown novel *The Flying Cross*, the film featured Walter Connolly in the title role. As a sleuthing priest, he is matched against jewel thief M. Hercule Flambeau (Paul Lukas). Father Brown, along with Inspector Valentine (Robert Loraine) and Sir Leopold Fischer (Halliwell Hobbes) receive identical notes from Flambeau stating that he is intent on stealing the ten "Flying Star" diamonds. Father Brown is in possession of four of the diamonds, which are part of a crucifix, with the remaining six safely stored in Leopold's vault.

Flambeau visits Father Brown at his home and roughs him up as he tries to get the priest to tell him where the diamonds are. Father Brown has been waiting a long time to get Flambeau in his grasp and then reform him. A young couple eager to speak to Father Brown burst into the rectory just in time, forcing the thief to leave.

Late at night Leopold is woken by smoke which is quickly filling the house. The smoke is being emitted by a smoke bomb, ignited to cover the theft of his diamonds. Flambeau has fallen in love with Leopold's daughter Evelyn (Gertrude Michael) and tells her that there is no better way to show his affection than to steal the "Flying Stars" for her. She attempts to persuade him not to steal the remaining diamonds, as he might get hurt in the process. Father Brown attempts to show Flambeau the differences between good and bad choices, without success, and Flambeau steals the jewels from him.

Flambeau eventually converts to good and returns all of the diamonds. Father Brown reunites him with Evelyn, but the thief thinks that the priest has set a trap as the police arrive to arrest him. Promising him sanctuary, Father Brown takes him into the bell tower, where Flambeau escapes by climbing down a rope to the church's courtyard. Flambeau has a change of heart and turns himself over to the authorities, knowing in his heart that Evelyn will be waiting for him after he serves his sentence.

Edward was hitting his stride with *Father Brown, Detective*. The success of this thriller proved his ability to effectively direct genres other then comedy. He convincingly gave the movie a British air. Walter Connolly, who was often cast in supporting roles as a doctor or judge, and excelled at portraying businessmen and newspapermen, was the perfect choice for Father Brown. Una O'Connor as Father Brown's maid Mrs. Boggs and E.E. Clive as the sergeant supplemented the excellent cast.

Edward, however, was starting to experience disappointments as projects that he was promised were reassigned or never materialized. He was originally slated to direct a November release for Paramount titled *The Milky Way*. But instead the directorial responsibility of the Harold Lloyd comedy was transferred to Leo McCarey. Berg, Stebbins, Allenberg and Blum, the agency Edward was now working with, placed advertisements in trade journals announcing that he was preparing his 100th picture, *The Army Rides Again*. He experienced yet another disappointment after MGM shelved the project.

Edward continued to publicly long for the "good old days" of making movies without the restrictions and demands of the new order. In an article for *The Hollywood Reporter*, "Did the Chump Like It?" Edward complained about the critics who were demanding that films have more artistic merit than entertainment values for the common moviegoer:

> Sometimes I think that today, in pictures with our ideas of high art with our complicated conferences on motivation, narration, delineation, characterization and all the other "ations" to which the screen has become heir, we lose sight of this fundamental principle that has come down the years from the tent shows ... but which still today rules us as potentially as it did then.... We have erected a Colossus in the picture industry. We have progressed from primitive flickers to our great spectacles. We have developed from hasty scripts written on the cuff to filming the world's greatest literature. But the final test of it all is, as then ... "will the chumps like it?"

Edward despised camera screen tests. Commenting on his next MGM film he admitted that he didn't like the process, as it made actors nervous, which makes it difficult to get to know an actor's true capability. The *lack* of a screen test was something that would likely have made Irving Thalburg even more nervous, and which might have prevented Edward from getting future quality assignments.

Edward's first assignment for 1935, and the 99th film on his résumé, was a May release, MGM's *Murder in the Fleet*. The naval thriller gave Edward the opportunity to once again

In the MGM naval thriller *Murder in the Fleet* (1935) Edward directed Robert Taylor (center), a young actor who was on the verge of stardom.

pen a film scenario. The premise wasn't far off from the story used for *Death on the Diamond*, which may have been intentionally used as a surefire whodunit formula. With technical assistance from Lieutenant Commander Frank Wead, Edward wrote a yarn set aboard the U.S.S. *Carolina*, a newly commissioned cruiser selected by the Navy to have test equipment. The fire control gear, responsible for automatically aiming and firing artillery at its target, would revolutionize Naval warfare by making the action free of human operators.

The film featured Robert Taylor, a young actor on the verge of stardom. After signing a seven-year contract with the studio for $35 a week, Taylor became one of MGM's lowest-paid actors of 1934. Within a year MGM focused their resources on his growing popularity, promoting him as "The Heartthrob of the Nation."

MGM originally planned to feature Maureen O'Sullivan, known for her role as Jane in the lucrative Tarzan adventure films, as the female interest, but instead gave the role to Jean Parker. Parker, a fairly new face in Hollywood, had just appeared in a run of successful films, including *Little Women* (1933), *Operator 13* (1934) and *Sequoia* (1934). Ted Healy and Nat Pendleton were reunited, playing off of each other to furnish the thriller's comedy relief as they compete for the attention of Una Merkel.

The story opens with a race to install the device on the ship by noontime the following day ... or else its contract would be voided, making the equipment available to foreign countries. According to Capt. John Winslow (Arthur Byron), the gear, supposed to have been delivered to the U.S.S. *Carolina* ten days ago, was suspiciously lost in transit. Intelligence intercepted it as it was being transported towards the Mexican boarder.

Lt. Tom Randolph (Taylor) is placed in charge of the installation. A crane transferring some of the gear to the cruiser malfunctions and drops its cargo, nearly killing a sailor. It is discovered that the winch was sabotaged. A civilian engineer working on the machine's wiring is shot and killed. All visitors to the ship are suspects, including the competing manufacturer, Harry Jeffries (Richard Tucker), and a foreign consul named Kamchukan (Mischa Auer). While a diversion distracts the investigators, the gear is again sabotaged. As the chief electrician attempts to trace a damaged cable, he is stabbed in the back with a bayonet.

Down below, as a sailor enters a powder magazine room, he is knocked unconscious. Another sailor sounds an alarm. Randolph rushes to the room, and as he enters it he discovers a man trying to light a charge which would blow up the ship. The man, Victor Hanson (Jean Hersholt), turns out to be the original inventor of the fire control gear. He explains that his idea was stolen from the company that he worked for; they then sold the plans to another company without giving him any compensation. He is now taking his revenge by preventing its successful installation.

In their struggle, some explosive is ignited. Realizing what is happening in the locked magazine room, orders are issued to flood the room. Randolph subdues the mad Hanson and the door is opened just in time to let the rising water rush out. In the end the equipment is installed successfully, and just in time to honor the contract's deadline.

Aside from writing the scenario, Edward also directed. As was the case with the other MGM films he directed, he was given quality cast, crew and scenery to work with—and, considering the restrictive studio system he was forced to work under, it was a gratifying trade-off. Edward's direction was exceptional, using various shots that realistically portrayed the cramped rooms of a battle cruiser. His technical adviser was Prince Sigvard Bernadotte of Sweden, a navy lieutenant who gave up his royalty to marry Erika Patzek, a commoner and German actress. Experienced at UFA, he was placed under contract at MGM.

A bonus for Edward was directing John Hyams and Leila McIntyre, two vaudeville actors whom he admired as a child. The couple, whose daughter was actress Leila Hyams, was making their first screen appearance, playing comical tourists.

Paramount asked Edward to direct a release planned for September, *The Virginia Judge*. Walter C. Kelly, assigned to the role of Judge Davis of Tidewater, Virginia, was well known on the vaudeville circuit for his portrayal of the Virginia Judge, a peacekeeper who enacted the parts of his monologue standing behind a dais. According to advance material for the film, his screen appearance was the 17,000th time he had offered his act, with the only things missing being his well-remembered yarns about quaint Southern characters. Advertisements for *The Virginia Judge* promoted the judge's bucolic sentiments: "The Judge's heart held the whole town ... even that poor wayward step-son of his" and "He'd rather give a man $30 than 30 days."

Aside from performing the judge characterization in his dialogue stories on stage, which were influenced by observing Virginian police court judges, Kelly often portrayed African Americans who were being tried in his court. His depictions of the poor defendants were racist, as he characterized them as slow-witted and lazy, a portrayal of African Americans which unfortunately became a stereotype for black actors in the early years of film.

Taking full advantage of this stereotype African American character, actor Stepin Fetchit filled in as the defendant Spasm Johnson. Fetchit's role wasn't too different from the character he played in *Judge Priest*, in which he co-starred with the late Will Rogers the previous year. Reaching star status, and in the process becoming a millionaire, Fetchit became a controversial movie actor as his portrayals offended blacks. But he eventually gained support for opening the doors for future African Americans entertainers.

As a physical comedian, Fetchit was prone to accidents. During the filming of a *Virginia Judge* scene in which Fetchit played the human target at a carnival's "hit the man and win a cigar" concession, an actor picked up a real ball instead of a prop ball, hitting Fetchit and leaving him with a bad head gash.

Newcomer Robert Cummings was cast as Judge Davis's ungrateful stepson Jim Preston. Cummings, a light comedian who up until that time only had small parts in films, was on his way to becoming a popular actor, eventually getting his own television shows *The Bob Cummings Show* (1955) and *My Living Doll* (1964).

Jim's best friend Bob Stuart was played by Johnny Downs, a seasoned actor who was hired by Hal Roach in 1923 as one of the rascals in his *Our Gang* comedy shorts. After appearing in twenty-four of Roach's two-reelers, Downs followed a career of singing and dancing on the vaudeville stage, eventually returning to movies as an all–American type in college musicals which were popular during the late 1930s. Newcomer Marsha Hunt played the part of Mary Lee Calvert, Jim and Bob's love interest. Hunt was a 17-year-old fashion model who was encouraged to try out in Hollywood, even though she hadn't any acting experience.

The story was simple, with a predictable ending. In a quarrel over Mary, Jim shoots Bob. Jim is arrested and his stepfather Judge Davis is forced to step in. The judge is able to judiciously resolve the crisis.

Edward teamed with Hal Roach Studios for *Mister Cinderella*, an October 1936 release. Edward had now been in the business for 23 years. This was his 102nd production, and his only film for that year. *Mister Cinderella* was a significant departure for the studio, as Roach recently announced that he was deserting the two-reel comedy field to concentrate on feature comedies. Only his *Our Gang* series was to remain on the Roach schedule, but now as one-reel shorts.

Edward's move to Hal Roach Studios seemed to be a perfect match: It was clear that the success of *Mister Cinderella* was due to the skilled director's ability to transform the script into a classic slapstick film. The comedy features Jack Haley as Joe Jenkins, a hotel barber who thrives on reading reports of society life. Betty Furness plays the part of Patricia Randolph, an attractive young socialite.

Joe is mesmerized by Patricia, the daughter of the president of Randolph Automotive Company, Peter Randolph (Raymond Walburn). Peter is developing a new engine that will run on diesel fuel. His company is on the brink of bankruptcy, and without an additional five million dollars will have to close its doors. Peter enlists Patricia to help him get the attention of a wealthy socialite and company stockholder named Aloysius P. Merriweather (Monroe Owsley), hoping to propose their project to him and get his funding.

Aloysius, a reveler who spends most of his time in an inebriated state, is avoiding all calls during his hotel stay. Joe has a scheduled appointment to cut Aloysius's hair and arrives to find the partygoer passed out on his bed in last night's tuxedo. He attempts to sober him up and get him to answer the phone, which has been ringing nonstop. Aloysius tells Joe to answer the phone; when he does, Joe finds that it is Patricia, who thinks she is speaking with Aloysius, similar to the contrivance used in *Here Comes the Groom*. She has invited him to a formal reception at her parents' mansion and Jack enthusiastically accepts the invitation for Aloysius. Aloysius refuses to go, sending Joe in his place as a Cinderella.

Joe arrives at the party and becomes even more smitten with Patricia in person. Peter will be arriving with a business partner later in the evening and Patricia needs to ensure that Aloysius (Joe) is still there when they arrive. Staling for time, she takes him on a boat ride. She pretends that it's out of gas and they row to her father's fishing shack on a remote island.

Mishap after mishap strands them on the island. As they wait to be rescued, Joe confesses to Patricia that he isn't Aloysius. Wanting to get even with Aloysius, Patricia starts to scheme and asks Joe to keep up the ruse when they return home.

They are rescued the following morning and return to Patricia's house where they are accused of having a scandalous relationship. The gossip becomes front-page headline news, reporting on socialite Patricia Randolph's engagement to Aloysius.

From here on the movie follows a script that continually adds to the cavalcade of characters. First Aloysius's wife Maizie (Rosina Lawrence) shows up at the Randolph estate looking for her husband—causing mayhem when everyone finds out that Aloysius is a two-timer who is already married. Next Spike Nolan (Tom Dugan), a gangster who wants to kill Aloysius because of a grudge, also shows up. At the same time Detective McNutt (Edward Brophy) arrives, following a report that there is going to be a killing at the house that night.

Aloysius arrives at the Randolph home, adding to the chaos. Spike demands to know who is the real Aloysius. Thinking that Joe is a detective who was hired to save her husband, Maizie points out Joe is Aloysius. A mad race around the house ensues and Spike is apprehended.

Edward teamed up with Hal Roach Studios to direct *Mister Cinderella* (1936). The comedy featured Jack Haley as a hotel barber who thrives on reading reports of society life, and Betty Furness, the socialite he dreams of.

    The hope of getting five million dollars from Aloysius is dashed after they realize that the money is tied up in Randolph Automotive Company's stock. Joe gets an idea: If he can get Randolph's competitor Emmett Fawcett (Morgan Wallace) to think that the prototype works, he might get Fawcett to pay Randolph the five million to keep the vehicle out of production. He gets Fawcett's attention as he drives by his anchored yacht. What Fawcett doesn't know is that the Randolphs' butler Watkins (Arthur Treacher) is in the engine compartment pedaling a makeshift foot-powered engine. Fawcett pays the ransom of five million dollars to have the engine put out of production. In the end Joe saves the Randolph Auto Company, becomes vice-president, and wins over Patricia.

Featuring a cast of quality B actors, *Mister Cinderella* turned out to be a first-class comedy. Furness, who at 14 started her career modeling with the Powers agency, received a film contract with RKO-Radio within a couple of years. Later in her career, after leaving moviemaking, she shifted her career to Broadway and television. Owsley, usually cast as a heavy, gave an amusing performance as the intoxicated millionaire.

One *Mister Cinderella* scene involved the tossing of four hundred pies in a prerequisite slapstick routine. The blueberry and custard pies, purchased from a local bakery, were treated at the studio with whipped cream and powdered sugar, with the sugar used to make them stick better to the face. With the exception of close-ups, Bob Sanders and Charles Oelzo, two prop men who were experienced at tossing pies, were the pie-slingers, with some direct hits made at a distance of over 15 feet. Actors, including Haley and Dugan, went through eight changes of clothing during the filming of the scene.

Syndicated entertainment columnist Harrison Carroll reported that for Edward to get the proper effect it was necessary to take the victims by surprise, due to the fact that even old-timers were apt to flinch when they saw the pie coming.

> Sedgwick works a ruse. He has the players rehearse the scene several times up to the point where the pies are thrown. Then he takes it several more times calling "cut" just before the barrage.
> Finally, when the victims' suspicions are lulled he gives a secret signal to the prop men. They let go.
> The expressions of the four players as they get the gooey mess right in the face are something to watch.
> Tommy Dugan however, is a quick thinker. As the shot ends he drops to one knee, throws his arms out, and puts up his blueberry-smeared features.
> "Mammy!" he shouts
> The company howls.

During the production of *Mister Cinderella* Haley and Furness' stand-ins, Billy Baxter and Eleanor Crooker, announced that they would be getting married. The entire company was invited to attend the ceremony, which took place at the Crescent Heights Methodist Church in Hollywood.

Edward's second Hal Roach production, which once again teamed him with Jack Haley, was the May 1937 release *Pick a Star*. The song-and-dance comedy took advantage of the renewed interest in musicals, mainly due to the popularity of the sensational dance team of Fred Astaire and Ginger Rogers.

Pick a Star's storyline was very similar to *Free and Easy* (1930), Buster Keaton's talkie premiere which Edward directed: small town beauty queen wins the grand prize of a trip to Hollywood with a promise to appear in motion pictures, and in the process is wooed by a caddish movie star. Mr. Stone (Russell Hicks), the talent scout for Excel Pictures, is on hand at a small-time movie theater to present the winner with a $2,000 prize and tickets to Hollywood. While Joe Jenkins (Haley), the master of ceremonies, announces the winner onstage—Miss Waterloo's Cecilia Moore (Rosina Lawrence)—Stone is backstage stealing the show's proceeds. After finding out that the contest was a scam, Joe faints on stage. Joe, who is in awe of Cecilia, recovers and promises that he will do whatever is takes to finance the trip on his own and make sure she becomes a famous actress.

Edward's second Hal Roach production teamed him with Jack Haley again in the star-studded *Pick a Star* (1937). Charles Halton, Leila McIntyre, James Finlayson, Jack Haley, Rosina Lawrence, Mischa Auer, Patsy Kelly, Stan Laurel, and Oliver Hardy, following a pie fight, are pictured around Edward (courtesy Niles Essanay Silent Film Museum).

In a quest to make some money and connections, Joe travels to Hollywood and becomes a busboy at the star-studded Colonial Club. Hiding the fact that he is working in a restaurant, his letters home to Cecilia and her sister Nellie (Patsy Kelly) report that he is doing well and has been forming contacts—which is far from the truth.

An airplane routed for Hollywood makes an unscheduled landing at Waterloo's airport due to poor weather conditions. Cecilia and Nellie take the passengers into their home for the night. One passenger is the debonair but caddish actor Rinaldo Lopez (Mischa Auer), who immediately takes an interest in Cecilia. Two other passengers, Mr. and Mrs. McGregor (John Hyams and Leila McIntyre), become fed up with the delay and plan to return to New York on their own. They give their tickets to Hollywood to Cecilia and Nellie.

Arriving in Hollywood, the sisters make a reservation at the Colonial Club to see Joe perform. Joe attempts to hide his lowly status by getting up on the dance floor to join in with an entertainer who is performing. He quickly makes a comedy out of the routine as he stumbles through the dance steps and mangles the song's lyrics.

Once Cecilia finds out that Joe is a busboy, she becomes upset. As he chases her out to the street, a car hits him. Mr. Klawheimer (Charles Halton), the head of Excel Pictures and owner of the car, promises to give Joe a job reference if he doesn't report the accident.

Eight. A Hollywood in Transition and the Fate of the Silent Idol 215

The following day Joe arrives at Excel and reports to the studio boss, a man named Johnson. Instead of getting a job as an actor, the gruff Johnson makes him a studio chauffeur. Once again Edward appears in a cameo, this time as the studio boss who is only seen with his back to the camera.

Cecilia eventually gets her chance at doing a screen test, but gets camera-shy when it is time to perform. Joe joins her and they sing a duet while imagining themselves in a spectacular musical production.

The dance scene allowed Edward the opportunity to direct a musical spectacular. Although the movie was produced on a small budget, the segment was shot with camera angles that effectively made the dozens of dancers seem to be appearing in an extravagant routine from a Busby Berkeley musical.

Although the promotions for *Pick a Star* hyped the appearances of Stan Laurel and Oliver Hardy, their parts were minimal. At the end of the big dance number, the duo appears on the set out of character as they discuss their scene with the director, which eventually evolves to having the two busting up a Western saloon. They're also seen playfully performing a routine using toy instruments.

The spectacular dance scene in *Pick a Star* (1937) allowed Edward the opportunity to effectively make the dozens of dancers seem like they were appearing in an extravagant routine from a Busby Berkeley musical (courtesy Niles Essanay Silent Film Museum).

Edward had been looking forward to working on a comedy for MGM titled *The 44th Floor* as his next feature, but once again the production was shelved. He was asked to direct *Riding on Air* for David L. Loew Productions. Working for Loew meant that Edward would not only be responsible for directing yet another "B" movie, but one which had lower production values then he was used to working with.

The slapstick movie featured Joe E. Brown, a comedian who found previous success working at Warner Bros. The wide-mouthed Brown was the sort of comedian filmgoers either loved or hated—he could appear as a humorous hero to one person, or as an irritating buffoon to another. As a ten-year-old, Brown ran away from home to join a tumbling act known as the Five Marvelous Ashtons, which led to experience on the vaudeville and burlesque stage. He eventually worked his way to Broadway and then to appearances in silent films throughout the 1920s. With the advent of sound, he was able to make use of what would become his trademark booming yell, which was always accompanied by a wide-mouthed grin.

Warner Bros.' *Elmer the Great* (1933) made him one of the top ten moneymakers that year. In 1937 he accepted a contract with Loew for six pictures at $100,000 a picture. Similar to Buster Keaton's disastrous move, Brown was given poor advice: His popularity dipped while working for David L. Loew Productions. According to Brown, "None of the independent pictures were up to the standards set at Warners."

Directing Joe E. Brown (left) in *Riding on Air* (1937) for David L. Loew Productions meant that Edward would not only be responsible for directing yet another "B" movie, but one which had lower production values than he was used to working with. Harlan Briggs and Florence Rice appear in a scene with Brown.

Over the next couple of years Edward would direct Brown in four comedies. Two of them, *Fit for a King* (1937) and *Gladiator* (1938), turned out impressively, considering their so-so production values. In *Riding on Air*, originally promoted as *All Is Confusion*, Brown plays the role of Elmer Lane, managing editor for the *Claremont Daily Chronicle*, a small-town newspaper. Elmer is also an amateur inventor who has discovered a way to fly planes remotely through the use of radio waves. A con artist, Doc Waddington (Guy Kibbee), hears that Elmer just won $5,000 in a radio contest. Doc introduces himself to Elmer as a financier and convinces him to invest his winnings in a new company that will produce his radio beam apparatus, adding that Elmer would become president of the venture.

Elmer's girlfriend Betty Harrison (Florence Rice) is concerned that he is investing the prize money foolishly, and demands that he gets his money back from Doc. Meanwhile, Doc is getting the town's businessmen to purchase company shares for twenty-five dollars each. Harvey Schuman (Vinton Haworth), Elmer's competition for newsworthy stories and rival for Betty, finds the bullet-riddled body of Bug Fuller on the side of the road. The autopsy says that the gangster was first beaten to death, shot in the back five times, and then thrown from an automobile. Elmer becomes suspicious and wonders why the body was found ten feet away from the road. He deduces that he might have been thrown from an airplane. Elmer's theory expands: Each Wednesday a plane files over the area, and it's possible that Fuller was dropped from that plane.

After purchasing $5,000 worth of shares from Doc, Harvey gets a call from the *Chicago Daily Blade* to let him know about the story of a con artist selling fraudulent stock to the people in Clearmont. Harvey has Doc arrested and blames Elmer for the mess, getting the cheated investors to turn on Elmer.

The Wednesday night plane passes by on schedule and its occupants turn out to be perfume smugglers. Elmer takes off to follow them and is fired on by the smugglers. Elmer realizes that there's a shotgun in his plane and shoots off the propeller of the gangsters' plane. After the gangster's plane lands, they are arrested.

The runway is now crowded with townsfolk waiting to welcome Elmer back as a hero. Out of gas, he parachutes out over another part of town while Bill guides the plane in with the radio beam. Elmer lands safely and kisses the ground as his neighbors arrive. In the end Elmer is not only a hero but also has also sold his radio beam technology to the Chicago airport for $10,000.

Edward made a cameo appearance, this time in footage which could have easily been left on the cutting room floor. The segment has Elmer racing from the barber shop. As he runs in front of a police officer, he slows down and slinks away suspiciously. Edward, who unconvincingly played the police officer, is casually dressed in a jacket, sans a tie, with a police officer's cap on his head and a nightstick in his hand. Edward's musical talent was put to good use as well. In one scene where Brown is taking a bath, he sings "I'm Tired of Trying to Make You Mine," a song with lyrics by Edward and music by Henry Cohen.

Fit for a King, a September release, was a remake of *I'll Tell the World*, the action-filled romance Edward directed in 1934, now transformed into a comedy. Although Lincoln Quarberg and Frank Wead were responsible for writing the original story, Richard Flournoy was given the credit for writing *Fit for a King*'s screenplay.

Brown, the film's main attraction, played Lee Tracy's old role of news reporter Stanley Brown, but with the character's name changed to the preposterous Virgil Ambrose Jeremiah

Christopher "Scoop" Jones. Helen Mack filled the part of Jane Hamilton aka Princess Helen, which was originally played by Gloria Stuart, with Paul Kelly cast as the competing reporter Briggs, Harry Davenport as Archduke Julio (originally Grand Duke Ferdinand), Halliwell Hobbes as Count Strunsky, and Donald Briggs as Prince Michael.

The filmed scenes were almost identical reshoots of the original version, only substituting Tracy's serious character with Brown's slapstick persona. *Fit for a King* gave Brown a chance to demonstrate both his famous howl and the acrobatic skills he learned onstage. For Edward, it meant another tedious film in the can. From this point on, Edward's films would be mediocre features, and far from challenging compared to his previous endeavors.

Nineteen thirty-seven was a sad year for silent serial fans, as one of the Sedgwicks' closest friends passed away. Ruth Roland, remembered as the Queen of the Thriller Serials, died on September 22 after her battle with cancer. Roland had decided to retire from acting in 1923, living comfortably on the profits from her real estate investments. Making only four motion pictures after her retirement, including two sound films, Roland never considered returning to the silver screen permanently, but instead continued her entertainment career on the vaudeville stage. As she was a close personal friend of the Sedgwicks, Clarence Hutson, Eileen's husband, was asked to act as one of the pallbearers, along with Joseph Breen, District Attorney Burton Fitts, Sid Grauman, Bartley Hezvrun, Robert Z. Leonard and Harry Zepner. W.S. Van Dyke, who directed Roland in her adventure films, delivered the eulogy.

Edward's next collaboration with Joe E. Brown was a comedy produced for Columbia. An August 1938 release, *The Gladiator* was freely based on Philip Wylie's 1930 science fiction novel *Gladiator*, in which a scientist invents a serum that gives test animals super-strength. When he discovers that his wife is pregnant he injects her with the drug. Their son, who is born with superhuman strength, speed, and bulletproof skin, spends much of his life learning to hide his powers, occasionally using them for good. It's been widely speculated that the novel was the inspiration for the comic book character Superman, who made his first appearance in June 1938 in *Action Comics* #1.

The Gladiator borrowed portions of the novel's plot, with Professor Abner Danner (Lucien Littlefield) intent on creating a superhuman being. The unlikely experimental subject turns out to be Hugo Kipp (Joe E. Brown), a recently unemployed administrative assistant who worked at Twin Springs Children's Orthopedic Hospital. The hospital's committee decided to give the position to the son of a benefactor who has a college degree. Hugo purchases the winning ticket at a local movie theater's $1,500 cash jackpot night. He decides that he will use the money to go back to Webster College to finish his degree.

Hugo decides to stay at Professor Danner's boarding house, the lodging he used a dozen years earlier when he attended college. The professor has developed a serum that will change a human into a superman who, like an ant, would be able to lift fifty times his own weight and, like a grasshopper, jump a hundred times his height. While Hugo sleeps, the professor injects him with the serum, which give him superhuman strength. Upset, he confronts the professor about giving him the serum without being consulted.

On his first day on campus Hugo meets Iris Bennett (June Travis). Thinking that Hugo is athletically gifted like his grandfather and father, both graduates of the college, she encourages him join the school's football team. Hugo joins the team and, with the help of the serum, helps them win the big game. Iris starts to fall for Hugo.

Hugo takes Iris to the hospital where he used to work to meet Bobby (Dickie Moore), one of Hugo's biggest fans. An invalid, Bobby is slowly getting back his ability to walk. Hugo is concerned that the hospital will be sending Bobby to an orphanage once he makes a full recovery. He's prepared to adopt Bobby but he must prove that he can support the child. Serendipitously, he notices a headline on the newspaper reporting on an upcoming wrestling match that is looking for a contender to take on Man Mountain Dean, with a $10,000 prize. Hugo is convinced that he can wrestle as well as he plays football and signs up for the challenge.

The wrestling event begins with Hugo flipping Man Mountain Dean over and over again and knocking him unconscious. During the second round the drug wears off. Hugo can hardly stand up and takes a beating as Mountain Man Dean pounces on him.

Professor Danner, Iris and Bobby arrive at the wrestling event. The professor alerts Hugo that he doesn't have any more of the serum and that he has destroyed the formula. Hugo is on his own for the next round, as he is sent back in to get a further beating. Finding a lit cigar on the edge of the wrestling mat, he proceeds to burn Man Mountain Dean's butt. Mountain Man Dean slips and Hugo accidentally kicks him in head, knocking him out cold. Hugo wins the $10,000 purse, which is more than enough to adopt Bobby. In addition, he

Over the next couple of years Edward would direct Joe E. Brown (center, standing) in four more comedies with *Gladiator* (1938) turning out impressively, considering its independent production values. *The Gladiator* was freely based on Philip Wylie's 1930 science fiction novel *Gladiator*, which is widely speculated as being the premise for the comic book character Superman.

finds that he will also need to have a wife before can adopt a child. Iris looks longingly at Hugo and suggests that they get married.

Brown took advantage of the film to make good use of his quirky voice characterizations throughout. Missing, though, was his trademark howl.

After years of working in a tumbling act, Brown had an athletic ability that allowed him to perform many of his own physical stunts. One of the *Gladiator* stunts required Brown to twirl giant wrestler Man Mountain Dean over his head. The prop department installed invisible wire rigging for the stunt, but Man Mountain insisted that Brown could perform it on his own. Brown was convinced, so when the time came to stop the filming and rig him up with the wiring, Brown just continued on, almost effortlessly picking up the 327-pound wrestler. The film continued to roll and Edward thought the shot worked well, requesting the same scene shot at four additional angles. On the fifth try of lifting and twirling the wrestler over his head, Brown felt something tear inside his groin area; he had a double hernia.

While recuperating from surgery, Brown experienced a bad accident driving along Sunset Boulevard where it passes through the UCLA campus. He found that his station wagon's brakes weren't working as he rounded a curve that paralleled a steep 30-foot embankment. Brown lost control and the car somersaulted down the hillside, leaving him in an almost paralyzed state. Brown's injuries included a severed septum, his back broken in two places, and one collapsed lung. In the operating room, Brown lost his pulse for about 40 seconds.

Edward was called back to MGM to direct a January 1939 release, *Burn 'Em Up O'Connor*. Working on the racing thriller for MGM meant that his assignment would bring him up a notch quality-wise. Milton Merlin and Byron Morgan worked with Edward on the scenario. Although it was based on Sir Malcolm Campbell's novel *Salute to the Gods* it was very similar to the formula used in *Death on the Diamond* and *Murder in the Fleet*, with racecar drivers being killed instead of ballplayers and sailors.

The murder mystery revolves around a racecar team owned by Pinky G. Delano (Harry Carey), an aged driver. The car of one of Pinky's drivers uncontrollably races off of the track and flips, killing the driver. Jerry O'Connor (Dennis O'Keefe), an amateur racer, and his grease monkey friend Buddy Buttle (Nat Pendleton) are watching the newsreel in a movie theater when they both notice that something seems peculiar about the whole accident.

Jerry qualifies their midget racer for the next race and, along with Buddy, joins Pinky's team. The entire team feels that Pinky's cars are jinxed and the drivers worry who will be the next to die in a crash. In the meantime, Jerry becomes fixated on Pinky's daughter Jane (Cecilia Parker).

The next three drivers lose control of their cars and get into deadly wrecks. Jerry and Buddy deduce that all of the drivers seemed to have had something affect their vision before crashing. Heading to the track at the next race before anyone else arrives, Jerry runs the course with his eyes closed. He has memorized the track and is assisted by Buddy's high-pitched whistling to alert him of the curves.

Just before the race, Jerry asks Buddy to get him a soda pop. Buddy places the cold bottle on the table and turns away for a moment. When he turns back, he notices that the bottle was moved, as a ring of condensation where it originally was placed is showing alongside where the bottle is now standing. Buddy, acting as a guinea pig, quickly gulps down the bottle. At first he appears to be fine, but then his eyesight starts getting blurry.

It's too late to warn Jerry, who drank a bottle offered to him by "Doc" Heath (Charley Grapewin) and is now racing on the track. It turns out that Doc was poisoning Pinky's drivers before they got into their cars, in revenge for the death of his son who died while he was racing for the Delano team. Jerry feels the effect of the drug and relies on his skills to run the course blind. He wins the race before he slams into a bale of hay. Having a change of heart about Jerry, Jane runs to him and, realizing that he is unscathed, caresses his head.

Dennis O'Keefe's portrayal of Jerry O'Connor was that of an annoying character, but it was effectively done. Cecilia Parker, better known to moviegoers for her role as the older sister of Mickey Rooney in MGM's "Andy Hardy" series, played her part well. Harry Carey, as always, turned in a decent performance.

Universal called in Edward to help direct a troubled project titled *You Can't Cheat an Honest Man*. The studio had teamed W.C. Fields with ventriloquist Edgar Bergen for a circus-themed comedy. The filming commenced in November 1938, and by the sixth week of production the unpleasantness between its two stars had become a serious obstacle. The two proved to be a successful combination on radio, Fields performing his character who had a soft spot for alcohol and Bergen's wiseguy dummy Charlie McCarthy; but once placed in front of a camera, the chemistry turned caustic.

To make matters worse, Fields, like Buster Keaton, employed an improvisational style

Edward was called back to MGM to direct *Burn 'Em Up O'Connor* (1939), in addition to contributing to its scenario. The racing thriller featured Cecilia Parker, Dennis O'Keefe, and Harry Carey.

throughout his movies. This drove the production off schedule. Once director George Marshall had started filming *You Can't Cheat an Honest Man*—a story that Fields claimed to have penned on an envelope—the scriptwriters frantically raced to keep up with Fields' ad-libbing.

Fields' reluctance to adhere to a finished script, compounded by his temperamental behavior (especially in dealing with Bergen), became a problem. Universal decided to separate the two stars, with the "Bergen unit" under the direction of Marshall and the "Fields unit" under Edward. Working with Fields became challenging for Edward, as Fields was soon at odds with him too. Before long Edward left the assignment, with the director position replaced by Eddie Cline, another veteran comedy director.

The comedy follows Fields as Larson E. Whipsnade, the owner of the money-losing Whipsnade's Circus. Constantly on the run from the law, Larson is trying to dodge authorities attempting to issue a summons to him for the $35,000 debt that his circus has incurred. Wealthy Roger Bele-Goodie (James Bush) is wooing his daughter Vicky (Constance Moore). Although she's in love with the circus' ventriloquist, the Great Bergen (Bergen), Vicky agrees to marry Roger instead, with the hope that Roger can bail out her father's circus. The Bele-Goodies prepare a party for Vicky and Roger's wedding, but once they realize that the Whipsnades are ordinary people the marriage is called off. In the end Vicky and Edgar renew their love for each other.

Had it not been for Fields' taxing style, Edward could have easily handled the direction for *You Can't Cheat an Honest Man*. The majority of the movie revolves around the McCarthy-Fields routines, with the two acts blending flawlessly. Remarkably, in the end, *You Can't Cheat an Honest Man* was completed on schedule and released in February 1939. And it turned out to be one of Fields' better films.

Beware Spooks!, Edward's third film direction featuring Joe E. Brown, was released by Columbia in October. In this comedy thriller, Brown played newlywed police officer Roy L. Gifford. Son of "Wild Bill" Gifford, an officer held in high regard by the commissioner, Roy is quite the opposite as a bone-headed coward. Commissioner Lester Lewis (Clarence Kolb) revokes leave for all officers as Slick Eastman (Marc Lawrence), the head of a narcotics ring and an alleged killer, is on the loose. This means the honeymoon plans for Roy and Betty Lou (Mary Carlisle) are postponed.

Roy is asked to turn in his service revolver and badge as he has let Slick slip through his fingers. Returning home he explains his jobless situation to Betty Lou. Since they can no longer afford a honeymoon trip to Bermuda, they settle for a stay at a disreputable hotel by the amusement pier. They soon discover that Slick resides at the same hotel; they follow him to the amusement pier. Slick is intent on killing gangster boss Nick Bruno (Don Beddoe), who once ratted him out to the law. He confronts Nick in his hideout in the spook house and fills him full of lead.

Slick attempts to escape but Roy chases and catches him. Slick is arrested and the commissioner pins Roy's badge back on him, awarding him an all-expenses-paid honeymoon to Bermuda.

Beware Spooks! borders on being tedious, with the obnoxious style of humor preventing it from being funny. The feature is very different from *Fit for a King*, which had limited Brown's trademark facial expressions and childish elocution. In *The Gladiator* Brown had used a similar dimwitted persona, but with the advantage of a halfway decent script. Edward was trapped, as he was still scheduled to make one more movie with Brown, *So You Won't Talk*, planned for 1940 release.

Ned Sedgwick, who died in 1932, lived long enough to see motion pictures become the family's livelihood. After a career in vaudeville, constantly traveling around in often-desperate searches for places to play, the Sedgwicks had found their real home in the Hollywood area, finally setting down roots.

In 1936 Eileen and Clarence adopted their daughter and son, Mary Eileen (Mimi) and Edward Thomas (Ed). The children were raised by an extended family which included Josie and Fenie. Their Beverly Hills neighborhood was populated with other entertainer families, many of which the Sedgwicks had working relationships with. Loretta Young and Jack Haley would become good friends of the Hutsons, with their children attending the same school. Mimi and Ed would take swimming lessons down the street from their home in George Burns and Gracie Allen's backyard pool.

Josie, who had taken countless risks while performing dangerous stunts in her films, was now paying the price as she was in constant pain from her old injuries, ones that sometimes required additional surgery.

The Sedgwicks enjoyed their social life, and often hosted parties or appeared as guests at functions that frequently included an impressive assortment of Hollywood notables. The parties were frequently referenced in Hollywood's society columns. On one occasion, the *Los Angeles Examiner* reported the November 11, 1934, opening of W.S. Van Dyke's bar. Styled with a marine theme, the bar displayed a large glass tank, revealing an underwater scene of an ancient shipwreck which was created by Roy Cornish of MGM's miniature department. Edward attended this event.

> Unfortunately, Ruth Mannix [Dyke's wife] was at home ill, but Van was charmingly assisted by his mother, Mrs. Laura Winston Van Dyke. Jean Harlow, in a black gown of simple lines, a tiny black hat a-top her platinum crowning glory, and with platinum fingernails, no less was radiant. Very much in attendance was the debonair Bill Powell. Nelson Eddy cavaliered Mitzi Cummings, and that duo of lively interest, Minna Gombell and Joe Sefton, were jolly well present.

The guest list for this occasion was quite a mix of actors, directors, writers, and miscellaneous public personalities, making it a paparazzo's dream. Invitees also included Col. William Fairbanks, Col. and Mrs. Berry, Sheriff Eugene Biscailuz, Col. Tim McCoy, Major and Mrs. Miller, Major McElwain, Judge and Mrs. Sproul, Major and Mrs. Walkup, Major and Mrs. Thrasher, Dr. Todd, Warner Baxter, Neil Hamilton, William Newberry, William K. Howard, Ted Healy, Douglas Shearer, Jean Hersholt, Joe Sherman, Vince Barnett, John Miljan, Vi-Seng Klang, Ulric Busch, Buck Jones, Hunt Stromberg, Harrison Carroll, Otto Kruger, Hardie Albright, Harry Carey, Jesse Lasky, Ralph Wheelwright, Harry Cohn, Hamilton MacFadden, Andy Hervey, J.J. Cohn, Robert Montgomery, Jimmy Durante, Jerry Mayer, Chester Morris, Clark Gable, Billie Burke, Irene Hervey, Kay English, Dorothy Sebastian, Muriel Evans, Conchita Montenegro, Toby Wing, Maureen O'Sullivan, Isabel Jewell, Charlotte Wood; Mesdames Kate Cummings, Ida Koverman, Pop Arnold, Raul Roulien, Max Baer, George E. Stone, Charles Butterworth, Jack Oakie, Howard Strickling, Lee Tracy, and Dashiell Hammett.

In honor of the March 23, 1936, marriage of actor Jack Oakie and Venita Varden, the Hutsons hosted a party for their friends at Lake Norconia. When the newlyweds returned from their honeymoon, Eileen and Clarence, along with Josie and Fenie, threw a welcome back party for the couple. The cocktail party, given at their Beverly Hills home, included an impressive list of Hollywood personalities and their spouses, including Wallace Berry, Jean Hersholt, Jack Benny, Joe E. Brown, Robert Young, Edward G. Robinson, Eddie Mannix, Harry Joe Brown, Ralph Morgan, Frank McHugh, Stu Erwin, Roscoe Karns, Harry Brown, W.S. Van Dyke, Henry Cohen, Wallace Ford, Jack Gardner, Irving Cummings, Harry Warren, Eddie Laemmle, Andy Devine, Dick Hunt, Richard Wallace, George Marshall, Ted Healy, David Butler, Lewis Stone, William Seiter, Joseph Seiter, Joseph Sugarman, Bing Crosby, Reginald Denny, Walter Jurman, John Ford, Harold Young, Robert Armstrong, Jack Haley, Henry King, Russell Simpson, Gary Cooper, Pat O'Brien, Otto Kruger, James Gleason, Tom Dugan, Minna Gombell, Gracie Allen, Pauline Brooks, Lois Wilson, Jeanne Robinson, Buff Cobb, Toby Wing, Ruth Roland, Babe Marx, June Gale, Una O'Connor, Helene Breen, Thyra Hagen, Mary Sedgwick, Mary Carlisle, Mary Eigan, Evelyn Offiel, Charles Ruggles, Fritz Tidden, George Burns, King Vidor, Hoot Gibson, John Miljan, Irvin Cobb, David Carlisle, Barney Carr, Tom Brown, Russell Gleason, Victor Orsatti, Frank Orsatti, Ernie Orsatti, and Joe Sefton.

The September 25, 1939, *Los Angeles Examiner* covered Tom and Marie Dugan's bar-

Retired from motion pictures, Eileen became a socialite. Eileen and her husband, Clarence Hutson (Eileen standing above kneeling Clarence), would often host parties at their home, inviting their celebrity neighbors (courtesy E. Hutson).

becue. Tom, a character actor and an occasional gag writer, had appeared in several of Edward's recent films. According to the write-up,

> A peeping Tom should have seen the tall, lanky Arthur Treacher frantically sliding all over the place in his effort to give histrionic expression to the title, *Slide, Kelly, Slide*, and the all a dither Charles Ruggles even more a dither while he thumped money with his fist and carried on with football gesticulations in his portrayal of *$1,000 a Touchdown*. And if this Peeping Tom had still lingered to watch these screwball antics he should have seen Lucille Ball giving her acting all to *The Rains Came*.

Others guests attending the barbecue included William and Mary Gargan, Charlie Ruggles and Marion LaBarba, Arthur and Virginia Taylor, the Robert Hopkins, the Al Malnecks, Flo and Jack Haley, Mr. and Mrs. Eddie Foy, Jr., the Jimmy Conlins, Ebba and Ed Sedgwick, the Jack Nortons, "Cookie" Cohen, Betty Byron and the James Hogans.

The mention of Edward and Ebba appearing at the same party as Lucille Ball, a struggling actress, is noteworthy, as the three would eventually form a close friendship. Their relationship would eventually guarantee Edward the exposure to a future Rubicon—the experience of television.

CHAPTER NINE

Nazis, Country Bumpkins, and a Couple of Redheads

By the 1940s the world was in the midst of its second major conflict of the century. Although the United States struggled to keep its neutrality, it could feel the ripples caused by the conflict reaching its shores. The motion picture industry in the U.S., however, was immediately affected as eleven countries were closed to English-language films.

The United States became enmeshed in the war following the attack on Pearl Harbor on December 7, 1941. Actors, including Clark Gable, James Stewart, Gene Kelly, Jackie Cooper, and Robert Taylor, enlisted in the armed services, and actresses, including Myrna Loy and June Allyson, signed up for work with the Red Cross. Many other stars volunteered their time performing for the troops overseas in USO shows, while others sold war bonds.

The movie industry was quick to capitalize on the global conflict by producing inspirational films that turned out to be Academy Award–winning box office draws, including director Howard Hawks' *Sergeant York* (1941), staring Gary Cooper, and director William Wyler's *Mrs. Miniver* (1942), featuring Greer Garson. Comedies contributed too, with Charlie Chaplin appearing in *The Great Dictator* (1940), his satire on Nazi Germany's Hitler, Bob Hope in *Caught in the Draft* (1941), and Bud Abbott and Lou Costello in *Buck Privates*, *In the Navy* and *Keep 'Em Flying* (all 1941).

Working alone in an office in the writers' building, Edward's position at MGM had evolved to that of a gagman and a troubleshooter for scripts in need of help. In 1940 Buster Keaton was rehired by MGM and assigned to work alongside Edward. Keaton, who was once earning $3,000 a week as an MGM star, was now on salary for $100 a week. Although their assignments were challenging, they were often followed by stretches of inactivity as they waited for their next job. An occasional directing job for Edward or an acting job for Keaton were welcome diversions from their routine positions.

With spare time on their hands they wrote spec scripts with expectations that one of them might be produced. In one script Edward and Keaton were hoping to capitalize on President Franklin Delano Roosevelt's new peacetime military draft of 1940 by creating a sequel to their 1930 film *Doughboys*, having the original actors, albeit older, play their roles as they re-enlist in the service. The two tried to sell their story to MGM, but the studio didn't think that it was prudent to poke fun at the war. Universal beat the two to the silver screen with a similar story idea when they released Abbott and Costello's *Buck Privates*.

Edward's directorial responsibilities were limited during the 1940s. His only assignment for 1940 was his final collaboration with Joe E. Brown, an October Columbia release titled *So You Won't Talk*, a spoof of the studio's 1935 crime drama *The Whole Town's Talking*. In this second-rate comedy Brown plays the role of Charles Augustus Hold, a *Star Chronicle* book reviewer who's known to his co-workers as "Whiskers" for his mustache and beard. His love interest Lucy Walters (Frances Robinson) encourages him to write books, rather than review them. In an effort to get him to change his image, she persuades him to shave off his facial hair. After "Whiskers" gets his beard and mustache shaved at the barber shop he looks exactly like Brute Hanson, a gang lord (also Brown) who was secretly released a year early from Alcatraz. Barber shop customers think that "Whiskers" is Brute, and word quickly gets out that the criminal is back in town. This is just the start of the confusion that ensues throughout the movie as "Whiskers" and Brute alternately pose as each other.

"Whiskers" discovers that Brute killed Red Mayberry and contacts the police. Disguised as Brute, he convinces Brute's thugs that Brute is "Whiskers" and gets them to tie up the gangster. When the police arrive, Lucy then has to convince them who's Brute and who's "Whiskers." The story ends with Lucy and "Whiskers" kissing.

One scene included was a tribute to a routine Edward directed and Buster Keaton performed in *Spite Marriage*: Hiding in a theater dressing room, Brown applies a long fake beard similar to the one Keaton wore when his character was also hiding backstage. Brown then proceeds to place a Union soldier cap on his head, making him look similar to Keaton's character.

Edward would also direct the MGM homefront comedy *Air Raid Wardens* starring Stan Laurel and Oliver Hardy, which was released in April of 1943. It was his only directorial job in the three years since *So You Won't Talk*.

Known for their visually physical style of humor, the English Stan Laurel and American Oliver Hardy became one the most recognizable comedy teams in the history of motion pictures. Their early stage experiences led them to work in silent comedy shorts, with the two first sharing the screen in *The Lucky Dog* (1921), a short for Sun-Lite Pictures. They didn't officially become a team until Hal Roach brought them together in 1926 for his comedy shorts. Offsetting each other's character with their size and style—Laurel thin and easygoing, Hardy with his large build and easily frustrated demeanor—the two were popular from the late 1920s to the mid–1940s.

With the expectation of having greater control over their work elsewhere, the two left Hal Roach Studios in 1940, signing on as free agents with 20th Century–Fox and MGM from 1941 to 1944. Their experience working at these studios, however, was not what they expected. As in the case of *Air Raid Wardens*, MGM engaged additional scriptwriters Martin Rackin and Harry Crane to assist Laurel and Hardy's longtime gagmen Jack Jevne and Charles Rogers, which resulted in the script becoming an overworked product. Similar to the disappointment Keaton experienced when he joined MGM, Laurel and Hardy quickly discovered that their input in the script process and freedom to improvise while filming were very limited.

Although the scenario was mediocre, the production benefited from MGM's polished production. In addition to the talent of Laurel and Hardy, *Air Raid Wardens* featured a decent supporting cast, which included comedian Edgar Kennedy as Joe Bledsoe, a radio repair shop manager. Kennedy became known as "the king of the slow burn" for his routine of making an exasperated look, which he followed by dragging his hand over his bald head and down his face. Horace (Stephen) McNally, an actor who was experienced in playing both heroes and villains, was cast in the role of Dan Madison, editor of the town's newspaper. Jacqueline White, another MGM contract player, filled the role of the paper's star reporter, Peggy Parker.

Air Raid Wardens opens in a small town caught up in the excitement generated following the attack at Pearl Harbor. The town is home to a new magnesium plant, a major concern for the town's citizens. It is up to the town to make sure that the supply of magnesium doesn't get into enemy hands.

Laurel and Hardy, two hapless entrepreneurs who have tried to run various businesses, are now owners of a bicycle shop. Believing that it is their patriotic duty to serve in the armed forces, the two travel to the city and attempt to enlist with the Army, Navy, and Marines, only to be classified as 4-F. Their only hope for serving their country is with the local Civil Defense chapter as air raid wardens.

When Laurel and Hardy return to reopen their bicycle shop, they discover that the owner of the building rented out the shop to a radio sales and repair business. The store's new occupant Eustace Middling (Donald Meek) turns out to be a Nazi. The two discover that Eustace is in charge of a group of Nazi spies who are planning to blow up the magnesium plant at 5:00 that afternoon while the rest of the town is busy performing a practice war incident.

Laurel and Hardy, who have proven to their Civil Defense unit to be unreliable, race off to the plant in an attempt to stop the attack. On their way they phone the board and, pretending to be an authority figure, announce that the drill will now take place at the magnesium plant.

The Nazi spies arrive at the plant, pistol-whip the two guards, and proceed to wire the plant with explosives. As the Civil Defense group arrives they find the guards unconscious. Upon awakening, one says that the spies went to the generator plant with dynamite. Dan confronts the spies and realizes that the attack is for real. Just as the spies fire a gun at Dan, patrol members aim a water hose at the spies, which moves them away from their detonator. Major Scanlon (Russell Hicks) arrives with the rest of the patrol to arrest them while Dan defuses the explosives. Laurel and Hardy capture Eustace as he attempts to escape and haul him to the plant tied up in some heavy rope. The boys have saved the day.

World War II adversely affected the real estate market in California, with potential customers becoming preoccupied with the possibility of being invaded by a foreign nation. Clarence Hutson's position as a real estate investor was terminated as his company hit hard times. Propitiously, Clarence was friends with Colonel Jason S. Joy, the Director of Public Relations for Fox, who was instrumental in getting him a job at the studio in 1942. Ten years earlier, as the head of the Motion Picture Producers and Distributors Studio Relations Committee, Joy had worked with Will Hays in enforcing the Production Code. The former national executive secretary of the American Red Cross had been appointed "liaison officer" between those who produced movies and those who desired to see them maintain "high

As a consolation for not having the opportunity to remake *Doughboys*, Edward would direct the MGM home-front comedy *Air Raid Wardens* (1943) starring Stan Laurel and Oliver Hardy, shown with Jacqueline Kennedy. It was his only directorial job in three years.

standards of art, entertainment, education and morals in motion pictures." Clarence was responsible for scouting out locations to be used in the studio's films. The films he was responsible for usually involved the armed forces. As a child Ed traveled with Clarence to Camp Pendleton Marine Corps Base in Oceanside, California, where he (Clarence) was working on production details for *Guadalcanal Diary* (1943). "We spent the whole summer down there. I was seven or eight, I guess. The head of the camp was General Fegan. I remember that quite well. We spent about three months there." In the meantime Clarence would have been busy securing houses, building and facilities to be used in the film.

By the mid–1940s Edward's career as a director was winding down, with his next major assignment coming three years after directing *Air Raid Wardens*. Edward and Keaton were asked to help out as uncredited directors on MGM's Technicolor movie *Easy to Wed*, a July 1946 release. Keaton had also contributed to the script, which was an adaptation of the 1936 hit *Libeled Lady*.

The romantic comedy featured Esther Williams and Van Johnson. An MGM talent scout first noticed Williams, a swimming champion, while she was employed at a Los Angeles department store. The studio created a special subgenre for her, "Aqua Musicals." Johnson was a young song-and-dance star who became popular during the war years. Due to injuries

Keenan Wynn, Van Johnson, and Lucille Ball are shown in a scene from *Easy to Wed* (1946). Edward and Buster Keaton, who both worked on the film as uncredited directors, encouraged Ball's comedic talent.

sustained in a near-fatal automobile accident, he was given a 4-F status, which disqualified him from service with the armed forces. Consequently he was able to fill in for the popular male stars of the day who had gone off to serve in the war.

Easy to Wed also featured a young actress named Lucille Ball. During the early 1930s, while working for Goldwyn and Fox, Ball was frequently cast as a chorus girl, as she was in Eddie Cantor's musical *Roman Scandals* (1933). By 1940 she was acting in predictable comedies for RKO, where she became known as the Queen of the B's. Although her move to MGM in 1943 gave her more prominent roles, the studio didn't give her movies the quality treatment that their productions were known for. Her uninspiring assignments were preventing her from getting more serious parts.

Edward had taken notice of Ball back while she was working as a chorine at Goldwyn, and would later reminisce about the moment he first recognized her hidden talent. "I saw this beautiful girl walking around the Goldwyn lot. She was one of the Goldwyn Girls. I'd see her tell a story and watch her facial expressions change. She'd illustrate it with everything she had. I got up my nerve to talk to her and said, 'Young lady, if you play your cards right, you can be the greatest comedienne in show business.'" Ball didn't realize how sincere Edward's compliment was until years later.

In the late 1930s Ball was reintroduced to Edward by Alexander Hall, a Paramount director she had been dating since 1937. Edward and Hall had common friends, most of whom had experience on the vaudeville stage earlier in their careers, including Jack Haley, Arthur Treacher, George Burns and Gracie Allen.

At MGM Keaton also took an interest in Ball and encouraged her to cultivate her unrealized talent. Edward and Keaton asked Louis B. Mayer to cast Ball as a comedienne, but the executive's response was that beautiful women sold more tickets than funny ones. Although Ball appreciated Edward and Keaton's advice, she felt that she wasn't ready to focus her attention on comedy. Yet in *Easy to Wed* Ball's comedic style is noticeably developed. It had traces of Lucy Ricardo, a character she would make tremendously popular on *I Love Lucy*, a pioneering television show that premiered in 1951.

As *Easy to Wed* opens, Gladys Benton (Ball) is the bride-to-be of Warren Haggerty (Keenan Wynn), a *Morning Star* newspaper reporter. At the last moment Warren jilts Gladys, who is waiting for him at the altar, when he is called in by Curtis Farwood (Paul Harvey), the publisher of his newspaper, to cover an important assignment. The affluent Allenburys are suing the paper for two million dollars for defamation of character because of a story they printed, and Curtis wants Warren get them to drop the case.

Warren comes up with an idea to frame Connie Allenbury by putting her in a scandalous situation with a married man. And he has just the man: Bill Chandler, a fellow reporter (Van Johnson). With the plan in place, Bill goes to Mexico City and is introduced to Connie. He attempts to convince her to drop the case, pointing out that if she wins the two million dollars, hundreds of people will be put out of work. She agrees to drop the lawsuit and put the money into a trust fund for the unemployed workers.

The plot progressively becomes convoluted as Warren, who's unaware of Connie's pact with Bill, continues to try to get Connie to change her mind. In the end Gladys is convinced that she really adores Warren and Connie stays will Bill.

Directorially, there are scenes that are clearly influenced by Edward and Keaton. In one scene, Bill Chandler is attempting to get into a boat with his hunting dog and equipment. The boat starts to slip away from the shore and he is left stretched out above the water, with his feet on land and his hands grabbing onto the back of the drifting boat.

Lucille Ball's comedic talent was also encouraged by their direction. The gestures and facial expressions and reactions upon which Edward had commented were all being utilized to her advantage in *Easy to Wed*. These routines would soon be used for her Lucy Ricardo *I Love Lucy* character.

In 1948 MGM assigned Edward to direct the Civil War comedy *A Southern Yankee* with Red Skelton, scheduled for August release. Trained on the vaudeville circuit, Skelton debuted on Broadway and radio in 1937 and on film in 1938. He would eventually move his talents to television, premiering *The Red Skelton Hour* in 1951 on NBC. For two decades his show stayed in the top twenty on both the NBC and CBS.

The film also featured Arlene Dahl, a fairly new face on the Hollywood scene. Dahl, voted the Rheingold Beer Girl of 1946, began her acting career in 1947 with Warner Bros. She was featured in only two Warner Bros. films before signing a contract with MGM, with *A Southern Yankee* being her fourth film.

Buster Keaton, employed as a gagman for Skelton, had suggested that Edward would be the ideal director for the production. Although Edward received the final credit as *A Southern Yankee*'s director, S. Sylvan Simon was responsible for redirecting many of the scenes. Skelton was disappointed with Edward's progress and insisted that Simon be brought in. Skelton and Simon had started their working relationship with Skelton's first feature, *Whistling in the Dark* (1941), with Simon going on to direct and produce for Columbia Skelton's box-office hit *The Fuller Brush Man* (1948).

Skelton's complaints about Edward's direction might not have been totally fair. The redheaded comedian was dissatisfied with his previous films produced by MGM and was looking for opportunities that would boost his career as Columbia's *The Fuller Brush Man* did. He was looking to be released from his MGM contract, so he might have been trying to give the studio a difficult time on *A Southern Yankee*, demanding that scenes be re-filmed.

Melvin Frank, Norman Panama, Harry Tugend, and Keaton wrote the *Southern Yankee* story. Keaton went uncredited onscreen but his influence is present throughout, with several gags lifted directly from his own movies. One scene includes a two-sided flag gag that Keaton used in silent days. John Ireland, Brian Donlevy, Charles Dingle, and Lloyd Gough supported Skelton in making it a decent spoof on Civil War films.

Set in St. Louis in 1865, *A Southern Yankee* revolves around "The Grey Spider," a South-

Buster Keaton had suggested to MGM that Edward would be the ideal director for the Civil War comedy *A Southern Yankee* (1948). Edward would be replaced after the film's star, Red Skelton (seated), complained of Edward's progress.

ern spy whose identity is known to only a handful of high-level Confederate officers. Skelton plays Aubrey Filmore, a bellboy for the Palmer Hotel; a Yankee, he dreams of being a heroic Secret Service agent.

A Yankee messenger delivers a confidential dispatch to Col. Clifford M. Baker (Art Baker). It states that once again the Grey Spider has struck a blow to the Union army, this time by blowing up an ammunition dump at the Jefferson barracks, killing 22 soldiers. It is evident that St. Louis is his next target. The colonel alerts the townspeople of his possible presence. Aubrey, who has been incessantly asking Col. Baker to make him an agent, annoys him to a point where the officer will say anything to get the bellboy off his back, telling him that he can help look for the Grey Spider (George Coulouris).

Aubrey falls for Sallyann Weatherby (Dahl), a Confederate spy. He then commences to bumble his way through a spy-chasing excursion that eventually takes him to the Confederate line where the North and South are engaged in battle. The Yankees are routed, with Aubrey left behind to change into a Confederate uniform. Afraid that the Yankees may fire on him, he dresses himself with his Yankee jacket exposed to the Northern side and his Confederate jacket to the Southern side. Similarly, he picks up a Union flag and a Confederate flag and disguises each against the other, with the Northern Stars and Stripes on one side and the Southern Stars and Bars on the other. Aubrey walks out to the front of line waving his flag, causing a ceasefire, with each side only seeing their color ... until the wind blows the flag around, revealing the opposite sides, and causing the battle to flare up again.

Behind the lines, Aubrey impersonates the Grey Spider, but it's only a matter of time before he's discovered to be a Northern spy and court-martialed. Just as he is placed in front of a firing squad, an announcement is made that the war is over. Sallyann rescues Aubrey from the firing squad just in time. They ride off into the sunset, with Aubrey falling out of the back of the wagon.

MGM attempted to capitalize on the success of Columbia's *The Fuller Brush Man* by duplicating the trend of pairing Skelton up with a highly visible and marketable trademark in *The Yellow Cab Man*. Edward was credited as comedy consultant in this March 1950 release. Any conflict that might have existed between Edward and Skelton during the filming of *A Southern Yankee* was apparently now a thing of the past. The two worked together one more time in *Excuse My Dust* (1951).

In *The Yellow Cab Man*, Skelton plays the accident-prone Augustus "Red" Pirdy, an amateur inventor who has recently been turned down by his insurance company for being a high-risk accident liability. As he crosses the street against traffic, he is hit by a Yellow Cab and is knocked unconscious. Ellen Goodrich, a Yellow Cab company claims adjuster (Gloria DeHaven), visits "Red" to settle his accident claim. Red confesses that it was his fault, at which point Ellen tries to get him to sign a document absolving the company. Just as he's about to sign, Martin Creavy (Edward Arnold), attorney at law and a defender of victims against corporations, enters the apartment and advises "Red" not to sign it. Martin is a thorn in the Yellow Cab Company's side, and Ellen's first reaction is to smack Martin with a pane of glass that is on display on Red's desk. Instead of shattering, the glass bounces off of his head. "Red" has invented a type of glass that is unbreakable and Ellen wants him to sell it to the Yellow Cab Company. She promises him a chance to demonstrate to the company his Elastiglass if he signs the paper.

Edward was the comedy consultant for *The Yellow Cab Man* (1950), starring Red Skelton (center), Gloria DeHaven, and Herbert Anderson. Apparently any conflict that might have existed between Edward and Skelton during the filming of *A Southern Yankee* was nonexistent in this production.

Martin wants to get *his* hands on "Red's" invention and demands that Yellow Cab employee Willis Tomlin (Herbert Anderson), whom he is blackmailing, replace the unbreakable glass with a pane of real glass before the demonstration. Mr. Hendrix (Paul Harvey), president of Yellow Cab, attends the demonstration and is asked to sit in the car to see how safe the Elastiglass is. When "Red" hurls a baseball into the windshield, the glass shatters and the ball beans Mr. Hendrix in the head.

"Red" insists on getting Mr. Hendrix to give him a second chance. This effort is thwarted throughout the story, as Martin is even more determined to get the formula from "Red." But in the end "Red" gets his opportunity to demonstrate the Elastiglass. This time Mr. Hendrix pitches the ball with Red behind the windshield. The glass proves to be successful as Hendrix tosses the ball ... which ricochets back and beans him in the head. "Red" runs through a door into a freight elevator shaft, ending up in the hospital in leg casts and Ellen kissing him.

Although *The Yellow Cab* featured a talented supporting cast which included James Gleason and Walter Slezak, the movie was a step down from *A Southern Yankee*. The Skelton character is dumbed-down, using a childlike voice throughout most of the feature. Although Edward was a comedy consultant, it was apparent that his influence wasn't used to full potential.

By this time in his career as director, Edward's pickings were becoming very slim. At one point he was considered for the directing job on *Abbott and Costello in the Foreign Legion* (1950), but was rejected due to his lackluster track record. His final achievement as a credited

Edward's final achievement as a credited film director was for *Ma and Pa Kettle Back on the Farm* (1951). Ma and Pa Kettle, played by Marjorie Main and Percy Kilbride, shown with Ray Collins (left), turned out to be a successful franchise for Universal.

film director was for *Ma and Pa Kettle Back on the Farm*, released by Universal International Pictures in March 1951. The Ma and Pa Kettle series was a spin-off from the successful romantic comedy *The Egg and I* (1947), which starred Fred MacMurray and Claudette Colbert. In the ensuing years, two of the supporting characters from *The Egg and I*, Ma and Pa Kettle (Marjorie Main and Percy Kilbride), turned out to be a successful combination for Universal. Neither Main nor Kilbride received important recognition as actors until they played the roles of Ma Kettle and Pa Kettle in *The Egg and I*, with Main receiving an Academy Award nomination for Best Supporting Actress. The success of their chemistry found the two of them returning to their roles together in seven Ma and Pa Kettle vehicles, with Main appearing in two final episodes without Kilbride.

Ma and Pa Kettle Back on the Farm, the third in the series, opens with Ma, Pa, and their brood of fifteen children living at the contemporary house that Pa won in a contest in their previous adventure. Their son and daughter-in-law Tom and Kim (Richard Long and Meg Randall) are now parents. Kim's parents, Jonathan and Elizabeth Parker (Ray Collins and Barbara Brown), have come to visit. Elizabeth, a bossy snob who quickly irritates the Kettles, forces them to move back to their ramshackle farm.

Two speculators with Geiger counters arrive on the Kettle property and get high readings for radioactivity, especially around the area where Pa is digging a new well. Thinking that the property contains uranium ore, they obtain it illegally. Jonathan helps the Kettles get their farm back, with the hope that Ma and Pa will become rich mining the uranium. However, it's discovered that the Geiger counter was reading uranium dust on Pa's coveralls: He got the clothing from his nephew who was in the navy and involved in atomic bomb testing. In the end the Parkers and Kettles put aside their differences and become good in-laws and grandparents.

Edward's contribution to the popular Kettle franchise was well-received, giving him a needed boost in the declining years of his film career.

By the late 1940s television networks were broadcasting scheduled programming from many of the major cities between New York and the Mississippi River, with commercial programming stretching to the West Coast by 1951. Movie studios no longer perceived the new medium as just a novelty. TV was damaging the motion picture industry as patrons were sticking to the comfort of their living rooms to be entertained. Even radio, previously blamed for the slump in box office receipts, was beginning to fear the loss of their audience to TV.

Red Skelton, both a movie and radio star, was at first a bit apprehensive about performing on TV. He was worried about the weekly grind of writing and memorizing brand new scripts which would be performed live, without having an opportunity to give the new routines a dry run and then fine-tune them as he was able to do in vaudeville.

In 1951 Skelton signed a contract with NBC to do a weekly half-hour series premiering that fall. Skelton would be writer and producer, but not director, the position he also vied for while doing films at MGM. The show turned out to be a success, with Skelton performing in *The Red Skelton Hour* for both NBC and CBS over a span of twenty years.

Skelton was still committed to fulfilling his contract with MGM and performed in a string of films that were mostly panned by critics. *Excuse My Dust* was one of them. Edward and Buster Keaton were brought on staff once again as uncredited directors, with Keaton involved in developing the scenario. The June release also featured Macdonald Carey, Sally

Excuse My Dust (1951) retained Edward and Buster Keaton once again as uncredited directors. The romantic comedy featured Red Skelton (right), along with Macdonald Carey and Sally Forrest.

Forrest, William Demarest, Raymond Walburn, Jane Darwell, Herbert Anderson, and Paul Harvey.

The comedy takes place in 1895, an era of primitive automobiles. Joe Belden's (Skelton) latest invention is a Gasmobile, a vehicle that runs on gasoline, a cleaning fluid he purchases at a drug store. Harvey Bullit (Demarest), owner of the local stable, is against motorized transportation as it's a threat to his livery business. His daughter Liz (Sally Forrest), however, thinks highly of Joe.

Joe enters his vehicle in a 20-mile "Road Race of Horseless Buggies" with a $5,000 first prize that would help him start his automobile assembly line. Harvey becomes a threat to the race as he attempts to get the authorities to prevent the automobiles from using town roads as a racetrack.

The race begins, with the participating autos using different sources of propulsion: naphtha, wet cell batteries, spring wind-up, steam, ether, and gasoline. Cyrus (Macdonald Carey), whose goal is to win the prize money as well as Liz's love, accidentally knocks Joe out with a hammer as they are repairing their vehicles after a collision. Cyrus takes off, leaving Joe behind.

Liz finds Joe unconscious and takes over the wheel until he comes to. They catch up with the others, with Cyrus in the lead. Liz jumps out of the auto to make it lighter, helping

Joe pass Cyrus and cross the finish line. Joe wins the $5,000 and the chance to start his automobile business.

Excuse My Dust turned out to be a decent production. Although Edward and Keaton were both involved, their broad-style humor was toned down for Skelton. Curiously, MGM re-released *Excuse My Dust* in 1973 as a children's matinee feature, retitled *Mr. Blendon's Amazing Gasmobile*.

Similar to Skelton, other film comedians jumped mediums to perform in their own television shows—not always successfully. Buster Keaton, one of the first to do so, performed on *The Buster Keaton Show*, followed by Bud Abbott and Lou Costello on *The Abbott and Costello Show* and Jimmy Durante on *The Jimmy Durante Show*.

The most influential of all was Lucille Ball, who starred in five different versions of her own series from 1951 to 1986. Edward was involved in the creation of the most memorable of the series, *I Love Lucy* (1951–1957).

CHAPTER TEN

Journey Beyond the Silver Screen

Over the years Edward and Ebba formed a close bond with Lucille Ball, becoming her surrogate family. On November 20, 1940, Ball married Desi Arnaz, a Latin bandleader, in a civil ceremony. The Arnaz marriage became troubled, partially due to Arnaz being away for extended periods as he toured with his band. In 1949, in an effort to strengthen their wedding vows, Arnaz asked Ball to marry him again, this time in a Catholic Church. The June 19 ceremony was only witnessed by a few close friends, with Edward escorting the bride to the altar.

By the late 1940s Ball's career was finally seeing success. From 1948 through 1951 she performed the role of Liz Cooper in the popular radio situation comedy *My Favorite Husband*. Starring opposite Richard Denning, who played her husband George Cooper, Ball appeared in 124 episodes. To keep their on-air personalities dynamic, the show's producer Jess Oppenheimer encouraged Ball and Denning to "act out their jokes and reactions," which created a playful interaction between their characters and the show's live studio audience. Riding on the success of the radio show, CBS became interested in developing the comedy into a television series, using both of the original actors. Transitioning *My Favorite Husband* to a visual medium was sure to be an easy task.

Ball, however, insisted that Arnaz should replace Denning in the role of George Cooper. Oppenheimer and Don Sharpe, Ball's agent, liked the idea enough to attempt to convince CBS and their sponsors to give it a try. CBS adamantly felt that viewers wouldn't perceive the two as a convincing enough married couple, even though in real life they were married for almost a decade.

In an attempt to prove that they could develop a successful television husband-and-wife team, the Arnazes tested their chemistry on the road, touring as a vaudeville act. Edward and Buster Keaton were on hand to give them creative advice. In April 1950, before heading out on their summer tour, the couple formed Desilu Productions, a company that would experience rapid growth within a year's time.

Ball, who was pregnant, had a miscarriage in July. After a brief recuperation period she and Desi continued their vaudeville show. The tour supported their case that audiences would accept them as a married couple. In December CBS gave the green light to go ahead with a pilot film for the series. The deal included Arnaz in the main male role.

The show's sponsor, Philip Morris, insisted that it be broadcast "live" from New York

City. With Ball pregnant again, the Arnazes decided that they wanted to stay on the West Coast. This proved to be a problem, as it was essential that the sitcom be broadcast from New York due to the technology involved. Without the coast-to-coast coaxial cable developed, live shows were typically sent from the east to west on low-quality 35mm or 16mm kinescope prints. The majority of smokers who purchased Philip Morris products lived east of Chicago, which meant they would be viewing the blurry episodes that were kinescoped in Hollywood, and not a clear live broadcast—something that the tobacco company would not stand for.

The pilot episode was filmed for promotional purposes in March 1951, and never publicly aired. The situation with the Arnazes remaining in Hollywood, where the comedy would be filmed, was resolved by May. There was a stipulation in the contract which stated that if the quality of the first couple of telefilms produced were not up to CBS's standards, the Arnazes would need to move to Manhattan to do the shows live until the coaxial cable was available. CBS was also concerned that the cost of filming would probably total twice the amount as it would have if the show were produced live.

Ball gave birth to a healthy girl on July 17. The Arnazes asked Edward to be their daughter Lucie's godfather, and he proudly accepted. In 1953 Edward also became godfather to their son Desi Jr. Ball's pregnancy with Desi Jr. was incorporated into seven Season Two episodes. It was the first pregnancy to appear on television, with the term "pregnant" replaced with "expectant," for fear that it might upset the public. It became a major event.

I Love Lucy premiered on October 15, 1951. Although the names of the sitcom's main characters were changed from Liz and George Cooper to Lucy and Ricky Ricardo, the essence of the radio version remained. The show pioneered the simultaneous use of three cameras (eventually known as the multicam system), which gave the director the flexibility of shooting scenes at multiple angles in front of a live audience. The result of filming in 35mm was high quality. The series was a runaway success, with its 1951–52 season ranking #3 in the Nielsen ratings. Taking over the top spot the following year, it continued to hold the #1 ranking through the end of its run in 1957, dropping only once to second place for its 1955–56 season. The encouragement which Edward had given Ball all those years ago, on how to develop her double-takes, stares, reactions and expressions, became the characteristics of her endearingly successful character Lucy Ricardo.

In *Lucy & Desi: The Legendary Love Story of Television's Most Famous Couple*, by Warren G. Harris, Lucy gave credit to Edward and Keaton's constructive advice. "Buster and Eddie Sedgwick were the first people to really sit me down and teach me all about slapstick comedy and the importance of props. They were masters at it, both were headliners on the stage when they were only tiny kids, believe it or not. Attention to detail, that's what it's all about. If I had to work with grapes, a loaf of bread, a cup of coffee, whatever, I had to test them first to know what I was eating or drinking, how hot or cold it was, how it got there, how it would ride on the tray."

After thirty-eight episodes, director Marc Daniels decided to leave Desilu due to differences he had with Oppenheimer and Ball. On May 16, the trade journals reported that he would be leaving once the May 23 show, filmed for Season Two, was completed. A few days after Daniels' resignation was mentioned in *Daily Variety*, Desilu announced that William Asher would direct the remaining two episodes that were planned before the show took a summer hiatus.

The same issue of *Daily Variety* also announced that Edward had been signed to direct

Ten. Journey Beyond the Silver Screen

The *I Love Lucy* episode "Lucy Goes to the Hospital" aired on January 19, 1953. The episode coincided with the birth of Lucille Ball's second child, Desi Jr. At the time of his death, which was five months after this episode aired, Edward, as a senior officer at Desilu, was busy preparing other projects. Shown left to right, William Frawley, Desi Arnaz, Lucille Ball, and Vivian Vance.

the remainder of the *I Love Lucy* episodes for the second season. As always, the Arnazes relied on Edward's invaluable advice to help them with their careers; in exchange, they would offer him a position working on their television series. Edward did not get the director job, but he was hired by Arnaz as production coordinator for Desilu. He was assigned to supervise the making of the theatrical film version of *I Love Lucy*. With the success of the series, Desilu had planned to produce a "one-a-year picture" based on several *I Love Lucy* episodes. At a time when only nine percent of U.S. homes had television sets, with only ninety-eight stations telecasting to the approximately 7,000,000 sets, the *I Love Lucy* theatrical feature would have brought the series to an even larger audience.

In the spring of 1952 the Arnazes asked Edward to transform three Season One half-hour episodes—"The Benefit," "Breaking the Lease," and "The Ballet"—into an eighty-minute feature film that was to be tested in the United States and Latin America. Edward was responsible for directing a new opening sequence, continuity segments to tie the three episodes together, and a closing sequence written by *I Love Lucy*'s staff writers. He suggested filming it as though it were a live show, including the cast making their introductions at the beginning and taking bows at the end. Filmed over a period of several days, the new scenes cost an estimated $25,000.

Edward died of a heart attack early in the morning of May 7, 1953. He had just completed the editing on the *I Love Lucy* movie. As a senior officer, he was also preparing other projects for Desilu, including a sitcom for comedian Eddie Quillan, which became *The Eddie Quillan Show*, a 1953 summer replacement for *I Love Lucy*. Desilu had plans to use Edward to direct an independent feature film production titled *Blazing Beulah of Butte*, which would have co-starred the Arnazes.

Edward turned 60 in November, and had celebrated his fortieth year in the movie industry just three weeks earlier. He was born at the dawn of cinema, entered the world of show business as a child performing vaudeville on stage, worked through the great studio era of the 1930s and 1940s, and was introduced to television during its Golden Age.

The May 8 *New York Times* carried Edward's obituary, with a résumé as embellished as one of Edward's scripts: "He came to Hollywood in 1913 and was credited with discovering Tom Mix and Hoot Gibson and directing them in their early Western films." In reality, Mix and Gibson were already matinee stars when Edward was assigned to work with them.

Edward's military record was inflated as well, making the overweight enlistee sound like an honored officer. "His military career included service as a Texas Ranger, an Army officer in 1908 and participation in World War II. In the Mexican Revolution Mr. Sedgwick handled the Associated Press wire."

Ed Hutson remembered his uncle as being a very funny man and a creative storyteller. "Each time he visited us, he would tell Mimi and me a chapter from a serial story he would make up as he went along, called 'The Crimson Guava.' The story elements usually had no rhyme or reason to them."

Lucie Arnaz recalled that when she and her brother Desi Jr. were young they thought the Sedgwicks were family relatives. "I don't recall much about Edward, since I was just three years old when he passed away. I do remember Ebba, as she was always at the taping for the later Lucy shows. Look-wise, she reminded me of Vivian Vance's character Ethel." And in real life Edward had a somewhat similar appearance to William Frawley's character Fred. They might have been instrumental in casting the Vance and Frawley as the Ricardos' neighbors.

The close relationship that the Sedgwicks and Arnazes enjoyed was implied in two *I Love Lucy* episodes. The Sedgwicks are mentioned as being party guests in the Season One episode "Drafted." In the Season Two episode "Lucy's Last Birthday," Edward and Ebba appear as guests at a surprise party for Lucy.

In her biography *Love Lucy*, Ball mentions Edward's generosity, which gave her career a boost. "I have a theory about the assists we get in life. Only rarely can we repay those people who helped us, but we can pass that help along to others." Ebba Sedgwick once commented, "When Lucy gives a down-and-out friend a job on *I Love Lucy*, she acts as if the friend is honoring her by taking the job, yet she gets this idea across with a wisecrack."

After Edward passed away, Ebba gave up their modest-sized home at 12634 Hortense Street in North Hollywood to move into an apartment. Greatly indebted to Edward, Ball offered Ebba a guest cottage to live in when she had surgery, and looked after her until her death on June 24, 1984, at the age of 73.

I Love Lucy, the movie, premiered in Bakersfield, California. It was another success and Desilu was ready to release it countrywide. MGM, however, felt that it would compete with *The Long, Long Trailer* (1954), a film which the Arnazes were contracted to do for the studio, and which was planned to be released the following year on Valentine's Day. Desilu complied and shelved the film, along with plans to repackage several *I Love Lucy* pregnancy-related episodes into a feature that was to be titled *Lucy Has a Baby*. Plans to do three non-pregnancy features, films that RKO, Columbia, and United Artists were bidding on, were scrapped.

Many of the Sedgwicks' contemporaries had already passed away: actress Ruth Roland lost her battle with cancer in 1937, actor Tom Mix had died in an automobile accident in 1940, Buck Jones perished in a fire in 1942, and William Desmond passed away in 1949, with director Romaine Fielding dying in 1923, William James Craft in 1932, and J.P. McGowan in 1952. The old guard was quickly being forgotten as new generations were being raised on television as the new choice for entertainment.

Edward posthumously received one of the first stars on the Hollywood Walk of Fame when it was dedicated in 1960. E.M. Stuart, who had served as a volunteer president of the Hollywood Chamber of Commerce, first proposed the concept for the visitor attraction in 1953. Between May 1956 and the fall of 1957 the process of selecting honorees from the five categories of the entertainment industry took place, with the selections including past and present motion picture, television, recording and radio personalities. High-profile mem-

Desi Arnaz and Lucille Ball look at a program with Eileen's daughter and son, Mimi and Ed Hutson (courtesy E. Hutson).

bers of the Motion Picture Selection Committee included Cecil B. DeMille, Walt Disney, Samuel Goldwyn, Jesse Lasky, Hal Roach, and Mack Sennett.

On August 15, 1958, the first eight stars were unveiled as a public demonstration of what the Walk of Fame would look like. Located at the intersection of Hollywood Blvd. at Highland Avenue, the names were Olive Borden, Ronald Colman, Louise Fazenda, Preston Foster, Burt Lancaster, Edward Sedgwick, Ernest Torrance, and Joanne Woodward.

The actual construction of the walk didn't begin until February 8, 1960, with Stanley Kramer being the first star installed on March 28, 1960, near the intersection of Hollywood Blvd. and Gower Street, just a short walking distance from Sunset Blvd. where Edward had started his Hollywood career almost 50 years earlier. Today Edward's star is located at 6801 Hollywood Blvd.

The moviemaking bug never quite took a hold of Edward's nephew and niece, Ed and Mimi Hutson, who both found the time-consuming process of filming stories boring. In spite of his feelings, as a child Ed was occasionally given minor roles in Fox features, appearing in *The Beautiful Blonde from Bashful Bend* (1949) with Betty Grable, and *Come to the Stable* (1949) with Loretta Young. Director Henry King, a good friend of Clarence, found a minor speaking role for Ed in *The Gunfighter* (1950) with Gregory Peck. Ed recalled that he even dreaded speaking the two sentences he was assigned. "I think it was, 'There he goes! Charlie's got him!' That was it! And I never liked doing it at all! I really didn't." Mimi, too, occasionally appeared in films. After graduating from Immaculate Heart, through a scholarship provided by ambassador Clare Boothe Luce, Mimi was given an uncredited role as a college girl in *A Man Called Peter* (1955) starring Richard Todd.

The two did enjoy accompanying their father on his job to scout out film locations across the United States. Clarence, who previously did public relations work for Fox, was promoted to head of the studio's Location Department. His experience as a flight instructor at March Field during World War I enabled him to fly the one-engine plane he took on his assignments by himself. Ed remembers on one occasion, when he was about eleven, Clarence and King took a trip to the East Coast. "They were looking for locations, but I have no idea what movie it was for. We flew to Florida, stopping every night, because you couldn't fly this little plane at night. This was 1948." The film Ed referred to was *Twelve O'Clock High* (1949), a war drama starring Gregory Peck.

Fox also owned a Grumman Mallard, a luxurious twin-engine plane stored at Santa Monica Airport, which Ed and Mimi enjoyed traveling in. "Quite often we would get out of grammar school and fly down to San Diego or someplace just for an hour or so, because he had some business down there, and come back. There was always some reason to go there, and we all went along with him."

Mimi and Ed, who were adopted by the Hutsons as infants, were born six months apart. Eileen and Clarence decided to separate them a grade level in school and held Ed back in first grade. At the time Clarence was an investment counselor for the Syndicate Mortgage Company, a real estate business that invested for actors who were interested in buying apartment and office buildings. Ed recalls that the family often took advantage of the housing opportunities made available through Clarence's company, and moved around the Los Angeles area quite often:

We first lived at 917 Roxbury Drive [in Beverly Hills]. Then my father sold that—I'm not sure exactly, maybe in '39—and we moved to Alpine Drive. But before that, I guess the house wasn't ready, so we lived in a house that belonged to Joe. E. Brown, on Walden Drive. They moved to Brentwood, and their house was empty, so we stayed there a few months, which I don't remember at all. And then we moved to 705 Alpine Drive [on and off].

Yeah, we lived on Warner for a while [in the Westwood area]. Then they brought a house on Rochester, which is just the next block over from there, and a block over. And then he built a duplex on Selby—we lived in the whole thing, both apartments. That was strange, having two kitchens. We moved back to Beverly Hills in 1950, and he died in August. I'd just graduated from grammar school, and [Clarence] died in August of 1950. So we just moved back to Beverly Hills. After about four years of my mother's spending there was no money left; then she sold that house and bought the one I have now, this house. So I lived here the longest in my life.

Clarence was very selective about the schools that his children attended, with Mimi attending Marymount High School and Ed attending Loyola High School, both preparatory schools. "Oh, my father didn't like the Catholic school in Beverly Hills," Ed remembered. "He liked the priests and nuns in Westwood, so we would rent the house in Beverly Hills and either buy or rent a house in Westwood until we would be in the right parish. We did that three times!"

The Hutsons' house in the Westwood section of Los Angeles, one of the smaller homes on their block, became a magnet for Mimi and Ed's friends. As Clarence was becoming frail due to a heart condition, Eileen encouraged their children to stay close to home at all times in case he fell ill. Situated directly across from St. Paul the Apostle Church, the Hutson home became a social gathering place for the teenagers, especially after the conclusion of the weekly meeting of the church's youth group, the Chi-Rho Club. Clarence (nicknamed "Poppy" by his children's friends) and Eileen thrived on welcoming them into their living room and always made sure that there was something warm cooking on the stove for the teens to eat when visiting. In later years, the Hutsons, who were known for their generosity, would often take in struggling actors, boarding them in a converted garage behind their house.

Upon entering Marymount High School, Mimi became best friends with Judy Lewis, the daughter of Loretta Young and Clark Gable. In her book *Uncommon Knowledge*, Lewis discusses being raised by her mother and stepfather, Tom Lewis, without knowing who her birthfather was. Her family moved to the heart of Beverly Hills in her freshman year of high school, and she first met Mimi. "[Mimi] arrived, late for class, wearing a tight black sweater, an even tighter black skirt, and two-inch black-suede high heels. (Her uniforms were late in arriving, she later explained.) Her thick black hair hung past her shoulders, and her lipstick was dark crimson. She had a voluptuous figure and an air of sophistication and sensuality far beyond her years."

As Lewis's parents were preoccupied with their careers, she found Mimi's family life to be "highly desirable" in comparison to hers. She soon found that the Hutson home was full of love and that they were willing to treat her as one of the family. Like many of her friends whose parents worked in the industry, she had assumed that she was also adopted, and the fact that Mimi and Ed were adopted too made her friendship with Mimi even more important. Looking back, Ed remembered that about 90 percent of their friends were adopted. "They were all mainly children of movie stars, and they were adopted. It was as if someone wasn't adopted, there was something wrong with them!"

Ed Hutson, Eileen's son, in the back addition at his home, furnished with a film projecting area and surrounded by personalized photographs from Hollywood legends. Eileen often used this converted garage to board struggling actors. Ed started working at Fox after he graduated high school. In 2011, after 55 years working for Fox, he retired from the studio.

Mimi and Lewis became part of a group of friends that included other teenagers whose parents worked in the movie industry: Jack Haley, Jr. (actor Jack Haley's son); Bob Doran (cinematographer Robert Doran's son); Gretchen Foster (Judy Lewis's cousin and daughter of actress Sally Blane and actor-director Norman Foster); Gary Crosby (actor Bing Crosby's son); Leslie Gargan (actor William Gargan's son); John "Bunky" Hearst, Jr. (son of Hearst Corporation executive John Randolph Hearst); and Bill Bashe.

The weekly church dances held in the basement of St. Paul the Apostle Church also attracted students from the local Catholic all-male schools like Loyola and Notre Dame, with many of the visiting boys taking an interest in Mimi and the other girls in her group. As the Hutsons were still living comfortably on Clarence's salary, they were able to celebrate Mimi's fifteenth birthday in style with a formal dance at the Beverly Hills Hotel. Mimi helped her mom compile the guest list. John Considine, a boy she was madly in love with, was her date for the celebration.

With Clarence's illness the Hutsons found it necessary to give up most of their upscale lifestyle. As medical insurance wasn't readily available as it is today, the Hutsons found Clarence's bills accumulating and the family realized that they would need to make sacrifices to pay them off. Eileen, who was comfortable living the life of a socialite and was used to carefree spending, was hit with the reality that she would need to sell their home in Beverly Hills.

Ed realized it was necessary to find a job after he graduated high school in 1956. Although he wanted to work at a studio he wasn't able to find an available position and took a job as a busboy, and then host, at the Pig and Whistle, a restaurant chain owned by friends of the family. Within a year Eileen was able to use her connections to find him a job in Fox's mailroom. Although Ed's goal was to work in the studio's art department, as he was interested in architecture, it would be another year before a position became available in the Scene Dock Department, which then comprised a manager and two assistants. Ed's responsibilities included cataloguing sets: As sets were built, all of their pieces were given numbers, including walls, fireplaces, windows and doors. He was responsible for making file cards for each item, which would then be referenced when a set director or art director was interested in knowing what items were available for reuse when designing new sets. Quite often a blueprint or drawing was attached to the card. "Well, if they wanted a Georgian [room], you could find a fireplace and some windows and maybe some doors—possibly some panel walls or something," Ed recalled.

When Ed started work in the Scene Dock Department, the art director in charge of the Art Department was Lyle Wheeler. As art director, Wheeler would work closely with the art director assigned for each movie—this is the reason why movie credits always listed two art directors.

> It was the same at the Property Department: It was always Walter Scott and somebody else. They were heads of departments, so they got credit too. And there was also a chief draftsman who was also an art director. The head of the department had a secretary. There was also an Art Department secretary. And there were maybe ten or twelve full-time art directors. Maybe on a normal time, twenty-seven set designers.
>
> And then later on, Jack Martin Smith was the head of the Art Department, and he was maybe five or six years, or seven years. And then the whole thing just sort of stopped being a big department.
>
> By that time, I was head of the Scene Dock Department. There was still another guy doing the set recording. And he retired, so they combined the two jobs, and I ended being the manager, too, because there was nobody else to manage.

Most of Ed's fondest memories came from working with John DeCuir, production designer for *The King and I* (1956), *Cleopatra* (1963), and *Hello Dolly* (1969), "I never saw him do it, but people would tell me, flying somewhere, he'd have little pieces of paper, and he'd be sketching what the set would look like. So he'd take a piece of paper from the pad and draw something. He'd draw another thing [and the set] ended up perfectly. He was an illustrator originally. In the old days, most of the art directors had been illustrators. Besides architects, they were artists too. He was about the most talented one that I can remember. There were all kinds of art directors over the years. Interesting people."

When Ed had started working at Fox, film production was already slowing down. "For a while there, it was very shaky. After *Cleopatra*, the whole place closed down, and I worked at Universal for six months in the Accounting Department. Then I came back, whatever year that was I don't know. And then the next few years, it was still sort of bad. When the TV season ended, everything collapsed, too. They weren't making enough movies on the lot to keep going."

The Sedgwick-Hutson family continued to live together as an extended family in their Westwood home. Fenie died October 22, 1964, at 92. As the matriarch of the family she experienced the evolution of the entertainment industry—from two-a-day performances on stages of gaslit opera houses to the introduction of broadcast television. Fenie was one of the founding members of the Motion Pictures Mother's Club, whose original members also included the mothers of notable actors Cesar Romero, Gary Cooper, Bing Crosby, Dorothy Lamour, John Howard, Lou Costello, Helen Mack, Tom Brown, and Marguerite Churchill.

At age 79, Josie died on April 30, 1973, of a stroke. Josie, who once ruled as the Queen of the Rodeo, proved onscreen that a female could ride just as tough as her male counterpart.

Eileen Sedgwick succumbed to pneumonia at Daniel Freeman Marina Hospital on March 15, 1991, at the age of 92. Making her mark on the silver screen as the Queen of the Serials, Eileen helped pave the way for the modern-day action film heroine. Her daughter Mimi, who had married and started a family, had died seven years earlier in 1984 at 48 years. In 2011, after 55 years working for Fox, her son Edward Hutson retired from the studio. He passed away on April 24, 2015.

The Sedgwicks' legacy continues to influence today's popular culture. Recently, Skinny Minnie, a fashion company, produced a line of designer women's shirts, one of which incorporated a vintage-looking illustration of a blond-haired cowgirl riding a horse. The design of the print announced Eileen Sedgwick as a fictitious Wild West show's "Girl in the Saddle."

In 1997 David White wrote a novel titled *Fantomas in America* which was influenced by Fox's long-lost serial *Fantomas in America* (1920). Without the serial available to reference (it was originally written by Edward Sedgwick and George Eshenfelder), White based his story of the famous French fictional character known as Fantomas, created by authors Marcel Allain and Pierre Souvestre in 1911, on the summaries of the episodes that he found in the chapterplay's exhibition book.

Creating a serial based on Fantomas would have been a welcome challenge for Edward, a passionate reader of dime novel adventure stories as a child. White explains that Fantomas' popularity would have been enough to convince Fox to invest in the serial:

> The character appeared in cheap, pulp novels once a month, through 32 volumes, and became a sensation. Fantomas himself is a master of disguise and master criminal that terrorizes Paris in a series of multiple identities. He commits horrifying acts of violence, often without any motive. He is constantly pursued by Detective Juve and Jerome Fandor, a young reporter. Every volume ends with Fantomas escaping and often with Juve and Fandor in some kind of death trap. In the final volume, he and Juve both perished aboard the *Titanic* (although it was renamed the *Gigantic*). The books were not only popular successes, but Fantomas became an icon of the new surrealist movement. Many of the early surrealists wrote essays on how the novels were examples of surrealism. Magritte even worked Fantomas images into several of his paintings and Kurt Weill and Robert Desnos wrote an operetta about the character that aired on French radio.
>
> Silent filmmaker Louis Feuillade made five film adaptations of the Fantomas novels. They were divided into chapters and exported to other countries where they became one of the first movie serials. They played in U.S. movie theatres around 1916–17 or so. Brentano's began publishing the books in English translation, but only got as far as the first seven volumes before giving up. Some of these translations were serialized in newspapers of the day. Today, these original translations are very difficult to locate although several have been reprinted in the last few years.
>
> The character was popular enough that Fox decided to do their own version in 1920. This new Fantomas serial was directed by Sedgwick, and was 20 chapters long. It featured Edward Roseman

as Fantomas, but the rest of the characters were completely new. The story was not based on any of the original stories by Allain and Souvestre.

Fantomas was, and still is, very popular. For some reason, however, his popularity did not last in the U.S. My own theory is that America's post–World War I isolationism kind of put a damper on foreign popular literature being imported to our shores. Starting in the '20s and '30s, there were a lot of homegrown pulp characters like the Shadow and the Avenger and I think they might have killed the market for characters like Fantomas.

In White's novel, Fantomas, who was previously thought to be dead, returns to the United States in 1917 and spreads his reign of terror through the streets of New York City. Detective Frederick Dickson traces him to the home of Samuel Cobblepot, a member of the elite Long Island Chapter of the Saint James Society. Other members have been invited to Cobblepot's home, including a slightly boisterous scriptwriter named Edward Sedgwick and a movie actor named Edward Roseman, both of whom were working at Fox Film Corporation at the time. "Putting Sedgwick and Roseman into the novel as characters became an important part of the story for me," White explains. "I had expounded on the original story so much that I felt like I needed to justify why they were so different. So I introduced Sedgwick as a way to explain that his film was based on the 'true' events that I had written about."

Over the years since it was first published, the success of White's novel has spurred on a line of adaptations of original Fantomas mysteries.

In 2003 the Columbia Broadcasting System produced *Lucy*, a made-for-television biography covering the life of Lucille Ball. The biopic took advantage of creative license and cast a bearded Ray Woolf in the role of Edward Sedgwick. Woolf, who was also a lot thinner than Edward, was given a sportier wardrobe than Edward would have ever worn, and was missing his trademark hat and cane.

Although Edward was portrayed as the compassionate mentor and friend that he was to Ball, his timeline was inaccurate. In the movie's reenactment of the filming for the final episode of *The Lucy-Desi Comedy Hour* Edward is shown sitting in the studio audience with Red Skelton. The final episode was shot in February 1960 for an April airing; Edward died in 1953.

Together, Edward, Josie and Eileen appeared in or worked on 286 known shorts and features. Their parents, Ned and Fenie, also appeared in movies during the silent era in uncredited roles. With very few exceptions, these films are no longer extant, and the few surviving silent-era titles are in the hands of private collectors and universities waiting to be restored. Early movies were intended to be circulated and then recycled for the nitrate used in the film's base; they were not meant to be stored for prosperity. The nitrate film itself was not conducive to long-term storage, as its cellulous nitrate base was highly flammable. But fortunately, every so often a reel of a feature or fragments of a serial's chapter is discovered, as was the case of *The Lure of the Circus* (1918).

Films like *Spring Fever, West Point, The Trail of '98*, and *Doughboys* have been restored and often shown on Turner Classic Movies, a network that reaches millions of viewers through cable and satellite broadcasts. There's hope that maybe someday, other films in the archives of universities or private collectors, such as Eileen's two-reeler *Lightnin' Wins*, which is in the possession of UCLA, will be restored for public viewing.

The Sedgwicks, along with countless other pioneers, were involved in building the foundation for today's motion picture industry. In the process Edward, Josie, and Eileen brought their dreams to life for generations of moviegoers in the films they created.

Sedgwick Family Filmography

1914

Beautiful Love: Eileen (Actor), Edward (Director, Writer)
The Heroes: Eileen (Actor), Josie (Actor), Edward (Actor, Director, Writer)
All for Love: Eileen (Actor), Edward (Actor)
The Belle of Breweryville: Eileen (Actor), Edward (Actor)
The German Band: Eileen (Actor), Edward (Actor)
On Circus Day: Eileen (Actor), Edward (Actor)
The Crooks: Eileen (Actor), Edward (Actor)
The Kid's Nap: Eileen (Actor)
The New Butler: Eileen (Actor)
Love and Flames: Eileen (Actor), Edward (Actor)

1915

Slim Fat or Medium: Eileen (Actor), Edward (Actor)
Lone Larry: Eileen (Actor)
The Eagle's Nest: Eileen (Actor), Josie (Actor), Edward (Actor)
The Mysterious Contragrav: Eileen (Actor)
Green Backs and Red Skins: Eileen (Actor), Edward (Actor)

1916

The Fascinating Model: Edward (Actor)
Room Rent and Romance: Eileen (Actor), Edward (Actor)
It's All Wrong: Edward (Actor)
He Became a Regular Fellow: Edward (Actor)
A Lucky Leap: Edward (Actor)
Some Medicine Man: Edward (Actor)
His Blowout: Edward (Actor)
Married a Year: Edward (Actor)
National Nuts: Edward (Actor)
When Slim Was Home Cured: Eileen (Actor), Edward (Actor)
When Slim Picked a Peach: Eileen (Actor)
Town That Tried to Come Back: Eileen (Actor), Edward (Actor)
Ain't He Grand?: Eileen (Actor), Edward (Actor)
Some Heroes: Eileen (Actor), Edward (Actor)
I'll Get Her Yet: Eileen (Actor)
His Golden Hour: Eileen (Actor), Edward (Actor)
Hired, Tired and Fired: Eileen (Actor), Edward (Actor)
Giant Powder: Eileen (Actor)
It's Great to Be Married: Eileen (Actor)
It Sounded Like a Kiss: Eileen (Actor)
The Emerald Pin: Eileen (Actor)
The Heritage of Hate: Eileen (Actor)
The Quitter: Eileen (Actor)
The Isle of Life: Eileen (Actor)
Kill the Umpire: Eileen (Actor)
Number 10, Westbound: Eileen (Actor)
The Gasoline Habit: Eileen (Actor)
Lily White and Centerville: Eileen (Actor)
Her Dream Man: Josie (Actor)
Missy: Josie (Actor)

1917

The Yankee Way: Edward (Actor, Writer)
The Varmint: Edward (Actor)
The Haunted Pajamas: Edward (Actor)
Who Said Chicken?: Edward (Actor)
Fat and Foolish: Edward (Actor)
The Temple of Terror: Eileen (Actor)
The Lion's Lair: Eileen (Actor)
The Last of the Night Riders: Eileen (Actor)
The Lure of the Circus: Eileen (Actor)
Jungle Treachery: Eileen (Actor)
The Paperhanger's Revenge: Eileen (Actor)
Money and Mystery: Eileen (Actor)
Man and Beast: Eileen (Actor)
Not Too Thin to Fight: Eileen (Actor)
Making Monkey Business: Eileen (Actor)
Dropped from the Clouds: Eileen (Actor)
Swearing Off: Eileen (Actor)
Flat Harmony: Eileen (Actor)
The Thousand-Dollar Drop: Eileen (Actor)
His Family Tree: Eileen (Actor)
The Woman in the Case: Eileen (Actor)
A Bare Living: Eileen (Actor)
It's Cheaper to Be Single: Eileen (Actor)
The Losing Winner: Eileen (Actor)
The High Cost of Starving: Eileen (Actor)
Good Morning Nurse: Eileen (Actor)
It's Cheaper to Be Married: Eileen (Actor)
The Honeymoon Surprise: Eileen (Actor)
The Maternal Spark: Josie (Actor)
Indiscreet Corinne: Josie (Actor)
Fighting Back: Josie (Actor)
One Shot Ross: Josie (Actor)
Ashes of Hope: Josie (Actor)
The Devil Dodger: Josie (Actor)
The Pullman Mystery: Josie (Actor)
The Boss of the Lazy Y: Josie (Actor)

1918

There and Back: Edward (Actor)
Why I Would Not Marry: Edward (Actor)
Don't Flirt: Edward (Actor)
Bruin Trouble: Edward (Actor)
Rough and Ready: Edward (Writer)
Cheating the Public: Edward (Writer)
The Fickle Blacksmith: Eileen (Actor)
Lure of the Circus: Eileen (Actor), Josie (Actor)
All for Gold: Eileen (Actor)
The Slow Express: Eileen (Actor)
The Human Tiger: Eileen (Actor)
Roped and Tied: Eileen (Actor)
Trail of No Return: Eileen (Actor)
Repeating the Honeymoon: Eileen (Actor)
Oh! Man!: Eileen (Actor)
Naked Fists: Eileen (Actor)
The Butler's Blunder: Eileen (Actor)
Quick Trigger: Eileen (Actor)
Passing the Bomb: Eileen (Actor)
The Shifty Shoplifter: Eileen (Actor)
A Kitchen Hero: Eileen (Actor)
Watch Your Watch: Eileen (Actor)
Hell's Crater: Eileen (Actor)
Flapjacks: Josie (Actor)
The Poor Fish: Josie (Actor)
Wild Life: Josie (Actor)
Beyond the Shadows: Josie (Actor)
Hell's End: Josie (Actor)
Wolves of the Border: Josie (Actor)
Paying His Debt: Josie (Actor)
Keith of the Border: Josie (Actor)
The Man Above the Law: Josie (Actor)

1919

The Winning Stroke: Edward (Writer)
Checkers: Edward (Actor)
The Jungle Trail: Edward (Assistant Director)
The Great Radium Mystery: Eileen (Actor)
A Pistol Point Proposal: Eileen (Actor)
Cyclone Smith Plays Trumps: Eileen (Actor)
Cyclone Smith's Comeback: Eileen (Actor)
The Wild Rider: Eileen (Actor)
A Phantom Fugitive: Eileen (Actor)
A Prisoner for Life: Eileen (Actor)
Jubilo: Josie (Actor)
The She Wolf: Josie (Actor)
Kingdom Come: Josie (Actor)

1920

Fantomas: Edward (Director, Writer)
The Face at Your Window: Edward (Writer)
Bride 13: Edward (Writer)
Sink or Swim: Edward (Actor, Writer)
Love's Battle: Eileen (Actor)
The White Rider: Eileen (Actor)

Putting It Over: Eileen (Actor)
The Lone Hand: Josie (Actor)
Daredevil Jack: Josie (Actor)
The Square Shooter: Josie (Actor)

1921

The Rough Diamond: Edward (Director, Writer)
Bar Nothing: Edward (Director, Writer)
Live Wires: Edward (Director, Writer)
A Battle of Wits: Eileen (Actor)
Dream Girl: Eileen (Actor)
Arrest Norma MacGregor: Eileen (Actor)
A Woman's Wit: Eileen (Actor)
Terror Trail: Eileen (Actor)
The Shadow of Suspicion: Eileen (Actor)
The Girl in the Saddle: Eileen (Actor)
The Heart of Arizona: Eileen (Actor)
The Diamond Queen: Eileen (Actor)
Duke of Chimney Butte: Josie (Actor)
Western Hearts: Josie (Actor)
Double Adventure: Josie (Actor)

1922

The Flaming Hour: Edward (Director)
Do and Dare: Edward (Director, Writer)
Boomerang Justice: Edward (Director)
The Bearcat: Edward (Director)
Chasing the Moon: Edward (Director, Writer)
Wolf Pack: Eileen (Actor)
False Brands: Eileen (Actor)
Judgement: Eileen (Actor)
The Open Wire: Eileen (Actor)
The Night Attack: Eileen (Actor)
Crimson Clue: Josie (Actor)

1923

The Thrill Chaser: Edward (Actor, Director, Writer)
The Ramblin' Kid: Edward (Director)
Blinky: Edward (Director, Writer)
Out of Luck: Edward (Director, Writer)
Shootin' for Love: Edward (Director, Writer)
Dead Game: Edward (Director)
Single Handed: Edward (Director)
The Gentleman from America: Edward (Director)

Romance Land: Edward (Director)
The First Degree: Edward (Director)
Beasts of Paradise: Eileen (Actor)
When Law Comes to Hades: Eileen (Actor)
Scarred Hands: Eileen (Actor)
In the Days of Daniel Boone: Eileen (Actor)
Making Good: Eileen (Actor)
Michael O'Halloran: Josie (Actor)
The Sunshine Trail: Josie (Actor)
Daddy: Josie (Actor)

1924

The Ridin' Kid from Powder River: Edward (Director)
Hit and Run: Edward (Director, Writer)
Sawdust Trail: Josie (Actor), Edward (Director)
Broadway or Bust: Edward (Director, Writer)
40-Horse Hawkins: Edward (Actor, Director, Writer)
Ride for Your Life: Edward (Director)
Hook and Ladder: Edward (Director)
The Riddle Rider: Eileen (Actor)
The Lone Round-Up: Eileen (Actor)
The White Moth: Josie (Actor)

1925

Two-Fisted Jones: Edward (Director)
Lorraine of the Lions: Edward (Director)
Let 'er Buck: Josie (Actor), Edward (Director, Writer)
The Saddle Hawk: Josie (Actor), Edward (Director, Writer)
The Hurricane Kid: Edward (Director)
The Spook Ranch: Edward (Writer)
Dynamite's Daughter: Josie (Actor), Edward (Writer)
Queen of the Round-Up: Josie (Actor)
The Girl of the West: Eileen (Actor)
Sagebrush Lady: Eileen (Actor)
Dangerous Odds: Eileen (Actor)
The Fighting Ranger: Eileen (Actor)
Daring Days: Josie (Actor)
The Outlaw's Daughter: Josie (Actor)
The Best Man: Josie (Actor)
The Fighting Schoolmarm: Josie (Actor)
A Battle of Wits: Josie (Actor)

Ropin' Venus: Josie (Actor)
The Phantom of the Opera (re-release): Edward (Director)

1926

Tin Hats: Eileen (Actor), Edward (Director, Writer)
The Runaway Express: Edward (Director)
The Flaming Frontier: Edward (Director, Writer)
Under Western Skies: Edward (Director, Writer)
There You Are: Edward (Director)
Lure of the West: Eileen (Actor)
Lightnin' Rage: Eileen (Actor)
Lightnin' Strikes: Eileen (Actor)
Lightnin' Wins: Eileen (Actor)
Lightnin' Flashes: Eileen (Actor)
Thundering Speed: Eileen (Actor)
Strings of Steel: Eileen (Actor)
Beyond All Odds: Eileen (Actor)
The Winking Idol: Eileen (Actor)
Temple of Terror: Eileen (Actor)
The Web: Eileen (Actor)
Mountain Molly'O: Josie (Actor)
Outlaw Love: Josie (Actor)
Montana of the Range: Josie (Actor)
Jim Hood's Ghost: Josie (Actor)
The Little Warrior: Josie (Actor)
Queen of the Hills: Josie (Actor)

1927

Spring Fever: Edward (Director)
The Bugle Call: Edward (Director)
Slide, Kelly, Slide: Eileen (Actor—uncredited), Edward (Director)
When Danger Calls: Eileen (Actor)
The Spider's Net (reissue of *Lightnin'* material): Eileen (Actor)
The Price of Youth: Eileen (Actor)
Red Pants: Eileen (Actor), Edward (Director)

1928

The Cameraman: Edward (Director)
Circus Rookies: Edward (Director, Writer)
West Point: Edward (Director)
Trail of '98: Josie (Actor)
Yellow Contraband: Eileen (Actor)

Beautiful But Dumb: Eileen (Actor)
Hot Heels: Eileen (Actor)
White Flame: Eileen (Actor)
A Girl in Every Port: Eileen (Actor)
The Vanishing West: Eileen (Actor)

1929

Navy Blues: Edward (Director—uncredited)
Spite Marriage: Edward (Director, Producer—uncredited)

1930

Parlor, Bedroom and Bath: Edward (Director)
Remote Control: Edward (Director, Producer)
Doughboys: Edward (Director, Composer)
Free and Easy: Edward (Director, Producer)
De frente, marchen: Edward (Director)
Estrellados: Edward (Director)
The Jade Box: Eileen (Actor)

1931

Maker of Men: Edward (Director, Writer)
A Dangerous Affair: Edward (Director)

1932

Sky Devils: Edward (Director—uncredited)
Speak Easily: Edward (Director)
The Passionate Plumber: Edward (Director)
Le plombier amoureux: Edward (Director)
Son of Oklahoma: Josie (Actor)

1933

Saturday's Millions: Edward (Director)
Horseplay: Edward (Director)
What! No Beer?: Edward (Director)

1934

Father Brown, Detective: Edward (Director, Producer)
Death on the Diamond: Edward (Director)
Here Comes the Groom: Edward (Director)
I'll Tell the World: Edward (Director)
The Poor Rich: Edward (Director)

1935

The Virginia Judge: Edward (Director)
Murder in the Fleet: Edward (Director, Writer)

1936

Mister Cinderella: Edward (Director, Producer, Writer—uncredited)

1937

Fit for a King: Edward (Director)
Riding on Air: Edward (Director)
Pick a Star: Edward (Director)

1938

The Gladiator: Edward (Director)

1939

Beware Spooks!: Edward (Director)
You Can't Cheat an Honest Man: Edward (Director—uncredited)
Burn 'Em Up O'Connor: Edward (Director, Writer—uncredited)

1940

So You Won't Talk: Edward (Director)

1943

Air Raid Wardens: Edward (Director)

1946

Easy to Wed: Edward (Director—uncredited)

1948

A Southern Yankee: Edward (Director—uncredited)

1950

The Yellow Cab Man: Edward (Comedy Consultant)

1951

Excuse My Dust: Edward (Director—uncredited)
Ma and Pa Kettle Back on the Farm: Edward (Director)

1953

I Love Lucy: Edward (Director)

Bibliography

Albee, Edward F. "Twenty Years of Vaudeville." *Variety* 72, no. 3 (September 6, 1923).

Balshofer, Fred J., and Arthur C. Miller. *One Reel a Week.* Berkley: University of California Press, 1967.

Blesh, Rudie. *Keaton.* New York: Macmillan, 1966.

Blum, Daniel. *A Pictorial History of the Silent Screen.* New York: Grosset & Dunlap, 1953.

Brady, Kathleen. *Lucille: The Life of Lucille Ball.* New York: Hyperion, 1994.

Braff, Richard. *The Universal Silents: A Filmography of the Universal Motion Picture Manufacturing Company, 1912–1929.* Jefferson, NC: McFarland, 1999.

Brown, Joe E., and Ralph Hancock. *Laughter Is a Wonderful Thing.* New York: A. S. Barnes, 1956.

Brownlow, Kevin. *The Parade's Gone By... .* New York: Alfred A. Knopf, 1968.

Carroll, David. *The Matinee Idols.* New York: Galahad, 1972.

Dempsey, Jack, and Barbara Piattelli Dempsey. *Dempsey.* New York: Harper & Row, 1977.

Dippie, Brian E. *Custer's Last Stand.* Lincoln: University of Nebraska Press, 1994.

Eames, John Douglas. *The MGM Story: The Complete History of Over Fifty Roaring Years.* New York: Crown, 1976.

Edmonds, I. G. *Big U: Universal in the Silent Days.* Cranbury, NJ: A.S. Barnes, 1977.

Eyman, Scott. *Lion of Hollywood: The Life and Legend of Louis B. Mayer.* New York: Simon & Schuster, 2005.

Fernett, Gene. *American Film Studios: An Historical Encyclopedia.* Jefferson, NC: McFarland, 1988.

Fowler, Gene. *Schnozzola.* New York: Viking Press, 1951.

Hay, Peter. *MGM: When the Lion Roars.* Atlanta: Turner, 1991.

Higham, Charles, and Joel Greenberg. *The Celluloid Muse: Hollywood Directors Speak.* Chicago: Henry Regnery, 1969.

Hiller, Jim, and Peter Wollen, eds. *Howard Hawks: American Artist.* London: British Film Institute, 1996. (Contains Jean-George Auriol's review, "A Girl in Every Port," *La Revue du Cinéma*, December 1928. Translated by John Moore.)

Keaton, Buster, and Charles Samuels. *My Wonderful World of Slapstick.* Garden City, NY: Doubleday, 1960.

Keaton, Eleanor, and Jeffrey Vance. *Buster Keaton Remembered.* New York: Harry N. Abrams, 2001.

Keith, B.F. "The Vogue of the Vaudeville." *National Magazine* 9 (November 1898): 146–53.

Kiehen, David. *Broncho Billy and the Essanay Film Company.* Berkeley, CA: Farwell, 2003.

Koszarski, Richard. *An Evening's Entertainment: The Age of the Silent Feature Picture 1915–1928.* Berkeley: University of California Press, 1994.

Laegreid, Renée M. *Riding Pretty: Rodeo Royalty in the American West.* Lincoln: University of Nebraska Press, 2006.

Lahue, Kalton C. *Bound and Gagged: The Story of the Silent Serials.* New York: Castle, 1968.

_____. *Continued Next Week: A History of the Moving Picture Serial.* Norman: University of Oklahoma Press, 1964.

Langman, Larry. *A Guide to Silent Westerns.* Westport, CT: Greenwood Press, 1992.

Lehmer, Kathy. "An Oral Interview with Ed Hutson." Los Angeles (Westwood), California, June 7 and 14, 1997, 20th Century–Fox, Inc., Oral History Project, 1997.

Lewis, Judy. *Uncommon Knowledge.* New York: Pocket, 1994.

MacQueen, Scott. "The 1926 *Phantom of the Opera*." *American Cinematographer*, September 1989, part I, 34–40; October 1989, part II, 34–40.

Mann, William J. *Wisecracker: The Life and Times of William Haines, Hollywood's First Openly Gay Star.* New York: Penguin, 1998.

Max, Arthur. *Red Skelton: An Unauthorized Biography.* New York: E. P. Dutton, 1979.

McCarthy, Todd. *Howard Hawks*. New York: Grove Press, 1977.

McPherson, Edward. *Buster Keaton: Tempest in a Flat Hat*. New York: Newmarket Press, 2005.

Meade, Marion Harper. *Buster Keaton: Cut to the Chase*. New York: HarperCollins, 1995.

Mix, Paul E. *The Life and Legend of Tom Mix*. Cranbury, NJ: A.S. Barnes, 1972.

Mordden, Ethan. *The Hollywood Studios: House Style in the Golden Age of the Movies*. New York: Alfred A. Knopf, 1988.

Page, Brett. *Writing for Vaudeville*. New York: The Writer's Library, 1915.

Paris, Barry. *Louise Brooks*. New York: Alfred A. Knopf, 1989.

Ramsaye, Terry. *A Million and One Nights: A History of the Motion Picture*. New York: Simon & Schuster, 1964.

Riley, Philip. *The Phantom of the Opera: Classic Silents Volume 1*. Absecon, NJ: MagicImage Filmbooks, 1999.

Roberts, Roberts. *Jack Dempsey, the Manassa Mauler*. Urbana: University of Illinois Press, 2003.

Sanders, Coyne Steven, and Tom Gilbert. *Desilu: The Story of Lucille Ball and Desi Arnaz*. New York: William Morrow, 1993.

Schickel, Richard. *The Men Who Made the Movies*. New York: Atheneum, 1975.

Sedgwick, Edward. *And Then There Were Five!* Los Angeles, CA, 1949 (unpublished manuscript).

Thompson, Frank. *Lost Films: Important Movies That Disappeared*. New York: Citadel Press, 1996.

Vidor, King. *A Tree Is a Tree: An Autobiography*. Hollywood, CA: Samuel French Trade, 1981.

White, David. *Fantômas in America*. Encino, CA: Black Coat Press, 2007.

Wortis Leider, Emily. *Becoming Mae West*. New York: Da Capo Press, 1997.

Zolotow, Maurice. *Shooting Star: A Biography of John Wayne*. New York: Simon & Schuster, 1974.

Index

Ain't He Grand? 52
Air Raid Wardens 227–229
Alba, Maria 157
All for Gold 61
All for Love 47
Allen, Gracie 223, 231
Anderson, Gilbert M. "Broncho Billy" 51, 108
Anderson, Herbert 234
Armstrong, Robert 156, 224
Arnaz, Desi 239–241, 243
Arnold, Edward 233
Arrest Norma MacGregor 92
Arthur, George K. 164, 176
Asher, William 240
Ashes of Hope 60
Astor, Gertrude 112
Auer, Mischa 209, 213, 214

Bakewell, William 153
Baldwin, Curley 130
Ball, Lucille: friendship with Edward and Ebba Sedgwick 225, 239, 240, 242; *I Love Lucy* 231, 238–243; working relationship with Edward Sedgwick 230–231
Balshofer, Fred 142
Bar Nothing 92
A Bare Living 55
Barry, Eddie 137
Barry, Phyllis 194
Bates, Les 137
A Battle of Wits (1921 release) 92
A Battle of Wits (1925 release) 122
The Bearcat 95–96
Beasts of Paradise 97–102
Beatty, May 196
Beautiful but Dumb 160
Beautiful Love 46
Beddoe, Don 222
Beery, Noah 104
The Belle of Breweryville 47
Benedict, Kingsley 50, 57
Bennett, Charles 112
Bennett, Mickey 160

Bergen, Edgar (and Charlie McCarthy) 221–222
Berke, William A. (Lester, William) 130
Bernoudy, Jane 51, 52
Bernstein, Isadore 45, 112, 128
The Best Man 122
Beware Spooks! 222
Beyond All Odds 137
Beyond the Shadows 64
Blane, Sally 185, 246
Blinky 103–104
Boardman, Virginia True 106, 108
Boland, Mary 204–205
Bond, Ward 201
Bonomo, Joe 100–102, 135, 163
Boomerang Justice 96
Borzage, Frank 92
The Boss of the Lazy Y 60, 64
Bower, Elsie 137
Boyd, William "Stage" 189
Bracey, Sidney 191
Bradbury, James, Sr. 159
Breamer, Sylvia 102
Brennan, Walter 128, 159, 182, 201
Bride 13 53, 75–79
Briggs, Donald 218
Brinley, Charles 97–99
Broadway or Bust 111
Broneau, Helen 131
Brooks, Louise 158, 159
Brophy, Edward 154, 168, 179, 184, 185, 194, 201, 206, 211
Brown, Barbara 236
Brown, Clarence 162, 172
Brown, Joe E. 216–220, 222–223, 227, 245
Brown, Johnny Mack 198
Bruin Trouble 68
The Bugle Call 154–155
Burn 'Em Up O'Connor 220–221
Burns, Bob 160, 162
Burns, George 223, 231
Bush, James 222
Bushman, Francis X. 44, 50, 51, 108, 149

The Butler's Blunder 64
Byron, Arthur 209

Calvert, E.H. 204
The Cameraman 165–170
Campeau, Frank 119
Canutt, Yakima 115, 160
Carewe, Arthur Edmund 105, 127
Carey, Harry 109, 116, 149, 162, 163, 220–221, 223
Carey, Macdonald 236–237
Carlisle, Mary 119, 222, 224
Carney, Augustus 51
Carter, Calvert 122
Casajuana, Maria 157
Chaney, Lon 80, 81, 125, 128, 129, 145, 148, 149, 176
Chasing the Moon 94
Cheating the Public 67–68
Checkers 70
Chester, George Randolph 97
Chester, Lillian 97
Childs, Ray 137
Christy, Dorothy 184
Church, Fred 51, 54, 57, 142, 160
Circus Rookies 164
Clements, Roy 51–52, 54
Clive, E.E. 201, 207
Cobb, Edmund 122, 135
Cody, Bill 119
Coghlan, Frank, Jr. 149
Cohen, Henry R. 129, 217, 224
Collins, Monte 119
Collins, Ray 235, 236
Conklin, Chester 127
Connolly, Walter 207
Coogan, Jackie 97, 105, 148, 154, 155, 177
Cooper, Gary 141
Cooper, George 143, 162, 163, 189
Corbett, Ben 124, 137
Cornwall, Anne 130, 132
Corthell, Herbert 119
Craft, William James 83, 87, 94, 97, 98, 100, 102, 115, 119, 159, 243
Crane, Ward 125, 130, 132

259

Crawford, Joan 151, 152, 154
Crimson Clue 97
Cromwell, Richard 186
The Crooks 47
Cummings, Robert 210
Cunard, Grace 131, 135
Cunningham, Jack 86
Curtis, Allen 55, 64
Cyclone Smith Plays Trumps 70
Cyclone Smith's Comeback 70

Daddy 105, 155
Dahl, Arlene 231
Dane, Karl 149, 150, 162, 163, 164, 172, 173, 176, 177, 200
A Dangerous Affair 185–186
Dangerous Odds 119
Daniels, Marc 240
Daredevil Jack 79–83
Daring Days 123–124, 162
Darwell, Jane 237
Davenport, Harry 218
d'Avril, Yola 189
Day, Marceline 145, 167, 168
Dead Game 103
Dean, Man Mountain 219–220
Death on the Diamond 204–206, 209
DeHaven, Gloria 233–234
del Rio, Dolores 162, 163
Demarest, William 237
Dempsey, Jack 79–83
Denning, Richard 239
Denny, Reginald 104, 184, 224
de Rochefort, Charles 113
Desmond, William 65–66, 78, 89, 100–101, 114–115, 130–131, 135–136, 243
The Devil Dodger 60
Devine, Andy 196–197, 201, 224
The Diamond Queen 87
Do and Dare 96–97
Donlin, Michael 112, 149, 150
Don't Flirt 68
Doran, Mary 182, 197
Double Adventure 83, 86–87
Doughboys 179–180; Spanish-language version (*De Frente, Marchen*) 181
Dougherty, Jack 119–122, 142, 160
Dove, Billie 104
Downs, Johnny 210
Dream Girl 92
Dropped from the Clouds 57
Du Crow, Tote 119
Dugan, Tom 211, 213, 224
Duke of Chimney Butte 92
Duncan, Lee 137
Durante, Jimmy 187–188, 191–192, 193–195, 201, 223, 238
Dvorak, Ann 189
Dwyer, Ruth 111
Dynamite's Daughter 122, 162, 175

The Eagle's Nest 49–50
Earle, Edward 171
Easy to Wed 229–231

Eburne, Maude 187
Edmunds, Lee 38
Edwards, Cliff "Ukulele Ike" 181
Eilers, Sally 179, 184
Elliott, John 130
Ellis, Frank 162
Ellis, Patricia 204–205
The Emerald Pin 54
Evans, Madge 204, 206
Excuse My Dust 223, 236–238

The Face at Your Window 85
Fahrney, Milton J. 119
False Brands 94
Fantomas 85–86, 248–249
Farnum, Dustin 44, 67, 132, 135
Farnum, Franklyn 83
Farnum, William 67–68, 69
The Fascinating Model 54
Fat and Foolish 60
Father Brown, Detective 207
Fawcett, George 130, 132, 151
Ferguson, Helen 97, 123
Fetchit, Stepin 210
The Fickle Blacksmith 64
Field, Elinor 103
Fielding, Romaine 46–50, 108, 243
Fields, W.C. 221–222
Fighting Back 60
The Fighting Ranger 119–122
The Fighting Schoolmarm 122
The First Degree 102
Fit for a King 217–218
Fitzroy, Emily 163
The Flaming Frontier 131–135
The Flaming Hour 97
Flapjacks 64
Flat Harmony 55
Fleming, Susan 185
Forbes, Ralph 162, 163
Ford, Francis 130, 135, 176
Forman, Tom B. 162
Forrest, Sally 237
40-Horse Hawkins 110
Francis, Alec B. 202
Frawley, William 241, 242
Free and Easy 176–178; Spanish-language version (*Estrellados*) 178
French, Charles K. 96, 119, 130, 135, 143
Friganza, Trixie 176–177
Fuller, Mary 75
Furey, Barney 137
Furness, Betty 211, 212, 213

Galveston hurricane of 1900 16–19
The Gasoline Habit 52
The Gentleman from America 102
The German Band 47
Gerry Society 32, 165
Gettinger, William (Steele, William) 59–60, 74, 103, 113, 116, 119, 128, 130, 135, 137, 143, 180
Giant Powder 54
Gibson, Hoot 72–73, 78, 95–96, 102–104, 106, 109–123, 125, 128, 132, 135, 150, 224, 242
A Girl in Every Port 156–159
The Girl in the Saddle 91
The Gladiator 218–220
Good Morning Nurse 55
Goodwin, Harold 132, 168
Gordon, C. Henry 206
Grant, Lawrence 202
Grapewin, Charley 212
Graves, Ralph 185, 186
Gravina, Cesare 105, 163
Gray, Lawrence 204
The Great Radium Mystery 71–72
Green Backs and Red Skins 47–48
Greenwood, Charlotte 184
Gribbon, Eddie 130, 135, 163

Haines, William 148–149, 151–153, 170, 173–174, 176, 182–183, 200
Hal Roach Studios 182, 211, 213, 227, 244
Haley, Jack 202, 204, 205, 211, 213–214, 223, 224, 225, 231
Hallett, Al 119
Halton, Charles 214
Hamilton, Mahlon 159
Hamilton, Neil 204–205
Hamlin's Wizard Oil Company 6
Hardy, Oliver 49, 214–215, 227
Harlan, Marian 112
Harvey, Paul 231, 234, 237
The Haunted Pajamas 60
Havez, Ebba: marriage to Edward Sedgwick 195–196; marriage to Jean C. Havez 181–182; scriptwriter 181, 188, 196
Hawks, Howard 156, 159, 226
Haworth, Vinton 217
He Became a Regular Fellow 52
Healy, Ted 205, 209, 223, 224
Hearn, Edward 81–82, 122–123, 124, 130
The Heart of Arizona 91
Hell's Crater 61
Hell's End 64–65
Her Dream Man 52
Here Comes the Groom 202–204
The Heritage of Hate 54
Hersholt, Jean 209, 223, 224
Hewston, Alfred 137
Hicks, Russell 213, 228
The High Cost of Starving 55
Hired, Tired and Fired 52
His Blowout 52
His Family Tree 55
His Golden Hour 51
Hit and Run 112, 150
Hobbes, Halliwell 207, 218
Hollings, Doc 20–21
Holmes, Helen 77, 110, 115, 138
Holt, Jack 145, 185–186, 209
Holtz, Tenen 163
Homans, Robert E. 189
The Honeymoon Surprise 55
Hook and Ladder 109–110
Horseplay 196–197

Horton, Edward Everett 201
Hot Heels 159–160
Hotex Film Manufacturing Company 46
Hoxie, Jack 116, 122
Hughes, Howard 188–189
Hulette, Gladys 113
Hull, George C. 103, 123
The Human Tiger 61
Humes, Fred 113, 119, 128, 164
Hunt, Marsha 210
The Hurricane Kid 115–116
Hurst, Paul 198
Hutchison, Charles 86–87
Hutson, Clarence 174, 196, 223, 224, 228, 244, 246, 258
Hutson, Edward: acting 244; adoption 223; birth 7; career at Fox 247
Hutson, Mimi: adoption 223; birth 7; growing up 244–246, 243
Hyams, John 210, 214
Hyams, Leila 171, 196, 197, 201, 210

I'll Get Her Yet 52
I'll Tell the World 202–203
Improved Order of Red Men 9, 26, 27
In the Days of Daniel Boone 97–99
Indiscreet Corinne 60
influenza pandemic of 1918 61, 63
Irving, Ethelyn 106
The Isle of Life 54
It Sounded Like a Kiss 52
It's All Wrong 54
It's Cheaper to Be Married 55
It's Cheaper to Be Single 55
It's Great to Be Married 54–55

The Jade Box 175–176
Jennings, DeWitt 207
Jewell, Isabel 203, 223
Jim Hood's Ghost 130
Johnson, Helen 117
Johnson, Noble 130, 135, 162
Johnson, Van 229–230
Jones, Buck 83–84, 92, 96, 187, 223, 243
Joslin, Margaret 51
Joy, Colonel Jason S. 228
Joyce, Natalie 157
Jubilo 72–74
Judgment 94; *The Problem Eternal* (1923 re-release) 94
Julian, Rupert 125
June, Mildred 110
The Jungle Trail 68–70
Jungle Treachery 57
Jurado, Elena 157

Karloff, Boris 102
Katz, Pitzy 180
Kearns, Jack "Doc" 79–81
Keaton, Buster: association with Edward 166, 231; early career 165–166; MGM 164; television series 238
Keefe, Cornelius 196

Keefe, Dennis 220, 221
Keith of the Border 64
Kelly, Paul 206, 218
Kelly, Walter C. 210
Kennedy, Edgar 81, 228
Kent, William 199
Kenyon, Charles 131
Kerry, Norman 104, 125, 128, 130
Key, Kathleen 130, 133
Kibbee, Guy 217
The Kid's Nap 47
Kilbride, Percy 235–236
Kill the Umpire 52
Kimball, Edward 122
King, Charles 176, 182
Kingdom Come 72–73
Kingston, Natalie 157
A Kitchen Hero 64
Kolb, Clarence 222
Korff, Arnold 179
Kyle, W.W., Sr. 21
Kyle Theater 23

Lackteen, Frank 141, 142
Laemmle, Carl 45, 51, 125, 129, 131–132
Laemmle, Ernst 122, 123
La Marr, Barbara 113, 122
Landau, David 205–206
La Reno, Dick 119
Larkin, George 87, 96
Laroux, Carmen 190
The Last of the Night Riders 57
Laurel, Stan 49, 138, 176, 201, 214–215, 227
Lawrence, Marc 222
Lawrence, Rosina 211, 213–214
Lee, Duke R. 130
Let 'Er Buck 117–119
Levine, Nat 137, 160
Lewis, Judy 245–246
Lightnin' series (*Blitz*; *Claws*; *Fangs*; *Honor*; *Instinct*; *Lightnin' Flashes*; *Lightnin' Rage*; *Lightnin' Strikes*; *Lightnin' Wins*; *Rage*; *Speed*; *The Spider's Net*; *Vengeance*) 138–142
Lightnin' the Police Dog 138–142
Lily White of Centerville 52
The Lion's Lair 57
The Little Warrior 130
Littlefield, Lucien 218
Live Wires 91
London, Tom 141, 162
The Lone Hand 83
Lone Larry 50–51, 57
Long, Richard 236
Loraine, Robert 207
Lorraine, Louise 89, 102, 164, 176
Lorraine of the Lions 128, 159
The Losing Winner 57
Love and Flames 47, 49
Love's Battle 84
Lowery, William 142
Lubin Manufacturing Company 46, 49
A Lucky Leap 52–53
Lukas, Paul 207

The Lure of the Circus 57, 62–64
Lure of the West 137
Lyon, Ben 113
Lyons, Eddie 52, 54

Ma and Pa Kettle Back on the Farm 235–236
MacClean, Douglas 97
Mack, Helen 218, 248
MacRae, Henry 54, 57, 135, 175
Madison, Cleo 71
Main, Marjorie 235–236
Maker of Men 186–187
Making Good 104
Making Monkey Business 55
Maley, Dutch 137
Malone, Molly 62
Maloney, Leo 160–161
Malvern, Paul 100
Maly, Walter 141
The Man Above the Law 64–65
Man and Beast 54, 56–57
Maris, Mona 187
Married a Year 54
Marsh, Joan 186
Marshall, Tully 113, 162, 163
Martell, Alphonse 135
Marx, Max 135
The Maternal Spark 59–60
Mathews, Dorothy 157
Mayer, Louis B. 92, 129, 145, 148, 154, 178, 200, 231
Mayo, Frank 97, 102, 180
McComas, Ralph 55
McCoy, Tim 135, 187, 223
McDowell, Nelson 155
McGaugh, Wilbur 142
McGuire, Kathryn 128
McIntyre, Leila 210, 214
McLaglen, Victor 156
McNally, Horace (Stephen) 228
Meek, Donald 228
Mehaffey, Blanche 142–143
Merkel, Una 209
Merrill, Walter 184
Metcalfe, Earl 130
Michael, Gertrude 207
Michael O'Halloran 105–106
Miljan, John 223, 224, 182, 194, 201
Miller, Patsy Ruth 128, 159
Miller, Virgil 102, 125
Missy 52
Mister Cinderella 211–213
Mitchell, Grant 198, 201
Mix, Tom 42, 45, 78, 83, 92–94, 96–97, 102, 242, 243
Money and Mystery 57
Mong, William V. 159
Montagne, Edward J. 131
Montana of the Range 130
Montgomery, Robert 176, 177, 223
Moore, Constance 222
Moore, Dickie 219
Moore, Joe 83, 84, 94, 155
Moorhead, Natalie 184, 186
Moran, Lee 52, 54, 151

Moran, Polly 145, 176, 187
Morrison, Arthur 135
Morrison, Pete 65, 73, 104
Moses, Major Raymond G. 153
Mountian Molly O' 130
Mower, Jack 97–98
Murder in the Fleet 208–209
Murphy, Edna 86, 91, 114
The Mysterious Contragrav 50

Nagel, Conrad 143, 144, 145, 148, 176
Naked Fists 64
National Nuts 52
Navy Blues 172–174
Neill, James 104
Nesbit, Evelyn 53
The Night Attack 94
Nixon, Marion 116, 119
Not Too Thin to Fight 55
Novak, Eva 93–94
Number 10 57
Nye, G. Raymond 69, 119

O'Brien, John B. 122, 123, 130
O'Brien, Tom 102, 142, 145, 155
O'Connor, Una 196, 201, 207, 224
Oh! Man! 64
O'Keefe, Dennis 220–221
Oliver, Edna May 201
On Circus Day 47
One Shot Ross 60, 64, 162
O'Neil, Sally 149
The Open Wire 94
Oppenheimer, Jess 239, 240
Ortego, Artie 119, 130
Osborne, Bud 120, 162
Out of Luck 103–104
Outlaw Love 103
The Outlaw's Daughter 122–123
Ovey, George 135
Owsley, Monroe 211, 213

Padden, Sarah 155
Padjan, Jack 130
Page, Anita 172–173, 176–177
The Paperhanger's Revenge 55
Parker, Jean 209
Parlor, Bedroom and Bath 183–185; French-language version (*Buster Se Marie*) 85; German-language version (*Casanova Wider*) 85
Passing the Bomb 65
The Passionate Plumber 187–188; French-language version (*Le Plombier Amoureux*) 188
Patterson, Walter 162
Patton, Bill 162
Paying His Debt 65
Payton, Claude 119
Peacock Military Academy 24, 46
Pearson, Virginia 127
Peers, Joan 184
Pegg, Vester 162
Pendleton, Nat 205, 209, 220
Pendleton Round-Up 117–119
Percy, Eileen 151

A Phantom Fugitive 70
The Phantom of the Opera 125–128
Philbin, Mary 104, 125, 128, 170
Pick a Star 213–215
Pickford, Jack 58, 59, 149
A Pistol Point Proposal 70
Plimpton, Horace G., Jr. (Plympton, Horace) 85
Plympton, George H. 87, 94
Polo, Eddie 62–64, 70, 78
The Poor Fish 64
The Poor Rich 201–202
Porcasi, Paul 198
Potel, Victor 51, 52, 54, 180
The Price of Youth 155
A Prisoner for Life 70
Pryor, Roger 202
The Pullman Mystery 60
Purcelle, Irene 187

Queen of the Hills 130
Queen of the Round-Up 122
Quick Trigger 61
The Quitter 54

The Ramblin' Kid 104
Rand, Sally 157
Randall, Meg 236
Rawlinson, Herbert 154
Ray, Allene 89, 135
Red Pants 150–151
Reeves, Bob 71
Remote Control 182
Repeating the Honeymoon 64
Rice, Florence 217
Rice, Frank 213
Richardson, Jack 65, 97, 131, 137
Rickson, Joe 130, 162
The Riddle Rider 114–115
Ride for Your Life 110
The Ridin' Kid from Powder River 112–113
Riding on Air 216–217
Roach, Bert 143
Roberts, Edith 58, 105, 145
Robinson, Frances 227
Rodgers, Walter 133
Rogers, Will 73–74, 210
Roland, Gilbert 187
Roland, Ruth 77, 78, 89, 97, 243, 108, 218, 224
Romance Land 102
Room Rent and Romance 52
Rooney, Mickey 205, 221
Roped and Tied 61
Ropin' Venus 122
Roseman, Edward 69, 85–86, 248
Rough and Ready 67–68
The Rough Diamond 93–94
Rubin, Robert 148
The Runaway Express 142–143

The Saddle Hawk 119
Sagebrush Lady 137
Saturday's Millions 197–199
Sawdust Trail 111
Sawyer, Joe 186, 198

Sax, Samuel 137–138
Saylor, Syd 131, 143
Scarred Hands 104–105
Schayer, Richard 109
Schenck, Nicholas 148, 166
Schrock, Raymond L. 70, 109, 119, 123, 125, 131
Sebastian, Dorothy 170, 177, 223
Sedgwick, Edward Martin: birth 8; death 242; Desilu Productions 240–242; Hollywood Walk of Fame 243; song writing 129
Sedgwick, Edward W. (Ned): birth 6–7; death 193
Sedgwick, Eileen: birth 14; death 248; Gretel Yoltz 156; product endorsements 106
Sedgwick, Josephine (Fenie) Walker: birth 7; death 248
Sedgwick, Josephine (Josie): birth 11; death 248
Selwyn, Ruth 191
Semels, Harry 142
Shackelford, Floyd 130
The Shadow of Suspicion 91
The She Wolf 72–73
The Shifty Shoplifter 64
Shootin' for Love 103–104
Silvera, Karl 137
Sims, Milton 55
Single Handed 103
Sink or Swim 85
Skelton, Red 231–232, 233, 236
Sky Devils 188–189
Slide, Kelly, Slide 149–151
The Slow Express 64
Smith, Clifford 83, 91, 105
So You Won't Talk 227
Some Heroes 52
Some Medicine Man 52
Son of Oklahoma 189–191
A Southern Yankee 231–235
Speak Easily 191–193
Spite Marriage 170–172
The Spook Ranch 123
Spring Fever 151–152
The Square Shooter 83
Stanton, Ralph 85
Stanton, Richard 53, 60, 67, 68, 70, 79, 85
Steele, Bob 189
Stewart, Roy 64, 66, 83
Stone, Fred 92
Stratton-Porter, Gene 105
Strings of Steel 135–136
Stuart, Gloria 202–203, 218
Summerville, Slim 196–197
The Sunshine Trail 105
Sutch, Bert 131
Swearing Off 55

Taylor, Ray 175
Taylor, Robert 208–209, 218, 226
Tearle, Conway 113
The Temple of Terror 57, 142
Terror Trail 87
Thayer, Fran N. 41

There and Back 68
There You Are 145
Thorpe, Richard 160
The Thousand-Dollar Drop 55
The Thrill Chaser 104
Thundering Speed 137
Tin Hats 143–145
Todd, Harry 51, 128, 130, 135, 143, 155
Todd, Lola 115
Todd, Thelma 191, 201
Toler, Sidney 189, 191, 204
Tollaire, August 187
Tourneur, Maurice 113
Town That Tried to Come Back 52
Tracy, Lee 202, 203, 217, 223
Tracy, Spencer 189
Trail of '98 162–163
Trail of No Return 61
Travis, June 218
Treacher, Arthur 204, 212, 225, 231
Trent, Jack 130
Tryon, Glenn 159
Tucker, Richard 193, 209
Tully, Marshall 113, 162, 163
Turpin, Ben 49, 51, 52, 54
Two-Fisted Jones 129–130

Under Western Skies 130
Universal Film Manufacturing Company 45, 50, 51, 54

Vale, Vola 92, 127

Vance, Vivian 241, 242
Van Dyke, W.S. "Woody" 80–83, 86, 218, 223–224
The Vanishing West 160
The Varmint 58–59
Vidor, King 46, 129, 143, 163, 180, 224
The Virginia Judge 210

Walburn, Raymond 211, 237
Walker, Johnnie 86, 91
Walker, Robert 122, 142
Wallace, Morgan 212
Walsh, George 85
Watch Your Watch 64
Water, Hal 142
Wayne, John 115, 186–187
The Web 137
West, Mae 81, 142, 199
West Point 152–154
Westbound 57
Western Hearts 91–92
What! No Beer? 193–195
When Danger Calls 155
When Law Comes to Hades 104
When Slim Picked a Peach 52
When Slim Was Home Cured 52
White, David 248–249
White, Jacqueline 228, 229
White, Pearl 77–78, 89, 108, 115
White Flame 159
The White Moth 113–114
The White Rider 83–84

Whitlock, Lloyd 159
Who Said Chicken? 60
Why I Would Not Marry 67
Wild Life 64, 65
The Wild Rider 70
Willard, John 85
Williams, Esther 29
Williams, Kathlyn 77
Williamson, Robin 47, 48, 49
Wilson, Al 110, 119, 121–122
Wilson, Ed 135
Windsor, Claire 143, 145, 154
The Winking Idol 130–131
The Winning Stroke 70
The Wolf Pack 94
Wolves of the Border 64
The Woman in the Case 55
A Woman's Wit 92
Woodruff, Bert 151
Worne, Duke 137
Wynn, Kennan 230–231

The Yankee Way 60
The Yellow Cab Man 233–235
Yellow Contraband 160–162
You Can't Cheat an Honest Man 221–222
Young, Loretta 170, 223, 244, 245
Young, Robert 197, 204, 206, 224
Young, Tex 130

Zany, King 111
Zarana, Zalla 141

www.ingramcontent.com/pod-product-compliance
Ingram Content Group UK Ltd.
Pitfield, Milton Keynes, MK11 3LW, UK
UKHW050537150426
5217IPUK00026B/1978